EXPLAINING SOCIAL PSYCHOLOGY TO A SOCIOLOGIST

EXPLAINING SOCIAL PSYCHOLOGY TO A SOCIOLOGIST

FIRST EDITION

Edited by M. Nicole Warehime

University of Central Oklahoma

Bassim Hamadeh, CEO and Publisher
Mazin Hassan, Acquisitions Editor
Amy Smith, Project Editor
Berenice Quirino, Associate Production Editor
Jackie Bignotti, Production Artist
Sara Schennum, Licensing Associate
Natalie Piccotti, Director of Marketing
Kassie Graves, Vice President of Editorial
Jamie Giganti, Director of Academic Publishing

Cover image copyright © 2015 Depositphotos/hobbit_art.

Printed in the United States of America.

ISBN: 978-1-5165-3970-3 (pbk) / 978-1-5165-3971-0 (br)

CONTENTS

MAKING INTRODUCTIONS

Just like it sounds, social psychology has elements of both sociology and psychology. Both disciplines claim to be a home for the subfield of social psychology; however, both disciplines approach the study of social psychology from different perspectives. This anthology strives to find the understanding of both perspectives while emphasizing the important role of sociology. Figure 1 illustrates the home of social psychology as the bridge between sociology (the systematic study of human group behavior) and psychology (the systematic study of individual behavior).

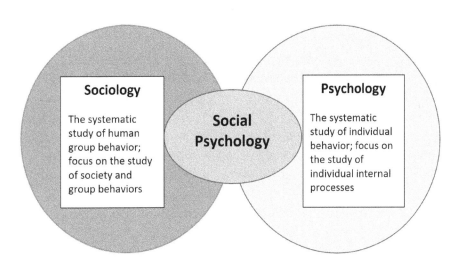

Figure 1   Social psychology, the bridge between sociology and psychology

In social psychology, we find that we are already experts in the field. We have spent our entire lives observing and measuring the behaviors of others. We have been influenced by those around us: family, peers, the media, and nations; individually, we have influenced others around us simultaneously. So, why take a course in social psychology if we are already aware of our social surroundings? Well, social psychology allows researchers to understand behaviors and find patterns of social behaviors in our society. Gordon Allport (1924) refers to social psychology as an understanding and explanation of "how the thought, feeling and behavior of individuals are influenced by the actual, imagined or implied presence of other human beings." In more basic terms, social psychology is the study of the interaction between society (sociology) and individuals (psychology).

Social psychology understands the society as goal oriented. People interact with others with a purpose. Behaviors work toward a goal and are not accidental. Social behavior is also dispositional (individual ascription) in nature as well as situational (environment). This means that individuals maintain a fairly stable personality; however, we change our behaviors based on the situation. For example, how an individual acts with their parents at a religious ceremony may be different from how an individual acts with their friends at a nightclub. Our personalities remain somewhat the same, but we change our behaviors based on the situation we are facing. Further, group behavior is influenced by the viewpoints of the individuals within the group. As an illustration, if an individual views the world as a hostile place, they may interact with hostility toward other individuals within the group. On the other hand, if an individual views the world as a helpful place, they may interact with other individuals within the group with understanding. Finally, individuals bring cultural influence to the social behavior. Culture refers to the common beliefs, norms, and behaviors of a group, including language, religion, food, and clothing. To summarize, social behavior is (1) purposively goal oriented; (2) modified by individual personality and the situation; (3) altered by worldview perceptions; and (4) cultural.

The foundations of social psychology stem from the aftermath of the atrocities of World War II. Researchers aimed to comprehend how the role of authority (one individual, like Adolf Hitler) could influence the behaviors of many (groups, like the Schutzstaffel, or SS). Hitler created the SS as a paramilitary unit to carry out the atrocities of the concentration camps and to enforce the various policies of the Nazi Regime. This "elite" group was known for committing the worst war crimes of World War II. Upon trial, many members of this group argued that they were simply "carrying out orders" and should not be held individually responsible for their behaviors. Social psychology initially attempted to test whether or not this could occur. Further research and application have investigated how group behavior can be influenced in other ways; for example, when buying a car. The salesperson uses techniques from social psychology to influence the car buyer's decisions during the process. We will investigate the role of social psychology in making choices and persuasion later in the anthology. Social psychologists also investigate altruism (helping behavior) and aggression (destructive behavior). Other researchers study why we like the people we like in interpersonal attraction and attitude development.

As the title implies, the goal of this anthology is to explain social psychology to a sociologist. How does the role of the individual influence the study of group behavior? Sociologists primarily tend to focus on the role of group behavior, while psychologists typically focus on the role of individual behavior. So, the bridge of social psychology is an important opportunity for sociologists to understand this important influence of individual units in our society.

References

Allport, G. (1924). *Social Psychology*. New York: Houghton Mifflin.

UNIT I

INTRODUCTION TO SOCIAL PSYCHOLOGY

Introduction

Individuals in society engage in social psychology every moment of their lives. As one studies social psychology, immediately the person can recognize the basic tenets of social psychology throughout their day. Early on in life, humans learn that survival depends on interaction with other humans. Babies cannot survive without the intervention of other humans. This requirement for interaction continues until the human dies. So, why is this interaction important? How does this interaction influence the individual beyond basic survival? And how do individuals interacting with others influence society?

After reading this paragraph, one may immediately think about the men and women who live "off the grid," as isolated as they possibly can be. However, as we cannot overlook these individuals, they are not the norm of expected behavior in society. At some point, these individuals did interact with others. Throughout this book a discussion will unfold about both the good and the bad of these interactions. So, what exactly is social psychology?

Social psychology refers to the study of the interaction between individuals and society. By the name of this subfield, one can see the overlap between sociology and psychology. Sociologists would focus more on the larger (meso- to macro-level) interactions, while psychologists would focus more on the smaller (micro- to meso-level) interactions. The first reading selection will detail this foundational understanding of social psychology.

An important understanding of social psychology is the emphasis on "the study of" portion of the definition. Social psychology discusses theory from a scientific perspective. The use of the scientific method is very important to social psychologists. However, unlike other sciences (e.g., physics, chemistry), social psychology requires the use of humans in the study. Consequently, social psychologists have a strong focus on the ethics of scientific research. But social psychology does have a dark past that further influences and defines the ethics of the field. For example, Carney Landis in 1924 wanted to study social influences of facial expressions. He hypothesized that there would be universal facial expressions. To test this hypothesis, he assigned test subjects to do a series of tests while he monitored the facial expressions. At one point he had his test subjects, including individuals under age 18, decapitate live rats! Today, we would classify this research as unethical for human involvement due to psychological distress. And Landis did not find any support for his research hypothesis in this experiment. This section also includes a reading on the research methods and ethics of social psychology.

As you read this section, focus on the foundation of the field of social psychology. With this understanding, the rest of the study of social psychology will be easier to understand and observe in your daily interactions with society. While reading this section, think about the social psychology of the next decision that you make, whether it is to go to the party this weekend or to attend a study session.

How to Think Sociologically

Steven M. Buechler

People have always tried to make sense of the world around them. Myths, fables, and religion provided traditional ways of making sense. More recently, science has provided additional ways of understanding the world. Sociology is part of the rise of science as a means of making sense of the world.

As we know in our own time, there can be tension between religious and scientific views. Contemporary disputes over evolution, sexuality, marriage, and even the age of our planet often pit religious values against scientific interpretations. More broadly speaking, both at home and abroad, religious fundamentalisms rest uneasily alongside modern, secular worldviews. These familiar tensions have a history that takes us back to the origins of sociology itself.

Sociology and Modernity

The rise of sociology is part of a much larger story about the emergence of the modern world itself. Modernity emerged in European societies through a long process of social change that unfolded from the sixteenth to the nineteenth centuries. During this time, virtually everything about organized social life in Europe was fundamentally transformed. In our day, we speak of globalization as a force that is changing the world in the most basic ways. But current patterns of globalization can be traced back to the rise of modernity itself; in many respects, they are a continuation of the changes that ushered in the modern world.

Economically, modernity transformed most people from peasants to workers in a complex division of labor. Politically, modernity created distinct nation-states with clear boundaries. Technologically, modernity applied scientific knowledge to producing everything from consumer goods to lethal weapons. Demographically, modernity triggered population growth and massive migration from small, familiar, rural communities to large, urban, anonymous cities.

When social worlds change like this, some people benefit while others are harmed. In addition, most people find rapid change and its inevitable conflict to be unsettling, and they seek to understand what is happening. It was this moment that gave rise to sociology. Explaining modernity became sociology's task at the same time that modernity was making sociology possible in the first place.

The link between modernity and sociology was the Enlightenment. This intel-lectual revolution accompanied other revolutionary changes occurring throughout Europe. In the broadest terms, the Enlightenment challenged religious belief, dogma, and authority. It sought to replace them with scientific reason, logic, and knowledge.

Four basic themes pervaded Enlightenment thought (Zeitlin 1987). First, human reason was the best guide to knowledge, even if it meant that scientific skepticism displaced religious certainty. Second, reason must be paired with careful, scientific observation. Third, Enlightenment thought insisted that social arrangements be rationally justified; if not, they must be changed until they could be rationally defended. Finally, Enlightenment thought assumed that with the systematic application of reason, the perfectibility of people and the progress of society were all but inevitable.

Enlightenment thought contained some potentially fatal flaws. It was a Eurocentric worldview, created by privileged white men, that made universal pronouncements about all people in all times and places. While applauding Europe's progress, it ignored the colonial domination of the rest of the world that provided the labor, goods, and wealth that underwrote that progress. Generalizations about "humanity" meant "males," to the exclusion of women, and pronouncements on the "human race" meant white Europeans, to the exclusion of darker people, who were viewed as subhuman.

The Enlightenment was much more than a justification of imperialism, sexism, and racism, but it could become that as well. More than two centuries later, the jury is still out on whether Enlightenment biases can be overcome and its promises be fulfilled. Some postmodernists see little hope for this to happen. Others, myself included, think that the critical spirit of the Enlightenment can help uproot its biases. The project is already under way as feminists, people of color, and postcolonial writers find their way into contemporary sociological discourses (Lemert 2013).

In its own day, the Enlightenment provoked a "romantic conservative reaction" (Zeitlin 1987) that rejected the elevation of reason and science over faith and tradition. It defended traditional customs, institutions, and ways of life from the new standard of critical reason. The debate between Enlightenment progress and conservative reaction set the agenda for sociology as the social science of modernity. Progress or order? Change or stability? Reason or tradition? Science or religion? Individual or group? Innovation or authority? Such dichotomies framed the subject matter of the new science of sociology.

The classical era of sociology refers to European thinkers whose ideas brought this new discipline to maturity from the late eighteenth to the early twentieth centuries. The very different sociologies of Auguste Comte, Herbert Spencer, Ferdinand Toennies, Karl Marx, Max Weber, Georg Simmel, Emile Durkheim, and others are variations on sociology's main theme: How do we understand modern society? Given these efforts, we might think of sociology as the ongoing effort of human beings to understand the worlds they are simultaneously inheriting from earlier generations and maintaining and transforming for future generations.

This approach has been described as the "sociological imagination." It arises when people realize that they can only know themselves by understanding their historical period and by examining others in the same situation as themselves. We think sociologically when we grasp how our historical moment differs from previous ones and how the situations of various groups of people differ from each other (Mills 1959).

The sociological imagination is guided by three related questions. The first concerns the social structure of society. How is it organized, what are its major institutions, and how are they linked together? The second concerns the historical location of society. How has it emerged from past social forms, what mechanisms promote change, and what futures are possible based on this historical path? The third concerns individual biography within society. What kinds of character traits are called forth by this society, and what kinds of people come to prevail? The sociological imagination is thus about grasping the relations between history and biography within society.

The sociological imagination sensitizes us to the difference between "personal troubles" and "public issues." A personal trouble is a difficulty in someone's life that is largely a result of individual circumstances. A public issue is a difficulty that is largely owing to social arrangements beyond the individual's control. The distinction is crucial because common sense often interprets events as personal troubles; we explain someone's difficulties as springing from individual shortcomings. The sociological imagination recognizes that such difficulties are rarely unique to one person; they rather happen to many people in similar situations. The underlying causes derive more from social structures and historical developments than the individual alone. If our goal is "diagnosis," the sociological imagination locates problems in a larger social context. If our goal is "treatment," it implies changing the structure of society rather than the behavior of individuals.

This applies to success as well. Common sense often attributes success to individual qualities. The sociological imagination asks what social and historical preconditions were necessary for an individual to become a success. Many successful people, in Jim Hightower's memorable phrase, "were born on third base but thought they hit a triple." The point is that whereas common sense sees the world in individual terms, sociological thinking sees it in structural terms. Only by seeing the connections between structure, history, and biography can we understand the world in a sociological way.

This discussion implies that professional sociologists and ordinary people see the world differently. This is often true, but the issue is more complicated. Modernity has also led ordinary people to develop a practical sociology in their everyday lives. Think about it this way. Sociology sees the world as a social construction that could follow various blueprints. Indeed, social worlds *are* constructed in very different ways in different times and places.

In our time, an awareness of the socially constructed nature of social worlds is no longer the privileged insight of scholars, but has become part of everyday understanding. Whether owing to rapid change, frequent travel, cultural diffusion, or media images, many people understand that we live in socially constructed worlds. Some people are distressed by this fact, and others rejoice in it, but few can escape it. Thus, an idea that was initially associated with professional sociology has become part of the everyday consciousness of ordinary people today.

The result is that many people without formal sociological training understand social processes quite well. Put differently, the objects of sociological analysis are people who are quite capable of becoming the subjects of the sociological knowledge created by that analysis. Although few people can explain how quantum mechanics governs the physical world, many can describe sociological processes that shape the social world.

Certain circumstances prompt people to think sociologically. Perhaps the key stimulant is when familiar ways of doing and thinking no longer work. It is when people are surprised, puzzled, challenged, or damaged that they are most likely to think sociologically (Lemert 2008). People then develop sociological competence as they try to make sense out of specific, individual circumstances by linking them to broader social patterns. In this way, sociological awareness begins to understand bigger things as a by-product of wrestling with the practical challenges of everyday life.

Circumstances do not inevitably provoke sociological consciousness. Some people redouble their faith or retreat into ritualism. So perhaps we can conclude this way. Societies confront people with problems. These problems have always had the potential to promote a sociological awareness. In our times, there is a greater awareness of the socially constructed nature of the world. This makes it even more likely that when people in this society are confronted with practical challenges, they will develop sociological competence as a practical life skill. In late modernity, everyone can become a practical sociologist.

Thinking Sociologically

The sociological perspective involves several themes. They overlap with one another, and some may be found in other social sciences as well as everyday consciousness. Taken together, they comprise a distinctive lens for viewing the social world. Here are some of those themes.

Society is a Social Construction

People construct social order. Sociology does not see society as God-given, as biologically de-termined, or as following any predetermined plan beyond human intervention. At the same time, this does not mean that everyone plays an equal role in the process or that the final product looks like what people intended.

Social construction begins with intentions that motivate people to act in certain ways. When many people have similar goals and act in concert, larger social patterns or institutions are created. Goal-driven action is essential to the creation of institutions, and it remains equally important to their maintenance and transformation over time. Put succinctly, society is a human product (Berger and Luckmann 1966).

Basic human needs ensure some similarities in the goals that people pursue in all times and places. But these pursuits also unfold in specific historical circumstances and cultural contexts that have led to a dazzling variety of social worlds. This variety is itself the best evidence of the socially constructed nature of social worlds. If biology or genetics were the determining force behind social worlds, wouldn't they look a lot more similar than what we actually see around the globe?

Social constructionists thus insist that society arises from the goal-driven action of people. But they also recognize that the institutions created by such actions take on a life of their own. They appear to exist independently of the people who create and sustain them. They are expe-rienced by people as a powerful external force that weighs down on them. When this external force becomes severe enough, people are likely to lose sight of the fact that society is a social product in the first place.

The value of the social constructionist premise is this dual recognition. On one hand, society is a subjective reality originating in the intentions of social actors. On the other hand, it becomes an objective reality that confronts subsequent generations as a social fact that inevitably shapes *their* intentional actions—and so it goes. Understood this way, the idea that society is a social construction is at the heart of the sociological perspective.

Society is an Emergent Reality

Another premise of sociology is emergentism. This reveals sociology's distinctive level of analysis. For psychology, the level of analysis is the individual, even if it is acknowledged that individuals belong to groups. For sociology, the level of analysis is social ties rather than individual elements. Emergentism recognizes that certain realities only appear when individual elements are combined in particular ways. When they are, qualitatively new realities emerge through these combinations.

Take a simple example. Imagine a random pile of ten paper clips. Now imagine linking these paper clips together to form a chain. There are still ten paper clips, but a new emergent reality has appeared that is qualitatively different from the random pile because of how the elements are related to one another. Or consider human reproduction. Neither sperm nor egg is capable of producing human life on its own; in combination, qualitatively new life begins to emerge from a particular combination of elements.

Sociology specializes in the social level of analysis that emerges when elements are combined to create new, larger realities. Emergentism also implies that when we try to understand elements outside of their context, it is at best a simplification and at worst a distortion. The parts derive meaning from their relationship with other parts, and the sociological perspective is fundamentally attuned to such relationships.

Society is a Historical Product

Thinking historically is a crucial part of the sociological imagination (Mills 1959). Classical sociologists thought historically because they lived in times of rapid social change and it was a major challenge to understand such change. Modern sociology tends to be more static, and modern people tend to be very present-oriented. Both professional and practical sociologists would benefit from a more historical perspective on the social world.

Seeing society as a historical product means recognizing that we cannot understand the present without understanding the past. Historical knowledge of past social conditions provides crucial comparisons. Without such benchmarks, it is impossible to understand what is genuinely new in the present day. Without a historical referent for comparison, sociology is clueless when it comes to understanding social change. Historical knowledge also provides the raw material for categories, comparisons, typologies, and analogies that are crucial to understanding both the present and possible future worlds.

The concept of emergentism applies here because the importance of seeing relationships between elements also works chronologically. If we look at society at only one point in time, we sever it from its past and its potential futures. Its very meaning arises from these relationships; to ignore them is to distort even the static understanding of society at one point in time. Consider the difference between a photograph and a film that presents a succession of images. We can learn something from the still photo, but its meaning often changes dramatically when we see it as one of a series of interrelated images.

Society Consists of Social Structures

Sociologists use the term *structure* to refer to the emergent products of individual elements. Structure implies that the social world has certain patterns or regularities that recur over time. Put differently, sociologists are keenly interested in social organization.

Structures are products of human purposes, but they acquire an objective reality and become a powerful influence on human action. Think about how physical structures like buildings shape action. We almost always enter buildings through doors; in rare cases we might do so through windows, but walking through walls is not an option. Social structures are less visible and more flexible than buildings, but they also channel people's actions, because they make some actions routine and expected, others possible but unlikely, and still others all but impossible.

Like buildings, social structures often have a vertical dimension. Social structures ensure that some people are better off than others and that some are not very well off at all. Some residential buildings have penthouses at the top, premium suites near the top, standard accommodations below them, and housekeeping staff in the basement. Social structures are also stratified, granting power, privilege, and opportunity to some while limiting or denying them to others. Sociologists are especially interested in the hierarchical dimension of social structures.

Sociologists traditionally thought of social structures as powerful forces weighing down upon the individual. In this image, structures constrain freedom of choice and behavior. But this is a one-sided view. Structures are constraining, but they are also enabling. These established patterns of social organization also make many actions possible in the first place or easier in the second place. Without preexisting social structures, we would have to do everything "from scratch," and the challenge of sheer survival might overwhelm us. The trick is thus to see social structures as simultaneously constraining and enabling social action (Giddens 1984).

Society Consists of Reflexive Actors

People in society are aware of themselves, of others, and of their relationships with others. As reflexive actors, we monitor our action and its effects on others. We continue, modify, or halt actions, depending on whether they are achieving their intended effects. According to one school of thought, we are literally actors, because social life is like a theatrical performance in which we try to convince others that we are a certain kind of person (Goffman 1959). To stage effective performances, we must constantly be our own critic, judging and refining our performances. Reflexivity thus means that when we act, we are conscious of our action, we monitor its course, and we make adjustments over time.

To stage such performances, we must undergo socialization. Along the way, we acquire a language that provides us with tools for reflexive thinking. We also acquire a self. Oddly enough, to have a self requires that we first have relationships with others. Through those relationships, we imaginatively see the world from their perspective, which includes seeing ourselves as we imagine we appear to them. It is this ability to see ourselves through the perspective of others—to see ourselves as an object—that defines the self. Reflexive action only becomes possible with a self.

Reflexivity makes ordinary people into practical sociologists. To be a competent person is to be a practical sociologist. We cannot help being sociologists every time we ponder a potential relationship, reconsider a hasty action, or adopt someone else's viewpoint. All such situations call upon and refine the reflexivity that is the hallmark of social action as well as a defining characteristic of the sociological perspective.

Society is an Interaction of Agency and Structure

Social structures and reflexive actors are intimately connected. Unfortunately, much sociology emphasizes one side of this connection at the expense of the other. Agency-centered views stress the ability of people to make choices out of a range of alternatives in almost any situation. The emphasis on choice implies that people control their own destiny, at least within broad limits.

Structure-centered views stress the extent to which people's choices are limited by social structures. The emphasis on structures implies that people's options—if not their lives—are essentially determined by larger social forces over which they have little control. Both approaches have merit, but the challenge is to see structure and agency in a more interconnected way.

Marx once said that people make their own history (acknowledging agency), but under circumstances they do not choose but rather inherit from the past (acknowledging structure). Here's an analogy from the game of pool. Each time you approach the table, you "inherit" a structure left by your opponent when they missed their last shot. Yet, for every layout of balls on the table, there is always a shot that you can attempt, and that action will alter the structure of the table for subsequent shots. In this analogy, structure (the position of balls on the table) both limits and creates opportunities for agency (taking a shot), which in turn alters the structure for the next round of shooting. If pool is not your game, chess is also a good analogy. The point is that agency and structure are two sides of the same coin; each conditions the possibilities of the other as we make our own history in circumstances we don't choose.

The close connection between structure and agency has led one theorist to reject the notion of structure altogether, because it implies something that exists apart from agency. Anthony Giddens (1984) talks about a *process* of structuration. In this view, actors use preexisting structures to accomplish their goals, but they also re-create them as a by-product of their actions. Consider a wedding ceremony. It is a preexisting cultural ritual people use to accomplish the goal of getting married. The by-product of all these individual marriages is the perpetuation of the cultural ritual itself. Generalize this to any situation in which we draw upon an established part of our social world to achieve a goal; in using this part we also sustain (and perhaps transform) it as a part of social structure.

Society has Multiple Levels

Although society has multiple levels, sociologists often focus on one level at a time. Think about using Google Maps to locate a destination. You can zoom out to get the big picture at the expense of not seeing some important details. Alternatively, you can zoom in on some key details at the expense of not seeing the big picture. Combining these differing views will orient you to your destination, but we must remember it is ultimately all one interconnected landscape.

Sociologists nevertheless distinguish between macro and micro levels of society. When we look at the macro level, we typically include millions of people organized into large categories, groups, or institutions. The macro level is the "big picture" or "high altitude" perspective in which society's largest patterns are evident and individuals are invisible. When we look at the micro level, we might inspect no more than a dozen people interacting in a small group setting. Here, the role of particular individuals is very prominent, and larger social patterns fade into the background.

Some of the best sociology involves understanding not only structure-agency connections but also micro-macro links. Every macro-structure rests on micro-interaction, and every micro-interaction is shaped by macro-structures. The previous example of a wedding also illustrates this point. On the macro level, weddings are a cultural ritual that inducts people into the institution of marriage and the family. However, weddings, marriage, and the family would not exist on the macro level without countless, micro-level interactions. The macro-level institution depends on micro-level actions to sustain it. At the same time, anyone who has ever gotten married will tell you that macro-level, cultural expectations about weddings impose themselves on people as they plan for this supposedly personal event. Every micro-level wedding depends on a macro-level, cultural blueprint for its social significance. The micro and macro levels of society are one interdependent reality rather than two separate things.

Society Involves Unintended Consequences

One of the more profound insights of the sociological perspective concerns unintended and unanticipated consequences of action. Much human action is purposive or goal-directed. People act because they want to accomplish something. Despite this, they sometimes fail to achieve their goals. But whether people achieve their goals or not, their actions always create other consequences that they don't intend or even anticipate. Shakespeare made a profoundly sociological point when he had Juliet fake her own suicide to dramatize her love for Romeo. Unfortunately, the plan never reached Romeo. Juliet neither intended nor anticipated that Romeo would find her unconscious, believe that she was really dead, and take his own life in response. Nor did he intend (or even realize) that she would awaken, discover his real death, and really take her life in response. Talk about unintended consequences!

This principle acknowledges the complexity of the social world and the limits on our ability to control it. It says that despite our best efforts, the effects of social action cannot be confined to one intended path; they always spill over into unexpected areas. The principle is also a cautionary message for those seeking to solve social problems. Such efforts might succeed, but they often bring other consequences that are neither positive nor intended.

Efforts to control crime provide an example. Consider policies to "get tough" on crime through harsher treatment like capital punishment and mandatory sentencing. Because the human beings who serve as judges and juries are reflexive actors who take these facts into account, they are often less likely to convict suspects without overwhelming evidence because of the harshness of the sentence. Thus, the unintended consequence of an attempt to "get tough" on crime might be the opposite, because fewer suspects are convicted than before.

A related idea is the distinction between manifest and latent functions. A manifest function is an outcome that people intend. A latent function is an outcome that people are not aware of; it can complement, but it often contradicts, the manifest function. Crime and punishment provide yet another example. The manifest function of imprisonment is punishment or rehabilitation. The latent function is to bring criminals together where they can meet one another, exchange crime techniques, and become better criminals upon their return to society.

The concept of latent functions is crucial to sociological analysis. Sometimes we observe behavior or rituals that seem irrational, pointless, or self-defeating. This is the time to begin looking for latent functions. What we will often find is that such "irrational" behavior reinforces the identity and sustains the cohesion of the group that performs it. Thus, before we dismiss the tribal rain dance (because "rain gods" don't exist), we must explore its latent function. Even when people don't (manifestly) know what they are (latently) doing, their behavior can be crucial to group cohesion.

Recognizing unintended consequences and latent functions is not just for professional sociologists. Daily living requires managing risk, and ordinary people in everyday life recognize the tricky nature of goal-directed action. The folk wisdom that "the road to hell is paved with good intentions" acknowledges the potential disconnect between goals and outcomes. Such recognition, however, never completely prevents outcomes we neither intend nor expect. These principles give social life some of its most surprising twists, and sociology some of its most fascinating challenges.

No attempt to capture the sociological perspective in a small number of themes can be complete. Other sociologists would doubtless modify this list. But most would recognize these themes as central to thinking sociologically. As such, they provide a foundation for the more detailed investigations to follow.

Sociology's Double Critique

This final theme deserves special emphasis as the foundation of this book. Last but not least, thinking sociologically means looking at the social world in a critical way.

In everyday language, *critical* implies something negative. Being critical is often seen as being harsh, unfair, or judgmental. When we say someone is "critical," we often mean that their behavior is inappropriately mean-spirited. This is a perfectly reasonable use of everyday language, and the point it makes about how people should treat one another is also perfectly reasonable.

In sociological language, *critical* means something else. Doing sociology in a critical way means looking beyond appearances, understanding root causes, and asking who benefits. Being critical is what links knowledge to action and the potential of building a better society. Being critical in the sociological sense rests on the profoundly *positive* belief that we can use knowledge to understand the flaws of the social world and act to correct them.

The sociological perspective contains a double critique. First, mainstream sociology brings an inherently critical angle of vision to its subject. Second, some particular approaches in sociology carry this critique further by building on values that make sociological analysis especially critical of power and domination.

The critical dimension of mainstream sociology derives from the Enlightenment. Despite the flaws noted earlier, the Enlightenment advocated the use of reason, science, and evidence to critically examine religious truth, established doctrine, and political authority. Given its

Enlightenment roots, sociology has always cast a critical eye on all types of claims, forms of knowledge, and exercises of power.

It is this quality that Peter Berger (1963) called the "debunking" tendency of sociological consciousness. Debunking means that the sociological perspective never takes the social world at face value and never assumes that it is what it appears to be. The sociological perspective rather looks at familiar phenomena in new ways to get beyond the immediately obvious, publicly approved, or officially sanctioned view. In this way, sociology sees through the facades of social structures to their unintended consequences and latent functions. Sociologically speaking, the problem might not be crime but laws, not revolution but government. Berger concludes that sociology is not compatible with totalitarianism, because the debunking quality of sociology will always be in tension with authoritarian claims to knowledge and power.

Although the world has changed since Berger wrote, the need for debunking is greater than ever. The political fundamentalisms of Cold War and rival superpowers have been replaced by other fundamentalisms that are logical targets for sociology's debunking insights. A world in which more and more people feel they know things with absolute certainty is a world that drastically needs the sociological perspective.

At the same time that some people embrace fundamentalist beliefs, others become suspicious and cynical about everything. This stance ("debunking on steroids") is too much of a good thing. For the ultra-cynical poser, all ideas, values, and beliefs are suspect, and none deserve support. Against this stance, sociology offers nuance and judgment. The sociological perspective recognizes that some ideas, values, and beliefs have more merit, logic, or evidence than others. Careful sociological thinkers make such distinctions. Indeed, the ultra-cynical mind-set itself needs debunking. Cynicism helps people avoid action or evade responsibility. A sociological perspective suggests that such inaction, or evasion, *is* action that tacitly supports dominant powers by refusing to challenge them in any way.

Mainstream sociology does not take the world for granted. Just when we think we have the answers, it poses another level of questions. For all these reasons, sociology in its most generic form has always included a critical angle of vision.

Although mainstream sociology is inherently critical, some versions of sociology take critique to another level by adopting certain values as the basis for their critique. In contrast to mainstream sociology, these approaches are devoted to a critical analysis of how social structures create relations of domination.

This fully critical sociology is best understood in contrast to mainstream sociology. Although mainstream sociology is critical because of its debunking tendency, it also adopts a scientific posture of detachment. Mainstream sociology seeks to be value-free, value-neutral, or objective. Put differently, mainstream sociology deliberately refrains from taking sides that would jeopardize its scientific neutrality. Mainstream sociology recognizes that *as citizens*, sociologists can be political actors. But it insists that in their role as scientific sociologists, they must maintain their objectivity.

Critical sociology differs from mainstream sociology on these issues. It emphasizes that in social science, humans are both the subjects and the objects of study. Notions of objectivity derived from the natural sciences don't necessarily translate into social science. But even if sociology could approximate objectivity, critical sociologists reject such a stance. It is not desirable, because the quest for objectivity diverts sociologists from asking the most important questions and from taking a more active role in the resolution of social problems.

Think of the contrast in this way. Mainstream sociology is primarily committed to one set of Enlightenment values having to do with science and objectivity. Critical sociology is primarily committed to another set of Enlightenment values having to do with freedom and equality. The latter values demand critical scrutiny of any social order that imposes unnecessary inequalities or restrictions on people's ability to organize their lives as they wish. These values require critical analysis of social arrangements that create conflicting interests between people and allow one group to benefit at the expense of another.

Critical sociologists deliberately focus on relations of domination, oppression, or exploitation, because these actions so obviously violate the values of freedom and equality. Critical sociologists are willing to advocate for groups who are victimized by such arrangements. Good critical sociologists realize they cannot speak for such groups. But they can explore how social arrangements make it difficult for some to speak for themselves, and they can underscore the importance of changing those arrangements.

Other issues distinguish mainstream from critical sociology. Mainstream sociology's commitment to science means it maintains a strict divide between scientific questions of what *is* and normative questions of what *ought* to be. Critical sociology wants to transcend this divide by linking critical analysis of how the world is organized now with normative arguments for how the world should be organized in the future. Behind such arguments are hopeful, or even utopian assumptions about alternative worlds that might be constructed. Critical sociology is simultaneously pessimistic about the current state of the world and optimistic about its possible futures. It examines our potential for living humanely, the social obstacles that block this potential, and the means to change from a problematic present to a preferable future.

The debate between mainstream and critical sociology is important and complex, and it will not be resolved by anything said here. But what can be said is that sociology is better because of the debate. Each side provides a corrective to the faults of the other. At the extreme, mainstream sociology becomes an inhumane, sterile approach that reduces human beings to objects of scientific curiosity; it needs a course correction through the humane values of critical sociology. At the extreme, critical sociology becomes an empty, ideological stance that denies the complexities of its own value commitments; it needs a course correction through the scientific caution of mainstream sociology.

Sociology's double critique thus derives from mainstream and critical sociology, respectively. My primary goal in this book is to illustrate critical sociology, but I also include the critical insights of mainstream sociology. I do so because these approaches sometimes speak to different issues, because neither seems adequate on its own, because they are often complementary, and because this best conveys the richness of our discipline itself. In the end, it is less important which side is "right" than that both sides coexist and continually provoke us to be reflexive about our role as sociologists and as actors in the world.

Sociology's double critique is also crucial to rethinking the flaws of the Enlightenment itself. Mainstream sociology's notion of debunking accepted truths grew out of the Enlightenment struggle against religion, but there is no reason it can't also foster critical examination of the Enlightenment itself. Critical sociology's challenge to domination also seems tailor-made to examining and overturning those forms of domination that the Enlightenment ignored, accepted, or promoted. Thus, for all its flaws, the Enlightenment provides tools for its own examination, critique, and transformation.

References

Berger, Peter. 1963. *Invitation to Sociology.* New York: Doubleday.

Berger, Peter, and Thomas Luckmann. 1966. *The Social Construction of Reality.* Garden City, NY: Anchor.

Giddens, Anthony. 1984. *The Constitution of Society.* Berkeley: University of California Press.

Goffman, Erving. 1959. *The Presentation of Self in Everyday Life.* Garden City, NY: Anchor.

Lemert, Charles. 2008. *Social Things.* 4th ed. Lanham, MD: Rowman & Littlefield.

———. 2013. *Social Theory: The Multicultural and Classic Readings.* 5th ed. Boulder, CO: Westview Press.

Mills, C. Wright. 1959. *The Sociological Imagination.* New York: Oxford University Press.

Zeitlin, Irving. 1987. *Ideology and the Development of Sociological Theory.* Englewood Cliffs, NJ: Prentice Hall.

How We Become Who We Are

Steven M. Buechler

The previous chapter traced the history of the individual. We learned that the individual is a late arrival who appears only with the rise of modernity. All societies contain people, but only modern ones have individuals.

This chapter traces the biography of the individual. Here, the individual arrives late in a different sense. We become individual only through socialization. We begin this process utterly dependent on others. Only after extensive social support do we develop self-awareness, become individuals, and acquire identity. In both historical and biographical terms, individuals only emerge through social connections with others. We are always social before we are individual (Lemert 2008).

When we ponder what makes one person different from another, there are at least two types of answers. A psychological answer seeks unique traits to explain personal differences. A sociological answer examines the relationships people have with others. Here individuality arises not from something internal, but rather from our external ties to others. A classic version of this idea sees the individual existing at the center of a "web of group affiliations" (Simmel 1908).

A modern variant is the sociograph. You can construct your own. Draw a small circle in the center of a piece of paper to symbolize you. Now draw spokes radiating out to other circles that represent the people in your life. Your relationships with those people differ in many ways: the length of time you have known them, the closeness or intensity of your bonds with them, and the like. Imagine drawing spokes in differing colors, thicknesses, or lengths to capture such nuances.

If you took this exercise seriously, the resulting sociograph would be different from those constructed by others. Sociographs illustrate how no two people occupy the same location in a web of group affiliations. Put differently, we all have unique locations in social networks.

A sociological perspective thus explains the uniqueness of individuals not by focusing inward on personal traits but rather by focusing outward on social networks. We differ from others because we occupy different locations in different networks. Even individuality is not "personal" as much as it is "social."

Take the exercise a step further. Imagine moving to some other circle in your sociograph and constructing that person's sociograph. Their web would include you and some people you know in common, but it would also include people who aren't in your web. Now imagine constructing a sociograph for everyone in your sociograph. As the number of spokes multiply exponentially, the circles representing individuals become less prominent than the ties linking them together. Indeed, the circles representing people come to look like fleeting interruptions in a flow of social forces and connections between them.

This imaginary exercise dramatizes how individuals don't exist apart from social ties with other individuals and groups. Moreover, individuality itself (even with its connotation of uniqueness) is best seen as a product of our distinctive ties with others rather than a purely personal set of traits.

In what follows, we explore how individual selves emerge through social processes. The exploration begins with C. H. Cooley's looking-glass self and proceeds to the synthesis of George Herbert Mead. We then examine symbolic interactionism and identity theory. The chapter closes with observations about how human beings are reflexive actors who bring self-awareness to every situation they encounter.

Cooley's Contributions

Charles Horton Cooley made two vital contributions to understanding how selves emerge through a social process. His work anticipates that of George Herbert Mead, who inspired the symbolic interactionist tradition, which remains sociology's best guide to unraveling questions about self and society.

The first of Cooley's (1998) contributions concerns the role of primary groups in social life. Primary groups involve intimate, face-to-face interaction with others. Within primary groups, we know others and are known to them as whole people, because our involvement is ongoing, all-inclusive, and central to our sense of self.

People also belong to secondary groups, but their connections to such groups are less personal, less intimate, more formal, and often shorter lived than with primary groups. In the sociograph you imagined a moment ago, your primary group consists of the people with whom you have the strongest (and often longest) bonds. They are probably the people closest to you in the sociograph. Farther away from you and your primary group, there are probably other nodes and networks that represent your secondary groups.

The vast majority of people begin their lives within a primary group of family members and perhaps others who are regarded as "family." For better or worse, whether "functional" or "dysfunctional," such familial primary groups are the first and most important social group through which most of us are socialized and develop a sense of self and individuality.

As our self develops, we venture out and join other groups. On the first day of school, we become members of a secondary group of other students. What might start as a frightening social encounter with strangers often develops into another primary group. As we come to know, interact, and play with the same circle of kids, we might form increasingly intimate bonds that become primary relationships.

In adolescence, such peer groups often become more primary and intimate than our family groups. When young people feel as if their friends understand them in ways their parents no longer do (and when parents feel the same way), it is a good indication of multiple primary ties (and tension between them). A more intense emotional tie might then arise, as a romantic partner displaces both the peer group and the family. And somewhat later, we might marry one of those partners and begin a family that will become our next primary group.

Throughout the life cycle, our web of group affiliations consists of shifting combinations of primary and secondary groups. But primary groups remain central to who we are. Our sense of self is intimately connected to these groups. In somewhat different sociological language, primary groups are crucial reference groups; we refer ourselves to these groups to judge who we are, what to do, how to act, and where to find validation for the people we have become. For all these reasons, our webs are held together by our thickest social ties to primary groups.

Cooley's second major contribution is his notion of the self, which is closely tied to primary groups. The key point is simply that there is no self or individual apart from our relationships with other people. "From Cooley's vantage point, then, the self is a social product, a product 'produced' largely in the primary group. It is a product best labeled a 'looking-glass self,' in that a child obtains an identity only with the realization that his or her picture, idea or image of himself or herself 'reflects' other people's picture of him or her" (Reynolds 2003, 63–64).

Imagination is crucial to Cooley's notion of the self. To say that we live in an imaginary world sounds like a put-down. But imagining involves basic processes of thought and cognition; to imagine is to think about the world, about people in the world, about our impressions of them, and about their impressions of us. In this sense, we inevitably live in an imaginary world, because we routinely try to understand the world by thinking about it. These processes are central to how we construct, maintain, or undermine our sense of self and identity.

When we combine primary groups and imagination, we can see the logic in Cooley's "looking-glass self." A crucial part of our imaginary lives involves speculation about the thoughts of others. The thoughts of others, in turn, contain impressions about who we are (and we're pretty disappointed if they don't). It is through this interactive process that we arrive at our sense of self.

This self has three components. First, we imagine how we appear to others. Second, we imagine how they evaluate our appearances. Finally, we construct a sense of self, based on our imaginary understanding of how others evaluate us (Reynolds 2003, 64). Put more succinctly: I am who I think you think I am.

Although the term *looking-glass* sounds quaint, the metaphor of a mirror still makes the point. Without others to reflect who we are back to us, we would have no reliable means of arriving at a sense of self. Common sense might dismiss this as "imaginary," but sociological insight says that this is all we have to base a self on.

We can even dispense with the metaphor. We use real mirrors when we want to assess, modify, or repair our physical appearance. The mirror is essential to get outside ourselves and see ourselves from the perspective of other people. In parallel fashion, our self only becomes known to us through the perspective of other people.

Cooley claimed we also develop strong, emotional responses to the selves that we construct through the looking-glass process. The emotions Cooley regarded as most central were pride and shame. When our judgments of others' judgments about us suggest we are viewed positively, then our self incorporates pride in who we are. When our judgments of others' judgments about us suggest we are viewed negatively, then our self incorporates shame about who we are. For Cooley, the looking-glass self was as much about emotional responses as cognitive processes (Scheff 2005).

Popular culture often tells people to "be positive" and "feel good about themselves," as if this could be accomplished by sheer will. More sociologically informed advice would say surround yourself with people who are positive about and feel good about you. Easier said than done, but if Cooley is right, our self-feelings do not arise on their own and cannot long exist in contradiction to the feelings we imagine others have about who we are.

Mead's Synthesis

Building on the work of Cooley and others, George Herbert Mead formulated a distinct perspective on self and society. Mead wrote little but was a gifted lecturer at the University of Chicago. Upon his retirement and death in 1931, his students assembled his ideas into a sociological classic titled *Mind, Self and Society* (Mead 1934).

Mead's work synthesized ideas prevalent in late nineteenth- and early twentieth century social thought. Georg Simmel's web of group affiliations is one element. So is Max Weber's insistence that we can only understand social action if we see it from the perspective of the actor. Cooley's looking-glass self plays an obvious role. William James had also studied the social self. Mead also drew on the work of John Dewey, who approached mind not as a physical structure but as a process of interpretation and meaning. Finally, W. I. Thomas had discussed the "definition of the situation" and demonstrated that situations defined as real will be real in their consequences. The imagery of social actors imposing definitions on the world around them and acting on those definitions was central to Mead's work.

Mead's synthesis put him at odds with other sociological approaches. Many versions of sociology analyze social structures as static entities, but Mead saw society as a dynamic process of change and fluidity. For Mead, the social world is less like still pictures and more like a movie playing at multiple frames per second. Moreover, although some versions of sociology explain the world through casual relationships of independent and dependent variables, Mead saw social elements as interrelated and interdependent. Each part gained its meaning from its relationship to others and to the whole, so it is difficult to isolate elements that can be analyzed as cause and effect.

Having said that, Mead is clearly in the sociological camp by recognizing that society precedes and shapes the individual. Although grammatically awkward, a more conceptually accurate title for Mead's book might have been "Society, Mind, Self and Society," to suggest the priority of society as a social environment in which minds and selves develop in individuals who only then become competent social actors.

Mead's exploration of minds and selves develops some of the core ideas of interactionist sociology. The first challenge is to understand the development of individual minds. Mead's concern is not with the physical structure of the brain but with the social process of the mind. The focus is not neurons and synapses but rather consciousness and meaning.

Mead begins with behaviorist logic but quickly moves from static psychological behaviorism to symbolic social psychology. He defines a gesture as any action that serves as a stimulus and provokes a response. The response becomes a stimulus for the initial actor who then responds to it, which in turn becomes a new stimulus for the second actor. In this way, a conversation of gestures is an interactive spiral of stimuli and response between two or more actors.

Whereas behaviorists applied this logic to all human behavior, Mead thought conversations of gestures were primarily found in the nonhuman animal world (which is the basis for much behaviorist research going all the way back to Pavlov's salivating dogs). Such nonhuman animal behavior is largely rooted in instincts, meaning that animals are pre-wired to act in certain ways and do not rely on symbolic interpretations to do so. Mead's favorite example was a dogfight in which the behavior of each dog becomes a stimulus provoking an instinctive response in the other dog, leading to an escalation of barking, snarling, flattened ears, bared teeth, biting, and the like.

Mead departed from behaviorism by arguing that the vast majority of human action—and certainly the most sociologically interesting action—could not be understood as instinctual, unthinking patterns of stimulus and response. Humans differ from other animals because they formulate, interpret, and attribute *meaning* to actions and to people in their environment. This is why a boxing match is very different from a dogfight. Unlike dogs, boxers interpret, imagine, anticipate, and deceive as part of their strategy. It is this complex mental world—even in the brutality of the boxing ring—that qualitatively distinguishes human *action* from animal *behavior*.

To capture human action, Mead proposed different terminology. In contrast to the simple gestures of animals, human interaction involves significant symbols. Simple gestures become significant symbols when they meet two requirements. First, they carry a specific meaning. Second, that meaning is shared within some community of people. Although this might sound obtuse, the best example is right here on the page. Human languages are vast collections of significant symbols known as words, which in turn can be put together in larger, meaningful units like phrases, sentences, paragraphs, and even books. Physical gestures (handshakes, applause, the finger) can also be significant symbols if they carry a specific, shared meaning.

Significant symbols arise from interaction, because it is only through interaction that they achieve significance. Consider that the meaning is in the response. If you utter a phrase that elicits immediate recognition, the odds are it is a significant symbol that carries the same meaning for others as it does for you. If your phrase is met with a blank stare, the odds are it's not a significant symbol, because it is not calling up a similar meaning in those around you.

Here's a simple example. I live with a cat that freaks out when someone rings the doorbell. After an especially traumatic episode, I tried a stopgap measure of taping a small piece of paper over the doorbell. To me, the paper meant "don't ring the doorbell—knock instead." The next day, a delivery person rang the doorbell (traumatizing the cat). The day after that, someone selling something I didn't need rang the doorbell (further traumatizing the cat). Neither person interpreted the paper over the doorbell in the way I intended. It was not a significant symbol, because there was no shared meaning between me and my visitors. The day after that, a neighbor came to borrow something and gently knocked on the door. In this instant, the piece of paper became a significant symbol, because she assigned the same meaning to it that I did and acted accordingly. She did so because she had also tried to keep people from ringing her doorbell and disturbing her child's afternoon nap.

The simple example illustrates several larger points. Significant symbols are not static; they emerge through interaction only when it becomes evident that people assign the same meaning to some part of their environment. Moreover, what is a significant symbol to some people might not be a significant symbol to other people. This is most obvious when speakers of different languages attempt to communicate; it is a struggle to find even a minimal set of significant symbols so they can understand one another. But even within the same language group, there are subcultures of people who speak distinctive sublanguages known to them but not to outsiders. Indeed, the identity of many subcultures depends precisely on who "gets it" (that is, shares their significant symbols) and who doesn't have a clue. The abbreviations and shortcuts that comprise the vocabulary of texting (well understood by those who text and often impenetrable to those who don't) is merely a recent example of this long-standing aspect of human communication.

This demonstrates the social roots of individual minds. Here's the logic. "Mind" is shorthand for the process of thinking, involving consciousness and meaning. Thinking is really an internalized conversation of significant symbols. The focus of our thought could be anything: how to spend the weekend, whether we should call an elderly relative, pondering the motivation behind a friend's snide comment, or whatever. Regardless of the topic, to think is to have a silent conversation with oneself about that topic. Whereas interaction is an externalized conversation of significant symbols with others, thinking is an internalized conversation of significant symbols with ourselves.

Mead implies we cannot think without significant symbols; they are the building blocks of the internalized conversations that compose thinking. But if the symbols that comprise thinking are significant, this means they carry a shared meaning. Such shared meanings can only arise from interactions with others. The conclusion seems obvious. Humans are born with a physical brain but not a social mind. Minds are only acquired through social interaction with others. That social process provides us with the shared meanings of the significant symbols that allow us to think. When it comes to minds—as with so much else—we must first be social before we can be individual. Sociologically speaking, socialization makes us human by developing the capacities that distinguish us as a species.

Mead's argument might seem convoluted, but it resonates with common sense. Imagine encountering someone on a city street who is babbling incomprehensibly. What conclusions do we draw about their mental state? Now imagine that people who speak this person's language appear, and they have an animated discussion in Norwegian about how to find the subway station. We are likely to revise our opinion of their mental state when we recognize that they share meanings and a language with a group of people (just not us). But if no one ever comes along who understands our urban babbler, we are likely to conclude that they have "lost their mind." Even everyday language links making sense, shared meanings, and having a mind.

For Mead, the distinctive qualities of human interaction emerge from our ability to create, learn, and communicate significant symbols. They allow us to interpret stimuli and respond in meaningful ways. They allow us to develop abstract concepts that go beyond immediate experience and classify experiences into categories. This allows imaginative reflection on past experiences and future possibilities rather than learning only through trial and error. In the end, this makes intelligent action possible, as we use significant symbols, shared meanings, and abstract concepts to learn from the past, interpret the present, anticipate the future, and link them all together.

If minds only emerge through a social process, the same is true for selves. We are not born with a self but rather acquire one through socialization. Cooley's looking-glass self is an early statement of this position, and Mead builds on it.

The self has two components; one is there from the beginning. The "I" refers to impulses to act toward the world. This inborn "I" is later joined by a socialized "Me" to form a fully developed social self. Selves thereby involve interaction between the "I" and the "Me."

Although the impulses of the "I" are channeled by the socialization of the "Me," it never disappears. The "I" persists as an active subject; it is the part of us that acts in the moment. The persistence of the "I" even in the mature self means that people are always capable of spontaneous, creative, unpredictable actions. The self is never completely determined by larger social forces, because we always retain the capacity to act back upon those forces.

To have a self means to see oneself as an object. It is the capacity to be self-aware or self-conscious. The "I" can never achieve such awareness because it is always acting in the moment. It is the "Me" that provides this self-awareness. The "Me" only develops through "taking the role of the other." This is Mead's version of Cooley's looking-glass self. The underlying idea is quite similar: We arrive at a sense of self by imaginatively taking the role of other people in our social environment. From their perspective, we are an object in their world. When we imaginatively adopt their perspective, we are able to see ourselves as an object. We develop self-awareness.

Once again we must be social before we can be individual. Until we interact with others whose roles we imaginatively take, we cannot develop a concept of ourselves as an object. We need others whose roles we take to provide the mirrors that tell us that we have a self and who we are. Immersion in sustained interaction with others is the only way we develop a mind and a self; it is the way we become human.

To have a self is to be capable of observations, judgments, and feelings about the self that only become possible by taking the role of the other. If we act in ways that surprise others (and ourselves), this demonstrates the capacity of the "I" to act in novel ways. If we explain such action by saying "I'm not myself today," we are displaying a fully developed self. The statement is logically ludicrous but sociologically sensible. We are saying that some momentary action is inconsistent with a well-established sense of who we are based on a long process of role taking. Only the "Me" can offer such observations about the self.

The "Me" is thus the perspective of others internalized by the self. The "Me" is a developmental product of interaction that emerges in stages. As infants in the pre-play stage, we are incapable of getting outside ourselves and taking the role of others. Infants are all "I" and no "Me." As young children, however, we begin to develop both a mind and the ability to take the role of the other. In the play stage, we take the role of significant others in our social environment. These are specific people who are familiar to us. As we play, we model their behavior and imaginatively see the world from their perspective. This is the earliest version of seeing ourselves as an object; by imaginatively seeing ourselves through the eyes of our parents or primary caretakers, we begin to develop a sense of self.

As we become more skilled at role taking, we enter the game stage and simultaneously take the roles of multiple others in more complex situations. The famous example is playing baseball, but any team sport will do. To play such games well, each player must anticipate the actions of everyone else on the team. By anticipating their actions in different situations, good players align their actions to fit with overall team strategy. Such game playing presupposes an ability to take multiple roles that only emerges over time. This is why young children can handle some interactive play but are incapable of more complex team games.

As we progress from taking the role of significant others to multiple others, we eventually take the role of the generalized Other. This is not a particular person or group but rather the larger society and its norms and values. Returning to Cooley's language, the development of the self proceeds by switching mirrors. As very young children, it is particular, significant others who provide the mirror that tells us who we are. As older children, it is multiple others who provide that mirror. As socialization continues, the mirror becomes all of the attitudes, values, and beliefs that compose our society itself. The constant is that we look outside ourselves to know who we are. The variable is which "others" are most central in reflecting our self back to us.

The ability to take the role of the generalized Other signals a fully developed self. This "Other" is initially outside us, but it becomes incorporated inside us in the form of the "Me." The mature self combines the acting "I" and the socialized "Me." Because the self requires a "Me" and the "Me" requires taking the role of the other, the self only emerges through social interaction with others.

The development of mind and self go hand in hand. The internal conversation that comprises the mind can only occur with a corresponding self-awareness that signifies a self. Both emerge through interaction with others that provides shared meanings and role-taking opportunities. Although later sociologists have pursued many variations on these themes, Mead's synthesis provides a vital sociological understanding of the relationship between self and society.

Symbolic Interactionism

Mead's student Herbert Blumer took the lead in publishing Mead's (1934) ideas. Blumer also coined the term *symbolic interactionism* to underscore the importance of symbolic meanings in interpreting human action. The phrase sounds awkward, but conveys much about the assumptions of this approach.

Blumer (1969) subsequently claimed that symbolic interactionism could be summarized in three basic premises. The first is that human beings act toward things on the basis of the meanings things have for them. What is important is not the things but rather the meanings that we (and others) attach to them.

This seemingly subtle distinction makes a big difference. Consider the contrast between psychological behaviorism and symbolic interactionism. Behaviorists explain what we do as responses to stimuli in the environment. The environment determines behavior by providing stimuli that mechanistically lead us to seek rewards and avoid punishments. The stimuli, response, rewards, and punishments are assumed to be transparently self-evident to both the organism and the behaviorist. There is no need to explore the subjective "black box" of the mind; behaviorism rather seeks an external explanation linking behavioral responses to environmental stimuli.

This makes sense if people respond directly to things. It makes much less sense if they respond to the meanings of things, as Blumer claims. Interactionism sees action as a process of self-indication. Actors select which aspects of their environment are meaningful for them. Because they assign meanings to their surroundings, it could be said that actors determine their environment rather than the other way around. Because meanings vary across persons and situations, we must examine how minds shape meanings. Interactionism thereby seeks an internal explanation of action by linking minds, meanings, and actions.

The first premise establishes that meanings are central. The second is that meanings are derived from social interaction. This locates meanings between two polar opposites. They are not purely objective qualities attached to things in the same way in all times and places. But they are also not purely subjective choices of individuals outside interaction. Meanings are rather intersubjective accomplishments of social interaction. Like Mead's significant symbols, objects acquire meanings as a result of ongoing social interaction.

This premise explains variability in the meanings of objects over time and across groups. Why do people disagree about the appropriateness of Indian mascots for sports teams? How do people interpret the meaning of the Civil War in the South and the North? What does the word *gay* mean to different generations of people? When is graffiti a marker of gang affiliation, and when is it art? What does it mean to have a tattoo or a piercing? Such meanings are not fixed and objective; neither are they purely subjective and idiosyncratic. It is interactions in different groups that define the "same event" like the Civil War as a humiliating defeat or a glorious victory. Both meanings are "true" in different social worlds that sustain those definitions through interaction.

The variability of meanings reflects the pragmatist heritage of symbolic interaction in which things acquire meaning by how they are used or how people interact with them. Thus, a tree has different meanings and becomes a different object for the botanist, the timber company, and the poet. Take another example. A woman nursing an infant is interacting in a way that defines her breasts as nourishment and nurturance. That same woman making love with her sexual partner is interacting in a way that defines her breasts as erotic stimulation and gratification. That same woman undergoing an exam by her doctor is engaged in an interaction that defines her breasts as potential sites of disease and malignancy. Same woman, same breasts—but drastically different meanings arise from different interactions with different people.

The ways that interactions create and sustain meanings also establish the definition of the situation. Such definitions are intersubjective, cultural creations that provide cues about what to expect and how to behave in a given situation. Differing definitions of the situation create differ- ent meanings in "objectively" similar situations. A woman who bares her breast in public to nurse her infant might meet with acceptance, whereas a woman who does so in a strip joint might be condemned or even arrested (depending on local ordinances). A male doctor examining a female patient is engaging in behavior that could be construed as sexual assault in other settings, but is regarded as normal as long as the medical definition of the situation is maintained.

Blumer's third and final premise is that meanings are handled and modified through an interpretive process. This means that even when meanings are well established (and especially when they are not), people still tailor them to the specific situation at hand. This work begins with the process of self-indication in which people "create" their environment on the basis of intersubjective meanings.

The process continues because no two situations are exactly the same and general meanings must be adapted to specific settings. People are active throughout this process. "The actor selects, checks, suspends, regroups, and transforms the meanings in the light of the situation in which he is placed" (Blumer 1969, 5). This process of interpretation is a formative one in which meanings are used, revised, and modified as the actor fashions action that will be meaningful to all concerned.

Blumer's formulation of symbolic interactionism puts it at odds not only with psychological behaviorism but also with more structural approaches in sociology. Blumer insists that concepts like structure, system, function, or institution are really shorthand abstractions for people interacting with one another. Although the shorthand is convenient, it becomes a trap when we speak as if these abstractions act or even exist apart from the interactions that sustain them. For Blumer, good sociology avoids structuralist abstractions by focusing on the meanings and interactions that create, sustain, and modify social patterns.

Identity Theory

Interactionist theory provides sociology with its best understandings of identity. The starting point is that the self is the ability to see oneself as an object, evidenced by self-awareness or self-consciousness. This awareness originally emerges from, and subsequently depends on, interactions with other people.

We move from self to identity by asking what kind of object we see ourselves to be. If self is the object, identity is the meanings attached to that object. Identity emerges when meanings are attached to the object we call the self.

Blumer's first premise is that it is not objects but their meanings that are important. This applies to identity as follows. Everybody acquires a self. We couldn't interact with people if they didn't have a self through which to organize interaction. What is of interest in interactions is not the generic selves everyone possesses, but the particular identities or meanings of those selves. This is how we identify ourselves and others; who people are is a function of the meanings or identities linked to selves.

Blumer's second premise is that meanings arise through interactions with others. They are intersubjective accomplishments. The same applies to the meanings we call identities. Just as Mead's symbols become significant when they call up the same meaning in others as they do in us, identities become real when there is a shared understanding about who someone is. "One's identity is established when others *place* him as a social object by assigning him the same words of identity that he appropriates for himself or *announces*. It is in the coincidence of placements and announcements that identity becomes a meaning of the self" (Gregory Stone, cited in Vryan, Adler, and Adler 2003, 368; italics in original).

Take an extreme example. I might believe, and then announce to the world, that I am the second coming of Christ. If I persist in this claim, I will be dismissed as a nutcase. If I convince a small band of devoted followers of my claim, we will all be dismissed as mentally unstable (but perhaps dangerous because of our numbers). But if I somehow convince hundreds, then thousands, and finally millions of people around the world of my identity claim, and they relate to me as if I am that person, then don't I become that person? If my announcements and others' placements concur, does that not become my identity? In less extreme cases, the process is clear: identity emerges when an actor's announcements and others' placements coincide.

Blumer's third premise is that meanings are handled and modified through an interpretive process as people tailor meanings to fit specific situations. Applied to identity, this means that we continually reinterpret, select, check, regroup, suspend, and transform our understandings of who we and others are as part of ongoing interaction. For example, we understand that people (including ourselves) have different identities in different situations. When we encounter them in a certain situation, we selectively present some of our identities and expect them to do the same. If everyone enacts identities appropriate to the situation, interaction will proceed smoothly.

Each of Blumer's premises about meaning thus applies to identity itself. Interactionism also distinguishes several types of identities, including social, situational, and personal identities (Vryan, Adler, and Adler 2003, 367–372).

Social identities arise when we announce and others place us in positions within social structures. Identities based on class, race, gender, religion, or sexual orientation exemplify social identities. They are broad social categories that link us to others with similar traits and separate us from those with different traits. Social identities shape how people are enabled or constrained by social order; differing opportunities emerge from the statuses granted to or withheld from these identities.

Situational identities arise when we engage in face-to-face interactions with others and organize our action through situationally appropriate roles and definitions of the situation. Although they might be repetitive and patterned, situations are relatively short-lived. When we attend a baseball game, we become a fan; when we go on vacation, we become a tourist; when we leave for work, we become a motorist or commuter. We thus acquire a situational identity in a particular context. The ways we enact this identity are constrained by cultural norms and situational definitions, but there is always room for some individual creativity in enacting situational identities.

Personal identities arise when we construct biographical narratives about who we are. They distinguish us from others in the same positions or situations. Thus, part of my story is that when I was an undergraduate, I made my living (and more) as a drummer in a rock-and-roll band. Even though I stopped playing when I went to graduate school more than thirty-five years ago, it is part of who I am, because it is who I once was. Moreover, it helps establish my distinctiveness: not many college professors are former rock drummers, and not many rock drummers become college professors (and it's probably just as well that they don't).

Situational identities like baseball fan, grocery shopper, or wedding party member are short-lived and don't necessarily reveal much about who we are. Social identities are more permanent because they are difficult or impossible to change, although people can either embrace them or hold them at arms' length. Personal identities are more lasting in a different way, because they rest on a person's accumulated biography. Although we can distinguish different types of identity, the basic principles of identity theory still apply. Identities of all types are meanings attached to the self that emerge through announcements by self and placements by others.

Like all meanings, identities are socially constructed, maintained, and transformed. Most identity transformations are gradual, developmental transitions through the life cycle. Even though parenthood or retirement might feel sudden to the individual, they are routine in that they happen to many people and it is possible to anticipate and plan for them in advance. Other, less common identity transformations are quick and radical in nature. When prisoners of war are brainwashed, when people undergo a conversion experience, or when individuals are radicalized by extremist websites, they might renounce former identities and embrace dramatically different ones very quickly.

Another type of identity transformation involves "suspended identity" (Schmid and Jones 1991). This occurs when people must leave one identity behind while adopting another identity. If they intend to reclaim their former identity, it is not so much terminated or transformed as it is suspended. It's as if they hang that identity in the closet until they can wear it once again. When citizen soldiers are called up as army reservists or National Guard troops, they suspend their citizen identity and adopt a soldier identity. Unlike regular army troops, however, they are likely to see their citizen identity as the "real" one, which is temporarily suspended during military duty.

A classic case is people who go to prison. Before going to prison, people have a "pre-prison identity." Like the civilian anticipating becoming a soldier, these citizens anticipate becoming a prisoner as they move through the criminal justice system. A common response is self-insulation by minimizing contact with others, avoiding conflict or violence, and avoiding any situations that might undermine their preprison identity.

Despite these resolutions, inmates cannot take their pre-prison identity with them, nor can they live in complete isolation. They have to create a prison identity to relate to staff, guards, and other prisoners. Short-term inmates see this prison identity as temporary and situational, although they worry that it might displace their pre-prison identity. While serving time, inmates experience a dualistic self. They try to sustain a pre-prison identity, which is temporarily suspended, privately held, and rarely affirmed. They simultaneously enact a prison identity, which is self-consciously learned, enacted for self and others, and affirmed through prison interactions.

Toward the end of their sentence, prisoners develop a release identity that sets aside their prison identity and revives their suspended identity. Like earlier stages, this involves much self-talk about who they really are, how they might have changed, and how they can become the person they used to be. Upon leaving prison, former inmates acquire a post-prison identity that distances them from their prison experience and helps restore their suspended identity (Schmid and Jones 1991).

Prison thereby poses a particular identity challenge. Although most of us will not go to prison, all of us undergo processes of identity formation, maintenance, and transformation. Interactionist theory provides powerful tools for understanding them.

People as Reflexive Actors

Interactionist theory underscores how human action is guided by reflexivity. People are conscious of the meanings of selves, others, and objects in their world, and they use this knowledge to organize actions and pursue goals. The premise of reflexivity is shared by other theoretical perspectives as well.

[...] [T]here is a debate in sociology over the relationship between structure and agency. Structure-based approaches emphasize large social patterns that seem to dwarf individuals. Agency-based approaches stress individual choices and seem to deny the weight of external factors. Neither approach is completely satisfactory; the challenge is to strike a balance between the two.

One attempt is structuration theory (Giddens 1984). It rejects a view of structures as merely external and constraining forces that exist on their own. Rather than structures, it speaks of "structuration processes" as a way of linking structure and action. Here, structures are no more than the outcomes of past actions and the means for organizing current ones.

Seen this way, structuration processes sometimes constrain action because they are obstacles to what we want to do. But they can also enable action when they provide resources and means to pursue goals. Rather than seeing structures as external, controlling forces, we should see structuration processes as providing opportunities to act (within certain limits). Moreover, when people act, they unintentionally reproduce (and sometimes transform) those very structures.

This approach assumes people are reflexive actors. People in society "are vastly skilled in the practical accomplishments of social activities and are expert 'sociologists.' The knowledge they possess is not incidental to the persistent patterning of social life but integral to it" (Giddens 1984, 26). In other words, people routinely use practical consciousness in daily life to monitor their actions and the actions of others and to align both. This consciousness contains much practical knowledge about how things work in a particular society and culture.

People also incorporate sociological knowledge into practical consciousness; ideas like self-fulfilling prophecies, unintended consequences, or group-think have migrated from social science to everyday consciousness. It is difficult to appreciate the importance of this practical consciousness, because it becomes second nature once we're socialized. But if you've had any experiences with other cultures or languages that made you feel "dumb," it underscores how "smart" you are about your own culture and language and how unconsciously you call upon knowledge of it to do things.

Another way of describing reflexivity is sociological competence. "This seemingly native, highly practical, virtually ubiquitous capacity sustains us individually, but it also contributes mightily to our ability to form and keep social relations with others. Without it, social life would be impossible. Without it, every time we entered a new and different social situation, we would be forced to learn anew what to think of it and how to behave. But, most of the time, we understand what is going on and where we fit in" (Lemert 2008, 5). Like linguistic competence, sociological competence seems to be an inherent capacity to understand the social world. When it is matched with socialization, we use it in an almost effortless way.

Although acquiring sociological competence is *almost* effortless, it nonetheless requires practice. Charles Lemert (2008) draws on Pierre Bourdieu's (1977) notion of habitus to understand how sociological competence is sustained through practice. The concept of habitus underscores how much of social life involves habitual actions that once had to be learned but then became second nature—things that we do unthinkingly, and usually quite competently. Like Giddens's structuration, Bourdieu's habitus is where agency and structure meet and their seeming contradiction is resolved. Habitual practices simultaneously result from social rules (structures) and individual flourishes (agency) that produce action (Lemert 2008, 43).

From another angle, habitus is the intersection between actions experienced as novel by the individual while simultaneously conforming to social patterns. This is most evident when we first learn things that have yet to become habitual. The first time we drive a car, have a sexual encounter, or work at a job, the event is new to us but part of a larger pattern that happens in roughly similar ways for millions of people. The awkwardness that characterizes each of these original experiences demonstrates that these competencies must indeed be learned and practiced. At a certain point, driving, sex, or working are accomplished with much less awkwardness, signifying that we have learned and habitualized them. We have acquired sociological competence.

In everyday life, we focus on immediate concerns. We rely on sociological competence and acquired habits. It rarely occurs to us that our actions help sustain the society around us. Nonetheless, habitual actions performed by socially competent actors do precisely this. Giddens's structuration, Lemert's competence, and Bourdieu's habitus all point to the same conclusion. Social order rests upon the reflexivity of actors who use existing structures to do things while simultaneously (if unintentionally) sustaining, re-creating, and transforming those very structures. Without reflexivity, social order itself would be impossible.

Conclusion

Interactionist theory provides rich insights into mind, self, identity, and reflexivity. It is a good example of humanistic sociology. As such, it is critical in two ways. First, it is critical to an accurate understanding of the complex, dialectical connections between self and society, structure and agency, and micro and macro levels of society.

Second, it is critical by revealing that things are not always what they appear to be (Berger 1963). If we want to see beyond appearances to underlying realities, this theory is like a back-stage pass in the theater of social life. Consider individualism one more time. As noted earlier, US culture is probably the most individualistic in human history. If any culture assumes we are individual before we are social, it is ours. Interactionist theory is thus critical to seeing all the ways we are unavoidably social before we can become individual (Lemert 2008).

The third sense of critical sociology explicitly examines power, domination, exploitation, and oppression. Here, interactionism has been largely silent. It critically examines US individualism, but it uncritically accepts US egalitarianism.

US culture has always emphasized its distance from European traditions, where rank, status, class, and distinction are crucial. US ideology describes a "classless" society where everyone gets a chance and no one is held back by artificial social barriers. Although not necessarily embracing these specific ideas, interactionism's image of society also downplays vertical hierarchies and emphasizes horizontal lifeworlds. The interactionist image of society is multiple social worlds of distinctive meanings and identities coexisting alongside one another. It implicitly sees society as a pluralistic conglomeration of such worlds.

What is lacking in this image is the role of power in social life. Although it is true that different social worlds construct different meanings, it is also true that some worlds have the privilege and power to make their meanings normative while marginalizing others. The meanings central to interactionist theory are often hierarchically organized so that some groups benefit at the expense of others.

This is nicely captured in the notion of ideology as meaning in the service of power (Thompson 1990). Interactionism has provided a rich vocabulary for analyzing meanings in social life, but it will only reach its fully critical potential when it examines the relationships between meaning and power.

References

Berger, Peter. 1963. *Invitation to Sociology*. New York: Doubleday.

Blumer, Herbert. 1969. *Symbolic Interaction: Perspective and Method*. Englewood Cliffs, NJ: Prentice Hall.

Bourdieu, Pierre. 1977. *Outline of a Theory of Practice*. London: Cambridge University Press.

Cooley, Charles Horton. 1998. *On Self and Social Organization*. Chicago: University of Chicago Press.

Giddens, Anthony. 1984. *The Constitution of Society*. Berkeley: University of California Press.

Lemert, Charles. 2008. *Social Things*. 4th ed. Lanham, MD: Rowman & Littlefield.

Mead, George Herbert. 1934/1962. *Mind, Self and Society*. Chicago: University of Chicago Press.

Reynolds, Larry T. 2003. "Early Representatives." In *Handbook of Symbolic Interactionism*, ed. Larry T. Reynolds and Nancy J. Herman-Kinney, 59–81. Lanham, MD: AltaMira.

Scheff, Thomas. 2005. "Looking Glass Self: Goffman as Symbolic Interactionist." *Symbolic Interaction* 28(2):147–166.

Schmid, Thomas J., and Richard S. Jones. 1991. "Suspended Identity: Identity Transformation in a Maximum Security Prison." *Symbolic Interaction* 14(4):415–432.

Simmel, Georg. 1908/1955. *Conflict and the Web or Group Affiliations.* New York: Free Press.

Thompson, John. 1990. *Ideology and Modern Culture.* Stanford, CA: Stanford University Press.

Vryan, Kevin D., Patricia A. Adler, and Peter Adler. 2003. "Identity." In *Handbook of Symbolic Interactionism*, ed. Larry T. Reynolds and Nancy J. Herman-Kinney, 367–390. Lanham, MD: AltaMira.

Research Methods in Social Psychology

Leonard Newman and Ralph Erber

Solomon Asch's Story: A Beautiful Idea

Consider the case of the late Solomon Asch, who became widely known for his work on conformity and how people form impressions of others. By his own admission, Asch became a social psychologist because he was intrigued by the ideas that researchers in the field pursued (Tesser, 1990).

Asch's interest in conformity was rooted partly in Muzafer Sherif 's (1935, 1936) work on that topic, which made use of the autokinetic effect. In his studies, Sherif had asked participants to look at a bright source of light presented in front of a dark background. The autokinetic effect is the perception that after a time, the bright light appears to move. This illusion, which has to do with our visual-perceptual system, explains why we perceive stars in the night sky to be stationary objects, as long as we don't focus on any single one. Once we do focus on a single star, it appears to wander after a few seconds. The precise reasons for this experience, which happens to everyone, were of little concern to Sherif and Asch.

What mattered to both was that any judgment about the apparent motion of the bright light is entirely subjective and open to interpretation. This particular feature of the autokinetic effect made it a perfect vehicle for studying conformity—that is, people's propensity to go along with a majority. Sherif asked research participants to report on the movements of the bright light. In some instances, they made their judgments in the presence of other apparent research participants, who always gave their answers first. The participants who answered first were really confederates of Sherif, who had been instructed to give a particular answer (for example, "It's moving six inches to the right"). Under these conditions, participants went along with the majority. That is, they adopted the answers given by the confederates.

Asch was both intrigued and troubled by these findings. He felt that participants' reactions, though they clearly indicated conformity, were within reason. After all, the autokinetic effect is a visual illusion; thus, there was no clear right or wrong answer. And when the right answer is less than obvious, agreeing with others makes sense. Yet Asch couldn't help wondering what would happen if the right answer were obvious. Would participants still conform to others' judgments?

Solomon Asch's question would prove to be a fruitful one. What makes a good research idea, and how does it develop into a scientific study? In this chapter, we will begin at the beginning of the research process, with the ideas that eventually develop into research questions. Then we will discuss the research methods social psychologists use, including experiments and surveys. We will see how to analyze experimental data and survey results and interpret their meaning. And we'll see how Asch's question led to some surprising—and disturbing—conclusions.

Asking the Question

Whether any field of inquiry can rightfully call itself a science depends on the sophistication and rigor of its methods. Few would disagree with this general idea that good methods translate into good science. Yet great methodology doesn't get us very far if we don't ask the right questions, or ask good questions in the right way. In some ways, researchers are less concerned with establishing facts than they are with exploring the world of ideas. We could even argue that there is an art to every science, one that is exemplified by the beauty of the ideas we pursue.

Intriguing Ideas: The Seemingly Banal, the Surprising, and the Bizarre

Ultimately, what makes for a beautiful idea? Some ideas that seem utterly trivial on the surface may become intriguing because of their surprising implications. Take, for example, the idea that people like to be consistent: it's obvious, boring, and almost embarrassingly trivial. Yet as Leon Festinger (1957; Festinger & Carlsmith, 1959) showed, the consistency principle has some rather unexpected implications for our behavior vis-á-vis our attitudes. Imagine that you think baseball is boring. Imagine further that someone offers you either $5 or $100 to tell a foreign student who knows nothing about the game that baseball is fun. Would your attitude about baseball change as a result of receiving either $5 or $100 for telling this small lie?

According to cognitive dissonance theory (Festinger, 1957), your attitude will not change much if you receive a large reward. The tidy sum of $100 provides enough justification for your lie: You did it for the money. On the other hand, a measly $5 generally won't be enough to justify your false claim about baseball. The only way to resolve this inconsistency is to adjust your attitude to fit your behavior (Festinger & Carlsmith, 1959). Thus, you come to believe that baseball isn't so boring, after all.

Other ideas can be intriguing, not so much because they have wide applications or surprising implications, but because they seem downright bizarre. Do you think you know yourself in a way that others don't? The answer seems obvious—of course you do! However, Daryl Bern (1965) suggested instead that you have no privileged insight into your own attitudes and feelings. According to his self-perception theory (Bern, 1965), when asked whether you like opera, you don't retrieve a stored attitude from memory. Instead, you retrieve memories of opera perfor-mances you have attended, count the number of opera CDs you own, and so on. Low totals would suggest that you don't care for opera that much; high totals might suggest you are an opera buff.

That, however, is exactly the way an outside observer would go about assessing your attitude toward opera. In other words, you draw conclusions about your attitude by examining your own behavior, just as others would. Although it seems to violate common sense, self-perception theory explains why doing a small favor for someone makes us more willing to do a large favor later on. Doing a small favor makes us see ourselves as helpful, a self-perception that later comes into play when we are asked to do a large favor (Cialdini, 2008). Similarly, if we are rewarded for doing something we already enjoy, will we like the activity more or less? The answer is less, because we now infer that we're doing it for money rather than pleasure.

Although the research ideas we have introduced up to this point are compelling for different reasons, they share a common feature: None of them is based on the conventional wisdom that good goes with good and bad goes with bad. Applications of this approach, including theorizing about individual differences, often take the form "Do people with high self-esteem have better intimate relationships than people with low self-esteem?" or "Do people who enjoy thinking process a persuasive message more deeply than people who don't?" Research questions of this nature are not particularly compelling, because the answer most often is "yes," although in most cases the reverse is also true. Consequently, there is a limit to how much we can learn by posing such questions.

Translating Intriguing Ideas into Research Questions

No matter how compelling an idea is, it must pass one final test before it can be translated into a research question: we must ask the question at the appropriate level of abstraction. Think about violence, for example. We could ask, "Why are humans as violent as they are?" This kind of question could provoke hours of debate in a coffeehouse, but it cannot easily be translated into a research idea. Now think about the question "Why do people riot after their team wins a championship?" This question, too, concerns violence, but it is raised at a less abstract, more concrete level. It, too, could be debated for hours, but unlike the first question, it can also be translated into a fairly concrete, researchable question.

The process of translating curiosity into a research question requires two important and related steps. First, we need to translate our question into a **hypothesis**. At the most basic level, a hypothesis is a hunch about the relationship between the crucial elements of our question. For example, we could put our question about what makes people violent into the context of exposure to media violence. That would allow us to hypothesize that increased exposure to media violence may lead to increased aggression. Because people *vary* in the extent to which they watch violence on television and in the movies, and because they also *vary* in the extent to which they aggress against each other, these elements of our question are called **variables**. Our hypothesis connects the two variables in a causal fashion by proposing that a change in one will lead to a change in the other.

Restating our question in the form of a hypothesis isn't all we need to do, however. To be viable, our hypothesis must be connected to some existing theory, the second step in converting an idea into a research question. Without theory, our speculations about the relationship between the two variables would be little more than a hunch—not enough to justify the time and effort that goes into research. Employing a theory turns a hypothesis into an educated guess.

Without theory it is difficult to generate viable hypotheses.

Let's return to our hypothesis about the link between aggression and exposure to media violence. We could guess that there is probably *some* relationship between the two variables, such that *more* exposure probably would produce *more* aggression. That hunch would be insufficient grounds for research, however. To strengthen our hypothesis, we might ground it in the social learning theory of aggression (Bandura, 1973), which holds that exposure to aggressive models leads to aggressive behavior. To the extent that media images of violence can serve as vicarious models for aggression, then, we can safely speculate that exposure to media images of violence may have the same effect as exposure to real-life models for aggression.

Asking the Question: A Summary

Social psychologists ask questions about human behavior in a social context. The questions they ask are rooted in ideas about our social world. Ideas can be intriguing if they lead to questions that explain a variety of seemingly unrelated phenomena, or that show surprising implications of seemingly banal truths, or that lead to seemingly bizarre conclusions. Research ideas that are based on individual differences—to the extent that they postulate that good things go with good and bad things go with bad—often are not intriguing. To translate an intriguing idea about human behavior in a social context into a research question, we must first state it as a hypothesis—that is, a statement that specifies the suspected relationship between two or more variables and then ground the idea in theory.

Think Like a Social Psychologist

Thinking Critically
—On the night before an important test, the obvious thing for a student to do would be to spend as many hours as possible studying. Knowing that people like to feel good about themselves, however, what benefits might you suspect a student could derive from not preparing at all?

Designing Research
—To satisfy your curiosity about self-esteem, you decide to test the hypothesis that people with high self-esteem are happier with their jobs than people with low self-esteem. What possibly important question would your study fail to answer?

Answering Questions with Data

Solomon Asch's Story, Continued: When the Obvious Right Answer Isn't Obvious

As Solomon Asch continued to think about Sherif's experiment, he wondered what would happen if the right answer were obvious to participants. Would they still conform to others' judgments?

To answer his question, Asch (1955) conducted an experiment very similar to Sherif's. Instead of asking participants to make judgments about an ambiguous stimulus, he presented them with a vertical line drawn on a board, along with a set of comparison lines of obviously varying lengths. He asked participants to pick the one line that matched the target line. The right answer was so obvious that most participants, left to their own devices, could give it immediately.

Yet once again, the results were complicated by the presence of several confederates, who in some cases had been instructed to give the wrong answer. Under these circumstances, a startling number of participants went along with the majority, even though their answers clearly were wrong. What was going on?

Once a question has been translated into a hypothesis and connected to a theory, researchers are in a position to test whether it is, in fact, true. To that end, social psychologists can draw on an extensive array of research tools available to most social scientists. They include naturalistic observations of behavior, surveys, and longitudinal techniques that track people's behavior over long periods. More than any other method, social psychologists like to use experiments to test their hypotheses. As we will see, however, there is a limit to how much we can learn from experiments. Let's look first at the advantages the experimental method has to offer.

The Logic of Experimentation

The most important advantage of the experimental method is that it allows researchers a maximum amount of control in testing hypotheses concerning the causal influence of an **independent variable** (for example, exposure to video game violence) on a **dependent variable** (for example, aggression). Conducting an experiment requires researchers to create a laboratory analog of a real-world phenomenon. That is, they must recreate the real-world conditions surrounding their hypothesis, but in a controlled way that eliminates other variables.

The key elements in this process are *control*, *random assignment*, and *comparison*. To *control* for extraneous variables, experimenters hold all other variables constant and allow only the variable of interest—the independent variable—to fluctuate. They accomplish this by creating different experimental conditions. Any measurable changes in the behavior of interest—the dependent variable—can then be attributed to differences in the experimental conditions. This type of control minimizes the chances that extraneous variables (those not of interest) might influence the results of the experiment. Extraneous variables—for example, the location of the experiment or the experimenter's demeanor—can subtly and unintentionally influence research participants' responses to the variable of interest. Experimenters can maximize control over these variables by keeping them constant for all participants.

A second form of control, just as important, is **random assignment** of participants to the experimental conditions. The fact that no two people are exactly alike creates a problem for researchers who are trying to determine the relationship between an independent and a dependent variable. One way to control for the myriad individual differences among research participants is to randomly assign them to the different experimental conditions. Random assignment means that every participant has an equal chance of being assigned to any of the experimental conditions. Assigning participants to conditions in this way distributes individual differences evenly across all the different conditions. It is a way of controlling variables that are otherwise beyond the experimenter's control.

Finally, to allow any kind of *comparison*, an experiment must have more than one condition. How many there are depends in part on the number of independent variables that are of interest you (we'll go into this in more detail in the next section). In its most basic form, an experiment compares the results from an experimental condition with those obtained in a control

The coin toss at the annual Army-Navy game. In an experiment, flipping a coin is a perfectly appropriate way to randomly assign participants to conditions.

condition. Even a seemingly simple experiment requires careful consideration of the appropriate control condition, as will become clear in the next section. When researchers do a good job of controlling the influence of extraneous variables, assigning participants to conditions randomly and providing appropriate comparisons, they can be confident that any difference they observe in the dependent variable is due, in fact, to variations in the independent variable.

The Nuts and Bolts of Experimentation

Let's illustrate how control, random assignment, and comparison work by designing a hypothetical experiment. Suppose you are interested in discovering whether exposure to violent video games causes young children to become more aggressive. There is good reason to suspect that might be the case, based on the results from hundreds of studies of the effects of media violence (Anderson & Bushman, 2002). Still, most of the research done in the past has primarily looked at TV violence, so your hypothesis regarding video game violence is somewhat novel, though it is grounded firmly in theory. Before you can begin your research, you must make a series of decisions, the first of which is how to specify the independent variable.

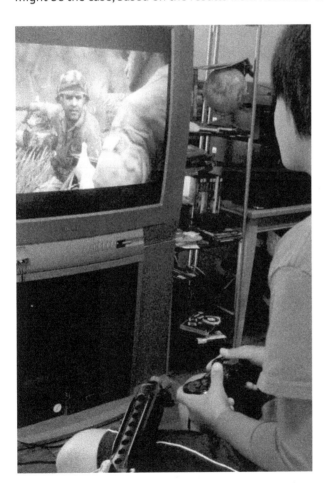

Will he become more aggressive as a result of playing a violent videogame? Social psychologists have a number of methods at their disposal to answer this question.

Specifying the Independent Variable

First, you need to decide on how many levels your independent variable (exposure to video game violence) should take on. Clearly, you need to expose one group of children to some form of video game violence and then find a way to measure their aggression. But to whom will you compare them? One obvious comparison would be to children *not* exposed to video game violence. However, you need to allow for the possibility that playing any kind of video game may increase aggression to some extent, whether the game in question is *Grand Theft Auto* or *Backyard Baseball*. To take this possibility into account, you could choose three different levels of the independent variable: (1) exposure to a violent video game; (2) exposure to a nonviolent video game; and (3) no exposure, with the last two levels serving as control conditions.

Given the huge selection of commercially available video games, how would you decide which ones to use in your study? This question relates to the way in which you *operationalize* your independent variable. **Operationalization** of an independent variable means identifying a version of the variable that can be made to work in the somewhat sterile and artificial laboratory environment. For your study, you would probably pick a game that is rated as moderately violent. Using a hyper-violent game might limit your ability to draw conclusions about the effects of violence more generally; using a game that is not violent enough might obscure any differences among the conditions. For the nonviolent condition, you probably would pick a game that is rated as nonviolent. What about the group of children who don't get to play a video game, though? Asking them to simply sit around for a while would be both awkward and impractical. Thus, you might want to operationalize "no exposure" by asking these children to draw for a comparable period.

Choosing the Participants

With the levels of the independent variable set and properly operationalized, you can turn to running the experiment. How will you select your participants? Your hypothesis pertains to the effects of video game violence on young children, so you might decide on first, second, or third graders at the local elementary school, making your final decision based on their teachers' enthusiasm for your study. You might even find a room at the school that you could convert into a lab with little more than a chair, a desk, and a video game console. After obtaining consent from the children's parents, you are almost ready to run the experiment. You should, of course, randomly assign the children to your experimental conditions. You could do so in several ways — pulling numbers representing your conditions out of a hat would suffice, or you might decide to use a more high-tech solution, like a random number generator. The point is that the assignment should be random rather than haphazard.

Measuring the Dependent Variable

One decision you must still make is how to measure aggression, your dependent variable. Doing so should not be difficult, since aggression manifests itself in a fairly limited number of observable behaviors. You could observe the children at play after the experiment, and simply count the number of times they push, shove, or kick other children. You could then use the totals you compile over a predetermined period to construct an index of aggression. If you see a higher incidence of pushing, shoving, and kicking among the children who played the violent video game compared to those who played a nonviolent game or played no game at all, your hypothesis will be supported.

This example may suggest that measuring the dependent variable is fairly simple, but that is far from the case. When you decide how to measure a dependent variable, you operationalize it in the sense that you pick one of many possible forms of measurement. Although there is nothing wrong with measuring aggression as the number of pushes and shoves a child engages in, aggression can manifest itself in other ways, including verbal aggression and indirect aggression. Operationalizing aggression as you have tells you little about the effects of violent video games on other forms of aggression.

Furthermore, much of social psychology is devoted to the study of behavior that is not clearly observable, such as thoughts and feelings. [...] [S]ocial psychologists study attitudes, impressions, and perceptions that frequently do not manifest themselves in overt behavior. Just as frequently, they study hidden influences on behavior, thoughts, and feelings, which by definition tend to occur without a person's conscious awareness.

To ascertain what participants think and how they feel as a result of some variation in their environment, social psychologists often rely on paper-and-pencil measures of everything from their transient moods to their racial attitudes. Scales like these usually include multiple items that measure different aspects of the underlying construct. Mood scales, for example, often contain items that tap into both the positive-negative dimension of moods (for example, happy versus sad) and the arousal dimension (for example, serene versus joyful). Scales designed to measure sexist attitudes include measures of both hostile sexism and benevolent sexism, a seemingly positive but ultimately paternalizing form of prejudice (Glick & Fiske, 1996). Finally, increasing interest in hidden influences has created a cottage industry of methods for measuring implicit prejudice, such as the Implicit Association Test (Greenwald, Banaji, Rudman, Farnham, Nosek, & Mellott, 2002; Greenwald, McGhee, & Schwartz, 1998). For a firsthand experience with the IAT, visit www.yale.edu/implicit

Ensuring Validity and Reliability

Scales like the ones we just described must live up to two relatively independent standards. First, they must have **validity**—that is, they must measure what they claim to measure. Second, they must have **reliability**—that is, they must measure what they claim to measure consistently.

Validity and reliability can be established in a number of ways. To demonstrate the *validity* of a scale, for example, you could compare its results to those obtained with another scale that measures essentially the same concept. You could also compare its results to a scale that measures something entirely different. A high degree of similarity with the first measure, along with a high degree of dissimilarity with the second measure, would suggest that the scale is, in fact, a valid one. Because it measures the underlying construct, it is said to be high in *construct validity*. To establish the *reliability* of the scale, you can simply administer it repeatedly. If it yields consistent results over time, you can consider it reliable.

Validity and reliability do not always go hand in hand. A prime example is the spring-operated bathroom scale you use to weigh yourself. Though it often consistently shows the same weight

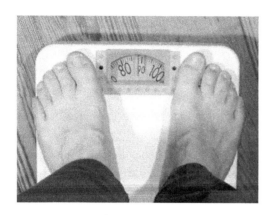

A bathroom scale provides you with a reliable estimate of your weight because it measures it consistently. However, it lacks validity because it does not provide a true estimate of your weight.

and thus can be considered a reliable measure, it may give a relatively poor indication of what you actually weigh. The counterweight scale used at your doctor's office provides a measure of your weight that is both valid and reliable. Because social psychologists go to great lengths to ascertain the validity and reliability of the scales they use in their experiments, those measures resemble the doctor's scale far more than your bathroom scale.

Laboratory experiments that present participants with a stripped-down version of reality in an otherwise controlled, somewhat sterile environment are powerful tools for examining potential cause-and-effect relationships. At the same time, however, the **internal validity** that researchers gain by exercising such a high level of control often compromises an experiment's **external validity**—that is, the ability to generalize the results beyond the laboratory. Quite simply, our experimental manipulations may not represent the richness of the underlying concept in the real world. For example, as a matter of convenience, researchers often rely on college students to participate in their experiments. How can we generalize the findings of such experiments beyond their unrepresentative samples?

One answer is that we cannot generalize them, at least not easily. To some extent, by testing hypotheses in the laboratory, researchers trade away generalizability for control, or external validity for internal validity. To the extent that we manage to replicate these experiments with slightly different operationalizations, however, we can be reasonably sure that we can generalize beyond a given operationalization. Yet we are still left with the artificiality of the laboratory setting, and the inability to generalize the experimental results beyond the chosen samples.

There are two ways of solving the dilemma of internal versus external validity. First, we can decide that our concerns about external validity are misplaced when our primary goal is to test predictions of what will happen in the lab, rather than what will happen in the real world (Mook, 1983). Take your hypothesis about the relationship between video game violence and aggression, for instance. If you test this hypothesis in the laboratory, all you are trying to do is show that the former *can* influence the latter—that is, that there is a cause-and-effect relationship between the two variables. You are fully aware that many real-life conditions may modify this relationship in important ways. For example, parents who condone violence may exacerbate the relationship; parents who condemn violence may attenuate it. Although the real world may often qualify cause-and-effect relationships established in the lab, it rarely invalidates them. Thus, we should evaluate laboratory research primarily in terms of its internal validity.

A second way to solve the dilemma of internal versus external validity is to identify variables and generate hypotheses that highlight concerns specifically with external validity. For example, if you have theoretical reasons to suspect that exposure to violent videogames might affect children differently depending on their age, it would be appropriate to test your hypothesis using children from other age groups. If you have theoretical reasons to suspect that the results of your experiment might not hold up outside the laboratory, you should test your hypothesis in a real-life setting rather than in a lab. Compared to laboratory experiments, field experiments have both advantages and disadvantages.

Field Experiments and Quasi-Experiments

Conducting an experiment in a real-life setting has several advantages. First, it removes the artificiality of the laboratory, allowing us to observe changes in behavior, thoughts, or feelings in their natural context. For this reason, field experiments often give us an opportunity to look at the possible long-term effects of the manipulation of an independent variable. At the same time, the move to the real world means that we must relinquish some control.

Consider your hypothetical experiment concerning the effects of video game violence on aggression. Instead of ferrying groups of second graders back and forth to your lab, allowing them to play various video games and then observing them at play, you could randomly assign them to take either of the two games home. You could then observe their behavior the next day and again in two weeks, which would give you a measure of both the short- and long-term effects. The problem, however, is that even though you assigned participants randomly, you have little or no control over how much time they actually spend playing the video games. You also have little control over the extent to which the children talk with each other about the games. For all you know, a subset of children may be trading the games. Lack of control over these aspects of the experiment threatens its internal validity. That is not to say that field experiments are always a poor way of testing a hypothesis. Quite the contrary; they are often the only way to study relationships such as the predictability of visitors and the well-being of people who live in retirement homes (Schulz, 1976).

Some research questions may force us to relinquish random assignment to conditions. That is often the case when researchers want to study the effects of social interventions—that is, programs designed to reduce drug use, prevent date rape, or increase the likelihood that students will remain in college. In these cases, decisions about who receives a treatment or intervention are often made by others. Given the possible beneficial effects of the treatments, to do otherwise might be unethical. However, the lack of randomly assigned treatment and control groups leaves us unable to control what happens to whom, hampering our ability to draw any kind of comparison.

Do these problems mean that we cannot study the effects of social interventions? The answer is no, because we can still study them through **quasi-experiments**. In fact, we can even study cause-and-effect relationships by gathering data at additional times and places, in order to rule out alternative explanations for the observed results (Cook & Campbell, 1979).

Suppose, for example, that your university has implemented an innovative program to increase the number of freshmen who return for their sophomore year. Suppose further that a wise administrator has given you a grant to study the effectiveness of the new program. One easy way to test whether or not it has made a difference would be to compare the retention rate in the year before the intervention to the retention rate after the intervention. However, such a design would hamper your ability to draw conclusions about cause and effect, for two reasons. First, you are looking at two different groups of people. There may be something unique about either or both freshmen classes that could explain any difference in retention rates that you might observe. Second, you are looking at the two groups a couple of years apart. Much may have happened during that period—for example, the nature of the economy or the availability of financial aid may have changed, either of which could provide an alternative explanation for any difference in retention rates.

A quasi-experiment would provide data on whether these college freshmen may be more likely to return for their sophomore year in response to an intervention aimed at freshmen retention.

To rule out these alternative explanations, you could use one of several quasi-experimental designs. To address the explanation based on the uniqueness of one or both classes, you could compare several freshman classes prior to implementation, with several freshman classes following implementation. To rule out the influence of extraneous events such as changes in the economy, you might want to look at retention rates at a comparable school that does not have such a program. This approach would allow you to identify differences that might result from the intervention, as well as any preexisting differences between the groups. In essence, it would allow you to compare your school's students to students who were subject to the same extraneous influences, but did not experience the intervention.

Quasi-experiments clearly have a place in social psychology, particularly when researchers are interested in studying cause-and-effect relationships in the real world, but cannot make use of random assignment. At the same time, quasi-experiments tend to be costly and time consuming, and are therefore used far less often than they should be.

Survey Methods

Many research questions do not require an experimental procedure; for others, conducting an experiment would be impractical. If we are interested in the relationship between material wealth and life satisfaction (Diener & Biswas-Diener, 2002; Nickerson, Schwarz, Diener, & Kahneman, 2003), do we really want to conduct an experiment? If we want to know whether individuals who idealize their partners are happier with their relationships than those who do not (Murray, Holmes, & Griffin, 1996), can we really devise an experimental procedure to find out? In both cases, we have independent variables (material wealth, partner idealization) and dependent variables (life satisfaction, relationship satisfaction), but we cannot manipulate the independent variables. Nor could we do anything in the lab to affect people's satisfaction with their lives or their life partners.

Questions like these call for the use of nonexperimental methods, chief among them the **survey method**. In doing survey research, we collect data from all or part of a population in order to examine the incidence, distribution, and relationships among naturally occurring phenomena such as life satisfaction. Among the first questions we would ask before conducting such a survey is the extent to which we want to generalize our findings. For example, when we want to know how satisfied people are with a politician's performance in office, we obviously want to generalize our findings to all constituents. The same would be true of the relationship between wealth and life satisfaction.

Selecting the Sample

In both the cases just described, it is important to obtain a representative sample. A sample is representative to the extent that every member of the population has an equal chance to be selected. A **random sample** meets this requirement, because choosing survey respondents from the population in random fashion all but assures that every member of the population has an equal chance of being picked.

When generalizability is not a major concern, a nonrandom sample, also called a **convenience sample**, will often suffice. For example, Murray et al. (1996) wanted to test a hypothesis about the relationship between partner idealization and relationship satisfaction. Consequently, they structured their sample to include couples who had been together for varying amounts of time. Of course, they could have studied a representative sample of American couples, but the additional cost and effort would not have been justified by the additional benefit of increased generalizability. Because the researchers were primarily interested in simply showing a link between partner idealization and relationship satisfaction, that benefit would have been small to negligible. If anything, anyone who wished to challenge the findings on the grounds that they lacked generalizability would need to explain why a representative sample might produce different results.

To be recruited for a survey is a fact of life in many contexts.

Asking Survey Questions: It's not as easy as you Think

Issues of generalizability aside, what we can learn from surveys depends on both the nature of the questions and how we ask them. There is ample research to suggest that the wording of the questions, the order in which we ask them, and the response format can have a surprisingly strong influence on the answers we get (Schwarz, 1999). When respondents read a survey question, for example, they do more than interpret its *literal* meaning; they try to infer its *pragmatic* meaning. A question like "What did you do on Sunday?" is simple enough to allow most respondents to decipher its literal meaning, but which of the respondent's Sunday activities does the researcher want to know about? The question's literal meaning might suggest activities such as tooth brushing and toenail clipping, but its pragmatic meaning—inferred from the questioner's perceived intentions—would suggest more uncommon activities, such as sleeping in or going for a walk.

In settling such questions, respondents tend to invoke conversational rules. In other words, they limit their reports to the kinds of activities they would report to a friend or colleague. Thus, survey questions should be worded so as to take conversational rules into account. For example, if we are interested in obtaining a detailed account of respondents' Sunday activities, rather than just the highlights, we need to ask the question in a way that will elicit the desired response.

Choosing the Response Format

In a number of ways, the response format can also influence the answers researchers obtain. An open response format to the "What did you do on Sunday?" question allows respondents to list everything they did that day, though what they include will ultimately depend on how they interpret the question. The same respondents who omit activities that seem un-interesting from an open response format may include them if asked to check them off on a list. The difference between the two formats can produce profound differences in results. For example, in one study (Schuman & Presser, 1981) researchers asked respondents what they considered to be "the most im-portant thing for children to prepare them for life." Almost two thirds of respondents picked "To think for themselves" from a list of possibil-ities. However, when presented with an open-response format, less than five percent of respondents listed that activity as most important. Obviously, the results obtained in the two different formats would suggest very different conclusions.

Similar differences surface when survey participants respond to ques-tions using different rating scales. In one study (Schwarz, Knauper, Hippler, Noelle-Neumann, & Clark, 1991), a group of participants responded to the question "How successful are you in life?" using an 11-point rating scale that ranged from 0 (not at all) to 10 (extremely). Another group responded to the same question on an 11-point scale ranging from -5 to +5. The numerical values of the two scales had a profound impact on participants' responses. Only 13 percent of

CUSTOMER REVIEW
PLEASE, FILL SHORT CUSTOMER REVIEW FOR YOUR LAST PURCHASE

☐ **EXCELLENT**
☐ **VERY GOOD**
☐ **GOOD**
☐ **AVERAGE**
☐ **POOR**
☐ VERY POOR

THANK YOU FOR YOUR PURCHASE

The design and wording of a survey question can pro-foundly impact the answers researchers obtain.

the first group endorsed a value between 0 and 5; 34 percent of the second group endorsed a value between −5 and 0.

How can we account for this dramatic difference in the responses to the two scales? Presumably, when the scale was anchored with a 0, it prompted participants to interpret "not at all successful" to mean "lacking great achievement." But when the scale was anchored with a −5, it led participants to interpret "not at all successful" to mean "failed." Evidently, the 0 and the −5 led participants to recall different information. Again, the results suggest very different conclusions.

The Ethics of Social Psychological Research

The year was 1961; the place, Yale University. A young social psychologist named Stanley Milgram was about to embark on an experimental study of destructive obedience that would eventually become one of the most celebrated and controversial studies a psychologist ever produced (Milgram, 1963). The experiment he designed focused ostensibly on the effects of punishment on learning. Participants were to teach another person (called the learner) a list of word pairs, punishing him with an electric shock each time he made a mistake.

The experimental apparatus, a mock shock generator, contained a set of switches labeled in 15-volt increments, starting with 15 volts and ending with 450 volts. The switches were

Think Like a Social Psychologist: A Survey of Video Game Violence and Aggression

Suppose you have decided to use a survey to test your hypothesis about the relationship between exposure to video game violence and aggression among second graders. How would your choice of method affect the way you state your hypothesis? Should you be concerned about sampling? Whom would you ask to gather your data? What would you need to consider in wording and ordering the questions? Looking at the following response alternatives for video game consumption, would you expect your results to differ, depending on which alternative you use?

Response Alternative 1	Response Alternative 2
(a) Up to ½ hour	(a) Up to 2 ½ hours
(b) ½ hour to 1 hour	(b) 2 ½ hours to 3 hours
(c) 1 hour to 1 ½ hours	(c) 3 hours to 3 ½ hours
(d) 1 ½ hour to 2 hours	(d) 3 ½ hours to 4 hours
(e) More than 2 hours	(e) More than 4 hours

also labeled descriptively, ranging from "Slight Shock" to "Danger: Severe Shock" and an ominous "XXX" at the highest level. Participants were instructed to begin punishing the learner for incorrect responses at the lowest voltage level, and to increase the voltage each time the learner made a mistake. The learner, a confederate of Milgram, deliberately gave many wrong answers according to a predetermined schedule. Though the mock generator did not actually deliver any shocks, the learner's pretended protests and screams convinced the participants that it did.

Much to Milgram's surprise, most participants showed little reluctance to pull the switch that delivered potentially life-threatening shocks. Even those who balked continued after the experimenter assured them that the shocks were painful but not lethal, or simply demanded that they continue. Though the results of the experiment provided important insights into the nature and consequences of obedience, [...] the ethics of the experiment were questionable. Even though many participants willingly applied what they thought was the highest level of shock, most did not do so happily. In fact, participants often expressed discomfort and unease with the procedure.

Did Milgram act ethically in conducting his studies? There is no clear-cut answer to this question. Whether any social psychological experiment can be considered ethical depends on the extent to which the physical and psychological risks to participants are offset by the potential benefits to them or to society. This rule implies that when the risks are severe, the potential benefits must be great. When the risks are minimal, the potential benefits need not be great.

No experiment is ever completely free of risk. Even the most benign study has the potential to threaten participants' privacy and the confidentiality of their responses. Procedures that deceive participants about the true nature of an experiment may also cause them embarrassment. Considerations like these have led some (e.g., Rosenthal, 1994) to suggest that the quality of research should be taken into account in deciding whether it is ethical. This argument suggests that research that has no clear hypothesis, lacks a theoretical foundation, or is poorly conceived from a methodological point of view may not be ethically defensible.

By what process can we decide whether a research project meets a high enough standard of quality to be considered ethically defensible? Decisions of this sort were once left in the hands of researchers. However, all contemporary research in social psychology is conducted in accordance with safeguards that were instituted to minimize the chances of participants being put at unnecessary risk. Guidelines from the American Psychological Association require that at a minimum, researchers must obtain *informed consent* from participants after alerting them to potential risks. Researchers must also *debrief* participants about the nature and purpose of the research at the end of the study, and they must put in place procedures to assure the *anonymity* and *confidentiality* of the data. At most universities, institutional review boards review all research projects to assure their compliance with these safeguards, as well as with federal regulations.

Answering Questions with Data: A Summary

Experimentation is the method social psychologists use most often to test their hypotheses. Its key elements are control of extraneous variables, random assignment of participants, and the comparison of different experimental conditions. At a minimum, an experiment requires least one independent (causal) variable and one dependent (measured) variable. To measure the dependent variable, researchers can take direct measures of the behavior in question, or use paper-and-pencil scales that tap into the construct being measured. Paper-and-pencil measures must be both valid and reliable.

Well-designed experiments have high internal validity—that is, they allow conclusions about cause-and-effect relationships. At the same time, they often lack external validity, which is to say that they limit a researcher's ability to generalize findings to the real world. If the ability to generalize findings is important, social psychologists can use field experiments, quasi-experiments, and survey methods. However, the gains in generalizability that these methods provide come at a cost, for they often require additional research to allow causal inferences. Survey methods also require attention to the sampling of participants and to the wording and ordering of questions.

Regardless of which method a researcher chooses, all research must meet the ethical standards set forth by the American Psychological Association. At a minimum, these standards stipulate that researchers must minimize the potential risk to participants, as well as assure their anonymity and the confidentiality of the data. Researchers must also obtain informed consent from participants and debrief them fully at the end of the study.

Think Like a Social Psychologist

Designing Research

—You decide to conduct an experiment to test the hypothesis that participants who are in a happy mood will find mildly amusing jokes to be funnier than participants who are not in a happy mood. To create the happy mood condition, you ask one group of participants to spend ten minutes recalling a happy childhood memory. To create the neutral mood condition, you ask another group of participants to wait for ten minutes. Then you randomly assign 40 participants to either of your two conditions. How sound is your experimental procedure? How could you better operationalize the neutral mood condition?

—Suppose your experiment showed that as expected, the happy mood participants rated the jokes as funnier than the neutral mood participants. When you excitedly tell your best friend about these results, she questions them on the grounds that you didn't know what mood participants were in when they came to your experiment. What aspect of your procedure allows you to tell her that her objection does not matter?

Making Connections
—To obtain approval for a new drug, pharmaceutical companies commonly conduct drug trials in which research participants are randomly assigned to receive either the experimental drug or a placebo. Given that the new drug has potentially beneficial effects, how can this procedure be justified? What appears to be the most important consideration in such trials?

Thinking Critically
—A fellow student sends you an e-mail requesting that you complete a "quick survey" for his psychology honors thesis. For your convenience, he supplies you with a link to a website where the data are collected. When you click on the URL, you are taken to a page that asks for your name, along with your response to ten questions about your attitudes regarding safe sex and condom use. List all the ways in which your fellow student has violated the commonly accepted standards for the ethical conduct of research.

Making Sense of the Data

In every study, regardless of whether we use an experiment or a survey to test a hypothesis, we must eventually make sense of the data. To that end, we may first want to look at the distribution of scores for the variable we are interested in. Calculating the means—that is, the averages—can give us a quick overview of the pattern of results we obtained. Yet the means rarely tell the whole story, particularly for experimental results.

Analyzing Experimental Data

To illustrate this point, let's assume that you ran your experiment on the effects of video game violence and aggression with 30 participants, whom you assigned randomly to the three experimental conditions. **Table 3.1** shows the scores from this hypothetical experiment.

You can calculate the mean for the entire experiment by averaging all 30 scores (5.23). Note that this overall mean varies, to a greater or lesser extent, from virtually every individual score. The degree of variation between the individual scores and the overall mean represents the **total variance** in your experiment.

Table 3.1 Results from a hypothetical experiment on videogame violence and aggression: Number of pushes, kicks, and shoves observed during a 30-minute play period.

Violent Videogame Condition	Non-Violent Videogame Condition	Drawing Condition
8	6	3
7	5	3
11	9	4
6	4	2
6	4	2
9	5	3
10	5	2
5	2	1
12	6	3
8	4	2
———	———	———
M: 8.2	M: 5.0	M: 2.5

Next, you need to calculate the means for the experimental conditions (8.2, 5.0, and 2.5). They, too, vary to a greater or lesser extent from the overall mean. The degree of variation from one condition to the next—that is, the portion of the variance that is accounted for by the researcher's manipulations—represents the **systematic variance**. Finally, if you look at the scores within each condition, you find that few are identical, most likely because of individual differences among the participants. Some children may simply be more aggressive than others. Variation within a condition is called **error variance**, because it is due to variables that are out of your control.

Although a survey may measure all relevant variable, the correlational nature of the results makes conclusions about cause and effect difficult.

When you compare the means for your experimental conditions, you are interested in more than the relative magnitude of the differences between them. You also need to make sure that they were not caused by chance. To do that, you can use statistical procedures to partition the total variance into the systematic variance and the error variance. If more of the total variance is accounted for by your manipulations than by chance factors like individual differences, then the difference among the means is likely to be significant—that is, not due to chance.

Analyzing Survey Data

We've seen that surveys have some advantages over experiments. Surveys are often better suited than experiments to the study of naturally occurring phenomena. They also allow us to generalize, assuming that the participants were drawn from a random sample. These advantages come at a cost, however. Because in most surveys all variables are measured, drawing conclusions about cause-and-effect relationships is difficult. Instead, we are limited to assessing the degree of association between the variables that interest us.

The Nature of Correlations

Social scientists refer to the degree of association between two variables as a **correlation**. A correlation may be positive or negative, depending on the relationship between the two variables. Variables that are negatively correlated are inversely related; a zero correlation suggests the absence of a relationship. For example, if a survey on the relationship between material wealth and happiness reveals that happiness increases as wealth increases, the two variables would be positively correlated.

If the same survey showed that happiness decreases as wealth increases, the two variables would be negatively correlated. If the survey showed no relationship between wealth and happiness, the correlation would be a zero (see **Figure 3.1** for graphical representations of these outcomes).

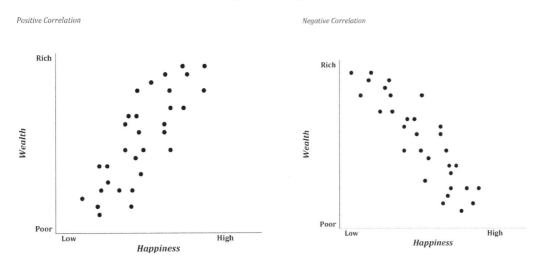

Figure 3.1 Three possible correlations in a hypothetical study on the relationship between wealth and happiness.

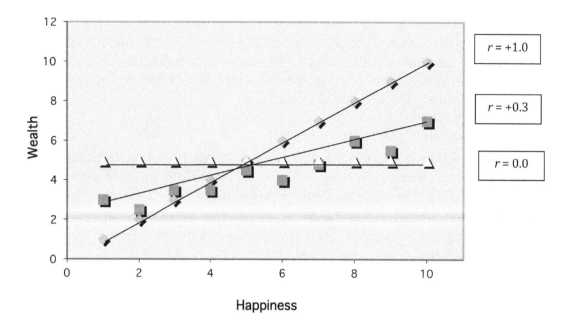

Figure 3.2   Correlations coefficients (r) of varying magnitudes in a hypothetical study on the relationship between health and happiness.

The correlation between two variables is expressed mathematically as a correlation coefficient. Its value can range from +1, indicating a perfect positive relationship between the two variables, to −1, indicating a perfect negative relationship. In social psychological research, we rarely find a perfect relationship between two variables. Instead, the correlation coefficients we observe are frequently on the order of .3 (or −.3). Because correlations of .3 are much closer to 0 (no correlation) than to +1 (perfect correlation) (see **Figure 3.2**), critics frequently dismiss them as too low to be meaningful.

Such criticisms are often misplaced, however. A correlation coefficient is much like a batting average in baseball. For the benefit of those who eschew America's favorite pastime, a batting average describes the degree of association between the number of times a player comes up to bat and the number of hits the player gets. As we all know, nobody bats a thousand, but a player with a .300 average is generally considered a slugger, even though his correlation between hits and at-bat appearances is a paltry .300. With the game on the line, any major league manager in need of a pinch hitter would prefer to bring in a player with a .300 average to a player with a .200 average. Similarly, if your life satisfaction survey shows a correlation of .3 between wealth and happiness and a correlation of .2 between a good sex life and happiness, you would have good reason to suspect that wealth may be more important to life happiness than sex.

Correlation versus Causation

In baseball, although coming up to bat is clearly necessary to get a hit, it does not *cause* the batter to hit the ball. In other words, correlation does not imply causation. Similarly, a positive correlation between two variables like wealth and happiness does not indicate causation. Instead, it can be interpreted in at least three ways: (1) the first variable could affect the second; (2) the second variable could affect the first' or (3) a third variable could affect both. So your .3 correlation could mean that wealth leads to happiness, but it could also mean that happiness leads to wealth (though that is unlikely). It could also mean that a third variable is responsible for the relationship you observed between wealth and happiness. That is, something about wealthy, happy people may affect their approach to work and life, creating both financial success and happiness. Similarly, an observed relationship between partner idealization and relationship satisfaction could indicate that continued idealization of one's partner leads to higher relationship satisfaction. Then again, it could mean that people who are happy with their relationships tend to idealize their partners.

Zero Correlation

In sum, survey data can provide valuable insights into the relationship between two or more variables. Even though a strictly causal interpretation of such data is problematic, the data allow researchers to speculate about the causal nature of a relationship. If one variable occurs before another, they can reasonably infer that the one that came first may have caused a change in the one that came second. Researchers can also measure additional variables and examine their relationship to the variable of interest. Of course, doing so can be fairly onerous, and thinking of every variable that could possibly be related to the variables of interest is often impossible. Ultimately, the choice between the survey method and the experimental method depends on what is more important to researchers. If studying naturally occurring phenomena and generalizing from the findings are of primary concern, the survey method may be more appropriate than an experiment. If drawing causal inferences is the primary goal, an experiment would be more appropriate.

Interpreting the Results

Successful data analysis can be a source of great satisfaction, or at least relief, especially when the data seem to support the hypothesis. Simply finding a significant effect, however, does not by itself imply support for the hypothesis. Rather, the pattern among the means or the correlation between the variables must point in the right direction. In terms of your study of video game violence and aggression, your statistical analysis would yield significant results whether you observed more aggression in the children who played the violent game or in those who played the nonviolent game.

Even if the pattern among the means breaks in the predicted direction, you need to ask some questions before you can draw firm conclusions about the extent to which the results support your hypothesis. Remember that in operationalizing an independent variable in a particular way, you are forgoing other possible ways of looking at the question. For example, there are many—some would say too many—violent video games on the market. *Grand Theft Auto* shares many of their features, but it also has some unique features. Thus, you need to ask whether your results may have been caused at least in part by the game's unique features. The same is true of the dependent variable. Counting the number of pushes, shoves, and kicks children engage in gives you a measure of direct physical aggression, but it tells you little about indirect forms of aggression such as spreading rumors about a classmate. Finally, even though your statistical analysis may suggest that your findings are not due to chance, you need to consider, and if possible rule out, *alternative explanations*.

Issues of this sort are often best addressed by collecting additional data. A successful *replication* of an experiment using different operationalizations of the independent and dependent variables can increase your confidence that you have truly studied what you set out to study. Just as important, multiple studies of the same hypothesis, done with different operationalizations and multiple samples, can add an element of generalizability to your experimental findings. A successful replication that is specifically designed to rule out an alternative explanation would further increase your confidence in your results. Finally, using another research method can compensate for any weaknesses in the original study. Under some circumstances, combining an experiment with a survey can give researchers the advantages of both methods: control and the ability to study naturally occurring phenomena.

Communicating the Results

Eventually, all scientists share the results of their research with others in the field, and sometimes with the public at large. Anthropologists often present their research in the form of a book, especially when it includes detailed observations collected over a long period of a group of people. Mathematicians tend to publish their results in scientific journals that are read by a fairly narrow audience. That makes sense, especially when the work involves the generation of mathematical proofs. Social psychologists fall somewhere between anthropologists and mathematicians in the way they communicate their results. They sometimes publish books on topics like prejudice, persuasion, and relationships, but more often they communicate their findings in one of the many journals devoted to the dissemination of social psychological findings.

Table 3.2 lists some of the most popular and most widely read social psychological journals. All these journals follow a rigorous process of **peer review** before publishing a manuscript. That is, the editors have the paper evaluated by other social psychologists who are familiar with the topic. Though the exact standards vary, all journals take into account the soundness of the methodology used in a study, the appropriateness of the data analysis, and the extent to which the research was conducted in accordance with accepted standards of ethical responsibility. Not surprisingly, most of the journals listed in Table 3.2 accept and publish only a small fraction of the submissions they receive—in some cases, as small as ten percent. As a result, the work published in these journals represents the best in the field.

"Let's round it off to 2 and go to lunch."

Although results can be informative, it's how we interpret them that really matters.

Table 3.2   Journals devoted to the publication of social psychological research.

Journal of Personality and Social Psychology
Journal of Experimental Social Psychology
Personality and Social Psychology Bulletin
Social Cognition
Basic and Applied Social Psychology
Journal of Social and Personal Relationships
Journal of Social Issues

Papers that are published in these journals share several other features. They generally are written according to the guidelines in the American Psychological Association's (APA) publication manual. APA guidelines stipulate that a research paper should have four distinct parts. The *introduction* presents the research question, along with a theoretical justification for the hypothesis. The *method* section contains information about who participated in the study, along with the details of how it was conducted. The *results* section describes the data that were obtained, along with detailed information on how they were analyzed. Finally, the *discussion* section includes a critical reflection on how the data relate to the hypothesis, along with a consideration of their limitations, implications, and possible applications.

This simple structure provides the backbone for every research article. Alas, because of the technical nature of the material, many students of social psychology—seasoned veterans included—often have difficulty communicating their findings in a compelling way. Articles that are compelling and interesting to readers share some additional features. First, they follow a four-part structure within each of the four parts of the paper. The *introduction* generally begins with a statement of the problem, followed by a review of the relevant literature, identification of the variable(s) of interest, and a theoretical justification for the hypothesis. The *method* section generally begins with a description of the sample of participants, followed by a description of how the variables of interest were operationalized, the design of the experiment, and a detailed account of how the experiment was run (the procedure). The *results* section includes information on what was done to the data, how they were analyzed, and what effects were observed, as well as information about any subsidiary analyses that may have been performed. Finally, the *discussion* section revisits the hypothesis, addresses how the data relate to it, considers possible alternative explanations, and notes the implications of the results beyond the experimental setting.

The way the author discusses the research also has an impact on an article's interest level. There are two ways to talk about science: the language of discovery and the language of debate. According to Wegner (2003), good science writing is all about discovery—about exploring, looking, suspecting, learning. This kind of writing conjures up images of truth seekers searching for something no one has ever seen before. The language of debate is more about battle: claiming, arguing, maintaining, holding. This kind of writing portrays science as a battle between scientists with competing views. Because the language of discovery is far more convincing than the language of debate (which implies that opposition is being mounted even as the findings are described), researchers are generally better off framing their papers in the language of discovery. It greatly increases the chances that an article will reflect the intriguing nature of its ideas, the elegance of its methods, and the sophistication of its data analysis. **Table 3.3** contrasts "discovery words" with "debate words."

Table 3.3   Discovery words versus debate words

Discovery Words	Debate Words
Suspect (We suspect that ...)	Argue (We argue that ...)
Find (We found ...)	Show (We showed ...)
Learn (We learned that ...)	Maintain (We maintain ...)
Possibility (It is possible that ...)	Position (Our position is that ...)
Suggest (We suggest ...)	Claim (We claim ...)
Indicate (The findings indicate ...)	Demonstrate (The findings demonstrate ...)
Idea (Our idea is ...)	Point (Our point is ...)
See (We can see that ...)	Hold (We hold that ...)
Expect (We expect to find that ...)	Hope (We hope to find that ...)

Compiled from: Wegner, D.M. (2003). Science Talk: Discover and Debate. Dialogue, 18, 10–11.

Making Sense of the Data: A Summary

The analysis of experimental data involves determining the variance accounted for by manipulations of its independent variables vis-à-vis the variance accounted for by chance factors. The more variance is explained by the manipulated variance, the higher the probability that differences among means are not due to chance. Survey data yield correlations between the variables of interest. Two variables can be positively correlated, negatively correlated, or uncorrelated. Regardless of what methods researchers use, they must consider and rule out alternative explanations for their results.

Social psychologists publish their research in journals. Rigorous peer review prior to publication ensures that researchers used sound methodology and appropriate data analysis, and complied with commonly accepted standards of ethical conduct. Journal articles generally have four parts: (1) an introduction to the research question; (2) a description of the method; (3) a description of the results and procedures for data analysis; and (4) a discussion of the results in light of alternative explanations, together with their theoretical implications. Although many journal articles are written in the language of debate, articles that are written in the language of discovery are particularly likely to reflect the intriguing nature of the ideas researchers pursue.

Epilogue: A Beautiful Idea with Unlovely Implications

What was going on in Asch's experiment, and what was so beautiful about his idea? Apparently, the desire to conform to others' thoughts and behavior is so profound, participants were willing to make patently false statements just to avoid contradicting one another. This conclusion has far-reaching implications. [...] Asch's findings became the cornerstone for a great deal of theorizing about the roots of atrocities committed during World War II. That is, perpetrators of those atrocities may have been motivated less by sadistic, evil motives than by a desire to conform.

Still, applicability to real life does not by itself render an idea intriguing, for just as we can be intrigued by a poem or painting, we can appreciate a research idea on its own merits. Asch's idea was intriguing because of its ability to explain a variety of seemingly unrelated phenomena as having a common cause. His findings not only helped to explain and predict why people would commit horrific crimes; they proved fundamental to our understanding of why people often fail to do the right thing, such as helping someone in need (Latane & Darley, 1970).

Key Terms and Definitions

Hypothesis: a statement about the relationship between the crucial elements of a research question

Variables: elements of a research question)

Independent variable: the causal variable of interest in an experiment

Dependent variable: the variable that is measured in an experiment

Random assignment: assignment of research participants in such a way that they have an equal chance to be assigned to any of the conditions of an experiment

Operationalization: the process through which a theoretical variable can be made to work in a laboratory environment

Validity: the extent to which a scale measures what it claims to measure

Reliability: the extent to which a scale yields consistent results

Internal validity: the extent to which an experiment allows conclusions about cause-and-effect relationships

External validity: the extent to which experimental results can be generalized beyond a specific sample or setting

Quasi-experiment: An experiment that is done without random assignment

Survey method: the collection of data from all or part of a population in order to examine the incidence, distribution, and relationships among naturally occurring phenomena

Random sample: a method of selecting survey respondents that assures that every member of a population has an equal chance to be selected

Convenience sample: a nonrandom sample, used when generalizability is not an issue

Total variance: the degree of variation among the scores obtained in an experiment

Systematic variance: the portion of the total variance that is accounted for by the conditions of an experiment

Error variance: the portion of the total variance that is accounted for by variables outside of the experimenter's control

Correlation: the degree to which two variables are associated; ranges from −1 to +1

Peer review: the process by which other scholars in the field evaluate the merits of a research paper submitted for publication in a journal

References

Anderson, C. A., & Bushman, B. J. (2002). The effects of media violence on society. *Science, 295*, 2377–2379.

Asch, S. E. (1956). Studies of independence and conformity: A minority of one against a unanimous majority. *Psychological Monographs, 70*, 1–70.

Bem, D. J. (1965). An experimental analysis of self-persuasion. *Journal of Experimental Social Psychology, 1*, 199–218.

Cialdini, R. B. (2008). *Influence: Science and practice* (5th ed.). Needham Heights, MA: Allyn and Bacon.

Cook, T. D., & Campbell, D. T. (1975). The design of quasi-experiments and true experiments in field settings. In M. D. Dunnett (Ed.), *Handbook of industrial and organizational psychology*. New York: Rand McNally.

Diener, E., & Biswas-Diener, R. (2002). Will money increase subjective well-being? *Social Indicators Research, 57*, 119–169.

Festinger, L., & Carlsmith, J. M. (1959). Cognitive consequences of forced compliance. *Journal of Abnormal and Social Psychology, 58*, 202–210.

Fiske, S. T. (2003). *Social beings: A core motives approach to social psychology*. New York: Wiley & Sons.

Greenwald, A. G., Banaji, M. R., Rudman, L. A., Farnham, S. D., Nosek, B. A., & Mellott, D. S. (2002). A unified theory of implicit attitudes, stereotypes, self-esteem, and self-concept. *Psychological Review, 109*, 3–25.

Greenwald, A. G., McGhee, D. E., & Schwartz, J. L. K. (1998). Measuring individual differences in implicit cognition: The implicit association test. *Journal of Personality and Social Psychology, 74*, 1464–1480.

Latane, B., & Darley, J. M. (1970). *The unresponsive bystander: Why doesn't he help?* Englewood Cliffs, NJ: Prentice-Hall.

Milgram, S. (1963). Behavioral study of obedience. *Journal of Abnormal and Social Psychology, 67*, 371–378.

Mook, D. G. (1983). In defense of external invalidity. *American Psychologist, 38*, 379–387.

Murray, S. L., Holmes, J. G., & Griffin, D. W. (1996). The benefits of positive illusions: Idealization and the construction of satisfaction in close relationships. *Journal of Personality and Social Psychology, 70*, 79–98.

Nickerson, C., Schwarz, N., Diener, E., & Kahneman, D. (2003). Zeroing in on the dark side of the American Dream: A closer look at the negative consequences of the goal for financial success. *Psychological Science, 14*, 531–536.

Rosenthal, R. (1994). Science and ethics in conducting, analyzing, and reporting psychological research. *Psychological Science, 5*, 127–134.

Schulz, R. (1976). Effects of control and predictability on the physical and psychological well-being of the institutionalized aged. *Journal of Personality and Social Psychology, 33*, 563–573.

Schuman, H., & Presser, S. (1981). *Questions and answers in attitude surveys*. New York: Academic Press.

Schwarz, N. (1999). Self-reports: How the questions shape the answers. *American Psychologist, 54*, 93–105.

Schwarz, N., Knauper, B., Hippler, H. J., Noelle-Neumann, E., & Clark, F. (1991). Rating scales: Numeric values may change the meaning of scale labels. *Public Opinion Quarterly, 55*, 570–582.

Sherif, M. (1935). A study of some social factors in perception. *Archives of Psychology, 27*, 1–60.

Sherif, M. (1936). *The psychology of social norms*. Oxford, UK: Harper.

Tesser, A. (1990, August). *Interesting models in social psychology: A personal view*. Paper presented at the annual meeting of the American Psychological Association, Boston, MA.

Wegner, D. M. (2003). Science Talk: Discover and Debate. *Dialogue, 18*, 10–11.

Post-Reading Activities

1   As you talk to classmates about what courses you are taking this semester, how would you describe the basics of social psychology and how it "fits" in the social sciences? How does this field compare/contrast to sociology and psychology?

2   Go to Philip Zimbardo's website to study the Stanford Prison Experiment at http://www.prisonexp.org/. Can you summarize the experiment in your own words (i.e., identify variables and the research methodology? Can you identify the ethical violations?

3   For more information on ethics, you can investigate the Nuremberg Code at https://history.nih.gov/research/downloads/nuremberg.pdf and the Belmont Report at https://www.hhs.gov/ohrp/regulations-and-policy/belmont-report/index.html.

Image Credits

UNIT II

THE INDIVIDUAL AND SOCIETY

Introduction

Socialization is a lifelong process of becoming a human. Of course, there are biological components to becoming a human, but there are social components as well. Social psychologists decipher which of these components are due to nature and which are due to nurture. What exactly does it mean to be human? Are we biologically born a human? Or is there something more to being a human than simply biology? Who are you? How did you become you? Social psychologists study the process of socialization as an explanation for how you became you. As the cycle highlights in Figure 2, socialization is critical to the development of the individual, but it also is critical in the development of a society. Without socialization, you do not become you and the society does not develop. What?

When an individual human is born, the individual human is incapable of survival without the intervention of others to provide food, shelter, love, etc. During this process of providing the basic needs of survival, the individual is taught skills to survive. Not only do these skills go beyond basic survival, but also social survival. Parents and guardians teach or socialize the children on how to behave at home and in public. If this socialization does not occur, children may remain alive but may not actually learn to navigate the social world. They can be deemed weird, socially awkward, which can lead to ostracism from society. If this occurs, the

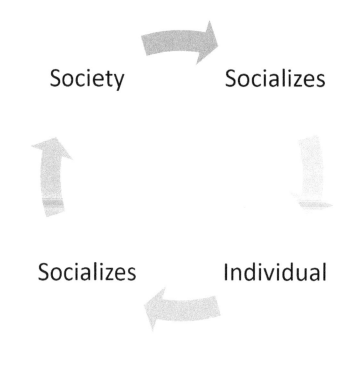

Figure 2. Socialization process

individual may not ever learn how to become a member of the society. So, this explains how an individual will not survive without the socialization provided by society.

To continue, if the individual is no longer socialized to be a member of the society, then the individual is not finding another individual with whom to procreate. If enough individuals do not procreate, then the society ultimately disappears. A bit extreme? Yes, but we can understand the importance of socialization with a less extreme example. If the socialization process changes from one generation to the next, society as we once knew it would no longer exist. We would have an evolved—but changed—society.

This socialization process is accomplished through interaction. The interaction provided by the agents of socialization (i.e., family, education, peers, media, religion, neighborhood) to the individual provides the individual with the tools to become what social psychologists and others would call a human. As Brooks highlights in the first reading, being a human is a long process and one that is not fully complete. It is more than just being born a member of *Homo sapiens;* rather, it is a distinction that is made from other life forms. Humans have the ability to develop symbolic communication through language and culture. With this ability humans become more than biological humans; biological humans can become social humans with individual personality, individuality, and social identity. Hogg provides an explanation of social identity theory and how nature and nurture contribute to the development of individual personality.

The readings in this unit illustrate the three components of socialization: (1) human biological potential; (2) culture; and (3) individual experiences. Brooks introduces the importance of both the biology of being born a human as well as the development of culture to becoming a member of the human society. Then, Hogg accentuates the individual experiences in the evolution of personality and identity.

What Is a Human? Anthropological Perspectives on the Origins of Humanness

Alison S. Brooks

[I]t would be impossible to fix on any point when the term "man" ought to be used.

Charles Darwin, *The Descent of Man*

Defining Human, Early Scientific Efforts

During the late seventeenth and eighteenth centuries, natural historians and biologists wrestled with the problem of defining humans within new conceptualizations of the natural world. In the context of the first anatomical studies of great apes, they found morphology (anatomical shape) alone was insufficient to achieve the appropriate degree of distinctiveness they felt was warranted, so many def initions and discussions fell back on distinctions in behavior such as language, innovation, or technology. In 1699, Tyson, in the first description of chimpanzee anatomy, named the chimpanzee *Homo sylvestris*, arguing that it was only the soul that differentiated this animal from ourselves, the brain and other anatomical parts being remarkably similar. Buffon (1749-67) wrote: "If our judgement were limited to figure [morphology] alone, I acknowledge that the ape might be regarded as a variety of the human species." Linnaeus in 1735 put *Homo sapiens* in the same order as the chimpanzee (*Homo troglodytes*) (Bendysche 1863), but Blumenbach (1779-80) and Lamarck (1809) put humans in a separate order, *Bimana*, emphasizing our reliance on bipedalism and free hands for making tools. However, Blumenbach's (1779-80) definition of human, "*Homo, erectus bimanus, mentum prominulum, dentes aequaliter approximati, incisores inferiores erecti*," would have excluded not only all the apes but also the large number of fossil human ancestors without chins. Lacking fossil evidence for human evolution, some early systematists who dealt only with living populations saw behavioral continuity from humans to "wild children" who lacked the essential ability to speak, to apes. Newly discovered peoples, such as the "Hottentots" of southern Africa, were sometimes accorded a less-than-human status.

The Fossil Record of Human Evolution

Beginning in the nineteenth century, the discovery of fossil remains attributable to human ancestors forced scientists to develop more explicit anatomical criteria for inclusion in the human lineage. Although the first discoveries bore the clearest resemblance to current humans and were associated with the bones of extinct animals, their robust skeletons were seen as evidence for a life of hard labor and possible disease in historic (e.g., Roman) times, and their great antiquity and associations were questioned. One of the earliest was the discovery by William Buckland (1823), reader in mineralogy at Oxford, of the "Red Lady of Paviland," which later research showed to be a ca. 26,000-year-old male burial in Paviland Cave near Swansea in Wales, with red ocher and ivory ornaments (Aldhouse-Green 1998). Despite the associated bones of extinct animals, Buckland interpreted this skeleton to be the remains of a camp follower of the Roman army, encamped nearby. "Whatever may have been her occupation, the vicinity of a camp would afford a motive for residence as well as the means of subsistence in what is now so exposed and uninviting a solitude" (Buckland 1823, p. 90). When even older fossils of Neanderthals began to turn up, beginning around 1835 with the first fossil Neanderthals from Engis in Belgium (Schmerling 1833-34), these also were attributed by Buckland and others (Grayson 1983) to socially marginal historic Europeans, as were the finds from the Neander Valley itself in 1856.[1]

Yet by the 1860s, the great antiquity of human ancestors and their association with extinct faunas in Europe had been demonstrated to the satisfaction of many natural scientists through archaeological finds in France and elsewhere. Beads, engraved bones, and other objects that were clearly of human manufacture had been recovered in association with extinct animals, including fossil elephants, rhinoceroses, monkeys, and cave bears (Lartet 1861). The establishment of the antiquity of life thus depended on parallel discoveries in stratigraphy, comparative anatomy, and geology, while acceptance of the antiquity of humanity depended in addition on emerging discoveries in paleontology.

Comparative anatomy and the geographic distribution of the apes most similar to humans had led Darwin (1871) to locate the likely origin place of humans in Africa. Only in 1891, however, was the first fossil attributed to a human ancestor recovered from outside Europe, not from Africa but from Trinil in Indonesia (Dubois 1894). Haeckel (1868) had already named the putative "missing link" between apes and humans "*Pithecanthropus alalus*" ("ape-man without speech"), but Dubois, struck by the human aspect of the femur found at Trinil (now thought to be the femur of a modern person and not associated with the fossil skull) preferred to emphasize the erect bipedal gait of his fossil: "*Pithecanthropus erectus*." This fossil, with its cranial capacity of only 900 cc, was incorporated later into the genus *Homo* as a separate species: *Homo erectus*. It had two important implications: that bipedalism was well established before the brain became modern, and that the early chapters in the story took place outside the European continent.

The first African fossils of Pliocene or Pleistocene Age relevant to human evolution were recovered only in 1924 at Singa (Sudan) and Taung (South Africa) (Woodward 1938, Dart 1925). The ca. 2-2.5 million-year-old Taung specimen of a small child with a chimpanzee-sized brain became the type fossil of *Australopithecus* (Dart 1925), a genus that is probably ancestral to our own (*Homo*), and provided support for Darwin's inference that humans originated in Africa. The Singa skull, on the other hand, at prior to ca. 133 thousand years ago (kya) had a relatively large brain cavity, high forehead, but robust brow ridges, placing it close to the origin of our own species *Homo sapiens* in the late Middle Pleistocene (McDermott et al. 1996).

Since the 1920s, Pleistocene-age (1.8-0.01 million years ago [mya]) fossil specimens belonging in the hominin lineage[2] have been recovered at an accelerating pace from Europe, Asia, Africa, and Australia, and now total more than a thousand individuals, many represented only by isolated teeth. Africa has yielded the oldest members of the lineage (Senut et al. 2001, Brunet et al. 2002, Haile-Selassie 2001, Haile-Selassie and WoldeGabriel 2009), the oldest artifacts (Semaw 2000, Semaw et al. 2003, Roche et al. 1999), the oldest members of our genus *Homo* (Kimbel et al. 1996, Deino and Hill 2002, Sherwood et al. 2002), and the oldest members of the species *Homo sapiens* (White et al. 2003, McDougall et al. 2005). Multiple genetic studies of mitochondrial, Y-chromosome, and nuclear DNA conclude that the greatest variability, the most ancestral lineages, and the likely region of origin all concur in indicating an African homeland for modern humans.

The hominin tree is bushiest at its Pliocene (5-1.8 million years ago) base, where we have relatively little fossil evidence (Figure 4.1). After ca. 1.4 mya, at the end of the early Pleistocene, all subsequent fossils are attributed to a small number (2-7) of species within the genus *Homo*, and most of these named species are either geographically or temporally distinct, rather than living at the same place and time.

The impressive complexity of the hominin fossil record has clarified some of the features that distinguished our lineage at an early stage from that of our closest simian relatives, as well as the order in which these distinctions appear. While we have very little evidence of chimpanzee or gorilla ancestry during the Plio-Pleistocene epochs of human emergence, studies of ancestral apes who lived more than 7 mya, prior to the ape-human split, together with comparative studies of present-day apes can help delineate what is peculiarly human. These unique human anatomical features include adaptations for bipedal locomotion, canine teeth that are similar in size and function to adjacent teeth in the dentition, adaptations for manual dexterity, and a large brain for our body size.

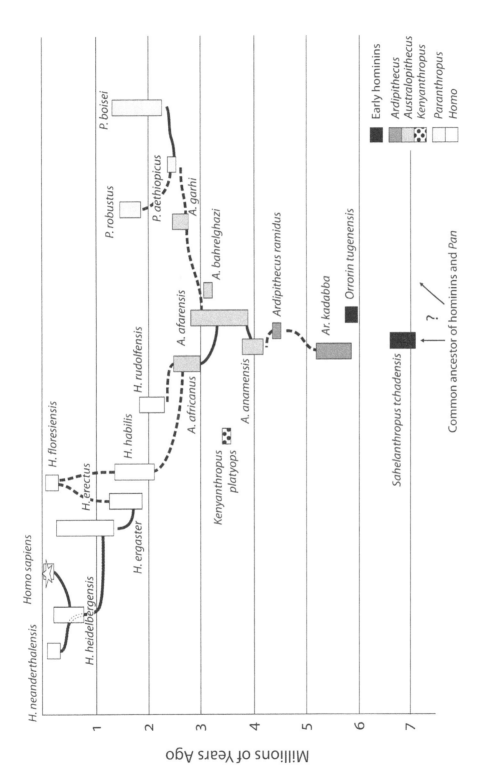

Figure 4.1 The hominin lineage, with dashed lines suggesting likely lines of decent (courtesy Brian Richmond). Note that relationships of the earliest hominins and of *Kenyanthropus* are unclear. *H. floresiensis* is the recently discovered small hominin from the Late Pleistocene of Flores in Indonesia, nicknamed "the Hobbit."

Bipedalism appears to have been present in the very oldest fossils attributed to the human lineage around 6 to 7 mya, based on the forward placement of the foramen magnum of *Sahelanthropus* where the spinal column enters the skull (Zollikofer et al. 2005), and on the morphology of the femur of *Orrorin tugenensis* (Richmond and Jungers 2008). Fully committed or obligate bipedalism, however, only appears in the genus *Homo* after 2.3 mya, and signals a commitment to terrestrial habitats, possibly including the development of endurance running as a major adaptation (Bramble and Lieberman 2004).

Ardipithecus fossils from Ethiopia, along with *Orrorin* and *Sahelanthropus*, suggest that while canine teeth, used by male apes in threat displays and occasionally as weapons in aggressive contests over social ranking, were reduced in the earliest fossils, their slashing function persisted to a certain degree in the earliest hominins (Haile-Selassie et al. 2004). While canines were further reduced in the earliest *Australopithecus afarensis* fossils from Ethiopia and Tanzania, only after 2.9 mya in the later australopithecines and early *Homo* did they reach proportions and morphology more similar to ours, suggesting a commitment to other forms of aggression or communication.

The small bones of the hand are rare in the fossil record, but those from *A. afarensis* such as "Lucy" (Figure 4.2a) and her Ethiopian fossil contemporaries of 3.7 to 2.9 mya and *A. africanus* (ca. 2.8-2.5 mya) show that hands by this time were capable of greater manual dexterity, with shorter palms and with fingers that could more adeptly grasp objects in opposition with the thumb (D. Green and Gordon 2008). The toe and finger bones were still somewhat curved, however, to promote tree-climbing (Stern and Susman 1983), and the wrist still exhibited a small projection, inherited from their ape ancestors, that stabilizes the wrist in African apes when walking on their knuckles (Richmond and Strait 2000).

The fossil record has demonstrated unequivocally that large brains were not a feature of early hominin evolution, but emerged only later within the genus *Homo*. The oldest members of this genus are found in Ethiopia at 2.3 mya (Kimbel et al. 1996), although a fossil temporal bone from Kenya points to the same early age for this genus throughout the East African Rift Valley (Deino and Hill 2002, Sherwood et al. 2002). Initially brain enlargement was not remarkable, teeth remained large, and body proportions suggested continued ability to navigate in the trees (Wood and Collard 1999). But by ca. 1.8 mya, brain size had increased to an average of about three-fourths the size of modern *H. sapiens*, along with full commitment to bipedalism, technology and manual dexterity, and something other than canine display for communicating relative dominance. Another increase in brain size to modern levels occurred about 700-600 kya, with no increase in body size, suggesting new and as-yet poorly understood cognitive developments. The oldest fossils with modern brain sizes are also African and include fossils from South, Central, and East Africa.

Clearly the expanding fossil record has blurred the morphological distinction between human and nonhuman primates that Blumenbach saw so clearly. But were all of these ancestors fully human? What do we mean by human? Are even all members of the genus *Homo*

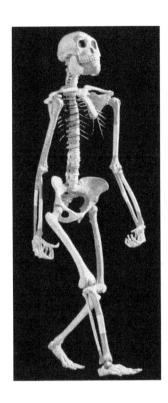

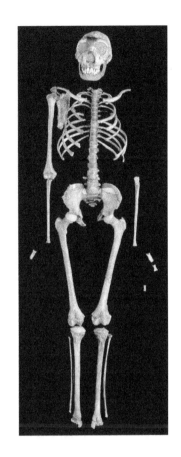

Figure 4.2 Fossil hominins: a) (*above left*) "Lucy" (Ethiopia) (*Australopithecus afarensis*), reconstructed by Owen Lovejoy. Note very long arms relative to legs, curved digits. Large face, small brain, ca. 3.7-2.9 mya (courtesy Owen Lovejoy, *National Geographic*); b) (*above right*) the Nariokotome "boy" (Kenya) *Homo ergaster/erectus* 1.5 mya (species range is ca. 1.8-0.8 mya, or younger in E/SE Asia) (courtesy National Museums of Kenya or *National Geographic*?); c) (*below right*) *Homo sapiens idaltu* (Herto, Ethiopia) 1.61 mya, one of the oldest fossil representatives of our own species (courtesy David L. Brill/Atlanta).

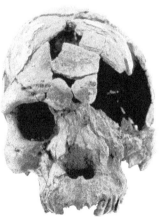

human? For that matter, anthropologists do not even agree on what should be placed in the genus *Homo*. Does it start with the appearance of stone tools 2.6 mya, the first signs of brain enlargement in Ethiopian and Kenyan fossils from 2.3 mya, or only with the humanlike suite of characteristics reflected in a complete skeleton (Figure 4.2b) with a larger brain, smaller teeth, modern body size, and modern limb proportions found in Kenya at 1.5 mya (Wood and Collard 1999)? Should we limit the definition of "fully human" only to members of the species *sapiens*, defined morphologically (Pearson 2000, Lieberman et al. 2004) by their large brains in relation to their body size, by their small teeth, their gracile skeletons, their chins, their minimal brow ridges and vertical foreheads, and by the way the face is tucked under the braincase, bringing the larynx closer to the mouth and tongue to facilitate speech? Can behavioral contrasts provide the distinction we seek?

Behavioral Perspectives on "What Is Human?"

Even for eighteenth- and nineteenth-century scholars, behavior played a major role in the definition of humans, as it did for Aristotle, Horace, and other ancient writers. Distinctions cited by these and other early scholars included language, shame, reason, use of fire and tools, a sense of justice, and a sense of the sacred. Once the great apes were known, these distinctions like the morphological ones became more nuanced. James Burnett (Lord Monboddo) argued in 1779-99 that orangutans and chimpanzees were human in every way—they had a guttural form of communication believed by native Indonesians to be language, and used simple stick tools. He also argued they had a sense of shame, built huts, used fire, and buried their dead, for which there is no modern evidence (Burnett 1779–99).

New research on great ape behavior has further blurred the behavioral distinctiveness of humans. All the great apes make and use simple tools, and for both chimpanzees and orangutans, tool use and other behaviors vary between populations, suggesting that a rudimentary form of "culture" is being handed down from one great ape generation to the next (Whiten et al. 1999). While spoken language is still a major defining feature of humans, many humans use other forms of communication, and apes have proven capable of learning and passing on a rudimentary ability for sign language[3] (Savage-Rumbaugh et al. 1989, Jackendorf 1999). Furthermore, there is now evidence that babies, who share with apes some of the same anatomical disadvantages in speaking, can communicate ideas in sign language long before they can talk, suggesting, if ontogeny recapitulates phylogeny, that sign language may have an older history in humans than spoken language (Petitto and Marentette 1997, Petitto et al. 2001). Psychologists (evolutionary and otherwise) are focusing on the expression, in humans, of such characteristics as "theory of mind," "ability to imitate," "empathy," "problem-solving abilities," and so on, but in almost every case, at least one of the great apes (and other animals as well) have shown a degree of these features that will not permit an absolute distinction between humans and other animals (Tomasello and Call 1997, Tomasello et al. 2005).

Genetics appears to provide another biological definition of humans, or at least of modern humans since the full decoding of the human genome in 2001. But genetic sequences, even those derived from fossils, actually do not shed much light on whether the bearers were fully human or not—only on their degree of relatedness to ourselves. The differences between the Neanderthal mitochondrial genome (R. Green et al. 2006, Noonan et al. 2006) and ours tell us nothing about the complexity of Neanderthal language(s) or whether Neanderthals shared ethical constraints, whether they held complex beliefs about death and the afterlife, whether they sang or made up poems or told stories about their ancestors. Genetics may be more informative on this issue in the future. Animal studies of behavioral genetics and the genetics of brain growth and development are just beginning to yield results (Fisher and Marcus 2006). Due to the essential unity of the genetic code in all living things, such results may carry implications for the evolution of human behavior.[4]

Defining Human: The Archaeological Approach

If we want to study the evolution of human behavior, we must necessarily turn to the fossil and archaeological records (Brooks 1996). Fossils can reflect behavior—in the shape of bones, their chemical composition, the position and strength of muscle markings, the damages suffered over a lifetime, and the disposition of the skeletal remains. Archaeological sites are formed by definition only through human activities, although Mercader et al. (2002, 2007) have shown that chimpanzees also leave archaeological traces of their behavior. The fossil and archaeological records are limited, however, in what they can say about the past, as they require definitions of humanness that are amenable to recovery in the material record. For example, one cannot recover fossil languages, at least not until the development of writing, although dead languages can be reconstructed up to a point from words preserved in living languages. But one can recover traces of symbolic behavior (D'Errico et al. 2003), or morphological traces of changes in brain or vocal tract morphology, that suggest an ability for language. Ideologies or the capacity for abstract thought are not preserved, but one can recover traces of practices that seem to conform to ideas about spirituality—burial of the dead and cave art. Problem solving and innovativeness cannot be directly observed in the past, but one can document increases in technological sophistication and rates of innovation. And while the social networks and societies in which humans live are abstractions that must be inferred from physical evidence even in living populations, through geochemical characterization of sources, one can trace the movement of materials over very long distances, rule out natural transport, and infer the size of such networks (Gamble 1998, Féblot-Augustins 1997, 1999). In addition, from patterns of variability in the material record, it is possible to infer whether or not people distinguished themselves from their neighbors through their material culture, and what the size of the distinctive groupings might have been. Signs of empathy may also be evident in the survival of individuals with crippling injuries or major deficits, who could not have survived long on their own.

From the perspective of modern humans, behavioral definitions of humanness include what could be called "living in our heads"—in reference to the fact that we do not live in a natural world but in one of our own imagination—an imagination that has led in many cases, perhaps inadvertently, to actual transformation of the natural world. Humans think up cultural solutions to scarcity, risk, and the quest for food, shelter, and mates, resulting in an astounding diversity of cultural forms, and the transformation (and endangerment) of vast areas of the earth's surface. Since humans' teeth and their two-legged gait are utterly inadequate for defense against natural predators, humans are totally dependent on invented technologies. Rather than living in a physical herd or a pack, humans live in what Anderson (1983) has called "imagined communities," populated by individuals one may never physically encounter— distant relatives, compatriots, ancestors, and spiritual beings. Humans use symbols extensively to represent themselves, their social groups, and their thoughts. In addition, symbols are used to reify social groups to the extent that disrespect to a symbol, especially a religious symbol, is tantamount to an act of violence against a person. And humans have the ability to imagine the feelings and lives of those around us as both separate from and similar to one's own—in a way that leads to extraordinary capacities for altruism and sympathy, even for individuals one may never meet.

The capabilities of modern humans must involve at least six different faculties:

- *Abstract thinking.* This is the ability to act with reference to concepts not limited in time and space. A chimpanzee can be taught to use symbols correctly to solicit a reward, but not to go to the grocery store with a shopping list and remember that she forgot to write down the milk.

- *Planning depth.* This is the ability to strategize in group context. Social carnivores share this ability in the immediate future, but lack our ability to plan for next year, or for contingencies that may never happen.

- *Problem solving through behavioral, economic, and technological innovation.* Many animals are good problem solvers, but modern humans solve problems that have not yet arisen, and devise entirely new ways of living in the process.

- *Imagined communities* (Anderson 1983). Our present communities, from family to nation, may include people we have never met, spirits, animals, people who have died, and the not-yet-born. These communities exist in our heads, and never meet face-to-face as a group.

- *Symbolic thinking* particularly regards information storage. This involves the ability to reference both physical objects/beings and ideas with arbitrary symbols, and to act on the symbol even if the person who planted it is no longer present. It is both the arbitrariness of such symbols and their freedom from time and space constraints that distinguish our symbolic behavior from that of animals.

- *Theory of mind* (C. Sherwood et al. 2008) involves the ability to recognize oneself as a separate intelligence but at the same time to read the emotions and thoughts of others (empathy). Apes and even domestic carnivores possess this to a degree, but only modern humans possess shared intentionality (Tomasello et al. 2005) and can even recognize and respond to humanity in individuals they will never meet.

The Early Record of Behavioral Evolution 2.6-0.6 MYA

When do these abilities first appear? It is difficult to say, not only because the record is sparse and patchy but because the capability may or may not be expressed for hundreds or thousands of years after it appears, and may depend on the development of other factors, or historical events. The capability for inventing computers may have existed in the late Pleistocene, but could not be expressed without the appropriate cultural and technological milieu. The limited evidence for early expression of some of these characteristics suggests, however, that the total package was not assembled over a short period.

Problem solving and technological innovation. The first stone tools date to 2.6 mya from Ethiopia (Semaw 2000, Semaw et al. 2003), slightly later in Kenya (Kibunjia et al. 1994, Roche et al. 1999). There is little evidence for abstract thinking in these artifacts as they consist of simple flakes directly related to the form of the raw material, although the ability to choose appropriate raw materials (Stout et al. 2005) and to derive multiple flakes from a single block (Delagnes and Roche 2005) is far beyond what even the smartest apes can be taught to do. The rate of change or innovation is initially very slow; new forms such as bifacially worked symmetrical hand-axes appear only after the first 900,000 years, and tools remain very static for more than I mya after that. Nevertheless, such tools made it possible for early humans to shift from the largely frugivorous diet of the great apes to one involving substantial carnivory (De Heinzelin et al. 1999, e.g.), and also to expand into the Near East, Indonesia, and China, far beyond their original range, by 1.9-1.6 mya (Anton and Swisher 2004, Gabunia et al. 2000, Zhu et al. 2001, 2008, Belmaker et al. 2002, Belmaker in press). Technology also seems to have made possible a shift in food preparation from teeth to tools, so that teeth become smaller while body size increases. Early human diets were probably omnivorous, with meat obtained largely by scavenging, although the "early access" pattern of marks on some bones suggests that at least some early humans confronted felid or canid carnivores at kill sites. Fire was controlled by 0.8 mya or earlier (Goren-Inbar et al. 2004), facilitating a new diet, the use of caves, hunting, new technologies, and social time at night.

There is no evidence from this time for *imagined communities* or *symbolic thinking*. Stone and other materials appear to have largely derived from within twenty-five km of the site (Féblot-Augustins 1997, 1999), and the shapes and technologies are very similar from India to England and from France to South Africa (Petraglia and Korisettar 1997). The early presence of language in some form is also debatable, as brain asymmetries exist in early *Homo*, but modern speech would have been difficult (Lieberman and McCarthy 2007). The symmetrical forms of stone tools after 1.7 mya may have carried a symbolic meaning, but since they are also utilitarian objects, their symbolic meaning, if any, is obscure.

Empathy, which appears very early in children before competent speech, may already be ref lected in a very early human skull from Dmanisi in the Caucasus at 1.9 mya (Lordkipanidze et al. 2005), of an individual who had lost almost all his teeth a considerable time before death, a condition that is rarely found in wild primates. Survival of this toothless individual required either a new, very soft diet or the assistance of others. The 1.5 mya *Homo ergaster* skeleton from Kenya also appears pathological in its vertebral column, yet survived into adolescence (Ohman et al. 2002).

The early appearance of these features does not mean they were as fully expressed as in modern humans or even that the full capacity existed as in ourselves. But it does indicate that the human capacity did not arise suddenly in full-blown form but developed or evolved over time from nonhuman antecedents.

Late Archaic Humans and Neanderthals

After 600 kya, most fossils exhibit essentially modern brain sizes, yet evidence of an increase in technological innovation, larger social networks, or symbolic behavior is minimal until ca.

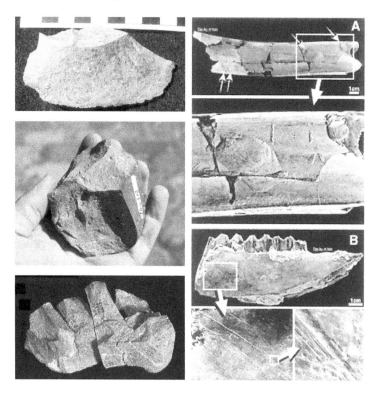

Figure 4.3 The oldest artifacts: a, b) *(above left top and middle)* flake and core from Gona, Ethiopia, 2.6 mya (courtesy Dietrich Stout); c) *(above right)* animal bones cut and broken open with stone tools, Bouri, Ethiopia, 2.6 mya (National Museum of Ethiopia, Addis Ababa; © 1999 David L. Brill/Atlanta); d) *(above left bottom)* refitted core and flakes, showing complexity of flaking sequence, Lokalalei 2C, Kenya, 2.34 mya (courtesy Hélène Roche; © MPK/WTAP).

Figure 4.4 Early traces of symbolic behavior before the oldest *Homo sapiens*: a) *(above top)* possible crude human figure—natural stone with groove delimiting the head, Berekhat Ram, Israel, ca. 250-280 kya (courtesy Francesco D'Errico); b) *(above middle and bottom)* ocher, Olorgesailie, Kenya, 220 kya (A. S. Brooks).

400 kya. A new stone technology (Levallois) required a degree of abstract thought to imagine the flakes whose shapes were predetermined by the shaping of the cores (Boeda 1995, Schlanger 1996, Tryon 2006, Monnier et al. 2006). The increased use of ocher in Africa might suggest body painting or alternatively a more utilitarian function (McBrearty and Brooks 2000, Barham 1998, Lombard 2005). And in Israel and Morocco, two slightly modified stones with traces of ocher dating to between 500 and 200 kya may or may not represent crude human images (D'Errico and Nowell 2000, Bednarik 2003). Wooden spears or javelins from Germany and numerous remains of large animals imply a more complex hunting technology (Thieme 1997), which may have

facilitated the occupation of much higher temperate latitudes by 600 kya, especially in Europe (Parfitt et al. 2005). One cave in Spain contains the remains of more than thirty individuals, mostly children and young adults, who lived ca. 400 kya. It is unclear if this concentration was due to deliberate disposal of the dead or some other factor (Arsuaga et al. 1997).

Neanderthals, who occupied Eurasia as far east as Uzbekistan between ca. 250 and 40 kya, were significantly more like modern humans in their behavior than their predecessors. They buried their dead, but without clear evidence of grave goods or associated symbols (Pettit 2001), used black and red mineral pigments found as powder, lumps, and "crayons," made stone-tipped spears (Boëda et al. 1998), and were competent hunters of large game (Mellars 1996, Chase 1989). Their fossil remains bear traces of both interpersonal aggression, in the form of a knife wound (Trinkaus 1983), and empathy, as elderly and handicapped individuals survived for much longer periods than previously. Evidence of cannibalism is also found at many sites (Defleur et al. 2000). Although Neanderthals occupied Europe for at least 200 kya, their technology shows very little innovation or regional differentiation until the end of this time. The Neanderthal brain was similar in size to ours when adjusted for their large body mass, but the relationship of the tongue and soft palate to the laryngeal space suggests that they may still not have been capable of all the complex speech sounds made by modern humans (Lieberman and McCarthy 2007). Clear evidence of symbolic behavior in the form of personal ornaments is only found at the most recent Neanderthal sites, dating to a time when anatomically modern humans were already on their periphery (Mellars 2006). Does this mean they possessed a capacity for innovation and symbolic behavior, or only a facility for imitation (Zilhao 2006)?

Into the 1970s it was thought that modern humans evolved in Europe. But with the advent of new fossils and better dating techniques, it became clear that the oldest anatomically "*Homo sapiens*" fossils were African. The oldest fossil attributed to *Homo sapiens* in Africa (McDougall et al. 2005) is more than five times as old as the oldest *Homo sapiens* in Europe. At the same time, genetic studies demonstrated that all living humans share a "recent" African common ancestor who lived between 100 and 200 kya, or more, while one group of African genetic lineages shares a common ancestor with all non-Africans that is considerably younger, perhaps 40–80,000 years ago. Although at first this result was disputed, repeated genetic analyses have confirmed our African origin. DNA sequences have been recovered from twelve Neanderthals who lived as far apart as Spain and Siberia, and the resulting sequences share similarities with one another but indicate at least three regional populations (Fabre et al. 2009) and contain many sequences not shared with living humans, suggesting around 600 kya or more of separate evolution (R. Green et al. 2006, Noonan et al. 2006).

The rapid appearance of modern-looking people in Europe was not some punctuated "human revolution" or "great leap forward" but was clearly an invasion of people with long tropical limb proportions (Pearson 2001). Asia has a more complicated but equally punctuated history, also suggesting invasion and ultimate dominance by outsiders (Akazawa et al. 1998). Indeed the first "out-of-Africa" migrations of *Homo sapiens* were to the Near East, with modern humans appearing first at Skhul and Qafzeh in Israel between ca. 110 and 90 kya, an initial wave that does not appear to have spread beyond this region until 50-60 ka. Modern humans then disappear from the Levant, as Levantine fossils from 90-50 ka are all Neanderthals (Hublin 2000), then re-expand at or before ca. 50 kya. Whether they used a northern route out of Africa via the Nile valley, or another "southern route" over the Babel-Mandeb strait (Foster and Matsumara 2005), they reached Australia by at least 50 kya and possibly slightly earlier (Stringer 1999, O'Connell and Allen 2004).

Becoming Fully Human: The Later Evolution of Behavior

The earliest *Homo sapiens* in Europe and Asia, ca. 40 kya and later, were almost certainly capable of the same range of behaviors as we are, as indicated by their cave paintings (Clottes 2000), sculptures (Conard 2003), musical instruments, beads and other jewelry (D'Errico et al. 2003), trade networks, technological innovations, regional diversity, economic flexibility, and ability to colonize the entire globe. About earlier humans in Africa who were physically similar to ourselves in many ways, there is considerable debate. Scholars like Richard Klein (2001 e.g.) argue that they were physically modern but behaviorally primitive. To him and others, modern behavior came about suddenly, a "Human Revolution" tied to a rapidly spreading genetic mutation for language. Sally McBrearty and I have argued otherwise, that the capabilities for these behaviors began to be expressed and therefore existed *before* modern physical appearance, with a gradual assembly of the kinds of behaviors we see later (McBrearty and Brooks 2000). This assembly was not unilineal but geographically and temporally spotty, with many reversals.

As archaeologists, we look especially for technological innovation and complexity as proxies for problem solving, long-distance exchange as a proxy for both planning depth and imagined communities, economic intensification (another proxy for problem solving and planning depth), regional styles that change over time (proxies for symbolic thinking and/or imagined communities), and beads, images, and notational pieces along with burial of the dead as proxies for symbolic thinking and theory of mind. For all of these material expressions of behavioral capabilities, there are modern, even living groups that lack them. While demonstrably capable of producing such items, they clearly lack the impetus or the history to do so, so absence may not be a good marker of nonmodernity. But absence of all of these over long archaeological stretches of time cannot be characterized as "modern behavior."

The rest of this paper will focus on three particular expressions of behavioral capabilities: technological innovation, long-distance exchange, and symbolic behavior. Since modern humans evolved in Africa, one should look particularly at the African evidence, which is still very scanty. There are more excavated sites dating to 250-35 kya in southwestern France than in the vast African continent. In particular the more typical tropical regions of Africa are poorly known; most of the evidence comes from the temperate regions at the northern and southern edges of the continent. Despite the limited quality of the evidence, more than 150 sites testify to the gradual assembly of innovative, social, and symbolic behaviors, and to a complex interrelationship between behavior and morphology, leading to modern humans.

Before ca. 200 kya, there are no known fossils attributed to *Homo sapiens sensu strictu*. The oldest examples to date are from Ethiopia, from the Middle Awash (160 kya, White et al. 2003), and from a second region in the far south, on the Omo river (195 kya, McDougall et al. 2005). All human remains found in Africa after this date are grouped in *Homo sapiens*, distinguished by smaller teeth, a chin, a vertical face tucked under the cranium, a vertical forehead, and vocal tract proportions conducive to spoken language. Several lines of evidence converge to suggest that East Africa rather than South Africa could be the cradle not only of our physical selves but also of our behavior. Not only are the oldest hafted points and the oldest *Homo sapiens* from there, but new mtDNA and Y-chromosome studies suggest that an East African population, the Sandawe, may reflect as deep a root of the human genetic tree as the southern African San (Tishkoff et al. 2007, Brooks et al. 2008). Genetics also suggests that the ancient East African population was larger. In central Kenya, as well as in northern Tanzania and areas of Ethiopia, archaeological remains suggest a density of human occupation that is quite rare outside this area, with the possible exception of the South African coast, where colder temperatures, a winter rainfall pattern, and rich marine resources concentrated human habitation in coastal areas (Marean et al. 2007).

But after more than a million years with little change in technology, the African record suggests that well before the appearance of *Homo sapiens*, before 285 kya, behavior had begun to change. New technologies produced standardized stone flakes and long thin blades (Johnson and McBrearty 2009, Gibbons 2009), ocher processing increased, and many sites have small quantities, up to 5 percent, of stone material derived from sources a considerable distance away— as much as 200 km or more, the first sign of an expanded social network. The increased use of ocher in Africa might suggest body painting or possibly a more utilitarian function. And in Israel and Morocco, two slightly modified stones with traces of ocher dating to between 500 and 200 kya may or may not represent crude images (D'Errico and Nowell 2000). The behavioral changes reflected in these finds are not sudden or directional. The evidence for them is interspersed with sites containing the old symmetrical large cutting tools, or simple flake technologies, or lacking evidence for ocher or exotic stone. But the general trend is toward more complex behaviors with time. By ca. 267 kya (e.g., Morgan and Renne 2008), several sites in South and East Africa include carefully made stone points, designed for hafting onto spear shafts.

New Technologies

More dramatic changes in behavior occur after the appearance of *Homo sapiens*. From South Africa to Egypt and from the western Sahara to Ethiopia, evidence for complex technologies and new tools increases especially after 100 kya. In the Middle Awash region of Ethiopia, the first *Homo sapiens* at ca. 160 kya are associated with both advanced flake technologies and the older symmetrical large cutting tools (Clark et al. 2003). Before 90 kya, stone points are large or thick, and were likely hafted onto thrusting spears in close encounters with prey. But after 90 kya, the points become tiny and light (Brooks et al. 2006, Yellen et al. 2005). We measured points from a number of other sites of about the same age from North, South, and East Africa and compared them to contemporaneous points made by Neanderthals. In comparing these to the range of points made by historic groups of hunter-gatherers, we concluded that the ancient African examples had to have served as armatures for a complex projectile weapons system, involving a point, a haft, and some sort of propulsion system, either a bow or a spearthrower. It is also likely that these very small points, which could not have delivered a lethal blow to a large animal, were associated with the use of poison.

A projectile weapons system has some parallels to a grammar (Ambrose 2001) in that it involves noninterchangeable forms: point, haft, binding, and propulsion agent, which can be combined in a limited number of ways, with each point or haft filling a role that can only be interchanged with another point or haft. Such a system provides tremendous advantages to the hunter, who can now kill at a distance, with much more success and less risk to himself (or herself), resulting in greater survivorship. What were they doing with these weapons? In the western Kalahari desert, we excavated a site dating to 77 kya on a seasonal pan, which today serves as an ambush hunting venue at the end of the rainy season, when other water sources are dry and game is concentrated around this resource (Brooks and Yellen 1987, Helgren and Brooks 1983). More than 600 small, finely made points constitute the dominant tool class, and associated animal remains suggest that humans were hunting large dangerous animals such as African buffalo, extinct giant zebra, and warthog with points weighing less than 10 grams, well within the range of arrowheads and spear-thrower darts known from historic peoples. At Klasies River in South Africa, one of these small points was actually stuck into the cervical vertebra of a giant buffalo (Milo 1998), providing proof of its use as a weapon.

At Mumba Shelter in Tanzania, there are also small projectile armatures, in levels dated to between 40 and 60-70 kya (Mehlman 1979, 1989, 1991, Hare et al. 1993, Prendergast et al. 2007). These are not only triangular but geometric crescents and trapezoids, designed for hafting multiple elements in a single haft in the manner of pre-dynastic Egyptian arrowheads. Again, this level of technological sophistication is also found in a very limited time and space in southern Africa, 60-65 kya. What is even more interesting in the Tanzanian case is that some of the tools are made of obsidian, not from Tanzania but from central Kenya, almost 300 km away (Merrick and Brown 1984). So we are not only looking at technological sophistication, but also at a likely exchange network. A few other African sites show comparable exchange distances in small amounts.

As early as 130 kya, another set of technological innovations appears to have focused on fishing. In eastern DR Congo (Zaire), we discovered a series of what appeared geologically and typologically to be Middle Stone Age localities along the river at a place called Katanda, following

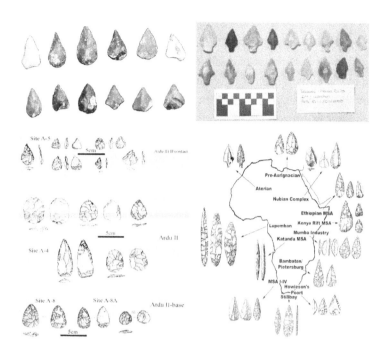

Figure 4.5 Small African projectile points dating to between 130 and 60 kya, which suggest early *Homo sapiens'* use of complex projectile technologies such as the spear-thrower and/or bow and arrow: a) (*above top left*) triangular points from ≠Gi, Botswana, 77 kya (A. S. Brooks); b) (*above top right*) tanged points from Tabelbala, Algerian Sahara, ca. 60-130 kya (A. S. Brooks); c) (*above bottom left*) point sequence from youngest (top) to older (base) at Aduma, Middle Awash Valley, Ethiopia, all younger than 90 kya (A. S. Brooks); d) (*above bottom right*) point diversity in Africa 90-60 kya, suggesting the possibility of largescale ethnic or interactive groups (S. McBrearty and A. S. Brooks).

an old land surface (Brooks et al. 1995). We excavated three sites, each with mammalian fauna and lithic artifacts but also with a series of barbed bone points (Yellen et al. 1995).[5] The dates for these sites have varied, but the trapped charge dating techniques suggest that an age of 80-90 kya would be likely, and that there is no evidence for an age of less than 60 kya. Again, this is a complex technology that appears to have been outside the competence of Neanderthals.

The associated fauna includes a very large component of fish remains, all of the same species (*Clarias*) and age, suggesting a seasonal fishing activity. The fish were very large; we caught one weighing seventy-four pounds, and the excavated ones were larger. Thus these three sites testify to both technological and economic innovation. In addition, fish provides important nutrients—omega-3 fatty acids—which nourish the brain (Crawford et al. 1999, Parkington 2003). Bone points very much like these are known from the Middle-Later Stone Age intermediate industry at White Paintings Shelter in Botswana (Robbins et al. 2000). The earliest Late Stone Age at White Paintings is dated to between 40 and 57 kya (Feathers 1997, Brooks et al. 2008). Very different cylindrical bone points resembling historical bone arrow points are known from ca. 77 kya at Blombos Cave (Henshilwood et al. 2001), from Peers Cave, and a number of other South African coastal sites,

Figure 4.6 Fishing and harpoon technology by early *Homo sapiens* at Katanda, eastern DR Congo, at 60-80 kya: a) (*above left top*) a few of the thousands of very large catfish bones recovered in excavations at three sites (A. S. Brooks); b) (*above left bottom*) very large catfish caught in 1990 in the Semliki River below the sites (A. S. Brooks); c) (*above right*) barbed bone harpoons with string wear in the basal grooves (A. S. Brooks).

predating 65 kya. In each case, fish bones have also been recovered. Bone points are a major technological advance, requiring considerably more time and effort to manufacture. Their advantage, according to ethnographic accounts, is that they float, allowing the fisherman to retrieve them easily.

Small projectile armatures in a complex weapons system could have given the edge to later modern humans, allowing populations to expand both within and outside Africa at the expense of the Neanderthals and other archaic populations. Neanderthals had many injuries from personal encounters with large dangerous animals (Berger and Trinkaus 1995); later moderns had very few. Neanderthals also had many more signs of dietary stress in their bones and teeth than the early moderns who succeeded them (Ogilvie et al. 1989).

These projectiles are also quite variable in time and space—at least as variable as the small arrow tips that succeed them. The patterning of regional variation is to a large extent independent of climate and raw material—a stone industry with geometric shapes (the Howiesons Poort), for example, is found from southern Namibia to the Cape Province of South Africa in a limited time band and is made on a wide variety of raw materials, from quartz to silcrete and chert. The distribution of regional styles of early *Homo sapiens* is thus as suggestive of ethnic or regional differences as any later African stone tools.

Symbolic Behavior

So far, we have demonstrated the presence of technological innovation, economic intensification, long-distance exchange, and regional styles in the behavioral repertoire of early modern humans. But is there hard evidence for symbolic behavior? Until very recently, there was little evidence before 40 kya. An image from the Apollo 11 Cave of an antelope with human hind legs was found in a level with an old date of 27,000 (Wendt 1976), although we have dated the industry found with it to 65,000 at that site (Miller et al. 1999). In 2002, an extraordinary piece of engraved ocher was described from Blombos cave in South Africa (Henshilwood 2002). It and a second similar piece clearly suggest that ocher had more than a utilitarian function. Many other pieces of ocher, bone, and eggshell with engraved geometric or linear designs are known from both this site and other sites in southern Africa, including fragments of decorated ostrich eggshell containers from ca. 65 kya at the Atlantic coastal site of Diepkloof (Rigaud et al. 2006).

Bead and other body ornaments are unequivocal evidence for symbolic behavior and for fully human status, as they have little utilitarian function. In traditional hunting societies, beads provide the basis of exchange networks that serve to tie distant people together in a mutual support network, which can be activated when times are bad. Individuals deliberately build these networks up as they grow into middle age, and acquire major responsibilities for raising and marrying off children or for supporting elderly parents (Wiessner 1984). As they age and their needs decrease, individuals begin to reduce the size of these networks. Beads and personal ornaments such as rings, or headpieces, also serve as markers of social identity or status worldwide, from wedding bands to the colorful collars of the Maasai to the diamond necklaces of society women (or men). Despite extensive excavation, no beads are known from Europe before ca. 40 kya. Early African sites have yielded a few ostrich eggshell beads in early sites—an unfinished one from South Africa (Boomplaas) dated to ca. 60-80 kya, and several from Tanzania (Mumba) dated directly to between 45 and 52 kya (Hare et al.1993). In 2004, a series of perforated shell beads from the coast of South Africa, dated to 76 kya, made headlines as the oldest evidence for personal ornaments (Henshilwood et al. 2004, 2005). Newer finds of shell beads, of the same genus, have been published from even older sites in North Africa and the Middle East, in direct association with modern humans at one site, but dated to as much as 110 kya (Vanhaeren et al. 2006, Bouzouggar et al. 2007). More and older bead sites are being reported as we excavate more sites with modern technologies.

The evidence for human burial practices with grave offerings indicative of symbolic behavior within Africa is limited, due in part to the relative dominance of open-air excavations where

Figure 4.7 Symbolic behavior by early *Homo sapiens* in Africa: a) (*above top left*) geometric design engraved on ocher from Blombos Cave, South Africa, 76 kya (courtesy Francesco D'Errico); b) (*above top right*) perforated shell beads from Blombos, 76 kya, with string wear in the holes. Beads from the same or similar species have now been found at multiple sites in South and North Africa, and the Levant, between 105 and 60 kya. Other shell beads have been recovered from East Africa dating to a similar antiquity (courtesy Francesco D'Errico); c) (*above middle*) small perforators for making holes or engraving from Aduma, Middle Awash, dating to ca. 80-90 kya (A. S. Brooks); d) (*above bottom*) geometric design engraved around lip of ostrich eggshell "canteen" (fragments), Diepkloof Rock Shelter, South Africa, ca. 60-65 kya (courtesy J.-Ph. Rigaud?).

bone preservation is poor, and in part to probable cultural practices of burial away from living sites. Two relatively elaborate cave burials at early dates, however, confirm the antiquity of this practice among modern humans at opposite ends of their early geographic range: the burial of a child at Border Cave in South Africa dated to 66-90 kya (Beaumont et al. 1978, Beaumont 1980, Miller et al. 1999, Millard 2006, Jacobs et al. 2008,) and an elaborate modern human burial at Qafzeh in Israel dated to 90-100 kya (Vandermeersch 1970, 1981, Hovers et al. 2003). The child burial is associated with what appears to be ocher and has a large perforated *Conus* shell in its

Figure 4.8   Oldest known figurative image from South Africa, Apollo 11 Cave, 27,000 BP (courtesy Heinrich Barthe Institut, Ralph Vogelsang).

chest area. The nearest source for the shell is the Indian Ocean ca. eighty km away. The Qafzeh individual was associated with seventy-one pieces of red ocher, and also with a perforated bivalve shell *(Glycymeris)* (D. Bar-Yosef 2005). Although the perforation could have been natural, the shell was brought to the site and placed in the burial, along with some possible offerings of animal remains. These two sites constitute the earliest clear evidence for symbolic burial with grave goods and red ocher, practices that suggest a belief in the survival of a spirit after death.

Summary: Why Humanness is a Gradual Process, Not a Sudden Event

The accelerating rate of technological innovation was a stepwise process, not a sudden event related to language. By 70 to 60 kya, well before the out-of-Africa event that apparently led to Neanderthal extinction, anatomically modern humans in Africa (and occasionally in the Levant) had light, complex projectile weaponry, fishing and bone fishing spears, long-distance exchange networks, ocher, deliberate burial with grave goods, regionally distinctive point styles, symbolic engravings, and personal ornaments. Within Africa, there is probably a complex web of interregional migration and local extinction that makes the record patchy and discontinuous. In addition, demographic and climatic factors may affect the degree to which any of these modern human capabilities are expressed; ethnographic studies suggest that symbolic expression, subsistence practices, and regional networks intensify under conditions of resource stress. It is also interesting that the first Australians, who must have come from

Figure 4.9 Examples of some of the first figurative sculptures and painted images from Europe: a) (*above left*) the "lion-man" in mammoth ivory, Hohlenstein-Stadel, Baden-Württemberg, Germany, ca. 32 kya (courtesy Ulmer Museum, Der Löwenmennsch: *Tier und Mensch in der Kunst der Eiszeit*, cover image and plate 13); b) (*above right*) a panel of horses from Chauvet Cave, France, ca. 30 kya (courtesy Jean Clottes et al., plate III.108 of *Cheavet Cave: The Art of Earliest Times*, photo by C. Fritz and G. Tosello).

Africa but entered an empty continent ca. 50 kya, lack evidence for any of these behaviors until after 30 kya when the population had grown to fill the available regions, and the climate turned hyper-arid.

Neanderthals, on the other hand, before 50 kya, had hafted spear points (Boeda et al. 1998), used a large amount of black coloring materials (they probably had light-colored skin), and practiced simple burials without offerings or ocher. There is little evidence in this early time range for Neanderthal fishing[6] and none for bone tools, musical instruments, cave art, or personal ornaments. After 40 kya, when the modern humans were already on their periphery or perhaps in their midst, Neanderthals responded to pressure by developing or adopting some of the same traits—particularly the beads, and stone technologies. But they still lacked small, light projectile armatures, they rarely if ever went fishing, and really long-distance raw material transport is only marginally present toward the end at the northeast end of their range in Eastern Europe and Central Asia, where we would expect human territories to be very large and populations sparse.

Why was *Homo sapiens* able to replace Neanderthals in Eurasia after 50 kya but not before? There seem to be three possibilities: one is the sudden genetic mutation theory, one is about technological superiority, and one concerns the development of more sophisticated social networks, supported by a greater use of symbols, which buffered human populations against risks, much like the naming and gift-giving relationships of the Kalahari hunter-gatherers.

While the answer is almost certainly more complicated than any of these simple hypotheses, and may involve combinations of them and other arguments, I would argue that the evidence against a revolutionary genetic event is strong when you look at Africa. That continent is characterized by the earlier appearance of technological and economic complexity, as well as of complex symbolic behavior. The patterning of change both during and at the end of the Middle Stone Age period of early *Homo sapiens* is also very different from that consistent with a revolution, as it is both spotty and gradual. Such patterning is much better explained by the existence in earlier anatomically modern humans of modern behavioral capabilities that are variably expressed when conditions call for them—when either climate or population growth creates effective crowding, in an otherwise sparsely inhabited landscape.

At what point did *Homo* become fully human? The more we know, the harder it is to draw a line between human and nonhuman or prehuman. The evidence suggests that the capabilities for "living in our heads" were present before 130 kya, and developed in a stepwise fashion, possibly in a feedback relationship with our morphology. Capacities for some of the most human qualities—creativity, empathy, reverence, spirituality, aesthetic appreciation, abstract thought, and problem solving (rationality)—were already evident soon after the emergence of our species.[7]

Notes

1   It should be noted that nineteenth-century physical anthropologists and anatomists argued that skeletons of the European lower classes were physically distinctive, bearing a slightly closer resemblance to apes in the shape of the forehead, chin, and upright stance (Gould 1996).

2   "Hominin" refers to humans and our extinct ancestors and close relatives, from the time of our divergence from the lineage of the African apes (Wood 2005).

3   Their anatomy does not facilitate the rapid production and distinction of multiple speech sounds.

4   According to some calculations, humans share 98.5 percent of their DNA with chimpanzees but also about 50 percent with bananas (Wood and Constantino 2004).

5   Francesco d'Errico is studying the manufacture and use of these points and has suggested that there is wear from some sort of line or string on the base, indicating probable use as a harpoon (Brooks et al. 2004).

6   Neanderthal fishing was argued for late Gibraltar Neanderthals by Stringer et al. (2008), but the fish remains in question are very limited and derive from small fish that possibly could have been brought in by a nonhuman mammal or avian predator.

7   I am extremely grateful to Brian Richmond for his comments on this manuscript and to Mary Ann Meyers for careful editing of the paper and its references.

References

Akazawa, T., K. Aoki, and O. Bar-Yosef, eds. *Neanderthals and Modern Humans in Western Asia.* New York: Plenum Publishers, 1998.

Aldhouse-Green, Stephen. "Paviland Cave: Contextualizing the 'Red Lady,'" *Antiquity* 72, no. 278 (1998): 756–72.

Ambrose, Stanley. "Paleolithic Technology and Human Evolution," *Science* 299, no. 5509 (2001): 1748–53.

Anderson, Benedict. *Imagined Communities: Reflections on the Origin and Spread of Nationalism.* London: Verso Books, 1983.

Anton, S. C., and C. C. Swisher III. "Early Dispersals of *Homo* from Africa," *Annual Review of Anthropology* 33 (2004): 271–96.

Arsuaga, J. L., I. Martínez, A. Gracia, J. M. Carretero, C. Lorenzo, N. García, and A. I. Ortega. "Sima de los Huesos (Sierra de Atapuerca, Spain): The Site," *Journal of Human Evolution* 33, nos. 2–3 (1997): 109–27.

Barham, L. S. "Possible Early Pigment Use in South-Central Africa," *Current Anthropology* 39 (1998): 703–20.

Bar-Yosef Mayer, Danielle E. "The Exploitation of Shells as Beads in the Palaeolithic and Neolithic of the Levant," *Paléorient* 31, no. 1 (2005): 176–85.

Beaumont, Peter B. "On the Age of the Border Cave Hominids 1–5," *Paleontologica Africana* 23 (1980): 21–33.

Beaumont, Peter B., Hertha de Villiers, and John C. Vogel. "Modern Man in Sub-Saharan Africa Prior to 49000 BP: A Review and Evaluation with Particular Reference to Border Cave," *South African Journal of Science* 74 (1978): 409–19.

Bednarik, Robert. "A Figurine from the African Acheulian," *Current Anthropology* 44, no. 3 (2003): 405–13.

Belmaker, Miriam, Eitan Tchernov, Sylvana Condemi, and Ofer Bar-Yosef. "New Evidence for Hominid Presence in the Lower Pleistocene of the Levant," *Journal of Human Evolution* 43, no. 1 (2002): 43–56.

Belmaker, Miriam. "On the Road to China: The Environmental Landscape of the Lower Pleistocene in Western Eurasia and Its Implication for the Dispersal of *Homo,*" in *Asian Paleoanthropology: From Africa to China and Beyond,* edited by Christopher J. Norton, David R. Braun, and John W. K. Harris. New York: Springer (Vertebrate Paleobiology and Paleoanthropology Series), in press.

Bendysche, Thomas. "On the Anthropology of Linnaeus: 1735–1776," in "The History of Anthropology," *Memoirs of the Anthropological Society of London,* 1 (1863): 421–26.

Berger, Thomas D., and Eric Trinkaus. "Patterns of Trauma among the Neanderthals," *Journal of Archaeological Science* 22 (1995): 841–52.

Blumenbach, Johann Friedrich. "I. Ordn. Bimanus. II. Quadrumana," in *Hand-buch der Naturgeschichte.* Dietrich, Göttingen (1779–1780) translated by R. T. Gore, as "Order I: Bimanus, II: Quadrumana," in *A Manual of the Elements of Natural History,* Section 4, 34–42. London: W. Simpkin and R. Marshall, 1825.

Boëda, Eric. "Levallois: A Volumetric Construction, Methods, and Technique," in *The Definition and Interpretation of Levallois Technology,* edited by Harold Dibble and Ofer Bar-Yosef. Philadelphia: University of Pennsylvania Press, 1995.

Boëda, Eric, Jacques Connajn, and Sultan Mohesen. "Bitumen as Hafting Material on Middle Paleolithic Artifacts from El Kowm Basin, Syria," in *Neanderthals and Modern Humans in Western Asia,* edited by Aoki Akazawa and Ofer Bar-Yosef, pp. 193–214. New York: Plenum Publishers, 1998.

Bouzouggar, A., N. Barton, M. Vanhaeren, F. d'Errico, S. Collcutt, T. Higham, S. Parfitt, E. Rhodes, J. L. Schwenninger, C. Stringer, E. Turner, S. Ward, A. Moutmir, and A. Stambouli. "82,000-Year-Old Shell Beads from North Africa and Implications for the Origin of Modern Human Behavior," *Proceedings of the National Academy of Sciences* 104 (2007): 9964–69.

Bramble, Dennis M., and Daniel E. Lieberman. "Endurance Running and the Evolution of *Homo,*" *Nature* 432 (2004): 345–52.

Brooks, Alison S. "Behavior and Human Evolution," in *Contemporary Issues in Human Evolution,* edited by W. E. Meikle, F. C. Howell, and N. G. Jablonski, pp. 135–66. Memoirs of the California Academy of Sciences no. 21, 1996.

Brooks, Alison S., David M. Helgren, Jonathan M. Cramer, Alan Franklin, William Hornyak, Jody M. Keating, Richard G. Klein, W. John Rink, Henry P. Schwarcz, J. N. Leith Smith, Kathryn Stewart, Nancy E. Todd, Jacques Verniers, and John E. Yellen. "Dating and Context of Three Middle Stone Age Sites with Bone Points in the Upper Semliki Valley, Zaire," *Science* 268 (1995): 548–53.

Brooks, A. S., and J. E. Yellen. "The Preservation of Activity Areas in the Archaeological Record: Ethnoarchaeological and Archaeological Work in North-west Ngamiland, Botswana," in *Method and Theory of Activity Area Research,* edited by S. Kent, pp. 63–106. New York: Columbia University Press, 1987.

Brooks, A. S., and J. E. Yellen. "Bones of Contention: Bone Tools and the Emergence of Modern Human Behavior," in *Abstracts of the 69th Annual Meeting of the Society for American Archaeology, March 31-April 4, Montreal, Canada,* p. 65 (Washington, DC: Society for American Archaeology, 2004).

Brooks, Alison S., F. James Feathers, Gideon Hartman, Noreen Tuross, Francesco d'Errico, and John E. Yellen. "Middle Stone Age Bone Points from Katanda (D. R. Congo): New Perspectives on Age and Association," in Abstracts of the Annual Meeting of the Palaeoanthropology Society, Montreal, Canada, March 30–31, 2004, *PaleoAnthropology* 1 (2004): p. A04.

Brooks, A. S., J. E. Yellen, L. Nevell, and G. Hartman. "Projectile Technologies of the African MSA: Implications for Modern Human Origins," in *Transitions before the Transition: Evolution and Stability in the Middle Paleolithic and Middle Stone Age,* edited by E. Hovers and S. Kuhn, pp. 233–55. New York: Kluwer Academics/Plenum, 2006.

Brooks, Alison S., Sarah A. Tishkoff, and John E. Yellen. "Origins of Modern African Diversity: Archaeological and Genetic Perspectives," in *Abstracts of the 73rd Annual Meeting of the Society for American Archaeology, Vancouver, BC, Canada, March 24–30, 2008.* Washington, DC: Society for American Archaeology, 2008.

Brunet, Michel, et al. "A New Hominid from the Upper Miocene of Chad, Central Africa," *Nature* 418 (2002): 145–51.

Buckland, William. *Reliquiae Diluvinae, or Observations on the Organic Remains Contained in Caves, Fissures and Diluvial Gravel, and on Other Geological Phenomena, Attesting the Action of a Universal Deluge.* London: J. Murray, 1823.

Buffon, Georges Louis Leclerc, Comte de. "Nomenclature des Singes," in *Histoire Naturelle, Générale et Particulière.* Paris: Imprimerie Royal (1749–67). Translated by W. Smellie, "The Nomenclature of Apes," in *Natural History, General and Particular,* vol. 10, pp. 1–36. London: T. Cadell and M. Davies, 1812.

Burnett, James (Lord Monboddo). "Of the Several Steps of the Human Progression from the Brute to the Man, Etc.," in *Ancient Metaphysics: or the Science of Universals,* book 1, ch. 2, pp. 25–34. Edinburgh: J. Balfour and Co., 1779–99.

Chase, P. G. "How Different Was Middle Palaeolithic Subsistence?: A Zooarchaeological Perspective on the Middle to Upper Palaeolithic Transition," in *The Human Revolution: Behavioral and Biological Perspectives on the Origins of Modern Humans,* edited by P. Mellars and C. B. Stringer, pp. 321–27. Edinburgh: Edinburgh University Press, 1989.

Clark, J. D., Y. Beyene, G. WoldeGabriel, W. K. Hart, P. R. Renne, H. Gilbert, A. Defleur, G. Suwa, S. Katoh, K. R. Ludwig, J-R. Boisserie, B. Asfaw, and T. D. White. "Stratigraphic, Chronological and Behavioral Context of Pleistocene *Homo sapiens* from Middle Awash, Ethiopia," *Nature* 423 (2003): 747–52.

Clottes, Jean. "Art between 30,000 and 20,000 bp," in *Hunters of the Golden Age: The Mid-Upper Palaeolithic of Eurasia 30,000–20,000 BP,* edited by Wil Roebroeks, Margherita Mussi, Jiri Svoboda, and Kelly Fennema, pp. 87–103. Leiden: University of Leiden Press, 2000.

Conard, N. J. "Palaeolithic Ivory Sculptures from Southwestern Germany and the Origins of Figurative Art," *Nature* 426 (2003): 830–32.

Crawford, M. A., M. Bloom, C. L. Broadhurst, W. F. Schmidt, S. C. G. C. Cunnane, K. Gehbresmeskel, F. Linseisen, J. Lloyd-Smith, and J. Parkington. "Evidence for the Unique Function of Docosahexaenoic Acid during the Evolution of the Modern Human Brain," *Lipids* 34 Supplement (1999): S39–S47.

Dart, Raymond. "*Australopithecus africanus:* The Man-Ape of South Africa," *Nature* 115 (1925): 195–99.

Darwin, Charles R. *The Descent of Man and Selection in Relation to Sex.* London: John Murray, 1871.

De Heinzelin, J., J. D. Clark, T. White, W. Hart, P. Renne G. Woldegabriel, Y. Beyene, and E. Vrba. "Environment and Behavior of 2.5-Million-Year-Old Bouri Hominids," *Science* 284, no. 5414 (1999): 625–29.

Deino, A., and A. Hill. "40Ar/39Ar Dating of Chemeron Formation Strata Encompassing the Site of Hominid KNM-BC 1, Tugen Hills, Kenya," *Journal of Human Evolution* 42, no. 1 (2002): 141–51.

Deino, A., and S. McBrearty. "40Ar/39Ar Chronology for the Kapthurin Formation, Baringo, Kenya," *Journal of Human Evolution* 42 (2002): 185–210.

Delagnes, A., and H. Roche. "Late Pliocene Hominid Knapping Skills: The Case of Lokalalei 2C, West Turkana, Kenya," *Journal of Human Evolution* 48 (2005): 435–72.

D'Errico, F., C. Henshilwood, G. Lawson, M. Vanhaeren, A.-M. Tillier, M. Soressi, F. Bresson, B. Maureillle, A. Nowell, J. Lakarra, L. Backwell, and M. Julien. "Archaeological Evidence for the Emergence of Language, Symbolism, and Music—An Alternative Evolutionary Perspective," *Journal of World Prehistory* 17, no. 1 (2003): 1–70.

D'Errico, Francesco, and April Nowell. "A New Look at the Berekhat Ram Figurine: Implications for the Origins of Symbolism," *Cambridge Archaeological Journal* 10 (2000): 123–67.

D'Errico, F., and C. S. Henshilwood. "Additional Evidence for Bone Technology in the Southern African Middle Stone Age," *Journal of Human Evolution* 52 (2007): 142–63.

Defleur, Alban, Tim White, Patricia Valensi, Ludovic Slimak, and Évelyne Crégut-Bonnoure. "Neanderthal Cannibalism at Moula-Guercy, Ardèche, France," *Science* 286, no. 5437 (2000): 128–31.

Dubois, Eugene. *Pithecanthropus erectus. Eine Menschenähnliche Uebergangsform aus Java.* Batavia: Landesdruckerei, 1894.

Fabre, Virginie, Silvana Condemi, and Anna Degioanni. "Genetic Evidence of Geographical Groups among Neanderthals," *PLoS One* 4, no. 4 (2009): e5151.

Feathers, James K. "Luminescence Dating of Sediment Samples from White Paintings Rockshelter, Botswana," *Quaternary Science Reviews* 16, nos. 3–5 (1997): 321–31.

Féblot-Augustins, J. *La Circulation des Matières Premières au Paléolithique* (2 vols.). Liège: ERAUL/CNRS no. 75, 1997.

Féblot-Augustins, Jehanne. "Raw Material Transport Patterns and Settlement Systems in the European Lower and Middle Palaeolithic: Continuity, Change and Variability," in *The Middle Palaeolithic Occupation of Europe*, edited by W. Roebrucks and C. Gamble, pp. 193–214. Leiden: University of Leiden, 1999.

Fisher, Simon E., and Gary F. Marcus. "The Eloquent Ape: Genes, Brains and the Evolution of Language," *Nature Reviews: Genetics* 7 (2006): 9–20.

Fitzsimmons, F. W. "Palaeolithic Man in South Africa," *Nature* 95 (1915): 615–16.

Forster, P., and S. Matsumura. "Did Early Humans Go North or South?" *Science* 308, no. 5724 (2005): 965–66.

Gabunia, Leo, Abesalom Vekua, David Lordkipanidze, Carl C. Swisher III, Reid Ferring, Antje Justus, Medea Nioradze, Merab Tvalchrelidze, Susan C. Antón, Gerhard Bosinski, Olaf Jöris, Marie-A.-de Lumley, Givi Majsuradze, and Aleksander Mouskhelishvili. "Earliest Pleistocene Hominid Cranial Remains from Dmanisi, Republic of Georgia: Taxonomy, Geological Setting, and Age," *Science* 288, no. 5468 (2000): 1019–25.

Gamble, Clive. "Palaeolithic Society and the Release from Proximity: A Network Approach to Intimate Relations," *World Archaeology* 29, no. 3 (1998): 426–49.

Gibbons, Ann. "Oldest Stone Blades Uncovered," *ScienceNOW* (April 2, 2009): http://sciencenow.sciencemag.org/cgi/content/full/2009/402/2 4/2/2009.

Goren-Inbar, N., et al. "Evidence of Hominin Control of Fire at Gesher Benot Ya'aqov, Israel," *Science* 304 (2004): 725–27.

Gould, Stephen J. *The Mismeasure of Man* (rev. ed.). New York: W. W. Norton, 1996.

Grayson, Donald K. *The Establishment of Human Antiquity*. New York: Academic Press, 1983.

Green, David J., and Adam D. Gordon. "Metacarpal Proportions in *Australopithecus africanus*," *Journal of Human Evolution* 54, no. 5(2008): 705–19.

Green, Richard E., Johannes Krause, Susan E. Ptak, Adrian W. Briggs, Michael T. Ronan, Jan F. Simons, Lei Du, Michael Egholm, Jonathan M. Rothberg, Maja Paunovic, and Svante Pääbo. "Analysis of One Million Base Pairs of Neanderthal DNA," *Nature* 444 (2006): 330–36 (and supplemental data).

Haeckel, Ernst. *The History of Creation: Or the Development of the Earth and its Inhabitants by the Action of Natural Causes: A Popular Exposition of the Doctrine of Evolution in General, and That of Darwin, Goethe, and Lamarck in Particular*. Chapter 23: "Migration and Distribution of Mankind. Human Species and Human Races," pp. 325–33. Translated from the German by E. Ray Lankester. New York: D. Appleton, 1868.

Haile-Selassie, Yohannes. "Late Miocene Hominids from the Middle Awash, Ethiopia," *Nature* 412 (2001): 178–81.

Haile-Selassie, Yohannes, Gen Suwa, and Tim D. White. "Late Miocene Teeth from Middle Awash, Ethiopia, and Early Hominid Dental Evolution," *Science* 303, no. 5663 (2004): 1503–5.

Haile-Selassie, Yohannes, and Giday WoldeGabriel, eds. *Ardipithecus Kadabba: Late Miocene Evidence from the Middle Awash, Ethiopia*. Berkeley: University of California Press, 2009.

Hare, P. Edgar, Glenn A. Goodfriend, Alison S. Brooks, Julie E. Kokis, and David W. von Endt. "Chemical Clocks and Thermometers: Diagenetic Reactions of Amino Acids in Fossils," *Carnegie Institution of Washington Yearbook* 92 (1993): 80–85.

Helgren, David H., and Alison S. Brooks. "Geoarchaeology at Gi, a Middle Stone Age and Later Stone Age Site in the Northwest Kalahari," *Journal of Archaeological Science* 10 (1983): 181–97.

Henshilwood, C. S., F. d'Errrico, M. Vanhaeren, K. von Niekerk, and Z. Jacobs. "Middle Stone Age Beads from South Africa," *Science* 304 (2004): 404. (See accompanying online material for pictures: DOI: 10.1126/science.1095905.) NB there is a longer treatment in *JHE* 48, no. 1 (2005): 3–24.

Henshilwood, C. S., F. D'Errico, C. W. Marean, R. G. Milo, and R. Yates. "An Early Bone Tool Industry from the Middle Stone Age at Blombos Cave, South Africa: Implications for the Origins of Modern Human Behaviour, Symbolism and Language," *Journal of Human Evolution* 41 (2001): 631–78.

Henshilwood, C. S., Christopher S. Henshilwood, Francesco d'Errico, Royden Yates, Zenobia Jacobs, Chantal Tribolo, Geoff A. T. Duller, Norbert Mercier, Judith C. Sealy, Helene Valladas, Ian Watts, and Ann G. Wintle. "Emergence of Modern Human Behavior: Engravings from South Africa," *Science* 295 (2002): 1278–80.

Hovers, Erella, Shimon Ilani, Ofer Bar-Yosef, and Bernard Vandermeersch. "An Early Case of Color Symbolism: Ochre Use by Modern Humans in Qafzeh Cave," *Current Anthropology* 44, no. 4 (August-October 2003): 491–522.

Hublin, Jean Jacques. "Modern-Non-Modern Hominid Interactions: A Mediterranean Perspective," in *The Geography of Neanderthals and Modern Humans in Europe and the Greater Mediterranean*, edited by Ofer Bar-Yosef and David Pilbeam, pp. 157–82. Cambridge, MA: Peabody Museum of Archaeology and Ethnography, Harvard University, 2000.

Jackendorf, Ray. "Possible Stages in the Evolution of the Language Capacity," *Trends in the Cognitive Sciences* 3, no. 7 (1999): 272–79.

Jacobs, Zenobia, Richard G. Roberts, Rex F. Galbraith, Hilary J. Deacon, Rainer Grün, Alex Mackay, Peter Mitchell, Ralf Vogelsang, and Lyn Wadley. "Ages for the Middle Stone Age of Southern Africa: Implications for Human Behavior and Dispersal," *Science* 322 (2008): 733–35.

Johnson, Cara Roure, and Sally McBrearty. "Cutting Edge: A New Date for the Earliest Blade Technology," in *Abstracts of the Paleoanthropology Society 2009 Meetings*. *PaleoAnthropology* 2009: A18.

Kibunjia, Mzalendo, Hélène Roche, Frank H. Brown, and Richard E. Leakey. "Pliocene and Pleistocene Archaeological Sites West of Lake Turkana, Kenya," *Journal of Human Evolution* 23 (1992): 431–38.

Kimbel, W. H., R. C. Walter, D. C. Johanson, K. E. Reed, J. L. Aronson, Z. Assefa, C. W. Marean, G. C. Eck, R. Bobe, E. Hovers, Y. Rak, C. Vondra, T. Yemane, D. York, Y. Chen, N. M. Evensen, and P. C. Smith. "Late Pliocene *Homo* and Oldowan Tools from the Hadar Formation (Kada Hadar Member), Ethiopia," *Journal of Human Evolution* 31 (1996): 549–61.

Klein, R. G. "Southern Africa and Modern Human Origins," *Journal of Anthropological Research* 67 (2001): 1–16.

Lamarck, Jean Baptist Pierre Antoine de Monet, Chevalier de. "Degradation and Simplification of Organization from one Extremity to the Other of the Animal Chain, Proceeding from the Most Complex to the Simplest. Bimana," in *Zoological Philosophy*, translated by H. Elliot, chapters 6 and 8, pp. 68–72 and 169–73. London: Macmillan Co., 1914. Original publ. *Philosophie Zoologiques*. Paris: Dentu, 1809.

Lartet, Édouard. "Nouvelles recherches sur la coexistence de l'Homme et des grands mammifères fossils," *Annales des Sciènces Naturelles (Zoologie)* 4ième série 15 (1861): 177–253.

Lieberman, Daniel E., Brandeis M. McBratneym, and Gail Krovitz. "The Evolution and Development of Cranial Form in *Homo sapiens*," *Proceedings of the National Academy of Sciences* 99, no. 3 (2002): 1134–39.

Lieberman, Phillip, and Robert C. McCarthy. "Tracking the Evolution of Language and Speech: Comparing Vocal Tracts to Identify Speech Capabilities," *Expedition* 49, no. 2 (2007): 15–20. (See also "Recent Origin for Modern Human Speech Capabilities," *Robert McCarthy, Florida Atlantic University* online computer reconstruction of Neanderthal speech at http://www.nasonline.org/site/DocServer/RobertMcCarthy.pdf?docID=38761.)

Lombard, Marlize. "Evidence of Hunting and Hafting during the Middle Stone Age at Kwa Zulu, Natal: A Multianalytical Approach," *Journal of Human Evolution* 48 (2005): 279–300.

Lordkipanize, David, Abesalom Vekua, Reid Ferring, G. Philip Rightmire, Jordi Agusti, Gocha Kiladze, Alexander Mouskhelishvili, Medea Nioradze, Marcia S. Ponce de León, Martha Tappen, and Christoph P. E. Zollikofer. "Anthropology: The Earliest Toothless Hominin Skull," *Nature* 434 (2005): 717–18.

Marean, C. W., M. Bar-Matthews, J. Bernatchez, E. Fisher, P. Goldberg, A. I. Herries, Z. Jacobs, A. Jerardino, P. Karkanas, T. Minichillo, P. J. Nilssen, E. Thompson, I. Watts, and H. M. Williams. "Early Human Use of Marine Resources and Pigment in South Africa during the Middle Pleistocene," *Nature* 449 (2007): 905–8.

McBrearty, S., and A. Brooks. "The Revolution That Wasn't: A New Interpretation of the Origin of Modern Human Behavior," *Journal of Human Evolution* 39 (2000): 453–563.

McDermott, F., C. Stringer, R. Grün, C. T. Williams, V. K. Din, and C. J. Hawkesworth. "New Late-Pleistocene Uranium-Thorium and ESR Dates for the Singa Hominid (Sudan)," *Journal of Human Evolution* 31, no. 6 (1996): 507–16.

McDougall, Ian, Francis H. Brown, and John G. Fleagle. "Stratigraphic Placement and Age of Modern Humans from Kibish, Ethiopia," *Nature* 433 (2005): 733–36.

Mehlman, Michael J. "Mumba-Höhle Revisited: The Relevance of a Forgotten Excavation to Some Current Issues in East African Prehistory," *World Archaeology* 11 (1979): 80–94.

Mehlman, Michael J. "Late Quaternary Archaeological Sequences in Northern Tanzania," Ph.D. diss., University of Illinois, 1989.

Mehlman, M. J. "Context for the Emergence of Modern Man in Eastern Africa: Some New Tanzanian Evidence," in *Cultural Beginnings: Approaches to Understanding Early Hominid Lifeways in the African Savanna,* edited by J. D. Clark, pp. 177–196. Bonn: Forschunginstitut fur Vor- und Fruhgeschichte, Romisch-Germanisches Zentralmuseum, Monographien 19, 1991.

Mellars, P. A. *The Neanderthal Legacy: An Archaeological Perspective from Western Europe.* Princeton: Princeton University Press, 1996.

Mellars, P. "The Impossible Coincidence: A Single-Species Model for the Origins of Modern Human Behavior in Europe," *Evolutionary Anthropology* 14 (2005): 12–27. (But see also Zilhao 2007, below.)

Mercader, Julio, Melissa Panger, and Christophe Boesch. "Excavation of a Chimpanzee Stone Tool Site in the African Rainforest," *Science* 296, no. 5572 (2002): 1452–55.

Mercader, Julio, Huw Barton, Jason Gillespie, Jack Harris, Steven Kuhn, Robert Tyler, and Christophe Boesch. "4,300-Year-Old Chimpanzee Sites and the Origins of Percussive Stone Technology," *Proceedings of the National Academy of Sciences* 104, no. 9 (2007): 3043–48.

Merrick, Harry V., and Frank H. Brown. "Obsidian Sources and Patterns of Source Utilization in Kenya and Northern Tanzania: Some Initial Findings," *African Archaeological Review* 2 (1984): 129–52.

Millard, Andrew. "Bayesian Analysis of ESR Dates with Application to Border Cave," *Quaternary Geochronology* 1, no. 2 (2006): 159–66.

Miller, Gifford H., Peter B. Beaumont, Hillary J. Deacon, Alison S. Brooks, P. Edgar Hare, and A. J. T. Jull, "Earliest Modern Humans in Southern Africa Dated by Isoleucine Epimerization in Ostrich Eggshell," *Quaternary Science Reviews* 8, no. 13 (November 1999): 1537–48.

Milo, R. "Evidence for Hominid Predation at Klasies River Mouth, South Africa, and Its Implications for the Behaviour of Early Modern Humans," *Journal of Archaeological Science* 25 (1998): 99–133.

Monnier, Gilliane F. "The Lower/Middle Paleolithic Periodization in Western Europe," *Current Anthropology* 47, no. 5 (2006): 709–44.

Morgan, Leah F., and Paul R. Renne. "Diachronous Dawn of Africa's Middle Stone Age: New 40Ar/39Ar Ages from the Ethiopian Rift," *Geology* 36, no. 12 (2008): 967–70.

Noonan, James P., Graham Coop, Sridhar Kudaravalli, Doug Smith, Johannes Krause, Joe Alessi, Feng Chen, Darren Platt, Svante Pääbo, Jonathan K. Pritchard, and Edward M. Rubin. "Sequencing and Analysis of Neanderthal Genomic DNA," *Science* 314, no. 5802 (2006): 1113–18.

O'Connell, J. F., and J. Allen. "Dating the Colonization of Sahul (Pleistocene Australia-New Guinea): A Review of Recent Research," *Journal of Archaeological Science* 31 (2004): 835–53.

Ogilvie, M. D., B. K. Curran, and E. Trinkaus. "Incidence and Patterning of Dental Enamel Hypoplasia among the Neanderthals," *American Journal of Physical Anthropology* 79 (1989): 25–41.

Ohman, J. C., C. Wood, B. Wood, R. H. Crompton, M. M. Günther, L. Yu, R. Savage, and W. Wang. "Stature-at-Death of KNM-WT 15000," *Human Evolution* 17, nos. 3–4 (2002): 129–42.

Parfitt, Simon A., René W. Barendregt, Marzia Breda, Ian Candy, Matthew J. Collins, G. Russell Coope, Paul Durbidge, Mike H. Field, Jonathan R. Lee, Adrian M. Lister, Robert Mutch, Kirsty E. H. Penkman, Richard C. Preece, James Rose, Christopher B. Stringer, Robert Symmons, John E. Whittaker, John J. Wymer, and Anthony J. Stuart. "The Earliest Record of Human Activity in Northern Europe," *Nature* 438 (2005): 1008–12.

Parkington, J. "Middens and Moderns: Shellfishing and the Middle Stone Age of the Western Cape, South Africa," *South African Journal of Science* 99, nos. 5–6 (2003): 243–47.

Parkington, J., C. Poeggenphl, J.-Ph. Rigaud, and P.-J. Texier. "From Tool to Symbol: The Behavioural Context of Intentionally Marked Ostrich Eggshell from Diepkloof, Western Cape," in *From Tools to Symbols: From Early Hominids to Modern Humans,* edited by F. d'Errico and L. Backwell, pp. 475-92. Johannesburg: Witwatersrand University Press, 2005.

Pearson, Osbjorn M. "Postcranial Remains and Modern Human Origins," *Evolutionary Anthropology* 9, no. 6 (2001): 229–47.

Petitto, Laura Ann, and P. F. Marentette. "Babbling in the Manual Mode: Evidence for the Ontogeny of Language," *Science* 251, no. 5000 (1991): 1493–96.

Petitto, Laura Ann, Siobhan Holowka, Lauren E. Sergio, and David Ostry. "Language Rhythms in Baby Hand Movements," *Nature* 413 (2001): 35–36.

Petraglia, Michael D., and Ravi Korisettar, eds. *Early Human Behaviour in Global Context: The Rise and Diversity of the Lower Paleolithic Record.* London: Routledge, 1997.

Pettitt, Paul A. "The Neanderthal Dead: Exploring Mortuary Variability in Middle Paleolithic Eurasia," *Before Farming* 1 (2001): 1–19.

Prendergast, M. E., L. Luque, M. Domínguez-Rodrigo, F. Diez-Martin, A. Z. P. Mabulla, and R. Barba. "New Excavations at Mumba Rockshelter, Tanzania," *Journal of African Archaeology* 5, no. 2 (2007): 163–89.

Richmond, Brian G., and William L. Jungers. "*Orrorin tugenensis* Femoral Morphology and the Evolution of Hominin Bipedalism," *Science* 319, no. 5870 (2008): 1662–65.

Richmond, Brian G., and David S. Strait. "Evidence That Humans Evolved from a Knuckle-Walking Ancestor," *Nature* 404 (2000): 382–85.

Rigaud, Jean-Philippe, Pierre-Jean Texier, John Parkington, and Cedric Poggenpoel. "Le mobilier Stillbay et Howiesons Poort de l'abri Diepkloof. La chronologie du *Middle Stone Age* sud-africain et ses implications," *Comptes Rendus Palévol* 5 (2006): 839–49.

Robbins, L. R., M. L. Murphy, G. A. Brook, A. Ivester, A. C. Campbell, R. G. Klein, R. Milo, and W. Downey. "Archaeology, Paleoenvironment, and Chronology of the White Paintings Rock Shelter, Tsodilo Hills, Northwest Kalahari Desert, Botswana," *Journal of Archaeological Science* 27 (2000): 1085–1113.

Roche, H., A. Delagnes, J. Brugal, C. Feibel, M. Kibunjia, V. Mourre, and P-J. Texier. "Early Hominid Stone Tool Production and Technical Skill 2.34 Myr Ago in West Turkana, Kenya," *Nature* 399 (1999): 57–60.

Savage-Rumbaugh, Sue, Stuart G. Shanker, and Talbot J. Taylor. *Apes, Language and the Human Mind.* New York: Oxford University Press, 1998.

Schlanger, Nathan. "Understanding Levallois: Lithic Technology and Cognitive Archaeology," *Cambridge Archaeological Journal* 6, no. 2 (1996): 231–54.

Schmerling, P.-C. *Recherches sur les Ossements Fossiles Découverts dans les Cavernes de la province de Liège, Vol 1 et 2.* Liège: Collardin, 1833–34.

Semaw, S., M. Rodgers, J. Quade, P. Renne, R. Butler, M. Dominguez-Rodrigo, D. Stout, W. Hart, T. Pickering, and S. Simpson. "2.6 Million-Year-Old Stone Tools and Associated Bones from OGS-6 and OGS-7, Gona, Afar, Ethiopia," *Journal of Human Evolution* 45 (2003): 169–77.

Semaw, S. "The World's Oldest Stone Artifacts from Gona, Ethiopia: Their Implications for Understanding Stone Technology and Patterns of Human Evolution between 2.6–1.5 Million Years Ago," *Journal of Archaeological Science* 27 (2000): 1197–1214.

Senut, Brigitte, Martin Pickford, Dominique Gommery, Pierre Mein, Kiptalam Cheboi, and Yves Coppens. "First Hominid from the Miocene (Lukeino Formation, Kenya)," *Comptes Rendus de l'Académie des Sciences— Series IIA — Earth and Planetary Science* 332, no. 2 (January 30, 2001): 137–44.

Sherwood, Chet C., Francys Subiaul, and Tadeusz Zawidzki. "A Natural History of the Human Mind: Tracing Evolutionary Changes in Brain and Cognition," *Journal of Anatomy* 212, no. 4 (2008): 426–54.

Sherwood, Richard J., Steven C. Ward, and Andrew Hill. "The Taxonomic Status of the Chemeron Temporal (KNM-BC 1)," *Journal of Human Evolution* 42, nos. 1–2 (2002): 153–84.

Stern, J. T., and R. L. Susman. "The Locomotor Anatomy of *Australopithecus afarensis*," *American Journal of Physical Anthropology* 60, no. 3 (1983): 279–317.

Stout, D., J. Quade, S. Semaw, M. J. Rogers, and N. E. Levin. "Raw Material Selectivity of the Earliest Stone Toolmakers at Gona, Afar, Ethiopia," *Journal of Human Evolution* 48 (2005): 365–80.

Stringer, Chris. "Has Australia Backdated the Human Revolution?" *Antiquity* 73, no. 282 (1999): 876–79.

Stringer, C. B., J. C. Finlayson, R. N. Barton, Y. Fernández-Jalvo, I. Cáceres, R. C. Sabin, E. J. Rhodes, A. P. Currant, J. Rodriguez-Vidal, J. F. Giles-Pacheco, and J. A. Riquelme-Cantal. "Neanderthal Exploitation of Marine Mammals in Gibraltar," *Proceedings of the National Academy of Sciences* 105 (2008): 14319–24.

Thieme, Hartmut. "Lower Palaeolithic Hunting Spears from Germany," *Nature* 385 (1997): 807–10.

Tishkoff, Sarah A., Mary Katherine Gonder, Brenna M. Henn, Holly Mortensen, Alec Knight, Christopher Gignoux, Neil Fernandopulle, Godfrey Lema, Thomas B. Nyambo, Uma Ramakrishnan, Floyd A. Reed, and Joanna L. Mountain. "History of Click-Speaking Populations of Africa Inferred from mtDNA and Y Chromosome Genetic Variation," *Molecular Biology and Evolution* 24, no. 10 (2007): 2180–95.

Tomasello, Michael, and Josep Call. *Primate Cognition.* New York: Oxford University Press, 1997.

Tomasello, Michael, Malinda Carpenter, Josep Call, Tanya Behne, and Henrike Moll. "Understanding and Sharing Intentions: The Origin of Cultural Cognition," *Behavioral and Brain Sciences* 28 (2005): 675–91.

Trinkaus, Eric. *The Shanidar Neanderthals.* New York: Academic Press, 1983.

Tryon, Christian A. "'Early' Middle Stone Age Technology from the Kapthurin Formation, Kenya," *Current Anthropology* 47 (2006): 367–75.

Tyson, Edward. *Orang-Outang: Or the Anatomy of a Pygmy Compared with that of a Monkey, an Ape and a Man. To which is Added a Philosophical Essay Concerning the Pygmies, the Cynocephalie, the Satyrs, and Sphinges of the Ancients. Wherein it will Appear that They are All either Apes or Monkeys and not Men, as formerly Pretended.* London: T. Bennett, 1699. (Note that "Orang Outan" was the general designation for all apes in the seventeenth and eighteenth centuries.)

Vandermeersch, Bernard. "Une sépulture moustérienne avec offrandes découverte dans la grotte de Qafzeh," *Compte Rendus de l'Académie des Sciences* 268 (1970): 298–301.

Vandermeersch, Bernard. *Les hommes fossiles de Qafzeh (Israël).* Paris: Editions du CNRS, 1981.

Vanhaeren, Marian, and Francesco d'Errico. "Aurignacian Ethno-Linguistic Geography of Europe Revealed by Personal Ornaments," *Journal of Archaeological Science* 33, no. 8 (2005): 1105–28.

Vanhaeren, M., F. d'Errico, C. B. Stringer, S. L. James, J. A. Todd, and H. K. Mienis. "Middle Paleolithic Shell Beads in Israel and Algeria," *Science* 312 (2006): 1785–88.

Wendt, W. E. "Art Mobilier from the Apollo 11 Cave, Southwest Africa: Africa's Oldest Dated Works of Art," *South African Archaeological Bulletin* 31 (1976): 5–11.

White, Tim D., Berhane Asfaw, David deGusta, Henry Gilbert, Gary D. Richards, Gen Suwa, and F. Clark Howell. "Pleistocene *Homo sapiens* from Middle Awash, Ethiopia," *Nature* 423 (2003): 742–47.

Whiten, A., J. Goodall, W. G. McGrew, T. Nishida, V. Reynolds, Y. Sugiyama, C. E. G. Tutin, R. W. Wrangham, and C. Boesch. "Cultures in Chimpanzees," *Nature* 399 (1999): 682–85.

Wiessner, Pauline. "Reconsidering the Behavioral Basis for Style: A Case Study Among the Kalahari San," *Journal of Anthropological Archaeology* 3, no. 3 (1984): 190–234.

Wood, Bernard A. *Human Evolution: A Very Short Introduction*. New York: Oxford University Press, 2005.

Wood, Bernard A., and Paul Constantino. "Human Origins: Life at the Top of the Tree," in *Assembling the Tree of Life,* edited by Joel Cracraft and Michael J. Donoghue, pp. 517–35. New York: Oxford University Press, 2004.

Wood, Bernard A., and Mark Collard. "The Changing Face of Genus *Homo.*" *Science* 284, no. 5411 (1999): 65–71.

Woodward, Sir Arthur Smith. "A Fossil Skull of an Ancestral Bushman from the Anglo-Egyptian Sudan," *Antiquity* 12, no. 46 (1938): 190–95, Plate I-VII.

Yellen, J., A. S. Brooks, E. Cornelissen, M. Mehlman, and K. Stewart. "A Middle Stone Age Worked Bone Industry from Katanda, Upper Semliki Valley, Zaire," *Science* 268 (1995): 553–56.

Yellen, J. E., A. S. Brooks, D. Helgren, M. Tappen, S. Ambrose, R. Bonnefille, J. Feathers, G. Goodfriend, K. Ludwig, P. Renne, and K. Stewart. "The Archaeology of Aduma: Middle Stone Age Sites in the Awash Valley, Ethiopia," *PaleoAnthropology* 10 (2005): 25–100.

Zhu, R. X., K. A. Hoffman, R. Potts, C. L. Deng, Y. X. Pan, B. Guo, C. D. Shi, Z. T. Guo, B. Y. Yuan, Y. M. Hou and W. W. Huang. "Earliest Presence of Humans in Northeast Asia," *Nature* 413 (2001): 413–17.

Zhu, R. X., R. Potts, Y. X. Pan, H. T. Yao, L. Q. Lu, X. Zhao, X. Gao, L. W. Chen, F. Gao, and C. L. Deng. "Early Evidence of the Genus *Homo* in East Asia," *Journal of Human Evolution* 55 (2008): 1075–85.

Zilhão, J. "Neanderthals and Moderns Mixed, and It Mattered," *Evolutionary Anthropology* 15, no. 5 (2006): 183–95.

Zollikofer, Christoph P. E., Marcia S. Ponce de León, Daniel E. Lieberman, Franck Guy, David Pilbeam, Andossa Likius, Hassane T. Mackaye, Patrick Vignaud, and Michel Brunet. "Virtual Cranial Reconstruction of *Sahelanthropus tchadensis.*" *Nature* 434 (2005): 755–59.

Personality, Individuality, and Social Identity

Michael Hogg

The study of collective behavior has a long and illustrious history in social psychology. It was the study of collective behavior that very much defined the new discipline of social psychology at its inception in the late 19th and early 20th century, and collective phenomena such as crowds, riots, deindividuation, and particularly group processes and intergroup relations have maintained a high profile ever since. However, at the same time social psychology has also focused on the self-contained individual person who processes and represents information, has feelings, engages in behavior, and interacts with individual others, an approach that often treats people as being fundamentally different from one another and having unique biographies and enduring personalities.

Because these latter individual and interpersonal concerns appear more focused on what happens in the head of the individual, they have come to characterize social psychology and are often invoked as the basic unit of analysis and level of explanation to make sense of collective and group behaviors. As a result, there is an ongoing tension, and often a metatheoretical disagreement, between social psychologists who feel you can explain collective behavior in terms of individual personality and those who believe you cannot. Over the past 40 years or so the most systematic, enduring, and sometimes strident, critique of personality explanations of collective and group phenomena has come from European social psychology—a critique that has framed the development of a number of key European social psychological theories, in particular minority influence (e.g., Moscovici, 1976; see Martin & Hewstone, 2003), social representations (e.g., Moscovici, 1988; see Lorenzi-Cioldi & Clémence, 2001), and social identity theory (e.g., Tajfel & Turner, 1979; see Hogg 2006).

In this chapter I focus only on social identity theory, broadly conceived, adopting its characterization of personality and individuality and describing how it views the relationship between personality/individuality and collective behavior. To do this, I first give some historical background as to how the study of collective and group behavior has been positioned in social psychology, with a particular emphasis on the European critique of personality explanations (also see Hogg, 2001a; Hogg & Williams, 2000; Turner, Reynolds, Haslam, & Veenstra, 2006). I feel this is important because it gives some insight into the way that social identity has conceived of personality.

I then describe how social identity theory has developed in this metatheoretical context and give a very brief overview of relevant aspects of the theory. The rest of the chapter textures the social identity perspective on the relationship between individuality/personality and the group, building in recent developments, clarifying misunderstandings, and identifying issues and directions for current and future research. In recent years there has been renewed interest among intergroup and social identity researchers in re-examining the relationship between individuality and the group—see Postmes and Jetten (2006) for a recent collection of chapters on this topic.

In this chapter I use the terms *personality* and *individuality* largely interchangeably, which is consistent with broad contemporary definitions of personality; for example Snyder and Cantor write "personality (loosely defined in terms of regularities in feeling, thought, and action that are characteristic of an individual)" (Snyder & Cantor, 1998, p. 635). Snyder & Ickes (1985) take this notion of regularities one step further by drawing a distinction between dispositional, interactional, and situational perspectives on personality.

Dispositional perspectives trace regularities to invariant properties of the individual person; this is very much the traditional perspective on personality (e.g., McCrae & John, 1992). *Interactional* perspectives acknowledge that situations unlock dispositions and allow them to be expressed (e.g., Baron & Boudreau, 1987); regularities arise because a situation prevails that enables the expression of a particular disposition. *Situational* perspectives attribute regularities in behavior to the fact that a person seeks out and remains in the same setting (e.g., Buss, 1987); people and their dispositions shape the settings that they find themselves in. Adopting the language of motivation, Snyder and Cantor characterize these three perspectives in terms of "individuals 'moved' by dispositions and 'moved' by situations, individuals 'moving' their social worlds" (Snyder & Cantor, 1998, p. 666).

From the perspective of the present chapter, although interactional and situational perspectives on personality view the social context as having an important influence on behavior, these perspectives share with the more traditional dispositional perspective a conception of the person as a largely idiosyncratic constellation of personal attributes and dispositions. As I hope to show below, it is this view of the person that some believe is problematic for explanations of group, intergroup, and collective behaviors as well as the collective nature of self.

Individual versus Collective in Social Psychology

Wundt is generally viewed as the founder of modern psychology as an extension of the natural sciences; he established a psychological laboratory in Leipzig in 1879 and launched a journal, *Philosophische Studien*, in 1881(for historical overviews of social psychology see Farr, 1996; Jones, 1998). However, between 1900 and 1920 he also wrote ten volumes of social psychology, which he called *Völkerpsychologie*, the psychology of a community or group of individuals (a *Volk*). For Wundt, social psychology was the study of "those mental products which are created by a community of human life and are, therefore, inexplicable in terms merely of individual consciousness since they presuppose the reciprocal action of many" (Wundt, 1916, p.3). Wundt's social psychology dealt with collective phenomena, such as language, religion, customs, and myth, that could not, according to Wundt, be understood in terms of the psychology of the isolated individual, the latter being his experimental psychology.

Wundt's collectivist approach to social psychology is evident in early non-experimental social psychology's analysis of the crowd, for example, LeBon's (1908) notion that the crowd caused a collective "racial unconscious"—containing primitive, aggressive, and antisocial instincts—to take hold, and McDougall's (1921) notion that out of the interaction of individuals there arose a "group mind" that had a reality and existence that was qualitatively distinct from the isolated individuals making up the group. Subsequent experimental social psychological research has indeed confirmed that human interaction produces emergent properties that cannot be properly understood by focusing on the psychology of the isolated individual; for example, Sherif's (1936) research on the emergence of norms, some of Asch's (1952) research on conformity to norms, and research on the emergence of social representations (see Lorenzi-Cioldi & Clémence, 2001).

Durkheim (1898), who was influenced by Wundt, agreed that collective phenomena could not be explained in terms of individual psychology. However, he also believed that such phenomena were not the province of psychology at all, but of the new discipline of sociology, which he sometimes called "collective psychology." Durkheim separated sociology from psychology, placing the psychology of collective phenomena in sociology and the psychology of the individual in psychology—an early disciplinary separation that, according to Farr (1996), helped create a psychological social psychology that prioritized the individual as the level of explanation of collective and group phenomena. The separation of sociology from psychology was complete by about 1925 (Manicas, 1987), separating social psychology and in particular the study of groups from its collectivist past.

Psychology's version of social psychology quickly had an uphill battle to promote collective behavior and the group as a separate level of analysis to personality and the individual. For example, although McDougall's "group mind" was not intended to refer to an extra-psychological entity, critics interpreted it in this way and were successfully able to discredit McDougall's approach and, by association, all collectivist perspectives in social psychology. Many consider the battle to have been lost with Floyd Allport's, authoritative and far reaching dictum that "There is no psychology of groups which is not essentially and entirely a psychology of individuals" (Allport, 1924, p. 4; see Graumann, 1986).

This metatheoretical framework has ensured that most subsequent social psychology of collective phenomena such as groups and intergroup relations has actually been a psychology of the individual person or of interpersonal interaction in dyads or small face-to-face aggregates (see Billig, 1976; Hogg, 1993; Taylor & Brown, 1979; Turner, 1982). For example, the substantial topic of group dynamics, which was dominant from the 1940s into the 1960s (see Shaw, 1981) and had its roots in Lewin's potentially collectivist field theory (e.g., Lewin, 1952), is essentially a study of interpersonal interaction in small face-to-face groups; and two of the major theories of prejudice and discrimination, the authoritarian personality (Adorno, Frenkel-Brunswick, Levinson, & Sanford, 1950) and the frustration-aggression hypothesis (Dollard, Doob, Miller, Mowrer, & Sears, 1939), were explanations in terms of dispositions and personality dynamics (see Billig, 1976). This agenda and emphasis has made it difficult to study large scale social categories, intergroup relations, or the collective self without resorting to personality, the individual, or largely dyadic interaction as the level of explanation.

The Problem of Reductionism

The principal problem that some social psychologists see with this kind of approach to the explanation of group and collective phenomena is one of level of explanation (e.g., Doise, 1986; also see Abrams & Hogg, 2004; Tajfel, 1972a; Turner & Oakes, 1986): It is a reductionist metatheory. The feeling is that if one tries to explain group and collective phenomena in terms exclusively of the individual, individual personality, or interpersonal interaction, many aspects of group behavior are left inadequately explained. It is a bit like asking why drivers stop at stop lights and being given an explanation solely in terms of nerve impulses from the brain to the hand: The level of explanation does not adequately answer the question. Nerve impulses are involved, but a full answer would probably also need some reference to conventions, norms, and the law. Doise (1986) argues that full social psychological explanations of collective and group phenomena require the *articulation* of different levels of explanation into an integrated conceptual framework; referring to individual level processes and structures alone is inadequate.

Concerns about reductionism have always been a part of social psychology, coming to the fore from time to time. For instance, the late 1960s and early 1970s witnessed a well-publicized crisis of confidence in social psychology (e.g., Elms, 1975; Strickland, Aboud, & Gergen, 1976). One major concern was that the psychology of groups had been reduced to interpersonal or individual psychology, in which collective phenomena were merely an aggregate of individual or interpersonal behaviors (e.g., Cartwright, 1979; Festinger, 1980; Steiner, 1974, 1986; Taylor

& Brown, 1979; Turner & Oakes, 1986). It was felt that this approach underemphasized the influence of groups and categories on self-conceptualization and social behavior and also provided at best only partial explanations of group phenomena, making it very difficult properly to theorize large scale group phenomena such as prejudice, intergroup conflict, social protest, social structure, social change, and crowd events.

One example of the limitations of reductionist theorizing comes from the group dynamics literature. The group dynamics concept of group cohesiveness captured both the essence of groupness and the psychology of group formation in terms of the development of bonds of interpersonal attraction among group members (e.g., Festinger, Schachter & Back, 1950). Although members of small face-to-face groups may like one another, interpersonal attraction is a very limited explanation of group formation and group cohesion and solidarity (Hogg, 1993). For example, it is implausible as an explanation of processes in large groups like organizations or even larger groups such as a religion; attraction may be a correlate or consequence rather than cause of group formation; and attraction among group members may be produced in a different way than interpersonal attraction, such that you might like someone as a group member but despise her as an individual. Other processes may be involved in group formation and solidarity, specifically—as proposed by social identity theory—ones having to do with people's cognitive representations of a collective and their sense of self-definition in terms of that collective, and their knowledge about the social status of their group and the nature of its relations to other groups.

The critique of reductionism resonated well with the emerging metatheoretical agenda of European social psychology. World War II destroyed social psychology in Europe, and it was not until the 1960s that it began to find its feet again. This resurrection—culturally contextualized by Europe's recent history of wars, revolutions, and ideological conflicts—was self-consciously and single-mindedly framed by a strong metatheoretical conviction and mission. As part of a reconstruction of the infrastructure of European social psychology (for example establishment of the European Association of Experimental Social Psychology in 1966 and the launching of the *European Journal of Social Psychology* in 1971), European social psychologists deliberately developed a European perspective on and agenda for social psychology that set itself up in contradistinction to what they believed was the individualism, reductionism, and asocial nature of mainstream, largely American, social psychology (see Jaspars, 1980, 1986; Tajfel, 1972b).

The European perspective was one that privileged the "social dimension" (e.g., Tajfel, 1984) and in so doing served to provide a distinctive scientific identity around which European social psychologists could organize themselves. The "social dimension" was defined as a

> view that social psychology can and must include in its theoretical and research preoccupations a direct concern with the relationship between human psychological functioning and the large-scale social processes and events which shape this functioning and are shaped by it. (Tajfel, Jaspars, & Fraser, 1984, p. 3)

In practice what this has meant is that many European social psychologists have placed a strong emphasis on research into society, intergroup relations, collective behavior, and the collective self and on theories that articulate concepts from different levels of explanation (e.g., Doise, 1986). There has also generally been a preference to view people as a product of society, rather than vice versa; a top-down analysis has prevailed. From this perspective personality and individuality alone do not adequately explain group phenomena; separate group level constructs are also required. People's sense of who they are, their sense of self, is not based in some form of fixed personality that is prior to society and the groups that make up society; on the contrary, self is constructed from the nexus of groups in society that have specific historical social relations to one another. It is not just that the self is socially constructed, which of course it must be (e.g., Simon, 1997), but that collective self-definition provides the context for more individual and interpersonal self-construal.

Because this metatheoretical orientation was central to the development of a distinct identity for European social psychology, it was particularly vigorously pursued, much like a scientific *jihad*, from the 1960s through 1980s (e.g., *European Journal of Social Psychology*, 1974, p. 4). It remains a distinct theme in European social psychology (e.g., Turner & Bourhis, 1996) but is less identity-defining for European social psychologists, who are now much more diverse in terms of their research foci and orientations.

However, what is important for this chapter is that social identity theory was explicitly developed and has been sustained by this European metatheory (e.g., Abrams & Hogg, 2004; Hogg, 2001a; Hogg & Williams, 2000), which is not surprising, given that it is a European theory, originally developed in Britain in the late 1960s and early 1970s by European social psychologists, key among whom was Tajfel, who was also a leader in the development of the infrastructure of postwar European social psychology.

Personality, Individuality, and Social Identity

Framed by the European metatheory, social identity theory was originally developed as a theory of intergroup relations—an explanation of prejudice, discrimination, and conflict and cooperation between groups (e.g., Tajfel, 1972c, 1974; Tajfel & Turner, 1979). Its development was predicated on a critique (e.g., Billig, 1976) of other dominant explanations of intergroup and group phenomena that relied on personality, such as the authoritarian personality theory (Adorno et al., 1950) and the frustration-aggression hypothesis (Dollarde, 1939), or on the psychology of the individual or of interpersonal interactions, for example small group dynamics (e.g., Shaw, 1981). Although Sherif's (e.g., 1966) realistic conflict theory of group behavior was more in keeping with the emerging social identity theory, it was considered to underemphasize the fundamental role of the socially defined self in group behavior.

Tajfel introduced the term social identity in 1972 to describe how self is conceptualized in intergroup contexts—how a system of social categorizations "...creates and defines an individual's *own* place in society" (Tajfel, 1972c, p. 293). He defined social identity as "... the individual's knowledge that he belongs to certain social groups together with some emotional and value significance to him of this group membership" (Tajfel, 1972c, p. 292). Social identity, the self-concept defined in terms of specific group memberships, was clearly distinguished from personal identity, the self-concept defined in terms of personal idiosyncrasies, personality attributes, and close personal relationships (e.g., Turner, 1982). Behavior, however, was always considered to vary on a continuum from being totally influenced by social identity to being totally influenced by personal identity; most situations were somewhere in the middle, but social identity theory was mostly, if not exclusively, interested in those group and intergroup behaviors located at the social identity end of the continuum.

Social identity theory had little further to say about personal identity; it was considered to play no significant role in group phenomena. Instead, the theory focused on social identity and its generative role in group behavior and the articulation of social cognitive processes associated with social identity and people's socially constructed beliefs about the nature of their group and its relations to other groups (Tajfel & Turner, 1979; also see Ellemers, 1993; Hogg & Abrams, 1988). The social identity and personal identity systems were separate, and within each the self was structured into discrete social and personal identities—constructions of self tied to specific group memberships, specific close relationships, and specific personality attributes (Turner, 1982).

However, people do generally feel they have an integrated and enduring sense of unique individuality, of an overall personality that differentiates them from all other people and provides them with a unique autobiography and a stable sense of who they are (Baumeister, 1998; Cantor & Kihlstrom, 1987; Markus, 1977). Social identity theory did not deny this. It maintained that, all things being equal, we probably never experience ourselves in this holistic manner; rather, we subjectively experience different facets of self in different contexts and situations (see discussion of salience, below). The social context brings into play different experiences of self. For example, in one context you may experience yourself as a psychologist (a social identity), in another as Italian (a social identity), in another as Mary's best friend (a personal identity), in another as a driven and ambitious individual (a personal identity), and so forth.

From a social identity perspective, it is social identity and collective self—not personal identity, individuality or personality—that is related to collective and group behaviors.

Self-Categorization Theory and The Individual

Social identity theory has a number of integrated conceptual foci (for contemporary overviews of social identity theory see Hogg, 2003, 2006; Turner, 1999a). Thus far I have largely discussed the original social identity theory of intergroup relations (e.g., Turner & Tajfel, 1979). A crucial development in the early 1980s was the social identity theory of the group, self-categorization theory (Turner, 1985; Turner, Hogg, Oakes, Reicher, & Wetherell, 1987), which focused on the role of the categorization process in group identification and group behavior. The main feature of this theory is its explanation of the way that social categorization depersonalizes perception so that people are viewed in terms of group prototypes rather than their individual attributes, and the way that categorization of self, self-categorization, depersonalizes self-construal, self-perception, and people's attitudes, feelings and behaviors.

Depersonalization is not the same as dehumanization or deindividuation (contrast Zimbardo, 1970, with Reicher, Spears, & Postmes, 1995). It does not refer to behavior in which people behave impulsively, antisocially or aggressively; rather it refers to a phenomenon where we represent and experience ourselves and others as relatively "interchangeable" members of a collective, rather than as unique separate individuals.

As with the earlier social identity research, most self-categorization research focused on group and collective phenomena such as stereotyping (e.g., Oakes, Haslam, & Turner, 1994), group cohesion and solidarity (e.g., Hogg, 1993), crowd behavior (e.g., Reicher, 1984), deindividuation phenomena (e.g., Reicher, Spears, & Postmes, 1995), and conformity and normative behavior (e.g., Abrams & Hogg, 1990). However, self-categorization theory left the door open for more serious attention to be paid to the study of individuality in the context of group life.

There were a number of reasons for this, all hinging on the new, more inclusive focus on group behavior as a whole rather than just intergroup behavior between large social categories. For example, when you study social identity processes in small interactive groups, you immediately confront the fact that although social identity processes play out in the usual way, individuality, personality, and interpersonal processes are also very obvious (Hogg, 1996; Hogg, Abrams, Otten, & Hinkle, 2004). The family is a good example—clearly a group, but also very clearly a context for personality and interpersonal processes.

Another example is the study of group norms and social influence in groups (Turner, 1991; also see Hogg & Smith, 2007). Although norms emerge to characterize a group as a whole in distinction to specific outgroups, there is absolutely no doubt that some individuals are more influential than others in shaping the group's norm. This suggested that social identity theory needed to properly consider the role of individual differences in the context of group life. As we shall see below, the problematic of relative influence was addressed, not in terms of idiosyncratic personality or individuality, but in terms of relative group prototypicality (e.g., Abrams & Hogg, 1990; Hogg, 2005; Turner & Oakes, 1989). This was the foundation of the social identity theory of leadership (Hogg, 2001b; Hogg & van Knippenberg, 2003) and social identity analyses of deviance (e.g., Marques, Abrams, Páez, & Hogg, 2001; Marques, Abrams, & Serôdio, 2001).

Some key elements of a self-categorization perspective on personality and individuality have recently been described by Turner and his colleagues (Turner, Reynolds, Haslam, & Veenstra, 2006). There are two key points to this perspective. The first is that all self-definitions and self-conceptions are based on self-categories defined by category prototypes. Self categories vary in size (inclusiveness); large, highly inclusive categories are social groups that define social identity, whereas small exclusive categories, which effectively only have one member, clearly define personal identity or individuality. Most categories are in the middle.

The second key point is that self categories are not stored in mind to be carried from one context to another; they are constructed in situ to define self in that particular context. In this way self-categories and attendant perceptions and behaviors are tied into contexts rather than invariant properties of individuals: If people's lives are circumscribed by a limited number of contexts, their behaviors will appear routinized, with the inference that it reflects invariant personality attributes; if their lives are in greater flux, then their behavior will appear more varied and less easily construed as personality.

Put this way, this second point veers towards social constructionism, appearing on the surface to argue that aspects of self are entirely *determined* by the immediate social context and are not stored in memory for the individual to bring into play to define self in a particular context. However, most social identity researchers do not take this stance, and a close reading of social identity theory, particularly its description of the process of salience (below), shows it to be quite consistent with Kurt Lewin's far reaching "person-situation" view that "every psychological event depends on the state of the person and at the same time on the environment, although their relative importance is different in different cases (Lewin, 1936, p. 12)

Psychological Salience

Context influences self-conception and behavior via a process of psychological salience (e.g., Oakes, Haslam, & Turner, 1994; Turner, Oakes, Haslam, & McGarty, 1994). People draw on accessible social categorizations—ones that are valued, important, and frequently employed aspects of self-conception and social perception (they are chronically accessible in one's memory) and/ or because they are self-evident and perceptually salient in the immediate situation (they are situationally accessible). People are very ready to use accessible categories to make sense of their social context, investigating how well the categorization accounts for similarities and differences among people (structural or comparative fit) and how well the stereotypical properties of the categorization account for why people behave as they do (normative fit).

If the fit of a particular categorization is poor, people cycle through other accessible categorizations until an optimal level of fit is obtained. This process is primarily fast and automatic; people strive to reduce feelings of uncertainty about self-conception, social interaction, and people's behavior (e.g., Hogg, 2000, 2007). However, it is also more deliberatively strategic because people strive to make psychologically salient those social categorizations that mediate a more evaluatively positive social identity and self-concept (cf. Tajfel & Turner, 1979). The categorization that has optimal fit becomes psychologically salient in that context as the basis of self-categorization, group identification, and prototype-based depersonalization. It triggers social identity related perceptions, cognitions, affect, and behavior.

The process of salience explains how self-construal and associated behavior are generated and configured by an interaction between, on the one hand, social categorizations and self-knowledge brought by the person to the situation and. on the other hand, information in the situation that points to certain social categorizations and situation-specific configurations of such categorizations.

However, salience is not entirely mechanical; it is influenced by chronically accessible categories and by people's motivations and goals and so forth (e.g., Hogg, 2003, 2006; Simon, 2004). Turner and colleagues write: "Self-categorization is not free to vary in any which way, but is always constrained by the motives, goals, values, experiences, theories and knowledge the perceiver brings to the situation, as well as by the psychological nature of the categorization process and the social situation within which the perceiver defines himself or herself" (Turner, Reynolds, Haslam, & Veenstra, 2006, p. 25).

Personality and individuality certainly play a role here, in so far as people differ in terms of chronic category accessibility and the subjective importance of particular identities, motives, goals, and life experiences; in any given context some of us may be more ready to use one social categorization than another to make sense of the situation and socially locate and define ourselves and others in that situation.

It is also worth noting that the social identity model of salience is not entirely inconsistent with contemporary perspectives on personality, discussed above, in which contexts evoke preexisting dispositions (the interactional perspective) and people are disposed to place themselves in particular situations (the situational perspective; Snyder & Cantor, 1998; Snyder & Ickes, 1985). However, it differs from and goes beyond personality treatments in its focus on a highly differentiated self that structures, and is structured by, the world in terms of social categories.

Personality and Individuality

Personality and individuality may also be a product of the particular level of social comparison that one employs: Where intergroup comparisons are made, then self is clearly defined in collective terms as a group member, but where self-other comparisons are made within a group, individuality may come to the fore (Turner et al., 1987). In this formulation the group is primary because it is the frame of reference that allows individuality and personality to emerge (Hogg, 2001a; Hogg & Williams, 2000). However, it is not clear whether self-other comparisons within a group are truly interpersonal comparisons resting on emergent individuality and personality or actually intragroup comparisons resting on appraisals of self and other as more or less prototypical members of the group (see below).

Another take on individuality within the context of social identity is provided by the notion of "relational self." Drawing on cross-cultural research showing that people in different cultures construe the relationship between individual and group in different ways (Markus & Kitayama, 1991; Oyserman, Coon, & Kemmelmeier, 2002), Brewer has described the relational self as a form of collective self-construal where social identity is defined in terms of networks of interpersonal relationships (Brewer & Gardner, 1996; Yuki, 2003). This form of social identity may be more prevalent in non-Western cultures, but it may also characterize friendship cliques and the family in Western societies.

This analysis does seem to suggest that the network of relations that defines the group is constructed from the bottom up, and thus individuality and personality are primary (e.g., Sedikides & Strube, 1997). However, this does not have to be the case; one can readily see how relational identity and selves can be constructed top down, as described by self-categorization theory.

The notion of relational identity raises the question of roles: Are they personal or social identities? The notion of role identities is important in more sociological social psychology (e.g., Ridgeway, 2001; Thoits & Virshup, 1997). From a social identity point of view, roles describe relationships between people and so can define social or personal identities, depending on whether the role relationship is constructed as being between individuals or between groups (Hogg, Terry, & White, 1995). So, for example, airline pilot vs. cabin crew and professor vs. undergraduate reflect intergroup relations and social identities, and "mother" is more a personal identity when played out between mother and daughter and more a social identity when configured as "soccer mom" vs. working woman.

Finally, Brewer's optimal distinctiveness theory opposes individuality to the group, much as does social identity theory, but argues that people strive for a balance between standing out as a unique individual within the group and being totally immersed in the group (Brewer, 1991; Pickett & Brewer, 2001; Pickett, Silver, & Brewer, 2002). There is a dynamic relationship between individual and group.

Overall, social identity perspectives on the self reject what Turner and Onorato (1999) have recently called the "personality model of self" (also see Hogg 2001a; Onorato & Turner, 2002, 2004) in which the self is a unique, idiosyncratic, enduring, fixed and bounded entity—the view that "I" and "me" rule supreme. Instead, the self is experienced differently depending on context, and individuality and personality are less likely to be behavioral and experiential progenitors than more transitory emergent properties of an interplay of contextual factors and motives, goals and experiences brought to the context. A subjective sense of self and personality does exist, but it is more context-dependent, less enduring and stable, and more group membership-based than allowed by most personality and individual differences research. And of course we habitually construct stable underlying personalities for other people through processes of attribution (e.g., Gilbert & Malone, 1995) and essentialism (e.g., Haslam, Rothschild, & Ernst, 1998).

Prototypicality, Individuality, and Influence

A key feature of the social identity analysis of self and group, as described above, is that when social identity is salient, people define themselves and others in terms of relevant ingroup and outgroup prototypes. In group contexts people are very attentive to prototype relevant information and to the relative prototypicality of self and fellow ingroup members (Haslam,

Oakes, McGarty, Turner, & Onorato, 1995; Hogg, 2005). The fact that groups are subjectively differentiated in terms of the ingroup prototypicality of members means that within groups there is a degree of paradoxical individuality—"paradoxical" because it is based upon perceived group prototypicality.

One consequence of this is that prototypical members are more influential over the life of the group than are less prototypical/marginal members. This idea underpins the social identity theory of leadership (Hogg, 2001b; Hogg & van Knippenberg, 2003; also see van Knippenberg & Hogg, 2003; van Knippenberg, van Knippenberg, De Cremer, & Hogg, 2004), which argues that prototypical members are better able to lead the group; they are more effective leaders who are better able to gain compliance and be innovative. They differ from other members in their ability to manipulate prototypicality (e.g., Reicher & Hopkins, 1996, 2003; Reicher, Hopkins, & Condor, 1997; Reid & Ng, 2000, 2003). Furthermore, group members go through an attribution process in which they construct a charismatic personality for prototypical leaders (e.g., Haslam & Platow, 2001; Platow & van Knippenberg, 2001). Unlike traditional treatments of charisma as a cause of leadership (e.g., Bryman, 1992; Conger & Kanungo, 1998), the social identity analysis sees it as an emergent property of group life.

Group members who are only marginally prototypical have a very different experience within the group. Typically they find it difficult to be influential. They are treated with suspicion, dislike, and sometimes hostility as norm violators and "black sheep" (e.g., Marques, Abrams, Páez, & Hogg, 2001; Marques, Abrams, & Serôdio, 2001; Marques & Páez, 1994) and can be attributed with deviant personality attributes and labeled as deviants (cf. Becker, 1963).

By focusing on differential prototypicality within a salient group, social identity theory can theorize personality as an emergent product of social identity-based perceptions and interactions, in this case focusing on the "construction" of charismatic and deviant personalities.

Personality and Prejudice

As discussed at the beginning of this chapter, an important aspect of the socio-scientific context in which social identity theory originally developed was the critique of personality and individual differences explanations of prejudice, discrimination, and intergroup behavior (e.g., Billig, 1976). In recent years this critique has been reinvigorated (e.g., Reynolds, Turner, Haslam, & Ryan, 2001; Turner, 1999b; Verkuyten & Hagendoorn, 1998) and focused not only on the theory of the authoritarian personality (Adorno et al., 1950) but also on the newer social dominance theory (e.g., Sidanius & Pratto, 1999) and the theory of right wing authoritarianism (e.g., Altemeyer, 1988).

Predicated on research showing that F-scale, social dominance orientation and right wing authoritarianism scores can all change rather quickly and as a result of influence attempts (e.g., Schmitt, Branscombe, & Kappen, 2003), the key point is that personality, as individual disposition, may, at very least, not be such a monolithic determinant of prejudice. At most, behaviors usually associated with prejudiced personality syndromes may be contextually malleable as a consequence of the social identity salience processes discussed above. Prejudiced personalities may reflect intergroup relations rather than create them.

In their social dominance theory, Sidanius and Pratto (1999) concede that although there are individual differences in social dominance orientation, the extent to which someone has a hierarchy-enhancing or hierarchy-attenuating social dominance orientation will be strongly influenced by whether one is actually a member of a dominant or subordinate group. Nevertheless, critics of social dominance theory argue that it is actually primarily a personality and individual differences theory of prejudice, discrimination, and conflict (e.g., Kreindler, 2005; Schmitt et al., 2003; Turner & Reynolds, 2003), although Sidanius and colleagues disagree with this characterization (Pratto, Sidanius, & Levin, 2006; Sidanius & Pratto, 2003).

Concluding Comments

Social identity theory developed within a metatheoretical tradition in social psychology that sought to explain group and intergroup phenomena in terms of processes associated with the construction and expression of self in collective terms. The idiosyncratic individual self, the classic self of personality theorists, was not seen to play a significant role in group behavior, and explanations of collective phenomena in terms of stable personality dispositions were seen at best to be only partial explanations.

Because social identity theory was initially devised as a theory of intergroup relations, once it had conceptually separated social identity(self defined in collective terms) from personal identity (self defined idiosyncratically), it focused only on the former. Developments in the early 1980s, specifically self-categorization theory, which broadened social identity theory into a general theory of group processes and self-conception, expanded the agenda to facilitate the study of intragroup phenomena. This re-acquainted social identity researchers with the fact that groups are patterned in terms of relative influence, role relations, and interpersonal dynamics. The issue of how social identity and collective self relate to individuality and personality was once more on the table. Specifically, there was a focus on variation in prototypicality within a group and its consequences for relative influence, leadership, and processes of marginalization and deviance.

In this chapter I have described social identity theory's metatheoretical roots, a grounding in the wider critique of explanations of group and intergroup phenomena in terms of individual personality or interpersonal relations. This metatheoretical background has meant that social identity theory has largely ignored literature on personality and individual differences, or has mainly engaged with a rather one-dimensional characterization of personality, what Snyder and Ickes (1985) have called the dispositional perspective on personality, where stable personality determines behavior. Interactional and situational perspectives on personality allow the social context a greater role in human behavior, but from a social identity perspective they nevertheless talk about dispositions being contextually-elicited or people being disposed to "choose" certain situations. This still underplays the notion of a multifaceted self and the role played by group membership and collective self-conception in behavior.

Overall, contemporary social identity research tends to view personality less as a cause of behavior than as a social construct in which people make inferences about stable underlying dispositions or human essences (e.g., Haslam, Rothschild, & Ernst, 1998), for example, in the construction of a charismatic personality for a group's leader or stereotype-consistent racial essences. In a similar vein individual differences are not so much viewed as idiosyncratic attributes that are brought to the group as socially constructed positions within the group based on perceived group prototypicality, positions that nevertheless have far reaching consequences for the group and the individual in terms of relative impact on group life and on how one is treated by the group (the psychology of social influence, persuasion, leadership, deviance, and marginalization).

One feature of individuality that remains relatively unexplored by social identity researchers is how close interpersonal relationships articulate with group life and social identity processes. There is little doubt that friendships are more likely to form and persist within than between groups, but do such friendships reinforce or undermine social identity? And how do such friendships impact the rest of the group? What about intergroup friendships? Wright and his colleagues have reported some intriguing data showing that hostile outgroup stereotypes can be reduced among people who know fellow ingroup members who have close and rewarding friendships with members of the outgroup (Wright, Aron, McLaughlin-Volpe, & Ropp, 1997). Another line of research focuses on the role of the relational self in group life (e.g., Brewer & Gardner, 1996): When do interpersonal relationships define or configure group membership and how do group membership configure relationships?

In conclusion, because social identity theory adopts a collectivist metatheory to focus on group behavior, intergroup relations, and the collective self, it has generally found the concept of personality, as a stable deterministic disposition, to be problematic in the highly context-responsive world of group behavior and social identity. Although in the past this has been a significant hurdle to engagement with research on personality and individual differences, developments in both social identity theory and the way that personality is now conceptualized may be lowering some of these hurdles and laying the groundwork for future dialogue.

References

Abrams, D., & Hogg, M. A. (1990). Social identification, self-categorization and social influence. *European Review of Social Psychology, 1,* 195–228.

Abrams, D., & Hogg, M. A. (2004). Metatheory: Lessons from social identity research. *Personality and Social Psychology Review, 8,* 98–106.

Adorno, T. W., Frenkel-Brunswick, E., Levinson, D. J., & Sanford, R. M. (1950). *The authoritarian personality.* New York: Harper.

Allport, F. H. (1924). *Social psychology.* Boston: Houghton Mifflin.

Altemeyer, B. (1998). The other "authoritarian personality." In M. P. Zanna (Ed.), *Advances in experimental social psychology* (Vol. 30, pp. 47–92). Orlando, FL: Academic Press.

Asch, S. E. (1952). *Social psychology.* Englewood Cliffs, NJ: Prentice Hall.

Baron, R. M., & Boudreau, L. A. (1987). An ecological perspective on integrating personality and social psychology. *Journal of Personality and Social Psychology, 53,* 1222–1228.

Baumeister, R. F. (1998). The self. In D. T. Gilbert, S. T. Fiske, & G. Lindzey (Eds.), *Handbook of social psychology* (4th ed., Vol. 1, pp. 680–740). New York: McGraw-Hill.

Becker, H. (1963). *Outsiders: Studies in the sociology of deviance.* New York: The Free Press.

Billig, M. (1976). *Social psychology and intergroup relations.* London: Academic Press.

Brewer, M. B. (1991). The social self: On being the same and different at the same time. *Personality and Social Psychology Bulletin, 17,* 475–482.

Brewer, M. B., & Gardner, W. (1996). Who is this 'We'? Levels of collective identity and self representation. *Journal of Personality and Social Psychology, 71,* 83–93.

Bryman, A. (1992). *Charisma and leadership.* London: Sage.

Buss, D. M. (1987). Selection, evocation, and manipulation. *Journal of Personality and Social Psychology, 53,* 1214–1221.

Cantor, N., & Kihlstrom, J. F. (1987). *Personality and social intelligence.* Englewood Cliffs, NJ: Prentice Hall.

Cartwright, D. (1979). Contemporary social psychology in historical perspective. *Social Psychology Quarterly, 42,* 82–93.

Conger, J. A., & Kanungo, R. N. (1998). *Charismatic leadership in organizations.* Thousand Oaks, CA: Sage.

Doise, W. (1986). *Levels of explanation in social psychology.* Cambridge, UK: Cambridge University Press.

Dollard, J., Doob, L. W., Miller, N. E., Mowrer, O. H., & Sears, R. R. (1939). *Frustration and aggression.* New Haven, CT: Yale University Press.

Durkheim, E. (1898). Représentations individuelles et représentations collectives. *Revue de Metaphysique et de Morale, 6,* 273–302.

Ellemers, N. (1993). The influence of socio-structural variables on identity enhancement strategies. *European Review of Social Psychology, 4,* 27–57.

Elms, A. C. (1975). The crisis of confidence in social psychology. *American Psychologist, 30,* 967–976.

Farr, R. M. (1996). *The roots of modern social psychology: 1872–1954.* Oxford: Blackwell.

Festinger, L. (1980). Looking backwards. In L. Festinger (Ed.), *Retrospection on social psychology* (pp. 236–254). New York: Oxford University Press.

Festinger, L., Schachter, S., & Back, K. (1950). *Social pressures in informal groups: A study of human factors in housing.* New York: Harper.

Gilbert, D. T., & Malone, P. S. (1995). The correspondence bias. *Psychological Bulletin, 117,* 21–38.

Graumann, C. F. (1986). The individualization of the social and the desocialization of the individual: Floyd H. Allport's contribution to social psychology. In C. F. Graumann & S. Moscovici (Eds.), *Changing conceptions of crowd mind and behavior* (pp. 97–116). New York: Springer-Verlag.

Haslam, S. A., Oakes, P. J., McGarty, C., Turner, J. C., & Onorato, S. (1995). Contextual changes in the prototypicality of extreme and moderate outgroup members. *European Journal of Social Psychology, 25,* 509–530.

Haslam, S. A., & Platow, M. J. (2001). Your wish is our command: The role of shared social identity in translating a leader's vision into followers' action. In M. A. Hogg & D. J. Terry (Eds.), *Social identity processes in organizational contexts* (pp. 213–228). Philadelphia: Psychology Press.

Haslam, N., Rothschild, L., & Ernst, D. (1998). Essentialist beliefs about social categories. *British Journal of Social Psychology, 39,* 113–127.

Hogg, M. A. (1993). Group cohesiveness: A critical review and some new directions. *European Review of Social Psychology, 4,* 85–111.

Hogg, M. A. (1996). Social identity, self-categorization, and the small group. In E. H. Witte & J. H. Davis (Eds), *Understanding group behavior (Vol. 2): Small group processes and interpersonal relations* (pp. 227–253). Mahwah, NJ: Erlbaum.

Hogg, M. A. (2000). Subjective uncertainty reduction through self-categorization: A motivational theory of social identity processes. *European Review of Social Psychology, 11,* 223–255.

Hogg, M. A. (2001a). Social identity and the sovereignty of the group: A psychology of belonging. In C. Sedikides & M. B. Brewer (Eds.), *Individual self, relational self, collective self* (pp. 123–143). Philadelphia: Psychology Press.

Hogg, M. A. (2001b). A social identity theory of leadership. *Personality and Social Psychology Review, 5,* 184–200.

Hogg, M. A. (2003). Social identity. In M. R. Leary & J. P. Tangney (Eds.), *Handbook of self and identity* (pp. 462–479). New York: Guilford.

Hogg, M. A. (2005). All animals are equal but some animals are more equal than others: Social identity and marginal membership. In K. D. Williams, J. P. Forgas, & W. von Hippel (Eds.), *The social outcast: Ostracism, social exclusion, rejection, and bullying* (pp. 243–261). New York: Psychology Press.

Hogg, M. A. (2006). Social identity theory. In P. J. Burke (Ed.), *Contemporary social psychological theories* (pp. 111–136). Palo Alto, CA: Stanford University Press.

Hogg, M. A. (2007). Uncertainty-identity theory. In M. P. Zanna (Ed.), *Advances in experimental social psychology* (Vol. 39, pp. 69–126). San Diego, CA: Academic Press.

Hogg, M. A., & Abrams, D. (1988). *Social identifications: A social psychology of intergroup relations and group processes.* London: Routledge

Hogg, M. A., Abrams, D., Otten, S., & Hinkle, S. (2004). The social identity perspective: Intergroup relations, self-conception, and small groups. *Small Group Research, 35,* 246–276.

Hogg, M. A., & Smith, J. R. (2007). Attitudes in social context: A social identity perspective. *European Review of Social Psychology, 18,* 1–43.

Hogg, M. A., Terry, D. J., & White, K. M. (1995). A tale of two theories: A critical comparison of identity theory with social identity theory. *Social Psychology Quarterly, 58,* 255–269.

Hogg, M. A., & van Knippenberg, D. (2003). Social identity and leadership processes in groups. In M. P. Zanna (Ed.), *Advances in experimental social psychology* (Vol. 35, pp. 1–52). San Diego, CA: Academic Press.

Hogg, M. A., & Williams, K. D. (2000). From I to we: Social identity and the collective self. *Group Dynamics: Theory, Research, and Practice, 4,* 81–97.

Jaspars, J. M. F. (1980). The coming of age of social psychology in Europe. *European Journal of Social Psychology, 10,* 421–428.

Jaspars, J. M. F. (1986). Forum and focus: A personal view of European social psychology. *European Journal of Social Psychology, 16,* 3–15.

Jones, E. E. (1998). Major developments in five decades of social psychology. In D. T. Gilbert, S. T. Fiske, & G. Lindzey (Eds.), *The handbook of social psychology* (Vol. 1, pp. 3–57). New York: McGraw-Hill.

Kreindler, S. A. (2005). A dual processes model of individual differences in prejudice. *Personality and Social Psychology Review, 9,* 90–107.

LeBon, G. (1908). *The crowd: A study of the popular mind*. London: Unwin. (French original 1896)

Lewin, K. (1936). *A dynamic theory of personality*. New York: McGraw-Hill.

Lewin, K. (1952). *Field theory in social science*. London: Tavistock.

Lorenzi-Cioldi, F., & Clémence, A. (2001). Group processes and the construction of social representations. In M. A. Hogg & R. S. Tindale (Eds.), *Blackwell handbook of social psychology: Group processes* (pp. 311–333). Oxford: Blackwell.

Manicas, P. T. (1987). *A history and philosophy of the social sciences*. Oxford: Blackwell.

Markus, H. (1977). Self-schemata and processing information about the self. *Journal of Personality and Social Psychology, 35*, 63–78.

Markus, H. R., & Kitayama, S. (1991). Culture and the self: Implications for cognition, emotion, and motivation. *Psychological Review, 98*, 224–253.

Marques, J. M., Abrams, D., Páez, D., & Hogg, M. A. (2001). Social categorization, social identification, and rejection of deviant group members. In M. A. Hogg & R. S. Tindale, (Eds.), *Blackwell handbook of social psychology: Group processes* (pp. 400–424). Oxford: Blackwell.

Marques, J. M., Abrams, D., & Serôdio, R. (2001). Being better by being right: Subjective group dynamics and derogation of in-group deviants when generic norms are undermined. *Journal of Personality and Social Psychology, 81,* 436–447.

Marques, J. M., & Páez, D. (1994). The 'black sheep effect': Social categorization, rejection of ingroup deviates and perception of group variability. *European Review of Social Psychology, 5,* 37–68.

Martin, R., & Hewstone, M. (2003). Social influence processes of control and change: Conformity, obedience to authority, and innovation. In M. A. Hogg & J. Cooper (Eds.), *The Sage handbook of social psychology* (pp. 347–366). London: Sage.

McCrae, R. R., & John, O. P. (1992). An introduction of the five-factor model and its applications. *Journal of Personality and Social Psychology, 60,* 175–215.

McDougall, W. (1921). *The group mind*. London: Cambridge University Press.

Moscovici, S. (1976). *Social influence and social change*. London: Academic Press.

Moscovici, S. (1988). Notes towards a description of social representations. *European Journal of Social Psychology, 18,* 211–250.

Oakes, P. J., Haslam, S. A., & Turner, J. C. (1994). *Stereotyping and social reality*. Oxford: Blackwell.

Onorato, R. S., & Turner, J. C. (2002). Challenging the primacy of the personal self: The case for depersonalized self-conception. In Y. Kashima, M. Foddy, & M. J. Platow (Eds.), *Self and identity: Personal, social, and symbolic* (pp. 145–178). Mahwah, NJ: Erlbaum.

Onorato, R. S., & Turner, J. C. (2004). Fluidity in the self-concept: The shift from personal to social identity. *European Journal of Social Psychology, 34,* 257–278.

Oyserman, D., Coon, H. M., & Kemmelmeier, M. (2002). Rethinking individualism and collectivism: Evaluation of theoretical assumptions and meta-analyses. *Psychological Bulletin, 128,* 3–72.

Pickett, C. L., & Brewer, M. B. (2001). Assimilation and differentiation needs as motivational determinants of perceived ingroup and outgroup homogeneity. *Journal of Experimental Social Psychology, 37,* 341–348.

Pickett, C. L., Silver, M. D., & Brewer, M. B. (2002). The impact of assimilation and differentiation needs on perceived group importance and judgments of ingroup size. *Personality and Social Psychology Bulletin, 28,* 546–558.

Platow, M. J., & van Knippenberg, D. (2001). A social identity analysis of leadership endorsement: The effects of leader ingroup prototypicality and distributive intergroup fairness. *Personality and Social Psychology Bulletin, 27,* 1508–1519.

Postmes, T, & Jetten, J. (Eds.) (2006). *Individuality and the group: Advances in social identity*. London: Sage.

Pratto, F., Sidanius, J., & Levin, S. (2006) Social dominance theory and the dynamics of intergroup relations: Taking stock and looking forward. *European Review of Social Psychology, 17,* 271–320.

Reicher, S. D. (1984). The St Pauls' riot: An explanation of the limits of crowd action in terms of a social identity model. *European Journal of Social Psychology, 14,* 1–21.

Reicher, S. D., & Hopkins, N. (1996). Self-category constructions in political rhetoric: An analysis of Thatcher's and Kinnock's speeches concerning the British miners' strike (1984–5). *European Journal of Social Psychology, 26,* 353–371.

Reicher, S. D., & Hopkins, N. (2003). On the science of the art of leadership. In D. van Knippenberg & M. A. Hogg (Eds.), *Leadership and power: Identity processes in groups and organizations* (pp. 197–209). London: Sage.

Reicher, S. D., Hopkins, N., & Condor, S. (1997). Stereotype construction as a strategy of social influence. In R. Spears, P. J. Oakes, N. Ellemers & S. A. Haslam (Eds.), *The social psychology of stereotyping and group life* (pp. 94–118). Oxford: Blackwell.

Reicher, S. D., Spears, R., & Postmes, T. (1995). A social identity model of deindividuation phenomena. *European Review of Social Psychology, 6,* 161–198.

Reid, S. A., & Ng, S. H. (2000). Conversation as a resource for influence: Evidence for prototypical arguments and social identification processes. *European Journal of Social Psychology, 30,* 83–100.

Reid, S. A., & Ng, S. H. (2003). Identity, power, and strategic social categorizations: Theorizing the language of leadership (pp. 210–223). In D. van Knippenberg & M. A. Hogg (Eds.), *Leadership and Power: Identity Processes in Groups and Organizations.* London: Sage.

Reynolds, K. J., Turner, J. C., Haslam, S. A., & Ryan, M. K. (2001). The role of personality and group factors in explaining prejudice. *Journal of Experimental Social Psychology, 37,* 427–434.

Ridgeway, C. L. (2001). Social status and group structure. In M. A. Hogg & R. S. Tindale (Eds.), *Blackwell handbook of social psychology: Group processes* (pp. 352–375). Oxford: Blackwell.

Schmitt, M. T., Branscombe, N. R., & Kappen, D. M. (2003). Attitudes to group-based inequality: Social dominance or social identity. *British Journal of Social Psychology, 42,* 161–186.

Sedikides, C., & Strube, M. J. (1997). Self-evaluation: To thine own self be good, to thine own self be sure, to thine own self be true, and to thine own self be better. In M. P. Zanna (Ed.), *Advances in experimental social psychology* (Vol. 29, pp. 209–296). New York: Academic Press.

Shaw, M. E. (1981). *Group dynamics: The psychology of small group behavior* (2nd ed.). New York: McGraw-Hill.

Sherif, M. (1936). *The psychology of social norms.* New York: Harper & Bros.

Sherif, M. (1966). *In common predicament: Social psychology of intergroup conflict and cooperation.* Boston, MA: Houghton Mifflin.

Sidanius, J., & Pratto, F. (1999). *Social dominance: An intergroup theory of social hierarchy and oppression.* New York: Cambridge University Press.

Sidanius, J., & Pratto, F. (2003). Social dominance theory and the dynamics of inequality: A reply to Schmitt, Banscombe, & Kappen, and Wilson & Liu. *British Journal of Social Psychology, 42,* 207–213.

Simon, B. (1997). Self and group in modern society: Ten theses on the individual self and the collective self. In R. Spears, P. J. Oakes, N. Ellemers, & S. A. Haslam (Eds.), *The social psychology of stereotyping and group life* (pp. 318–335). Oxford: Blackwell.

Simon, B. (2004). *Identity in modern society: A social psychological perspective.* Oxford: Blackwell.

Snyder, M., & Cantor, N. (1988). Understanding personality and social behavior: A functionalist strategy. In D. T. Gilbert, S. T. Fiske & G. Lindzey (Eds.), *Handbook of social psychology* (4th ed., Vol. 1, pp. 635–679). New York: McGraw-Hill.

Snyder M., & Ickes W. (1985). Personality and social behavior. In G. Lindzey & E. Aronson (Eds.), *Handbook of social psychology* (3rd ed., pp. 883–948). New York: Random House.

Steiner, I. D. (1974). Whatever happened to the group in social psychology? *Journal of Experimental Social Psychology, 10*, 94–108.

Steiner, I. D. (1986). Paradigms and groups. *Advances in Experimental Social Psychology, 19*, 251–289.

Strickland, L. H., Aboud, F. E., & Gergen, K. J. (Eds.) (1976). *Social psychology in transition*. New York: Plenum Press.

Tajfel, H. (1972a). Experiments in a vacuum. In J. Israel & H. Tajfel (Eds.), *The context of social psychology: A critical assessment*. London: Academic Press.

Tajfel, H. (1972b). Some developments in European social psychology. *European Journal of Social Psychology, 2*, 307–322.

Tajfel, H. (1972c). Social categorization. English manuscript of 'La catégorisation sociale'. In S. Moscovici (Ed.), *Introduction à la psychologie sociale* (Vol. 1, pp. 272–302). Paris: Larousse.

Tajfel, H. (1974). *Intergroup behaviour, social comparison and social change*. Unpublished Katz-Newcomb lectures. University of Michigan, Ann Arbor.

Tajfel, H. (Ed.) (1984). *The social dimension: European developments in social psychology*. Cambridge: Cambridge University Press.

Tajfel, H., Jaspars, J. M. F., & Fraser, C. (1984). The social dimension in European social psychology. In H. Tajfel (Ed.) (1984), *The social dimension: European developments in social psychology* (Vol. 1, pp. 1–5). Cambridge: Cambridge University Press.

Tajfel, H., & Turner, J. C. (1979). An integrative theory of intergroup conflict. In W. G. Austin & S. Worchel (Eds.), *The social psychology of intergroup relations* (pp. 33–47). Monterey, CA: Brooks/Cole.

Taylor, D. M., & Brown, R. J. (1979). Towards a more social social psychology? *British Journal of Social and Clinical Psychology, 18*, 173–179.

Thoits, P. A., & Virshup, L. K. (1997). Me's and we's: Forms and functions of social identities. In R. D. Ashmore & L. J. Jussim (Eds.), *Self and identity: Fundamental issues*. Rutgers series on self and social identity (Vol. 1, pp. 106–133). New York: Oxford University Press.

Turner, J. C. (1982). Towards a cognitive redefinition of the social group. In H. Tajfel (Ed.), *Social identity and intergroup relations* (pp. 15–40). Cambridge: Cambridge University Press.

Turner, J. C. (1985). Social categorization and the self-concept: A social cognitive theory of group behavior. In E. J. Lawler (Ed.), *Advances in group processes: Theory and research* (Vol. 2, pp. 77–122). Greenwich, CT: JAI Press.

Turner, J. C. (1991). *Social influence*. Milton Keynes: Open University Press.

Turner, J. C. (1999a). Some current issues in research on social identity and self-categorization theories. In N. Ellemers, R. Spears, & B. Doosje (Eds.), *Social identity* (pp. 6–34). Oxford: Blackwell.

Turner, J. C. (1999b). *The prejudiced personality and social change: A self-categorization perspective*. The Tajfel memorial lecture, invited keynote at the 12th general meeting of the European Association of Experimental Social Psychology. Oxford, UK,. July 6–11, 1999.

Turner, J. C., & Bourhis, R. Y. (1996). Social identity, interdependence and the social group. A reply to Rabbie et al. In W. P. Robinson (Ed.) *Social groups and identities: Developing the legacy of Henri Tajfel* (pp. 25–63). Oxford: Butterworth-Heinemann.

Turner, J. C., Hogg, M. A., Oakes, P. J., Reicher, S. D., & Wetherell, M. S. (1987). *Rediscovering the social group: A self-categorization theory*. Oxford: Blackwell.

Turner, J. C., & Oakes, P. J. (1986). The significance of the social identity concept for social psychology with reference to individualism, interactionism and social influence. *British Journal of Social Psychology, 25*, 237–252.

Turner, J. C., & Oakes, P. J. (1989). Self-categorization and social influence. In P. B. Paulus (Ed.), *The psychology of group influence* (2nd ed., pp. 233–275). Hillsdale, NJ: Erlbaum.

Turner, J. C., Oakes, P. J., Haslam, S. A., & McGarty, C. A. (1994). Self and collective: Cognition and social context. *Personality and Social Psychology Bulletin, 20,* 454–463.

Turner, J. C., & Onorato, R. (1999). Social identity, personality and the self-concept: A self-categorization perspective. In T. R. Tyler, R. M. Kramer, & O. Johns (Eds.), *The psychology of the social self* (pp. 11–46). Mahwah, NJ: Erlbaum.

Turner, J. C., & Reynolds, K. J. (2003). Why social dominance theory has been falsified. *British Journal of Social Psychology, 42,* 199–206.

Turner, J. C., Reynolds, K. J., Haslam, S. A., & Veenstra, K. E. (2006). Reconceptualizing personality: Producing individuality by defining the personal self. In T. Postmes & J. Jetten (Eds.), *Individuality and the group: Advances in social identity* (pp. 11–36). London: Sage.

van Knippenberg, D., & Hogg, M. A. (2003). A social identity model of leadership in organizations. In R. M. Kramer & B. M. Staw (Eds.), *Research in organizational behavior* (Vol. 25, pp. 243–295). Greenwich, CT: JAI Press.

van Knippenberg, D., van Knippenberg, B., De Cremer, D., & Hogg, M. A. (2004). Leadership, self, and identity: A review and research agenda. *The Leadership Quarterly, 15,* 825–856.

Verkuyten, M., & Hagendoorn, L. (1998). Prejudice and self-categorization: The variable role of authoritarianism and ingroup stereotypes. *Personality and Social Psychology Bulletin, 24,* 99–110.

Wright, S. C., Aron, A., McLaughlin-Volpe, T., & Ropp, S. A. (1997). The extended contact effect: Knowledge of cross-group friendships and prejudice. *Journal of Personality and Social Psychology, 73,* 73–90.

Wundt, W. (1916). *Elements of folk psychology: Outlines of a psychological history of the development of mankind.* London: Allen & Unwin. (German original 1912.)

Yuki, M. (2003). Intergroup comparison versus intragroup relationships: A cross-cultural examination of social identity theory in North American and East Asian cultural contexts. *Social Psychology Quarterly, 66,* 166–183.

Zimbardo, P. G. (1970). The human choice: Individuation, reason, and order versus deindividuation, impulse, and chaos. In W. J. Arnold & D. Levine (Eds.), *Nebraska symposium on motivation 1969* (Vol. 17, pp. 237–307). Lincoln: University of Nebraska Press.

Post-Reading Activities

1   In your own words, explain how nature and nurture work in harmony (not in dichotomy) in the development of the identity?

2   Provide an application of social identity theory. How did the individual (you or someone else) become a human with an identity?

3   Read a biography or autobiography. Can you identify the process of socialization through interaction and the development of a social identity?

UNIT III

MORAL BEHAVIORS

Introduction

Social psychologists study morality as a process of socialization. Are individuals socialized to follow the norms (expected behaviors) of conduct? But as we have discussed in this anthology, it is more than just the individual influences in making moral choices: situational influences also come into play. We make choices in deciding whether we will be altruistic based on our own motivations but also on the situation itself. In the first reading, "Altruism and Prosocial Behavior," the authors discuss the foundations of altruistic behaviors. The authors in the second reading, "Aggression," explore the social and individual influences on aggressive behaviors. Finally, the third reading, "Making Choices," discusses the social influences in decision making.

Overall, human life is filled with choices—a choice to be altruistic or ignore the one in need; a choice to be aggressive or flee the situation; a choice to marry the individual or move on to the next date, etc. Social influences that shape our choices include (1) risk aversion; (2) temporal discounting; (3) the certainty effect; and (4) keeping options open. When considering whether or not we will help an individual who has tripped along the sidewalk, we may want to avoid being injured also. This risk aversion allows us to weigh the pros and the cons (benefits and costs) of helping another person. Altruistic individuals will help another individual, even when there are no apparent benefits. Temporal discounting may influence our choice to become aggressive. Temporal discounting refers to the idea that what happens in the moment outweighs any future consequences. So, a person may decide to throw a punch at another individual because in that moment, it is the best choice. The aggressive individual will not consider the possible assault charges or punishment that could occur based on his or her action. Choices based on the certainty effect reflect the comfort of the known outweighing the uncertainty of the unknown. A person may choose to go to the university in their hometown because they are familiar with the town and the culture of the location, rather than exploring another university in a new city. The fear of the unknown contributes to the decision-making process for this individual. And finally, we may make choices based on the difficulty of the choice. We tend to want to postpone our decisions so that we can keep our options open. A person may not want to commit to marriage and choose to postpone engagement until the individual is certain there are no other better options available.

Altruism and Prosocial Behavior

John DeLamater, Daniel Myers, and Jessica Collett

Introduction

Jennifer Beyer, age 22, was driving along Old River Road in Appleton, Wisconsin, on a cold day in February. She was on the way to visit a friend, but when a soaking wet child flagged her down, she pulled over immediately. Shivering and frightened, Jeff Laszewski hurriedly explained that he and his friend, nine-year-old Colin Deeg, had been playing on the frozen Fox River when the ice gave way. Jeff had managed to climb back onto the ice and make it to shore, but Colin was still in the water and couldn't get out.

Starting down the river bank, Jennifer saw Colin splashing in the frigid water. At the point where many others would have stopped due to the great personal risk, she went onto the frozen river to rescue him. Inching her way onto the ice, she tried to use her scarf to pull Colin out, but the ice cracked and she plunged into the water. At this point, Colin was still conscious but fading fast. In the meantime, Jeff reached another adult, Cyndy Graf, who quickly dialed 911 for help and then ran to the river.

Jennifer grabbed Colin to keep him from going under and tried to get him out of the water. This proved impossible, however. Colin soon passed out and the weight of his wet clothes made him too heavy to push onto land. Jennifer's limbs were numb with cold by the time police arrived and fire teams reached the river with rescue equipment, but she had kept Colin's head above water and prevented him from drowning. Officers rushed the pair to nearby St. Elizabeth's hospital, where doctors used a bypass machine to warm Colin's blood, which had dropped in temperature to 78 degrees. Jennifer was treated for hypothermia. A week later, Colin was doing fine.

Jennifer Beyer's story is extraordinary for its valor and heroism, but everyday life is filled with smaller tales of people helping others in need. Individuals help others in many ways. They may give someone a ride, help change a flat tire, donate blood, make contributions to charity, return lost items to their owners, assist victims of accidents, and so on. Of course, the mere fact that someone needs help does not mean others will rush to give aid. Humans are capable of vastly different responses to persons in need. Although Jennifer Beyer went onto the ice to rescue Colin Deeg, many others would not have taken that risk. Some will not even stop to help a stranded motorist or make contributions to charitable causes. Thus, a challenge for social psychologists is to explain variations in helping behavior. When will people help others, when will they refuse to, and why? Drawing on research and theory, this chapter addresses the following questions:

1   What motivates us to help one another?

2   How do characteristics of the person in need of help influence giving by others?

3   What impact do cultural factors such as norms and roles have on helping behavior?

4   How do characteristics of the situation affect helping behavior?

5   In emergency situations, what factors determine whether bystanders will intervene and offer help?

6   When help is given, which factors determine the recipient's reactions?

When discussing the positive end of social behaviors, social psychologists use three interrelated terms. **Prosocial behavior** is a broad category of actions considered beneficial to others and as having positive social consequences. These include donating to charity, intervention in emergencies, cooperation, sharing, volunteering, sacrifice, and the like. This contrasts with antisocial behavior that is aggressive, violent, or destructive. **Helping** is prosocial behavior that has the consequence of providing some benefit to or improving the well-being of another person (Dovidio, Piliavin, Schroeder, & Penner, 2006). Intent is unimportant. There is no requirement that the helper intends to benefit another person with his or her action. Furthermore, the helper can also benefit from helping; under this definition, helping behavior may involve either selfish or egoistic motives. Another type of prosocial behavior is altruism. Although there is some disagreement on what behaviors count as altruistic (Kalmijn & De Graaf, 2012), here we define **altruism** as helping that is intended to provide aid to someone else without expectation of any reward (other than the good feeling that may result) and that comes at a cost to the helper. Note that, for altruism, intentions do matter. Under this definition, the helper must intend to benefit the other (Piliavin & Charng, 1990; Schroeder, Penner, Dovidio, & Piliavin, 1995; Simmons, 1991). In fact, this must be the primary goal of the altruistic action (Batson, 2011).

Motivation to Help

What motivates one person to help another? There are at least three major views on the issue, each rooted in different conceptions of human nature. The first view depicts humans as egoistic or selfish beings, concerned primarily with their own gratification. Helping originates from some ulterior, self-serving motive. Potential helpers weigh the costs and benefits of helping to decide whether they will do so. The second view depicts humans as rather more generous and unselfish beings, capable of real concern for the welfare of others. For instance, a bystander may rush to rescue an accident victim to relieve the victim's pain and anguish. Our human ability to empathize with others motivates us to alleviate their distress. The third view, from evolutionary psychology, sees prosocial behavior as an evolved trait that helps ensure individuals will pass along their genes to the next generation. In this section, we look at these three views in more detail.

Egoism

One view of human nature regards us all as fundamentally selfish beings, concerned primarily with our own gratification. This seemingly simple seed is used throughout the social sciences to explain a huge variety of social behavior, including prosocial acts. Although this view acknowledges that helping behavior occurs with considerable frequency, it treats helping as always originating from some ulterior, self-serving consideration (Gelfand & Hartmann, 1982). For instance, a student might help a peer with a difficult assignment to get admiration and approval from the other, to avoid feelings of guilt or shame, to obligate the other to her, or to bolster her own self-esteem. Helping behavior motivated by self-gratification is called **egoism**.

Even in the most other-oriented, charitable behavior, there is little doubt that considerations of reward and cost influence decisions to give or withhold help. Every helping act imposes some costs on the helper (danger, loss of time, financial costs, expenditure of effort). In general, the greater these costs, the less likely persons are to help (Kerber, 1984; Shotland & Stebbins, 1983). Would you be more likely to help someone study for an exam you are also studying for than for an exam you took last semester? If you are also studying for the exam, ensuring someone else understands the material takes little additional time and might actually help you understand the material better (in addition to the potential benefits of helping another student outlined above). Helping someone study for an exam for a class that you are not enrolled in, however, comes at a cost; it takes away valuable time that you could spend studying another subject and offers you fewer direct benefits.

There may also be some costs to potential helpers for *not* helping (public disapproval by others, embarrassment and loss of face, and condemnation by the victim). The evaluation of these costs is important in determining helping behavior, and many theorists believe individuals will generally not give help unless they think the rewards (even if not immediate) will outweigh the costs (Lynch & Cohen, 1978; Piliavin, Dovidio, Gaertner, & Clark, 1981).

The rewards that motivate potential helpers are many and varied. They may include such things as thanks from the victim, admiration and approval from others, financial rewards and prizes, and recognition for competence. People will help more if they anticipate rewards such as status enhancement (Bienenstock & Bianchi, 2004; Kerber, 1984). Even small rewards—like the small chocolate that the local Goodwill offers with every donation—tend to increase individuals' helping behavior. Getting something in return helps people make a self-interested justification for the behavior (Holmes, Miller, & Lerner, 2002; Perlow & Weeks, 2002).

The form of help that someone offers may depend on the specific rewards he or she seeks, and these may, in turn, depend on his or her own needs. For example, a study invited students to volunteer for a range of prosocial activities with similar rewards. When given a choice, students volunteered for activities related to their personal values and preferences. For example, those who enjoyed novelty volunteered more frequently to help with a project on unusual states of consciousness, ESP, and hypnosis, and those who liked close social relationships volunteered more frequently to help troubled high school students (Gergen, Gergen, & Meter, 1972).

Altruism and Empathetic Concern

People often react to the distress of others on an emotional level and offer help in response. The term **empathy** refers to the vicarious experience of an emotion that is congruent with—or possibly identical to— the emotion that another person is experiencing (Barnett, 1987; Eisenberg & Miller, 1987). For example, when a mother sees her child in pain, she may experience a very similar emotion to the child. There is considerable evidence that feelings of empathy for a person in need will lead to helping behavior (Batson et al., 1981; Dovidio, Allen, & Schroeder, 1990; Eisenberg & Miller, 1987; Fultz et al., 1986).

The Empathy-Altruism Model. The *empathy-altruism model* proposes that adults can experience two distinct states of emotional arousal while witnessing another's suffering: distress and empathy. Distress involves unpleasant emotions such as shock, alarm, worry, and upset at seeing another person suffer. Empathy, however, entails such emotions as compassion, concern, warmth, and tenderness toward the other (Batson, 1987, 1991; Batson & Coke, 1981; Batson & Oleson, 1991). These states of emotional arousal give rise to different motivations, but both can lead to helping behavior. If the bystander experiences distress at seeing another suffering, he or she may be motivated to reduce this distress (egoism). This contrasts with the situation in which a bystander experiences empathy when witnessing the suffering of another. Feelings of this type may cause the bystander to help the victim, but this help is motivated fundamentally by a desire to reduce the other's distress (altruism). The empathy-altruism model has received support from many experiments. Typically, the participants in these studies witness a person in distress and must decide whether to offer help. The independent variables in these studies are the level of empathy and the ease of escape from the situation. When empathy is high, the frequency of helping behavior is also high, irrespective of whether it was easy to avoid the situation. However,

Who will volunteer at this church charity drive? Who will donate goods? Personal characteristics sometimes drive the decision to help, but cost-benefit calculations, cultural norms, situational factors, and even genetics also play important roles. © Ocean/Corbis

when distress is high, the frequency of helping behavior drops off substantially when escape is easy; participants leave the situation rather than absorbing the costs of helping (Batson et al., 1983). Distress can be alleviated by leaving the situation; empathy cannot.

Altruistically motivated helping, fueled by empathy, appears to lead to more sustained giving than helping that is motivated by egoism (Piferi, Jobe, & Jones, 2006). In a study on the motivations for helping after the September 11 terrorist attacks, researchers found that individuals who gave money, blood, goods, or other forms of assistance because of other-focused motives (giving to reduce another's discomfort) were almost four times more likely to still be giving support one year later than those whose original motivation was to reduce personal distress (egoistic motives). This effect likely stems from differences in emotional arousal. The events of September 11 emotionally affected people throughout the United States. Those who gave to reduce their own distress reduced their emotional arousal with their initial gift, discharging that emotional distress. However, those who gave to reduce others' distress did not stop empathizing with victims who continued to struggle long after the attacks.

Evolutionary Perspectives

A third view on prosocial behavior takes an evolutionary perspective. The basic notion driving this theory is that any genetically determined physical attribute or trait that helps an individual survive will be passed on to the next generation. Eventually, individuals with the attribute will become more numerous than those without. The evolutionary perspective often points to others in the animal kingdom to demonstrate its propositions. For example, helping behaviors and even altruistic, self-sacrificing behaviors are common in nature. Ground squirrels, for instance, frequently sound alarm calls when a predator approaches. These calls warn other squirrels of the threat, but they also draw the attention of the predator to the individual sounding the alarm, thereby increasing the chances of that individual being killed (Sherman, 1980). Other animals sacrifice themselves to predators to protect the larger group (Wilson, 1971). At first, these patterns of self-sacrificing behavior seem to run counter to evolutionary theory. Altruism among animals often means that those who are the most helpful will be the least likely to survive. This means they will be less likely to have offspring and may not have any at all. How, then, could the altruistic tendency persist generations later? The same question can be posed, of course, with respect to humans.

Evolutionary psychology and a related theoretical perspective called *sociobiology* (Archer, 1991; Buss, 1999; Ketelaar & Ellis, 2000; Wilson, 1975, 1978) have constructed a response to the problem of altruism and have assembled evidence that supports the view that altruism has roots in evolution (Buss & Kenrick, 1998; Krebs & Miller, 1985). To understand how helping can make sense in an evolutionary context, it is important to appreciate that the "fittest" animal is the one that passes on its genes to subsequent generations. This can happen either by the animal itself producing offspring or by the animal's close relatives, such as brothers, sisters, and cousins (who share many of its genes), producing offspring. So although it is true that altruistic behavior will not have survival value for an individual, altruistic acts can increase the survival of one's genes if directed toward others who share the same genes (Hamilton, 1964; Meyer, 2000). Consider a mother bird who sacrifices herself to save the lives of her eight babies. Each of the babies carries half of the genes of the mother; thus, between them, they have four times as many of the mother's genes as she does herself.

Furthermore, some sociobiologists have argued that altruistic behavior is perpetuated because of reciprocation. If all the animals in a group engage in helping behavior, they will all be better off in the long run (Hardy & van Vugt, 2006). If, for example, the animals all take turns playing the role of sentry and warning the group of approaching predators, many more members of that group will survive and reproduce than if none of them had warned the group.

Evolutionary approaches to altruism have produced a considerable body of interesting research and theoretical propositions. For example, animals should be most altruistic toward those that most closely resemble them genetically—that is, they should help immediate family members more than distant cousins, and distant cousins more than outsiders or strangers (Burnstein, Crandall, & Kitayama, 1994; Rushton, Russell, & Wells, 1984). Second, parents will tend to behave altruistically toward healthy off-spring, who are likely to survive and pass on their genes, but less altruistically toward sick or unhealthy offspring, who are likely to die before reproducing (Dovidio et al., 1991). Third, helping behavior should only favor those who can still reproduce. Thus, helping behavior should be targeted more toward young women than to older women who are past the age of menopause (Kruger, 2001).

BOX 6.1 Research Update: Gossip as Prosocial Behavior

Gossip is a complex social behavior; although it is very common, it is also widely criticized. An evolutionary perspective would argue that gossip exists because it serves a purpose. According to psychologist Robin Dunbar, that purpose is a pro-social one. Dunbar (1996) hypothesized that gossip became more and more prominent as a linguistic practice as humans began to live in larger and larger groups. Without being able to directly observe others' behavior, group members would use gossip to track one another's reputation as trustworthy group members.

A team of social psychologists tested Dunbar's assumption about the prosociality of gossip in a series of experiments. Feinberg, Willer, Stellar, & Keltner (2012) put participants in situations in which they watched another participant (the transgressor) act selfishly. The researchers then gave the participants the opportunity to gossip about the transgressor to the participant who would interact with the transgressor next in the experiment. More than half the students chose to gossip, and 96% of those gossip messages moved beyond serving a selfish, personal end. Examples of prosocial gossip messages were: "[He] didn't send anything back last round. I'd advise not sending anything" or "Try to keep all the money you can, because [she] will not give you much in return."

Using a battery of self-reports and heart rate monitors, the researchers explored why gossip—and, particularly, prosocial gossip—was so common. They found that people with a more pro-social orientation, whose personality reflected more other-directed concerns, tend to gossip more than those with an egoistic orientation and that participants would gossip even if there was no potential of harm toward the transgressor and when it was costly to gossip. What made gossip so attractive?

Results suggest that witnessing the unfair acts of transgressors evoked negative arousal, especially among more prosocial individuals. The more negative affect participants felt, the more compelled they were to engage in prosocial gossip. Furthermore, engaging in prosocial gossip actually reduced their levels of negative affect. This was especially true for more prosocial individuals.

Gossip also had an important effect on behavior. Participants behaved more cooperatively when they knew that observers could potentially gossip about them.

Source: Adapted from Feinberg, Willer, Stellar, & Keltner, 2012.

Generally speaking, these evolutionary propositions have found support in studies. However, there are also exceptions and alternative explanations (Buss & Kenrick, 1998; Caporeal, 2001;

Dovidio et al., 1991). For example, Sime (1983) examined people in a fire emergency and found that they were much more likely to endanger themselves by searching for family members than by searching for friends. Rather than attributing this behavior to genetic kin selection, however, we may just as likely assume that people would sacrifice more to save someone they love than someone who is simply an acquaintance because losing the former would cause them more distress.

Although interesting, the sociobiological perspective is controversial, especially as applied to humans. For example, critics have questioned whether altruism is genetically transmitted (Buck & Ginsburg, 1991; Kitcher, 1985). By this model, animals and humans would help only close relatives and rarely or never help those who are genetically unrelated. Yet we know humans often help others who are unrelated—even total strangers. Some critics argue that to explain altruism among unrelated persons, it is necessary to rely on cultural constructs, such as religious values, that define unrelated others as appropriate recipients of help. At best, then, evolution is an incomplete explanation for altruism.

Characteristics of the Needy that Foster Helping

When in need, some people have a much better chance of receiving help than others do. Our willingness to help needy persons depends on various factors. Important among these are whether we know and like them, whether they are similar to or different from us, and whether we consider them truly deserving of help.

Acquaintanceship and Liking

We are especially inclined to help people whom we know and to whom we feel close. Studies of reactions following natural disasters, for example, indicate that whereas people generally become very helpful toward others, they tend to give aid first to needy family members, then to friends and neighbors, and last to strangers (Dynes & Quarantelli, 1980; Form & Nosow, 1958). Research suggests this tendency stems, in part, from an increased ability to empathize with those we know well (Maner & Gailliot, 2007). We are better able to take their perspective and vicariously experience their emotional distress, thereby motivating altruistic helping. Relationships increase helping because they involve relatively stronger normative obligations, more intense emotion and empathy, and greater costs if we fail to help. Even a brief acquaintanceship is sufficient to make us more likely to help someone (Pearce, 1980). A simple introduction or comment, and sometimes less, is enough to transform a complete stranger into a "familiar stranger" (Milgram, 1977) and increase the likelihood of helping.

We are also more likely to help someone we like than to help someone we do not like. This effect occurs whether our positive feelings about the other are based on his or her physical appearance, personal characteristics, or friendly behavior (Kelley & Byrne, 1976; Mallozzi, McDermott,

& Kayson, 1990). Moreover, we are more likely to help someone who likes us than to help someone who does not (Baron, 1971).

Similarity

In general, we are more likely to help others who are similar to ourselves than to help others who are dissimilar (Dovidio, 1984). That is, we are more likely to help those who resemble us in race, attitudes, political ideologies, and even mode of dress. For instance, with respect to race, several studies have reported that in situations where refusing to help may be easily justified, Whites are more likely to help other Whites than to help Blacks (Benson, Karabenick, & Lerner, 1973; Dovidio & Gaertner, 1981). Similarity of opinions and political ideologies also increases helping (Hornstein, 1978). In a series of field studies, New York pedestrians came across "lost" wallets or letters that had been planted by researchers in conspicuous places. These objects contained information indicating the original owner's views on the Arab-Israeli conflict, on worthy or unpopular organizations, or on trivial opinion items. The owner's views on these topics either resembled or differed from the views known to characterize the neighborhoods in which the objects were dropped. Persons finding the wallets or letters took steps to return them to the owner much more frequently when the owner's views were similar to their own. As Box 6.2 illustrates, even a characteristic as seemingly trivial as liking the same sport can influence the chances of helping (and hurting).

Much of the effect of similarity is a product of perceived group membership. [...] [P]eople tend to help in-group members (people who share a particular characteristic) more than out-group members (people who are different from them on a particular characteristic). This is, in part, because individuals are better able to ascribe emotions to in-group members. A study of helping after Hurricane Katrina illustrates this effect (Cuddy, Rock, & Norton, 2007). Researchers had White, Black, and Latino participants read a fictionalized account of a mother who had lost her child during Hurricane Katrina. Names cued readers into the victims' race (Tanesha/Amanda and Tyrell/Joshua). After reading the news story, participants were asked to describe the emotions the mothers were experiencing and whether they planned to volunteer or had already volunteered time toward Hurricane Katrina relief efforts.

Of primary interest to the researchers was the role of emotion in helping. They distinguished between two types of emotions—primary and secondary—to determine their relative effects. Primary emotions are emotions that are a direct result of an external cue. They are closely related to the situation at hand. For example, the moment an intimate relationship ends—the breakup—causes a rush of emotion that can be directly attributed to the breakup. You might experience sadness, hurt, and frustration. Secondary emotions are the more enduring effects of these immediate emotions. The rush of sadness may give way to insecurity, anxiety, or depression.

Results showed that participants inferred similar primary emotions—sadness, distress, pain, fear, and so on—for in-group and out-group members. In other words, whether a Black or White

BOX 6.2 Research Update: Group Boundaries and Helping Behavior

We tend to help others who are like us. A regular cyclist is more likely to stop to help a cyclist with a flat tire than to help a stranded motorist. Additionally, race, gender, and other strongly held group identities play an important role in our willingness to help others, but what impact might other, less salient identities have? For example, can similarity based on being a fan of a particular sport team or even a particular sport, like baseball, encourage helping behavior?

A group of researchers set out to explore the influence of these sports-related group memberships by using a choreographed accident in which a confederate fell down and feigned a painful injury in the presence of a subject. Prior to the accident, the subjects had taken a survey questionnaire about their favorite soccer team, thereby priming their identity as fans of their favorite team. Then, the subjects were directed to walk to a different location for the second part of the soccer study in which they were supposed to watch a video about soccer teams. Along the way, they passed the confederate, who fell and pretended to be hurt. The outcome of interest was whether the subjects stopped to help and, if so, how much help was offered.

The manipulation in the experiment was simple: The confederate wore a shirt identified with the subjects' favorite team, a shirt identified with the main rival of the subjects' favorite team, or a neutral shirt that did not identify with any team at all. The results were surprisingly stark. Confederates wearing the favorite team's shirt received help from the subjects over 90% of the time, whereas those wearing a plain shirt or the rival team's shirt received help less than one-third of the time.

In the second experiment, these same researchers attempted to examine a more diffuse identity: that of soccer fans in general rather than those of a particular team. This experiment followed a similar procedure as the first, except that instead of priming the subjects' identity about their favorite team, the researchers primed the subjects to think about their identity as soccer fans in general. They did this by telling the subjects that there are a few troublemakers among soccer fans who got into drunken brawls and, thereby, gave soccer fans a bad name. However, there are also many positive aspects about being soccer fans, and the purpose of the research was to examine these positive aspects. After hearing this information, the subjects filled out a survey about being soccer fans. The remainder of the experiment proceeded as before. Again, the primed identity had a strong effect on helping, but the pattern was different. If the confederate was wearing either soccer shirt, help was received about 75% of the time. If the confederate wore the generic shirt, help was received less than 25% of the time.

Source: Adapted from Levine, Prosser, Evans, and Reicher, 2005.

participant read the story of Tanesha or Amanda, they believed the mothers would feel similar levels of sadness. However, when participants were asked to rate secondary emotions—grief, sorrow, mourning, guilt, and so on—differences emerged. Specifically, participants inferred lower levels of secondary emotions to out-group members, thinking they would experience less grief than someone in their in-group. Importantly, empathizing with someone in need based on these secondary emotions has more of an influence on helping than simply empathizing on primary emotions.

Deservingness

After Hurricane Katrina, some Americans felt that the residents of New Orleans who stayed in the city during the storm did not deserve help. After all, it seemed like they decided to ignore officials' orders to evacuate. Whether we see someone as deserving help has important implications for our desire to act on their behalf.

Suppose you received a call asking you to help elderly people who had just suffered a sharp reduction in income after losing their jobs. Would it matter whether they lost their jobs because they were caught stealing and lying or because their work program was being phased out? A study of Wisconsin residents who received such a call showed that respondents were more likely to help if the elderly people had become dependent because their program was cut than because they had been caught stealing (Schwartz & Fleishman, 1978).

What matters in this situation is the potential helpers' causal attribution regarding the origin of need [...]. Potential helpers respond more favorably when a person's need is caused by circumstances beyond his or her control. Such people are true "innocent victims" who deserve help. In contrast, needs caused by a person's own actions, misdeeds, or failings elicit little desire to help (Bryan & Davenport, 1968; Frey & Gaertner, 1986). For instance, one study found that students were

ABC's program *What Would You Do* puts unsuspecting people in situations in which they can either intervene to help or choose to ignore someone in need. In one episode, *What Would You Do* had an actor—dressed like a homeless man—fall to the ground on a busy sidewalk. Although people stopped more quickly when the person who fell was a well-dressed woman, a number of onlookers did call 911 for the man. However, when the same man fell to the ground with a beer can in his hand, only one woman, named Linda Hamilton, stopped. She tried to get other people's attention, to no avail. Hamilton, who is sometimes homeless herself, then threw the beer can away, hoping it would elicit more help. After she realized that passersby would not stop on their own, she explicitly asked a woman to call 911. Immediately after this second woman stopped, others also came to the man's aid. © *ABC News*

less sympathetic and less likely to help a person who developed AIDS through promiscuous sexual contact than through a blood transfusion (Weiner, Perry, & Magnusson, 1988). In the United States, we tend to commit the fundamental attribution error (the tendency to overemphasize personality in making attributions) and assume that those in need are somewhat to blame for their situation and to downplay or ignore the importance of circumstances outside of their control that may have led to the need or made it difficult to overcome it. Needs thought to stem from illegitimate sources—including individual choices—undermine helping by inhibiting empathic concerns, blocking our sense of normative obligation, and increasing the possibility of condemnation rather than social approval for helping.

Even in emergencies, potential helpers are influenced by whether they consider a victim deserving. Consider responses to an emergency staged by experimenters on the New York City subway (Piliavin, Rodin, & Piliavin, 1969). Shortly after the subway train left the station, a young man (a confederate) collapsed to the floor and lay staring at the ceiling during the seven-and-a-half minute trip to the next station. In one experimental condition, the man carried a cane and appeared crippled. In another condition, he carried a liquor bottle and reeked of whiskey. Bystanders helped the seemingly crippled man immediately but waited several minutes, on average, before helping the man who appeared drunk.

Normative Factors in Helping

Would you intervene in a heated argument between a man and a woman you believe are married? In one experiment (Shotland & Straw, 1976), participants unexpectedly witnessed a realistic fight between a man and a woman in an elevator. The man attacked the woman, shaking her violently, while she struggled and resisted. In one treatment, the man and woman were depicted as strangers; the woman screamed, "Get away from me! I don't know you!" In the other treatment, she screamed, "Get away from me! I don't know why I ever married you!" This simple variation greatly affected the participants' propensity to help. Whereas 65% of the subjects intervened in the stranger fight, fewer than 20% intervened in the married fight.

This difference may have been due, in part, to the participants' perceptions of a greater likelihood of injury to the woman in the stranger fight than in the married fight. They assumed that an attack by a stranger might progress further than an attack by a husband. However, this reticence may have also been due to normative expectations. The participants who witnessed the married fight said they hesitated to take action because they were not sure their help was wanted. Almost all the participants who did not intervene said they felt the fight was "none of my business." Clearly, "wife" and "husband" are social roles, and some widely understood norms regulate the relations between wives and husbands (and outsiders). One of these is that, except in the case of physical abuse, outsiders should basically mind their own business and let married couples resolve disputes as they will. When the woman in the elevator identified herself as the man's wife, this norm suddenly became relevant and changed the meaning of intervention. To intervene in the fight would be an intrusion on the marital relationship and might invite reprisals from the husband, the wife, or both. In fact, participants who thought the attacker was the woman's husband believed he was more likely to attack them if they intervened than did participants who believed the attacker was a stranger. This fear of eliciting an attack on oneself when intervening makes men—who see themselves as more able to protect themselves in such an attack—more likely to intervene when they see a woman being abused than other women are (Laner, Benin, & Ventrone, 2001).

Norms of Responsibility and Reciprocity

Cultural norms mandate helping as appropriate under some conditions, and they define it as inappropriate under others. When mandated as appropriate, helping becomes an approved behavior, supported by social sanctions. Broad social norms indicate when helping is appropriate.

Social Responsibility Norm. The **social responsibility norm** is a general norm stating that individuals should help others who are dependent on them. People often mention their sense of what they "ought to do"—their internalized standards—when asked why they offer to help (Berkowitz, 1972). For example, Simmons (1991) reports the words of a bone marrow donor prior to giving: "This is a life and death situation and you must do anything you can to help that person, whether it is family, friends, or [someone] unknown" (p. 14). The word "must" in this statement suggests that a norm is operative.

Applicable in many situations, the social responsibility norm is readily activated. Some research suggests that simply informing individuals that another person—even a stranger—is dependent on them is enough to elicit help (Berkowitz, Klanderman, & Harris, 1964). Recognize, however, that there are stronger and weaker versions of the social responsibility norm. Whereas the norm that we must help dependent kin or needy friends is widely held, the belief that we must help needy strangers or unknown persons is not so universally accepted. Although the awareness of a stranger's dependency will sometimes elicit help, it does not always do so. Speeding passersby, for example, frequently disregard stranded motorists they notice on the roadside. Bystanders watch, apparently fascinated but immobile, during rapes and other assaults. Thousands of people reject charity appeals every day.

Some theorists have suggested that the social responsibility norm effectively motivates helping only when people are expressly reminded of it. In a test of this hypothesis (Darley & Batson, 1973), theological students were asked to write and record a talk. Some students prepared remarks on the parable of the Good Samaritan, others wrote about job opportunities. On the way to record their talk, the students passed a man slumped in a doorway. Although the students who wrote about the Good Samaritan were presumably thinking about the virtues of altruism as they passed the man, they helped the stranger only slightly more than the students who had prepared a talk on the unrelated topic. These findings suggest that the social responsibility norm is a fairly weak source of motivation to help and is easily negated by the costs of helping.

The Norm of Reciprocity. Another cultural standard, the **norm of reciprocity**, states that people should (1) help those who have helped them and (2) not help those who have denied them help for no legitimate reason (Schroeder et al., 1995; Trivers, 1983). Imagine your room-mate's car has broken down and he asks you for a ride to the grocery store to pick up a few things. You are much more likely to help him if he did a favor for you the last time you needed one. However, if he turned down a previous request to help you—say, when you needed a ride to campus from the bus station after returning from winter break—you are much less likely to agree. This reciprocity norm applies to anyone who has previously received some benefit from another. The norm is found in different cultures around the world (Gergen, Ellsworth, Maslach, & Siepel, 1975). Small kindnesses that create the conditions for reciprocity are a common feature of family, friendship, and work relationships.

People not only report that the reciprocity norm influences their behavior; behavioral stud-ies have actually demonstrated reciprocity in action (Bar-Tal, 1976; Wilke & Lanzetta, 1982). Reciprocity is especially likely when the person expects to see the helper again (Carnevale, Pruitt, & Carrington, 1982). People try to match the amount of help they give to the quantity they received earlier. By matching benefits, people maintain equity in their relationships and avoid becoming overly indebted to others. Understanding the norm of reciprocity, those in need are less likely to ask for help when they believe they will not be able to repay the aid in some form (Fisher, Nadler, & Whitcher-Alagna, 1982; Nadler, Mayseless, Peri, & Chemerinski, 1985). That said, people do not reciprocate every benefit they receive. Whether we feel obligated to reciprocate depends in part on the intentions we attribute to the person who helped us. We feel more obligated to reciprocate if we perceive that the original help was given voluntarily rather than coerced and that it was chosen consciously rather than accidentally (Gergen et al., 1975; Greenberg & Frisch, 1972).

Personal Norms

Although broad norms like social responsibility and reciprocity undoubtedly affect helping behavior, they are, by themselves, inadequate bases from which to predict the occurrence of helping behavior with precision. There are several reasons for this. First, given the wide variety of contingencies that people encounter, these norms are simply too general to dic-tate our behavior with any precision in all cases. Second, not everyone in society accepts these norms to the same degree; some individuals internalize them to a greater extent than others do. Third, the social norms that apply to any given situation occasionally conflict with one another; the social responsibility norm may obligate us to help an abused wife, for example, but the widely accepted norm against meddling in others' marriages tells us not to intervene.

In response to these criticisms, a different type of normative theory has been developed by social psychologists (Schwartz & Howard, 1981, 1984). This theory explains not only the conditions under which norms are likely to motivate helping but also individual differences in helping in particular situations. Instead of dealing with broad social norms, this theory focuses on **personal norms**—feelings of moral obligation to perform specific actions that stem from an individual's internalized system of values.

For example, a survey on medical transplants might ask, "If a stranger needed a bone marrow transplant, and you were a suitable donor, would you feel a moral obligation to donate bone marrow?" This survey would then be followed by an apparently unrelated encounter with a representative of an organization who would ask these individuals for help. In various studies, individuals' personal norms have predicted differences in their willingness to donate bone marrow or blood, to tutor blind children, to work for increased welfare payments for the needy (Schwartz & Howard, 1982), and to participate in community recycling programs (Hopper & Nielsen, 1991).

These personal norms may stem from role identities (Piliavin, Grube, & Callero, 2002). We are driven to act in ways consistent with our identities to experience ourselves as authentic and to uphold those identities [...]. For example, a religious person might help because it is "the Christian thing to do" or because they believe in the golden rule: "Do unto others as you would like done to you." Similarly, someone who has adopted an identity as a "blood donor" is more likely to give blood than someone who has not (Piliavin & Callero, 1991). Helping is most likely to occur when conditions simultaneously foster the activation of personal norms and suppress any defenses that might neutralize personal norms.

Gender Norms

Although there are not significant gender differences in how much people help, there are significant differences in the ways men and women help. These differences are related to gender role norms and expectations (Piliavin & Unger, 1985). For example, research findings suggest that men are more likely than women to intervene and offer assistance in emergency situations that entail danger (Eagly & Crowley, 1986). In a study of people who had been publicly recognized as heroes by the state of California (that is, persons who had intervened to protect someone during a dangerous criminal act, such as a mugging or bank robbery), all of the heroes but one was a man (Huston, Ruggiero, Conner, & Geis, 1981). Acting heroically by confronting risk and danger is often considered part of the traditional male role. Women, however, are more likely to help in situations requiring nurturance, caretaking, and emotional support. Women are more likely to help children they witness being abused than men are (Laner, Benin, & Ventrone, 2001) and women care for children and aging parents more on a day-to-day basis than men do, fulfilling an important help-giving function (Brody, 2004). Women are also more likely than men to provide their friends with personal favors, emotional support, and informational counseling (Eisenberg & Fabes, 1991; Otten, Penner, & Waugh, 1988).

Situational Influences

Prosocial behavior is influenced by not only normative factors but also situational influences on potential helpers. For example, we are more likely to help when we feel we have time to. In the earlier study of theological students who were on their way to give a speech on the parable of the Good Samaritan (Darley & Batson, 1973), being in a hurry had a much stronger effect on whether the students stopped to help than the topic of the speech did. Students who were in a hurry offered much less help than those who were not, in part because they felt a sense of social responsibility toward those who were waiting on them (Batson et al., 1978). In this section we consider a handful of other such factors: experiences with models of helping, mood, and the potential costs of helping (or not).

Modeling

An important factor that affects helping and aggression is the presence of behavioral models—someone else who is helping. The presence of a behavioral model tends to increase helping for several reasons. First, a model demonstrates what kinds of actions are possible or effective in the situation. Others who previously did not know how to help can emulate the model. As an example, even if a young college student wants to help a stranded motorist on the highway, he or she might not know anything about cars and, therefore, be unsure of how they might help the motorist. However, if the student had previously been in a car with someone else who, in a similar instance, made note of the mile marker and pulled out their cell phone and called highway patrol to notify the police of the stranded motorist and their location, the student would have a model of a possible behavior and would be more likely to respond similarly if a comparable situation occurred.

Second, a helping model conveys the message that to offer help is appropriate in the particular situation. A model may, for example, increase the salience of the social responsibility norm. Once aware of this norm, others may decide to help. A popular series of insurance commercials demonstrated this nicely, showing the sense of responsibility spreading through the city. It begins with a mother watching as a man stops to pick up her child's toy. She makes note of this and, later, in a restaurant, pushes a coffee cup—teetering on the edge of a table and at risk of falling—back toward the center of the table. A passerby witnesses this act of kindness and later stops to help a man up from a wet sidewalk. The commercial continues through a long series of models and observers who eventually become models for another observer.

Finally, a model provides information about the costs and risks involved in helping—a consideration that is especially important in situations involving danger. By offering help under conditions of danger or potential damage to self, models demonstrate to others that the risks incurred are tolerable or justified.

Mood

As discussed in Chapter 5, a mood is a transitory feeling, such as being happy and elated or being frustrated and depressed. Both good and bad moods can help or hinder a person's likelihood of helping another.

Good Moods and Helping. When individuals are in a good mood, they are more likely to help others than when they are in a neutral mood (Salovey, Mayer, & Rosenhan, 1991). Good moods promote both spontaneous helping and compliance with requests for help. There are several reasons that being in a good mood increases our propensity to help others (Carlson, Charlin, & Miller, 1988). First, people who are in a good mood are less preoccupied with themselves and less concerned with their own problems. This allows them to focus more attention on the needs and problems of others, which, through empathy, often leads to helping. Second, people in a good mood often feel relatively fortunate compared to others who are deprived. They recognize that their good fortune is out of balance with others' needs, and to restore balance, they use their resources to help others (Rosenhan, Salovey, & Hargis, 1981). Third, people in a good mood tend to see the world in a positive light and want to retain the warm glow of happiness. Thus, if they can maintain or even increase their own positive feelings through prosocial behavior, they will do so.

That said, good moods may also inhibit helping in particular situations. Those in a good mood may avoid forms of helping that involve unpleasant or embarrassing activities that threaten to interrupt or end their good mood (Cunningham, Steinberg, & Grev, 1980).

Bad Moods and Helping. The effects of a bad mood—feeling sad or depressed—can have rather complex effects on helping. Under some conditions, a bad mood inhibits helping. Under other conditions, however, it promotes helping (Carlson & Miller, 1987; Rosenhan, Salovey, & Hargis, 1981).

Bad moods can suppress helping for several reasons. First, a bad mood has an impact on the salience of others' needs. In contrast to those in a good mood, people in a bad mood are concerned about their own problems and less likely to notice others' needs than are people in a neutral or good mood. When others' needs do not grab the attention of a potential helper, help is less likely to be given (Aderman & Berkowitz, 1983; Rogers, Miller, Mayer, & Duval, 1982). Second, people in a bad mood often see themselves as less fortunate than others. Feeling relatively impoverished, they may resist using their own resources to help others, lest they become even more disadvantaged (Rosenhan et al., 1981).

Conversely, bad moods can sometimes increase helping. One explanation for this is the *negative-state relief hypothesis* (Cialdini, Kendrick, & Baumann, 1982; Cialdini et al., 1987). This hypothesis assumes that (1) individuals experiencing unpleasant feelings will be motivated to reduce them, and (2) people have learned since childhood that helping others will improve their own mood, often through the receipt of thanks or praise. The hypothesis predicts that people in bad moods will help others to boost their own spirits. Although this is an egoistic rather than altruistic motive for helping because individuals are offering help primarily to relieve sadness in themselves rather than to relieve suffering in others, the effect is the same. However, two important implications of this hypothesis are that (1) a negative mood will only motivate helping if people believe that doing so will improve their mood (Manucia, Baumann, & Cialdini, 1984), and (2) they will only help if there is not an accessible alternative way to relieve the bad mood (Schaller & Cialdini, 1988).

Costs

When making a decision to help, people usually make a calculation about the potential costs and benefits of their action. Cost calculations for helping involve both the costs to the helper and the needs of the victim. Helpers may be willing to endure higher costs to themselves if the costs to the victim of not receiving help are extremely high (Dovidio et al., 1991; Piliavin et al., 1981). Jennifer Byer realized that Colin would likely die if she did nothing. This potential cost was so great that she was willing to take the risk of falling into the frozen river herself to prevent it.

Bystanders often take into account several kinds of costs to themselves in emergency situations. First, bystanders consider the cost of giving direct help. This includes the costs to them if they offer help—lost time, exposure to danger, expenditure of effort, exposure to disgusting experiences, and the like. Second, bystanders consider the cost of not giving help. Costs borne by the bystanders if the victim receives no help include the burden of unpleasant emotional arousal while witnessing another's suffering and the costs associated with one's personal failure to act in the face of another's need (self-blame, possible blame from others, embarrassment, and the like).

Various studies have documented that cost influences prosocial behavior. First, research finds that the greater the cost to self of giving direct help, the less likely one is to help (Darley & Batson, 1973; Shotland & Straw, 1976). This was demonstrated, for instance, in a study conducted in the New York City subway (Allen, 1972). Aboard a subway car, a bewildered-looking man asked the participant (a passenger) whether the train was going uptown or downtown. The man in the neighboring seat—a muscular type reading a bodybuilding magazine—responded quickly but gave an obviously wrong answer.

Would you intervene here? High potential costs inhibit bystander intervention in this fight. Most bystanders would feel little responsibility for either man and would wish to avoid entanglement in the fight that is still in progress. © Cathy Yeulet/123rf

Both the bewildered man and the bodybuilder were confederates. The participant could help by correcting this misinformation, but only at the risk of challenging the bodybuilder. Whether the participants helped depended on how threatening the bodybuilder appeared to be. Threat was manipulated by varying his reaction to an incident a minute before. When the bodybuilder had previously threatened physical harm to a person who had stumbled over his outstretched feet, only 16% of the participants helped. When the bodybuilder had only insulted and embarrassed the stumbler, 28% helped. When the bodybuilder had given no reaction to the stumbler, 52% helped. Thus, the greater the anticipated cost of antagonizing the misinforming bodybuilder, the less likely people were to help the bewildered man.

Bystander Intervention in Emergency Situations

Some of the earliest and most interesting social psychological research on helping was inspired by the tragic murder of a young woman named Catherine (Kitty) Genovese. Shortly before 3:20 A.M. on March 13, 1964, Kitty was attacked near her home. Milton Hatch awoke at the first scream. Staring from his apartment window, he saw a woman kneeling on the sidewalk directly across the street and a small man standing over her. "Help me! Help me! Oh, God, he's stabbed me!" she cried. Leaning out his window, Hatch shouted, "Let that girl alone!" As other windows opened and lights went on, the assailant fled in his car. No one called the police. With many eyes now following her, Kitty dragged herself along the street—but not quickly enough. More than ten minutes passed before the neighbors saw her assailant reappear, hunting for her. When he stabbed her a second time, she screamed, "I'm dying! I'm dying!" Still, no one called the police. The third, fatal attack occurred in the vestibule of a building a few doors from Kitty's own entrance. Finally, at 3:55—35 minutes after Kitty's first scream—Harold Klein, who lived at the top of the stairs where Kitty was murdered, called the police. The first patrol car arrived within two minutes, but by then it was too late (Seedman & Hellman, 1975). It was subsequently discovered that a total of 38 people had witnessed the stalking and stabbing.

The tragic story quickly became front page news in New York and across the country, setting off a flurry of social psychological research. The fundamental questions raised by Kitty's murder were, "Under what conditions will bystanders and witnesses intervene in an emergency and give help?" and, "Why do people help in some emergency situations but not in others?" In this section, we will consider this issue in detail and look at various factors that influence whether a bystander will help a victim.

The Decision to Intervene

The term **bystander intervention** denotes a (quick) response by a person witnessing an emergency to help another who is endangered by events. Whether and how to intervene in an emergency is a complex decision because providing assistance often places the helper in considerable danger. These decisions require integration of a great deal of information about self and the environment. Given that there is not time to accurately assess the situation, it is not particularly difficult for the decision-making process to break down and prevent emergency intervention. Latané and Darley (1970) produced a model of this decision-making process made up of five steps. If any of these steps fail, the decision-making process ends and the bystander does not provide assistance.

1   The bystander must notice the situation. Some studies have manipulated how preoccupied potential helpers were, and unsurprisingly, those who were more caught up in their own thoughts were less likely to notice the emergency situation and, therefore, less likely to respond (Darley & Batson, 1973).

2   Once the bystander has noticed the situation, he or she must interpret it as an emergency. Most emergency situations are quite ambiguous, and failure to interpret them as emergencies will produce inaction among bystanders.

3   The bystander must decide that they have some personal responsibility in the situation. One famous study created a situation at a beach where the researchers staged the theft of a radio while its owner was swimming. Most people—about 80%—did nothing to try to stop the thief or to intervene in any manner. However, when the owner of the radio asked the person next to her to keep an eye on the radio while she was swimming, almost all of them confronted the person stealing the radio (Moriarty, 1975). Once they had taken on the responsibility for the radio, they were much more likely to act to help the victim. If bystanders interpret the situation to be "none of their business," they will not respond.

4   The bystander must believe that they know how to help. Sometimes, the assistance required is something

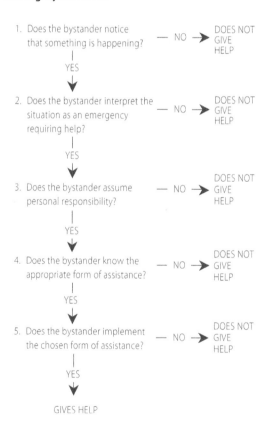

Figure 6.1   Decisions leading to intervention in an emergency

very simple, like dialing 911 for assistance. Other times, the situation is more complex. When witnessing an epileptic seizure, most people have no idea how to respond, and so they do nothing. People with medical training are much more likely to attempt to provide assistance at accident sites than are those without medical knowhow (Cramer, McMaster, Bartell, & Dragna, 1988).

5   The bystander must make the decision to act. Even if all of the first four conditions are fulfilled, people often will hesitate to act because they are afraid of negative consequences to themselves. Typically, people engage in some kind of risk calculation before they act in emergency situations (Fritzsche, Finkelstein, & Penner, 2000). For example, we are often hesitant to break up a fight between other individuals because we are afraid of getting hurt accidentally—or even that the two combatants will turn on us.

The Bystander Effect

In emergency situations, potential helpers are influenced by their relationship to other bystanders (Dovidio, 1984; Latané & Darley, 1970). This influence is apparent at each step in the decision-making process. To investigate the nature of bystander influence, researchers conducted a variety of laboratory studies that simulated emergencies of one kind or another. For instance, in an early experiment (Latané & Rodin, 1969), participants heard a loud crash from the room next door, followed by a woman screaming, "Oh my God, my foot! I ... can't move it. Oh my ankle. I ... can't get this thing off me." In another experiment (Darley & Latané, 1968), participants engaged in a discussion over an intercom suddenly heard someone in the group begin to choke, gasp, and call for help, apparently gripped by an epileptic seizure.

In each experiment, the number of people who were supposedly present when the emergency occurred varied. Participants either believed they were alone with the victim or that one or more bystanders were present. Time and again, the same finding emerged: As the number of bystanders increased, the likelihood that any one of them would help decreased (Latané & Nida, 1981). Bystanders helped most often and most quickly when they were alone with the victim. In other words, simply knowing that other potential helpers were also present inhibited intervention in an emergency. Furthermore, as the number of bystanders increases, the likelihood that any one bystander will help a victim decreases. Social psychologists termed this the **bystander effect**.

Theorists have identified several distinct processes that contribute to the bystander effect. These include social influence regarding the interpretation of the situation, evaluation apprehension, and diffusion of responsibility (Latané, Nida, & Wilson, 1981; Piliavin et al., 1981). Each of these processes affects specific steps in the decision-making process.

Interpreting the Situation. One important element of emergencies is the ambiguity of the situation. In retrospect, the Kitty Genovese situation does not seem that ambiguous at all, but in the heat of the moment, people are often not certain how to respond to unusual situations. Was she really stabbed? Is this a domestic argument that is being dramatized to embarrass one party? Is she acting as bait so the two of them can mug someone else? These and other questions delay reactions and stall a decision to act. During that pause, people look to the reactions of others for cues about what is going on and how to react. If others appear calm, the bystander may decide that nothing special is happening or that whatever is happening requires no help. Likewise, the failure of others to act may signal to the bystander that there is no appropriate way to help. In this way, they inhibit each other from helping.

Bystanders often try to appear calm, avoiding overt signs of worry until they see whether others are alarmed. Through such cautiousness, onlookers unintentionally encourage one another to define the situation as not problematic. The larger the number of apparently unruffled bystanders, the stronger their inhibiting influence is on one another. This effect is illustrated in Figure 6.2, using data from an experiment in which a false epileptic seizure was portrayed. However, consistent with this explanation, increasing the number of bystanders does not inhibit individual helping under certain conditions, such as (1) when observation reveals that

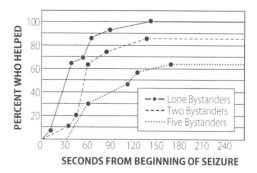

Figure 6.2   The Bystander effect

Students who were discussing, via intercom, their adjustment to college life heard one participant begin to choke, then gasp and call for help, as if he were undergoing a serious nervous seizure. Students intervened to help the victim most quickly and most often when they believed they were the lone bystander to witness the emergency. More than 90% of lone bystanders helped within the first 90 seconds after the seizure. Among those who believed other bystanders were present, however, fewer than 50% intervened in the first two minutes and fewer than 70% did so even after four minutes. The bystander effect refers to the fact that the greater the number of bystanders in an emergency, the less likely any one bystander will help.

Source: Adapted from Darley and Latane, "Bystander Intervention in Emergencies: Diffusion of Responsibility," *Journal of Personality and Social Psychology,* 8, 377–383. Copyright 1968 by the American Psychological Association.

others are indeed alarmed (Darley, Teger, & Lewis, 1973), and (2) when the need for help is so unambiguous that others' reactions are unnecessary to define the situation (Clark & Word, 1972).

Evaluation Apprehension. Bystanders are not only interested in others' reactions; they also realize that other bystanders are an audience for their own reactions. As a result, bystanders may feel evaluation apprehension—concern about what others expect of them and how others will evaluate their behavior. Evaluation apprehension can either inhibit or promote helping. On the one hand, evaluation apprehension inhibits helping when bystanders fear that others will view their intervention as foolish, inappropriate, or wrong. When they see that other witnesses to an emergency are not reacting (as in the Kitty Genovese case), they may infer that the others do not see a need to intervene or might even oppose intervention. In the decision-making sequence, evaluation apprehension mainly affects step 4 (choosing a way to react) and step 5 (deciding whether to implement a chosen course of action). On the other hand, evaluation apprehension promotes helping if there are no cues to suggest that other witnesses oppose intervention or if there is a sense of mutual awareness that some intervention is necessary (Schwartz & Gottlieb, 1976).

Diffusion of Responsibility. When one and only one bystander witnesses an emergency, the responsibility to intervene is focused wholly on that individual. But when there are multiple bystanders, the responsibility to intervene is shared, as is the blame if the victim is not helped. Therefore, a witness is less likely to intervene when others are present. The process wherein a bystander does not take action because others share the responsibility for intervening is called **diffusion of responsibility**. In the decision sequence, diffusion of responsibility operates primarily as step 3 (bystander decides whether he or she has the responsibility to act).

Diffusion of responsibility occurs only when a bystander believes that the other witnesses are capable of helping. We diffuse responsibility less to witnesses who are too far away to take effective action or who are too young to cope with the emergency (Bickman, 1971; Ross, 1971). Similarly, the tendency to diffuse responsibility is particularly strong if a bystander feels less competent than others who are present. Bystanders helped less, for example, when one of the other witnesses to a seizure was a premed student with experience working in an emergency ward (Pantin & Carver, 1982; Schwartz & Clausen, 1970).

Seeking and Receiving Help

Although the bulk of this chapter focused on giving help rather than receiving it, recipients' reactions to receiving help—and people's willingness to seek help in the first place—are important topics that also deserve attention. It seems obvious that the generally expected response to helping is gratitude and appreciation. But that is not always the case. In fact, help can elicit resentment, hostility, and anxiety.

Help and Obligation. When help is sought and received, resources (such as labor and materials) are transferred from one person to another. If the norm of reciprocity is salient in the situation, the person receiving help may feel obligated or indebted to the helper (Greenberg & Westcott, 1983). In consequence, needy persons (in nonemergency situations) sometimes experience a dilemma. On the one hand, they can ask for help and possibly endure some embarrassment or social obligation; on the other hand, they can suffer through the difficulties of trying to solve their problems on their own (Gross & McMullen, 1983). In cases in which the recipient has the opportunity and ability to reciprocate, there may be no problem. But in cases in which this is more difficult, it may create a lingering sense of indebtedness in the needy toward the helper (Nadler, 1991; Wills, 1992), and they may develop resentment and negative sentiments toward the benefactor (Clark, Gotay, & Mills, 1974; Gross & Latané, 1974).

Threats to Self-Esteem. In studying people's reactions to receiving help, theorists have proposed that an important determinant of whether help is appreciated or resented is the extent to which the help undermines the recipient's self-esteem (Nadler, 1991; Nadler & Fisher, 1986; Shell & Eisenberg, 1992). Although helping provides relief, it can also impair a recipient's self-esteem and sense of self-reliance. The avowed purpose of welfare, for instance, has been to aid impoverished individuals and to help families escape hunger while they establish themselves as self-supporting. Yet welfare and other forms of assistance are sometimes given reluctantly or in ways that do not promote these outcomes. Intentionally or otherwise, helpers may communicate the message that those who need and accept help are inferior in status and ability because they fail to display self-reliance and achievement (DePaulo & Fisher, 1980; Rosen, 1984). Taking help can cause embarrassment for recipients because it challenges the norm of self-reliance: an expectation that individuals should take care of themselves and their dependents. Similarly, students might be reticent to ask for help for fear that their professor or peers will consider them incompetent or unintelligent.

Similarity of Help Provider. Surveys regarding help seeking for personal and psychological problems indicate that we are most likely to ask people who are similar to us for assistance. Wills (1992) finds that persons looking for help of this type are several times more likely to seek it from friends, acquaintances, or family members than from professionals or strangers.

However, the helper's similarity to the recipient is a complex factor in help giving and help seeking. Help that implies an important inadequacy is often more threatening to our self-esteem when we receive it from those who are similar to us in attitudes or background than from those who are dissimilar (Nadler, 1987; Nadler & Fisher, 1984). Similarity can aggravate recipients' self-evaluations, because similar helpers are relevant targets for self-comparison (say, "If we are both alike, why do I need help while you can give it?"). People who accept aid from helpers similar to themselves on a task central to their self-concept report lower self-esteem, less self-confidence, and more personal threat than when they accept aid from dissimilar helpers (DePaulo, Nadler & Fisher, 1983; Nadler, Fisher, & Ben-Itzhak, 1983).

Other Forms of Prosocial Behavior

Although much of this chapter focused on helping specific others, there are more organizationally based forms of prosocial behavior that are also of interest to social psychologists. This final section highlights two specific types: philanthropy and volunteering.

Philanthropy. Charitable giving, or philanthropy, includes both small-scale donations (dropping your change in the plastic container at the grocery store counter) or large monetary donations (making a large gift to endow an annual scholarship at your local university). Such giving is particularly prevalent in churches and religious organizations, in which there is a tithing norm that encourages members to donate 10% of their income to charity or the church. In part because of the large amount of religious charitable giving, the United States is considered a "giving culture" (Wright, 2001). However, researchers suggest that this culture is sustained, in part, because people in the United Stated tend to feel that they have something to gain by giving, whether tax credits and deductions, enhanced social status, or something else.

People are more likely to give when certain factors are present. In addition to some discussed earlier (for example, an awareness of need and perceptions of deservingness), research suggests that individuals' are more motivated to donate money when they are directly asked to contribute. In other words, we are more likely to give when we are approached and made aware of the opportunity to give (Bryant, Jeon-Slaughter, Kang, & Tax, 2003). We are also more likely to give when the organization who needs contributions reflects values that are similar to our own and when we feel that our gift can make an important difference (Parsons, 2003). Giving not only helps charitable organizations but has also been shown to result in an enhanced mood—"a warm glow"—after giving (Meier, 2006).

Volunteering. Volunteering—freely giving time for the benefit of another person, group, or organization—also benefits organizations (Wilson, 2000). It has four distinct attributes that set it apart from other forms of prosocial behavior: *longevity* (it is usually institutionalized, ongoing, and quite often repeated), *planfulness* (it is thought out before being done), *nonobligatory* (it is not motivated by a concern for a specific individual with whom one has a relationship), and is done in *an organizational context* (most volunteering is not an individual acting alone) (Penner, 2002).

Certain qualities of individuals make them much more likely to volunteer. For example, greater social integration—being embedded in social networks—increases both the chances that someone will be asked to volunteer and their likelihood of agreeing to do so (Penner, Dovidio, Piliavin, & Schroeder, 2005). Being socially integrated might also give individuals greater awareness of problems that need attention. Research also suggests that those who are married, religious, and/or well educated are more likely to volunteer, as are women and those of higher social classes (Wilson, 2000; Wilson & Janoski, 1995; Wilson & Musick, 1997). Although findings are mixed, it appears that volunteering is beneficial to one's health, particularly mental health and well-being (Greenfield & Marks, 2004).

Summary

Prosocial behavior is any behavior that helps another. Helping is a specific type of prosocial behavior that benefits others. Altruism, another kind of prosocial behavior, is voluntary behavior intended to benefit another with no expectation of external reward. This intent is an important component of altruism.

Motivation to Help. Actors often engage in some kind of calculation of costs and benefits before engaging in prosocial behavior and will often help others for some type of reward. However, helping without intention of benefit (altruism) typically stems from humans' ability to experience empathy. Prosocial behavior may also be passed from parent to child through evolutionary processes that enhance the persistence of an individual's genes in future generations. Even self-sacrifice can be beneficial in perpetuating one's genes if targeted at those who share genetic material. If the net costs are too high, however, they will not act.

Helpers and Targets. Many characteristics of individuals affect the chance of receiving help from another. Acquaintanceship and liking of another person can increase the chances of helping behavior when that person is in need. Similarity between actors and targets can substantially increase the chances of helping behavior. Potential helpers also consider whether the target deserves help. Innocent individuals are more likely to receive help.

The Contexts of Prosocial Behavior. External factors, both norms and situational influences, can have powerful effects on prosocial behavior. We are more likely to help those who are dependent on us (the norm of social responsibility) and those who have helped us in the past (the norm of reciprocity). Personal norms that facilitate helping and determine how we help are often related to salient role and social identities, including gender. The presence of a model who demonstrates prosocial behavior facilitates helping. However, moods have mixed effects. In deciding when to help, we weigh the benefits and costs both to the persons in need and to ourselves. Individuals can learn about the costs and benefits through a social learning process.

Bystander Intervention in Emergency Situations. Prior to actually giving help in emergencies, bystanders go through a decision sequence. A bystander must realize that something is happening, interpret the situation as an emergency, decide that he or she has the responsibility to act, know or recognize an appropriate form of assistance, and decide to implement the chosen behavior. Ambiguous social situations cause participants to look for cues that might lead toward helping. Depending on others for these cues can produce a failure to provide help while everyone waits for cues from others that action is required, known as the *bystander effect*. The more observers there are to an emergency, the less likely any one person is to act because of a diffusion of responsibility.

Seeking and Receiving Help. Help is not always sought after or easily accepted by the targets because they are sometimes reticent to bear the obligations the help entails and because the assistance may threaten their self-esteem. The more similar a target is to a helper, the more embarrassing it may be to accept assistance.

Other Forms of Prosocial Behavior. Volunteering and philanthropy are prosocial behaviors that tend to benefit organizations rather than individuals.

List of Key Terms and Concepts

altruism (p. 132)

bystander effect (p. 151)

bystander intervention (p. 149)

diffusion of responsibility (p. 153)

egoism (p. 133)

empathy (p. 134)

helping (p. 132)

norm of reciprocity (p. 144)

personal norms (p. 145)

prosocial behavior (p. 132)

social responsibility norm (p. 143)

Critical Thinking Skill: Creative Thinking

Throughout this book, you have been exposed to research that may or may not relate to your personal experience. Although it might be interesting to you, you might ask what you can or cannot do with that information in your own life.

Take, for example, research suggesting that heterosexual married couples who engage in prosocial behaviors, like small acts of kindness and displays of respect and affection, and who are willing to forgive each other's faults or mistakes experienced more marital satisfaction and were less likely to imagine divorcing their partner (Dew & Wilcox, 2013). You likely know people who are married, so you could share this information with them in hopes of improving their relationship or helping to explain why they are so happily married. But could it have further-reaching influence? What might you take from it if you are not married?

To engage in critical creative thinking, we search for alternative applications of what we have learned.

The most obvious application would be to nonmarried couples. Whether cohabiting or simply dating, whether heterosexual or same-sex, these same behaviors from the Dew and Wilcox (2013) study likely strengthen relationships and lessen the chances of either person imagining ending the relationship. Can you think of examples of this?

But what about other types of relationships? Can you use these findings and the basis for them to enhance your platonic friendships or to create a better relationship with your mother or your daughter? What types of kindnesses, displays of respect, and forgiveness would be applicable in those relationships? What about your relationships with your neighbors or coworkers? Could you share the findings with your employer to help her think of ways she might increase employee satisfaction and reduce turnover?

Scientists often use this type of creative thinking to consider what questions to explore next. A sociologist reading this research might consider recruiting a sample of same-sex couples and asking similar questions to determine whether the relationship between prosocial behaviors and relationship satisfaction and commitment was as strong or perhaps stronger in those couples (Carrington, 1999). However, even if you are not planning to conduct your own research, you can benefit from this creative thinking as well. Considering alternative applications not only helps you understand the specific material but also encourages you to engage with the world in a deliberate and involved way.

References

Aderman, D., & Berkowitz, L. (1983). Self-concern and the unwillingness to be helpful. *Social Psychology Quarterly, 46*(4), 293–301.

Allen, H. (1972). Bystander intervention and helping on the subway. In L. Bickman & T. Henchy (Eds.), *Beyond the laboratory: Field research in social psychology*. (pp. 22–33). New York: McGraw-Hill.

Archer, J. (1991). Human sociobiology: Basic concepts and limitations. *Journal of Social Issues, 47*(3), 11–26.

Barnett, M. A. (1987). Empathy and related responses in children. In N. Eisenberg & J. Strayer (Eds.), *Empathy and its development* (pp. 146–162). New York: Cambridge University Press.

Baron, R. A. (1971). Reducing the influence of an aggressive model: The restraining effects of discrepant modeling cues. *Journal of Personality and Social Psychology, 20*, 240–245.

Bar-Tal, D. (1976). *Prosocial behavior: Theory and research*. New York: Halsted.

Batson, C. D. (1987). Prosocial motivation: Is it ever truly altruistic? In L. Berkowitz (Ed.), *Advances in experimental social psychology* (Vol. 20, pp. 65–122). New York: Academic Press.

Batson, C. D. (1991). The altruism question: Toward a social psychological answer. Hillsdale, NJ: Erlbaum.

Batson, C. D. (2011). *Altruism in humans*. New York: Oxford University Press.

Batson, C. D., Cochran, P. J., Biederman, M. F., Blosser, J. L., Ryan, M. J., & Vogt, B. (1978). Failure to help when in a hurry: Callousness or conflict? *Personality and Social Psychology Bulletin, 4*(1), 97–101.

Batson, C. D., & Coke, J. S. (1981). Empathy: A source of altruistic motivation for helping? In J. P. Rushton & R. M. Sorrentino (Eds.), *Altruism and helping behavior*. (pp. 167–187). Hillsdale, NJ: Erlbaum.

Batson, C. D., Duncan, B., Ackerman, P., Buckley, T., & Birch, K. (1981). Is empathic emotion a source of altruistic motivation? *Journal of Personality and Social Psychology, 40*, 290–302.

Batson, C. D., & Oleson, K. C. (1991). Current status of the empathy-altruism hypothesis. In M. S. Clark (Ed.), *Review of personality and social psychology: Vol. 12. Prosocial behavior* (pp. 62–85). Newbury Park, CA: Sage.

Batson, C. D., O'Quin, K., Fultz, J., Vanderplas, M., & Isen, A. M. (1983). Influence of self-reported distress and empathy on egoistic versus altruistic motivation to help. *Journal of Personality and Social Psychology, 45*, 706–718.

Benson, P. L., Karabenick, S. A., & Lerner, R. M. (1973). Pretty pleases: The effect of physical attraction, race, and sex on receiving help. *Journal of Experimental Social Psychology, 12*, 409–415.

Berkowitz, L. (1972). Frustrations, comparisons, and other sources of emotion arousal as contributors to social unrest. *Journal of Social Issues, 28*(1), 77–91.

Berkowitz, L., Klanderman, S. B., & Harris, R. (1964). Effects of experimenter awareness and sex of subject and experimenter on reactions to dependency relationships. *Sociometry, 27*, 327–337.

Bickman, L. (1971). The effect of social status on the honesty of others. *Journal of Social Psychology, 85*(1), 87–92.

Bienenstock, E., & Bianchi, A. (2004). Activating performance expectations and status differences through gift exchange: Experimental results. *Social Psychology Quarterly, 67*, 310–318.

Brody, E. M. (2004). *Women in the middle: Their parent care years.* New York: Springer.

Bryan, J. H., & Davenport, M. (1968). *Donations to the needy: Correlates of financial contributions to the destitute* (Research Bulletin No. 68–1). Princeton, NJ: Educational Testing Service.

Bryant, W. K, Jeon-Slaughter, H., Kang, H., & Tax, A. (2003). Participation in philanthropic activities: Donating money and time. *Journal of Consumer Policy, 26,* 43–73.

Buck, R., & Ginsburg, B. (1991). Emotional communication and altruism: The communicative gene hypothesis. *Altruism: Review of Personality and Social Psychology, 12,* 149–175.

Burnstein, E., Crandall, C., & Kitayama, S. (1994). An evolved heuristic for altruism: Evidence for a human propensity to calculate inclusive fitness. *Journal of Personality and Social Psychology, 67,* 773–789.

Buss, D. M. (1999). *Evolutionary psychology.* Boston: Allyn and Bacon.

Buss, D. M., & Kenrick, D. T. (1998). Evolutionary social psychology. In D. T. Gilbert, S. T. Fiske, & G. Lindzey (Eds.), *The handbook of social psychology* (4th ed., pp. 982–1026). Boston: McGraw-Hill.

Caporeal, L. R. (2001). Evolutionary psychology: Toward a unifying theory and a hybrid science. *Annual Review of Psychology, 52,* 607–628.

Carlson, M., Charlin, V., & Miller, N. (1988). Positive mood and helping behavior: A test of six hypotheses. *Journal of Personality and Social Psychology, 55*(2), 211–229.

Carnevale, P. J., Pruitt, D. G., & Carrington, P. I. (1982). Effects of future dependence, liking, and repeated requests for help on helping behavior. *Social Psychology Quarterly, 45*(1), 9–14.

Carrington, C. (1999). *No place like home: Relationships and family life among lesbians and gay men.* Chicago: University of Chicago Press.

Cialdini, R. B., Kenrick, D. T., & Baumann, D. J. (1982). Effects of mood on prosocial behavior in children and adults. *The development of prosocial behavior,* 339–359.

Cialdini, R. B., Schaller, M., Houlihan, D., Arps, K., Fultz, J., & Beaman, A. L. (1987). Empathy-based helping: Is it selflessly or selfishly motivated. *Journal of Personality and Social Psychology, 52*(4), 749–758.

Clark, M. S., Gotay, C. C., & Mills, J. (1974). Acceptance of help as a function of the potential helper and opportunity to repay. *Journal of Applied Social Psychology, 4,* 224–229.

Clark, R. D., & Word, L. E. (1972). Why don't bystanders help? Because of ambiguity? *Journal of Personality and Social Psychology, 24,* 392–400.

Cramer, R., McMaster, M., Bartell, P., & Dragna, M. (1988). Subject competence and minimization of the bystander effect. *Journal of Applied Social Psychology, 18,* 1132–1148.

Cuddy, A. J., Rock, M. S., & Norton, M. I. (2007). Aid in the aftermath of Hurricane Katrina: Inferences of secondary emotions and intergroup helping. *Group Processes & Intergroup Relations, 10*(1), 107–118.

Cunningham, M. R., Steinberg, J., & Grev, R. (1980). Wanting to and having to help: Separate motivations for positive mood and guilt-induced helping. *Journal of Personality and Social Psychology, 38*(2), 181.

Darley, J. M., & Batson, C. D. (1973). From Jerusalem to Jericho: A study of situational and dispositional variables in helping behavior. *Journal of Personality and Social Psychology, 27,* 100–108.

Darley, J. M., & Latané, B. (1968). Bystander intervention in emergencies: Diffusion of responsibility. *Journal of Personality and Social Psychology, 8,* 377–383.

Darley, J. M., Teger, A. I., & Lewis, L. D. (1973). Do groups always inhibit individuals' response to potential emergencies? *Journal of Personality and Social Psychology, 26,* 395–399.

DePaulo, B. M., & Fisher, J. D. (1980). The costs of asking for help. *Basic and Applied Social Psychology, 1,* 23–35.

DePaulo, B. M., Nadler, A., & Fisher, J. D. (1983). *New directions in helping: Help seeking* (Vol. 2). New York: Academic Press.

Dew, J., & Wilcox, B. W. (2013). Generosity and the maintenance of marital quality. *Journal of Marriage and Family, 75*(5), 1218–1228.

Dovidio, J. F. (1984). Helping behavior and altruism: An empirical and conceptual overview. In L. Berkowitz (Ed.), *Advances in experimental social psychology* (Vol. 17, pp. 362–427). New York: Academic Press.

Dovidio, J. F., Allen, J. L., & Schroeder, D. A. (1990). Specificity of empathy-induced helping: Evidence for altruistic motivation. *Journal of Personality and Social Psychology, 59*, 249–260.

Dovidio, J. F., & Gaertner, S. L. (1981). The effects of race, status, and ability on helping behavior. *Social Psychology Quarterly, 44*, 192–203.

Dovidio, J. F., Piliavin, J. A., Gaertner, S. L., Schroeder, D. A., & Clark, R. D. (1991). The arousal/cost-reward model and the process of intervention: A review of the evidence. In M. S. Clark (Ed.), *Review of personality and social psychology: Vol. 12. Prosocial behavior* (pp. 86–118). Newbury Park, CA: Sage.

Dovidio, J. F., Piliavin, J. A., Schroeder, D. A., & Penner, L. (2006). *The social psychology of prosocial behavior.* Hillsdale, NJ: Erlbaum.

Dunbar, R. (1996). *Grooming, gossip, and the evolution of language.* Harvard University Press.

Dynes, R. R., & Quarantelli, E. L. (1980). Helping behavior in large-scale disasters. In D. H. Smith & J. Macaulay (Eds.), *Participation in social and political activities* (pp. 339–354). San Francisco: Jossey-Bass.

Eagly, A. H., & Crowley, M. (1986). Gender and helping behavior: A meta-analytic review of the social psychological literature. *Psychological Bulletin, 100*, 283–308.

Eisenberg, N., & Fabes, R. A. (1991). Prosocial behavior and empathy: A multimethod developmental perspective. In M. S. Clark (ed.), *Review of personality and social psychology, Vol. 12. Prosocial behavior* (pp. 34–61). Newbury Park, CA: Sage.

Eisenberg, N., & Miller, P. A. (1987). The relation of empathy to prosocial and related behaviors. *Psychological Bulletin, 101*, 91–119.

Feinberg, M., Willer, R., Stellar, J., & Keltner, D. (2012). The virtues of gossip: Reputational information sharing as prosocial behavior. *Journal of Personality and Social Psychology, 102*(5), 1015–1030.

Fisher, J., Nadler, D., & Whitcher-Alagna, S. (1982). Recipient reactions to aid. *Psychological Bulletin, 91*, 33–54.

Form, W. H., & Nosow, S. (1958). *Community in disaster.* New York: Harper.

Frey, D. L., & Gaertner, S. L. (1986). Helping and the avoidance of inappropriate interracial behavior: A strategy that perpetuates a nonprejudiced self-image. *Journal of Personality and Social Psychology, 50*, 1083–1090.

Fritzsche, B. A., Finkelstein, M. A., & Penner, L. A. (2000). To help or not to help: Capturing individuals' decision policies. *Social Behavior and Personality, 28*, 561–578.

Fultz, J., Batson, C. D., Fortenbach, V. A., McCarthy, P. M., & Varney, L. L. (1986). Social evaluation and the empathy-altruism hypothesis. *Journal of Personality and Social Psychology, 50*, 761–769.

Gelfand, D. M., & Hartmann, D. P. (1982). Response consequences and attributions: Two contributors to prosocial behavior. In N. Eisenberg (Ed.), *The development of prosocial behavior.* (pp. 165–196). New York: Academic Press.

Gergen, K. J., Ellsworth, P., Maslach, C., & Siepel, M. (1975). Obligation, donor resources, and reactions to aid in three cultures. *Journal of Personality and Social Psychology, 31*, 390–400.

Gergen, K. J., Gergen, M. M., & Meter, K. (1972). Individual orientations to prosocial behavior. *Journal of Social Issues, 28(3)*, 105–130.

Greenberg, M., & Frisch, D. (1972). Effect of intentionality on willingness to reciprocate a favor. *Journal of Experimental Social Psychology, 8*, 99–111.

Greenberg, M. S., & Westcott, D. R. (1983). Indebtedness as a mediator of reactions to aid. In J. D. Fisher, A. Nadler, & B. M. DePaulo (Eds.), *New directions in helping: Vol. 1. Recipient reactions to aid* (pp. 85–112). San Diego, CA: Academic Press.

Greenfield, E. A., & Marks, N. F. (2004). Formal volunteering as a protective factor for older adults' psychological well-being. *Journal of Gerontology, 59B*, 258–264.

Gross, A. E., & Latané, J. G. (1974). Receiving help, reciprocation, and interpersonal attraction. *Journal of Applied Social Psychology, 4*, 210–223.

Gross, A. E., & McMullen, P. A. (1983). Models of the help seeking process. In B. M. DePaulo, A. Nadler, & J. D. Fisher (Eds.), *New directions in helping: Vol. 2. Help seeking* (pp. 47–73). New York: Academic Press.

Hamilton, W. (1964). The genetical evolution of social behavior, I & II. *Journal of Theoretical Biology, 7*, 1–52.

Hamilton, W. D. (1964). The genetical evolution of social behaviour. I. *Journal of Theoretical Biology, 7*(1), 1–16.

Hardy, C., & Van Vugt, M. (2006). Nice guys finish first: The competitive altruism hypothesis. *Personality and Social Psychology Bulletin, 32*, 1402–1413.

Holmes, J. G., Miller, D. T., & Lerner, M. J. (2002). Committing altruism under the cloak of self-interest: The exchange fiction. *Journal of Experimental Social Psychology, 38*(2), 144–151.

Hopper, J. R., & Nielsen, J. M. (1991). Recycling as altruistic behavior: Normative and behavioral strategies to expand participation in a community recycling program. *Environment and Behavior, 23*, 195–220.

Hornstein, H. A. (1978). Promotive tension and prosocial behavior: A Lewinian analysis. In L. Wispe (Ed.), *Altruism, sympathy, and helping*. (pp. 177–207). New York: Academic Press.

Huston, T. L., Ruggiero, M., Conner, R., & Geis, G. (1981). Bystander intervention into crime: A study based on naturally-occurring episodes. *Social Psychology Quarterly*, 14–23.

Kalmijn, M., & De Graaf, P. M. (2012). Life course changes of children and well-being of parents. *Journal of Marriage and Family, 74*(2), 269–280.

Kelley, K., & Byrne, D. (1976). Attraction and altruism: With a little help from my friends. *Journal of Research in Personality, 10*, 59–68.

Kerber, K. W. (1984). The perception of nonemergency helping situations: Costs, rewards, and the altruistic personality. *Journal of Personality, 52*, 177–187.

Ketelaar, T., & Ellis, B. J. (2000). Are evolutionary explanations unfalsifiable? Evolutionary psychology and the Lakatosian philosophy of science. *Psychological Inquiry, 11*, 1–21.

Kitcher, P. (1985). *Vaulting ambition: Sociobiology and the quest for human nature*. Cambridge, MA: MIT Press.

Krebs, D. L., & Miller, D. T. (1985). Altruism and aggression. In G. Lindzey & E. Aronson (Eds.), *The handbook of social psychology* (3rd ed., pp. 1–71). New York: Random House.

Kruger, D. J. (2001). Inclusive fitness and judgments of helping behaviors: Adaptations for kin directed altruism. *Social Behavior and Personality, 29*, 323–330.

Laner, M. R., Benin, M. H., & Ventrone, N. A. (2001). Bystander attitudes toward victims of violence: Who's worth helping? *Deviant Behavior, 22*(1), 23–42.

Latané, B., & Darley, J. M. (1970). *The unresponsive bystander: Why doesn't he help?* New York: Appleton-Century-Crofts.

Latané, B., & Nida, S. (1981). Ten years of research on group size and helping. *Psychological Bulletin, 89*(2), 308–324.

Latané, B., Nida, S. A., & Wilson, D. W. (1981). The effects of group size on helping behavior. In J. P. Rushton & R. M. Sorrentino (Eds.), *Altruism and helping behavior: Social, personality, and developmental perspectives.* (pp. 287–313). Hillsdale, NJ: Erlbaum.

Latané, B., & Rodin, J. (1969). A lady in distress: Inhibiting effects of friends and strangers on bystander intervention. *Journal of Experimental Social Psychology, 5*(2), 189–202.

Levine, M., Prosser, A., Evans, D., & Reicher, S. (2005). Identity and emergency intervention: How social group membership and inclusiveness of group boundaries shape helping behavior. *Personality and Social Psychology Bulletin, 31,* 443–453.

Lynch, J. C., & Cohen, J. L. (1978). The use of subjective expected utility theory as an aid to understanding variables that influence helping behavior. *Journal of Personality and Social Psychology, 36,* 1138–1151.

Mallozzi, J., McDermott, V., & Kayson, W. A. (1990). Effects of sex, type of dress, and location on altruistic behavior. *Psychological Reports, 67,* 1103–1106.

Maner, J. K., & Gailliot, M. T. (2007). Altruism and egoism: Prosocial motivations for helping depend on relationship context. *European Journal of Social Psychology, 37*(2), 347–358.

Manucia, G. K., Baumann, D. J., & Cialdini, R. B. (1984). Mood influences on helping: Direct effects or side effects. *Journal of Personality and Social Psychology, 46*(2), 357–364.

Meier, S. (2006). *The economics of non-selfish behaviour.* Northampton, MA: Edward Elgar.

Meyer, P. (2000). The sociobiology of human cooperation: The interplay of ultimate and proximate causes. In J. M. G. van der Dennen, D. Smillie, & D. R. Wilson, (Eds.), *The Darwinian heritage and sociobiology.* (pp. 49–65). Westport, CT: Praeger.

Miles, R. H. (1977). Role-set configuration as a predictor of role conflict and ambiguity in complex organizations. *Sociometry, 40,* 21–34.

Moriarty, T. (1975). Crime, commitment, and the responsive bystander: Two field experiments. *Journal of Personality and Social Psychology, 31,* 370–376.

Nadler, A. (1987). Determinants of help seeking behaviour: The effects of helper's similarity, task centrality and recipient's self esteem. *European Journal of Social Psychology, 17*(1), 57–67.

Nadler, A. (1991). Help-seeking behavior: Psychological costs and instrumental benefits. In M. S. Clark (Ed.), *Review of personality and social psychology: Vol. 12. Prosocial behavior* (pp. 290–311). Newbury Park, CA: Sage.

Nadler, A., & Fisher, J. D. (1984). Effects of donor-recipient relationships on recipients' reactions to aid. In E. Staub, D. Bar-Tal, J. Karylowski, & J. Reykowski (Eds.), *Development and maintenance of prosocial behavior: International perspectives on positive morality.* (pp. 397–418). New York: Plenum.

Nadler, A., & Fisher, J. D. (1986). The role of threat to self-esteem and perceived control in recipient reaction to help: Theory development and empirical validation. In L. Berkowitz (Ed.), *Advances in experimental social psychology* (Vol. 19, pp. 81–122). San Diego, CA: Academic Press.

Nadler, A., Fisher, J. D., & Ben-Itzhak, S. (1983). With a little help from my friend: Effect of single or multiple act aid as a function of donor and task characteristics. *Journal of Personality and Social Psychology, 44,* 310–321.

Nadler, A., Mayseless, O., Peri, N., & Chemerinski, A. (1985). Effects of opportunity to reciprocate and self-esteem on help-seeking behavior. *Journal of Personality, 53,* 23–35.

Otten, C. A., Penner, L. A., & Waugh, G. (1988). That's what friends are for: The determinants of psychological helping. *Journal of Social and Clinical Psychology, 7*(1), 34–41.

Pantin, H. M., & Carver, C. S. (1982). Induced competence and the bystander effect. *Journal of Applied Social Psychology, 12*(2), 100–111.

Parsons, L. M. (2003). Is accounting information from nonprofit organizations useful to donors? A review of charitable giving and value-relevance. *Journal of Accounting Literature, 22,* 104–129.

Pearce, P. L. (1980). Strangers, travelers, and Greyhound terminals: A study of small-scale helping behaviors. *Journal of Personality and Social Psychology, 38*, 935–940.

Penner, L. A. (2002). Dispositional and organizational influences on sustained volunteerism: An interactionist perspective. *Journal of Social Issues, 58*(3), 447–467.

Penner, L. A., Dovidio, J. F., Piliavin, J. A., & Schroeder, D. A. (2005). Prosocial behavior: Multilevel perspectives. *Annual Review of Psychology, 56*, 365–392.

Perlow, L., & Weeks, J. (2002). Who's helping whom? Layers of culture and workplace behavior. *Journal of Organizational Behavior, 23*(4), 345–361.

Piferi, R. L., Jobe, R. L., & Jones, W. H. (2006). Giving to others during national tragedy: The effects of altruistic and egoistic motivations on long-term giving. *Journal of Social and Personal Relationships, 23*(1), 171–184.

Piliavin, I. M., Rodin, J., & Piliavin, J. A. (1969). Good samaritanism: An underground phenomenon. *Journal of Personality and Social Psychology, 13*(4), 289–299.

Piliavin, J. A., & Callero, P. L. (1991). *Giving blood: The development of an altruistic identity.* Baltimore, MD: Johns Hopkins University Press.

Piliavin, J. A., & Charng, H.-W. (1990). Altruism: A review of recent theory and research. *Annual Review of Sociology, 16*, 27–65.

Piliavin, J. A., Dovidio, J. F., Gaertner, S. L., & Clark, R. D. (1981). *Emergency intervention.* New York: Academic Press.

Piliavin, J. A., Grube, J. A., & P. L. Callero. (2002). Role as resource for action in public service. *Journal of Social Issues, 58*, 469–485.

Piliavin, J. A., & Unger, R. K. (1985). The helpful but helpless female: Myth or reality? In G. O'Leary, R. K. Unger, & B. S. Wallston (Eds.), *Women, gender and social psychology* (pp. 149–189). Hillsdale, HJ: Erlbaum.

Rogers, M., Miller, N., Mayer, F. S., & Duval, S. (1982). Personal responsibility and salience of the request for help: Determinants of the relation between negative affect and helping behavior. *Journal of Personality and Social Psychology, 43*(5), 956–970.

Rosen, S. (1984). Some paradoxical status implications of helping and being helped. In E. Staub, D. Bar-Tal, J. Karylowski, & J. Reykowski (Eds.), *Development and maintenance of prosocial behavior: International perspectives on positive morality.* (pp. 359–377). New York: Plenum.

Rosenhan, D. L., Salovey, P., & Hargis, K. (1981). The joys of helping: Focus of attention mediates the impact of positive affect on altruism. *Journal of Personality and Social Psychology, 40*(5), 899–905.

Ross, A. S. (1971). Effect of increased responsibility on bystander intervention: The presence of children. *Journal of Personality and Social Psychology, 19*(3), 306.

Rushton, J. P., Russell, R. J., & Wells, P. A. (1984). Genetic similarity theory: Beyond kin selection. *Behaviour Genetics, 14*, 179–193.

Salovey, P., Mayer, J. D., & Rosenhan, D. L. (1991). Mood and helping: Mood as a motivator of helping and helping as a regulator of mood. In M. S. Clark (Ed.), *Review of personality and social psychology, Vol. 12. Prosocial behavior* (pp. 215–237). Newbury Park, CA: Sage.

Schaller, M., & Cialdini, R. B. (1988). The economics of empathic helping: Support for a mood management motive. *Journal of Experimental Social Psychology, 24*(2), 163–181.

Schroeder, D. A., Penner, L. A., Dovidio, J. F., & Piliavin, J. A. (1995). *The psychology of helping and altruism: Problems and puzzles.* New York: McGraw-Hill.

Schwartz, S. H., & Clausen, G. T. (1970). Responsibility, norms, and helping in an emergency. *Journal of Personality and Social Psychology, 16*(2), 299–310.

Schwartz, S. H., & Fleishman, J. (1978). Personal norms and the mediation of legitimacy effects on helping. *Social Psychology, 41*, 306–315.

Schwartz, S. H., & Gottlieb, A. (1976). Bystander reactions to a violent theft: Crime in Jerusalem. *Journal of Personality and Social Psychology*, *34*(6), 1188–1199.

Schwartz, S. H., & Howard, J. A. (1981). A normative decision-making model of altruism. In J. P. Rushton & R. M. Sorrentino (Eds.), *Altruism and helping behavior*. (pp. 189–211). Hillsdale, NJ: Erlbaum.

Schwartz, S. H., & Howard, J. A. (1982). Helping and cooperation: A self-based motivational model. In V. J. Derlega & J. Grzelak (Eds.), *Cooperation and helping behavior: Theories and research* (pp. 327–353). New York: Academic Press.

Schwartz, S. H., & Howard, J. A. (1984). Internalized values as motivators of altruism. In E. Staub, E. Bar-Tal, J. Karylowski, & J. Reykowski (Eds.), *Development and maintenance of prosocial behavior: International perspectives on positive morality*. (pp. 229–255). New York: Plenum.

Seedman, A. A., & Hellman, P. (1975). *Chief!* New York: Avon.

Shell, R. M., & Eisenberg, N. (1992). A developmental model of recipients' reactions to aid. *Psychological Bulletin*, *111*, 413–433.

Sherman, P. (1980). The limits of ground squirrel nepotism. In G. Barlow & J. Silverberg (Eds.), *Sociobiology: Beyond nature/nurture?* (pp. 505–544). Boulder, CO: Westview.

Shotland, R. L., & Stebbins, C. A. (1983). Emergency and cost as determinants of helping behavior and the slow accumulation of social psychological knowledge. *Social Psychology Quarterly*, *46*, 36–46.

Shotland, R. L., & Straw, M. K. (1976). Bystander response to an assault: When a man attacks a woman. *Journal of Personality and Social Psychology*, *34*, 990–999.

Sime, J. D. (1983). Affiliative behavior during escape to building exits. *Journal of Environmental Psychology*, *3*, 21–41.

Simmons, R. G. (1991). Presidential address on altruism and sociology. *Sociological Quarterly*, *32*, 1–22.

Trivers, R. L. (1983). The evolution of cooperation. In D. L. Bridgeman (Ed.), *The nature of prosocial behavior*. New York: Academic Press.

Weiner, B., Perry, R. P., & Magnusson, J. (1988). An attributional analysis of reactions to stigmas. *Journal of Personality and Social Psychology*, *55*, 738–748.

Wilke, H., & Lanzetta, J. T. (1982). The obligation to help: Factors affecting response to help received. *European Journal of Social Psychology*, *12*, 315–319.

Wills, T. A. (1992). The helping process in the context of personal relationships. In S. Spacapan & S. Oskamp (Eds.), *Helping and being helped: Naturalistic studies* (pp. 17–48). Newbury Park, CA: Sage.

Wilson, E. O. (1971). *The insect societies*. Cambridge, MA: Belknap.

Wilson, E. O. (1975). *Sociobiology: The new synthesis*. Cambridge, MA: Harvard University Press.

Wilson, E. O. (1978). *On human nature*. Cambridge, MA: Harvard University Press.

Wilson, J. (2000). Volunteering. *Annual Review of Sociology*, *26*, 215–240.

Wilson, J., & Janoski, T. (1995). The contribution of religion to volunteer work. *Sociology of Religion*, *56*(2), 137–152.

Wilson, J., & Musick, M. (1997). Who cares? Toward an integrated theory of volunteer work. *American Sociological Review*, *62*(5), 694–713.

Wright, K. (2001). Generosity vs. altruism: Philanthropy and charity in the United States and United Kingdom. *Voluntas: International Journal of Voluntary and Nonprofit Organizations*, *12*(4), 399–416.

Aggression

John DeLamater, Daniel Myers, and Jessica Collett

Introduction

- On April 16, 2007, a single gunman, a senior at Virginia Tech, entered a residence hall on campus and gunned down two students. About two hours later, he entered the engineering building and chained the doors shut. He proceeded to enter a classroom and ended up killing 32 people before he finally killed himself. One professor, Livi Librescu, held the classroom door against the gunman's attempts to enter while his students escaped out the window. He was killed by bullets shot through the door he was holding shut.

- In November 2011, a 15-year-old-girl was sexually assaulted at a party by four young men. One of the boys took pictures of the assault that he passed on to his friends and their fellow schoolmates. The photos soon made their way onto social media websites, including Facebook. The girl in the photo, Rehtaeh Parsons, was taunted by her peers. She was bombarded with texts and messages. Some called her a slut, others asked to have sex with her, some claimed she only cried rape because she regretted that her actions became public. In April of 2013, unable to handle the bullying anymore, Rehtaeh committed suicide.

- Under investigation for murdering his wife, Josh Powell was allowed a supervised visit with his two young sons, Charlie, 7, and Braden, 5. As soon as the social worker pulled up to the rental house with his children, the boys ran toward the front door, anxious to see their father. Powell let the boys in, locked the social worker out, and proceeded to attack the boys with a hatchet. As the social worker called to report him for locking her out, Powell set the house on fire, killing both his sons and himself in a murder-suicide. These disturbing incidents are stark demonstrations of persons' ability to inflict pain and death on others. How can we account for such incidents and for the many forms of aggression that commonly occur in the United States and throughout the world? These phenomena are the focus of this chapter.

What is Aggression?

Defining aggression seems simple: Aggression is any behavior that hurts another, whether physically or emotionally. But further thought makes us recognize it is not the outcome so much as the intention that we must consider. We would not consider a surgeon an aggressor if a heart transplant patient died on the operating table despite heroic efforts to save the patient's life. Following Krebs (1982), we will define **aggression** as any behavior intended to harm another person (the target). Importantly, this harm must be something the target wants to avoid. According to this definition, a bungled assassination is an act of aggression, whereas heart surgery—approved by the patient and intended to improve his or her health—is clearly not aggression, even if the patient dies.

American culture tends to associate physical violence with aggression and ignores psychological and emotional abuse as additional types of aggression. If social service agencies and others can broaden individuals' conception of abuse, they can encourage more victims to seek help. © miriam-doerr

Aggression should not be equated with physical violence. Aggressive actions vary widely. The intended harm may be physical, psychological, or social—ranging from homicide or battery, to emotional abuse and cyber-bullying, to active neglect or harming a target's reputation.

Drawing on research and theory, this chapter addresses the following questions:

1   What motivates people to act aggressively?

2   How do characteristics of the target influence aggression?

3   How do characteristics of the situation influence aggression?

4   How can we reduce the frequency of aggressive behavior in society?

5   What influences the incidence of interpersonal aggression—abuse, bullying, assault, sexual assault, and murder—in our society?

Aggression and the Motivation to Harm

As the examples in the introduction show, human beings have a remarkable capacity to harm others—even those they love or are expected to protect. Why do people turn against others? What motivates human aggression? There are at least four possible answers: (1) people are instinctively aggressive; (2) people become aggressive in response to events that are frustrating; (3) people aggress against others as a result of aversive emotion; and (4) people learn to use aggression as a means of obtaining what they want. This section considers each of these in turn.

Aggression as Instinct

A deep history of psychological thought, going back at least to Sigmund Freud (1930, 1950), has considered aggression to be a basic human instinct—that is, an innate behavior that seems to emerge even without socialization or training. To Freud, the innate urge to destroy is as natural as our need to breathe. This instinct constantly generates hostile impulses that demand release. We often release these hostile impulses by aggressing against others, but we can also turn violently against ourselves (suicide) or suffer internal distress (physical or mental illness).

If our aggressive impulses are innate, that means they must be passed to us through our genetic code and are a result of long evolutionary processes. As discussed in earlier chapters, evolutionary theories rely on the Darwinian principle of survival of the fittest. According to Lorenz (1966, 1974), the aggressive instinct has evolved because it contributed to an animal's survival. For instance, in many species, the strongest and most aggressive animals occupy the top positions in the group's social hierarchy. To fight for position in this hierarchy is adaptive in a Darwinian sense, for it gives the animal control over food, shelter, and other resources needed to survive as well as access to mating partners.

Proponents of instinct theories are pessimistic about the possibility of controlling human aggression. At best, they believe, aggression can be channeled into approved competitive activities such as athletics, academics, or business. In these types of activities, there are social rules to govern the expression of aggression intended to prevent competition from degenerating into destructiveness. Quite often, however, socially approved competition stimulates aggression: Football and hockey players start throwing punches, soccer fans riot violently, and businesspeople destroy competitors or cheat the public through ruthless practices.

Although the propensity for aggression can be passed through human generations and aggression is common in social life, most social psychologists have not seen instinct theories of aggression as particularly useful. One reason is that generalizing findings about animal behavior to human behavior is hazardous. Moreover, cross-cultural studies suggest that human aggression lacks two characteristics that are typical of instinctive behavior in animals—universality and periodicity. The need to eat and breathe, for example, are universal to all members of a species. They are also periodic, for they rise after deprivation and fall when satisfied. Aggression, in contrast, is not universal in humans. It pervades some individuals and societies but is virtually absent in others. Moreover, human aggression is not periodic. The occurrence of human aggression is largely governed by specific social circumstances. Aggressive behavior does not increase when people have not aggressed for a long time or decrease after they have recently aggressed. Thus, our biological makeup provides only the capacity for aggression, not an inevitable urge to aggress.

Frustration-Aggression Hypothesis

The second possible explanation for aggressive behavior is that aggression is an internal state that is elicited by certain events. The most famous view of aggression as an elicited drive is the **frustration-aggression hypothesis** (Dollard et al., 1939). This hypothesis asserts that (1) every frustration leads to some form of aggression and (2) every aggressive act is due to some prior frustration. In contrast to instinct theories, this hypothesis states that aggression is instigated by external, environmental events.

In one early demonstration (Barker, Dembo, & Lewin, 1941), researchers showed children a room full of attractive toys. They allowed some children to play with the toys immediately while others were made to wait 20 minutes. The children who waited behaved much more destructively during play, smashing the toys on the floor and against the walls. Here, aggression is a direct response to **frustration**—that is, to the blocking of a goal-directed activity. By blocking the children's access to the tempting toys, the researchers frustrated them. This, in turn, elicited an aggressive drive that the children expressed by destroying the researchers' toys. More recent research suggests that the link between frustration and aggression may be an important cause for the positive link between video games and violence. More competitive games tend to increase aggressive behavior, supporting the role of frustration—from losing in a competitive situation—on increasing aggression (Adachi & Willoughby, 2011).

Several decades of research have led to modifications of the original hypothesis (Berkowitz, 1978). First, studies have shown that frustration does not always produce aggressive responses (Zillman, 1979)—frustrated individuals often restrain themselves due to fear of punishment. Take, for example, being laid off. Losing one's job is a frustrating experience. Researchers predicted that small increases in layoffs would lead to violence in communities. Large increases, however, would lead to reduced violence because those still working would be afraid of being laid off for causing trouble (Catalano, Novaco, & McConnell, 1997). Data from San Francisco supported these predictions. Frustration can also lead responses other than aggression, such as despair, depression, or withdrawal. Second, research indicates that aggression can occur without prior frustration (Berkowitz, 1989). The ruthless businessperson or scientist may attempt to sabotage competitors due to the desire for wealth and fame, even though the competitors have not blocked his or her goal-directed activity.

The frustration-aggression hypothesis implies that the nature of the frustration influences the intensity of the resulting aggression. Two factors that intensify aggression are the strength and the arbitrariness of frustration.

Aggressive acts often stem from frustration. Both the mother who yells at her children and a player who yells at an umpire do so because they are frustrated, one with her children fighting and the other with the umpire's call. *Left:* © Ocean/Corbis; *right:* © Gabe Palmer/Corbis

Strength of Frustration. The more we desire a goal and the closer we are to achieving it, the more frustrated and aroused we become if blocked. If someone cuts ahead of us just as we reach the front of a very long line, our frustration will be especially strong and result in a more aggressive response than if we were further back. Researchers demonstrated this in a field experiment (Harris, 1974). They had confederates cut ahead of people in lines at theaters, restaurants, and grocery checkout counters. The confederate cut in front of either the second or the twelfth person in line. Observers recorded the reactions of the person. As predicted, people at the front of the line responded more aggressively. They directed more than twice as many abusive remarks toward the confederate than people at the back of the line.

Cases of "road rage" also exemplify the frustration-aggression hypothesis and the relationship between the intensity of frustration and intensity of aggression. Road rage most commonly occurs when one motorist engages in a behavior that causes frustration in another driver, blocking the driver's attempt to reach a goal, such as arriving on time for an appointment or securing an available parking spot. This frustration may lead to many types of aggression. Social psychologists distinguish between driver aggression (honking, tailing, making obscene gestures) and driver violence (chasing the other car or its driver, throwing objects, or shooting at him or her). Mild frustration tends to cause the former, whereas stronger frustration causes the latter. Research finds that men and women are equally likely to report engaging in driver aggression in response to frustrating events, but only men reported driver violence (Hennessy & Wiesenthal, 2001).

Arbitrariness of Frustration. People are also apt to feel more hostile when they believe the frustration is arbitrary, unprovoked, or illegitimate than when they attribute it to a reasonable, accidental, or legitimate cause.

In a study demonstrating this principle, researchers asked students to make appeals for a charity over the telephone (Kulick & Brown, 1979). The students were frustrated by refusals

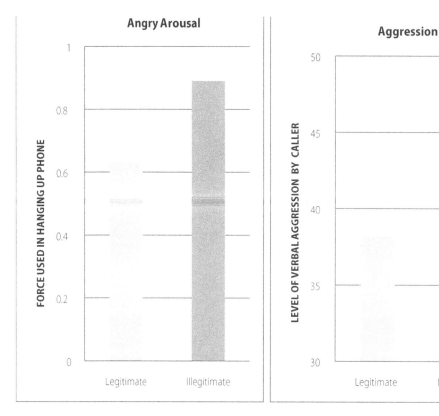

Figure 7.1 Effect of legitimacy of frustration on aggressive responses

Source: Adapted from "Frustration, Attribution of Blame, and Aggression" by Kulick and Brown, *Journal of Experimental Social Psychology,* 15: 183–194. Copyright 1979, with permission from Elsevier.

from all the potential donors (in reality, confederates). In the legitimate frustration condition, potential donors offered good reasons for refusing (such as "I just lost my job"). In the illegitimate frustration condition, they offered weak, arbitrary reasons (such as "charities are a rip-off"). As shown in Figure 7.1, individuals exposed to illegitimate frustration were more emotionally aroused than those exposed to legitimate frustration. They also directed more verbal aggression against the potential donors.

Aversive Emotional Arousal

In the eight decades since the original statement of the frustration-aggression hypothesis, research has identified several other causes of aggression. In one study, community residents and university students were asked what events upset or angered them (Averill, 1982). Some replied that legitimate actions by others and unavoidable accidents could trigger aggressive reactions.

Physical pain, such as stubbing one's toe, and verbal and physical attacks can arouse us and elicit an aggressive response. Insults—especially those involving traits that we value, perhaps intelligence, honesty, ethnicity, or attractiveness—can also provoke aggression. Repeated insults and bullying by classmates contributed to Columbine and other more recent school shootings by students.

Accidents, attacks, and insults tend to increase aggression because they all arouse **aversive affect**—negative emotion that people seek to reduce or eliminate (Berkowitz, 1989). When persons act aggressively in response to this negative affect, the aggression is often instrumental. That is, it is intended to reduce or eliminate the cause of the affect. Often, this affect is anger, but it can be pain or other types of discomfort. For example, one of the reasons violence is higher in the summer months is because the higher temperatures produce discomfort and people look for a way to discharge this aversive affect (Anderson, Anderson, & Deuser, 1996). Turning on the air conditioner, yelling at your little sister, kicking the dog, or shooting someone who insults you are instrumental actions to deal with the discomfort.

Aggression resulting from aversive affect is called **affective aggression**. Affective aggression is more common among persons who believe that acting aggressively will make them feel better. If someone believes that acting aggressively will not decrease the discomfort or negative affect, he or she will engage in other instrumental actions.

Social Learning and Aggression

Social learning theories provide a fourth explanation for aggressive behavior. Two processes by which aggression can be learned are imitation and reinforcement.

Imitation. Many people learn their aggressive behaviors by observing others commit aggressive acts and then enacting these same behaviors themselves. In one experiment, children observed an adult playing with a five-foot-tall, inflated rubber Bobo doll (Bandura, Ross, & Ross, 1961). In one experimental condition, the adult engaged in aggressive behavior toward the doll, including punching and kicking it and sitting on it. These actions, accompanied by the shouting of aggressive words and phrases, continued for nine minutes. Later, each child was intentionally frustrated and then left alone in a room with various toys, including a smaller Bobo doll. The children who had observed the aggressive model were much more aggressive toward the doll than those who had observed a nonaggressive model. They engaged in aggressive behavior such as kicking the doll and made comments similar to those they had observed.

Many children learn aggressive behavior from their parents. Indeed, 90% of parents in the United States report using physical punishment to discipline their children (see Chapter 3). Children who are spanked or slapped for transgressions are learning that if someone's behavior breaks rules or makes you angry, it is okay to punish them physically. A longitudinal study of 717 boys found that boys who experienced harsh parenting practices at ages 10 to 12 were more likely to be involved in violent dating relationships at age 16 (Lavoie et al.,

2002). Much of the other aggressive behavior within the family—child abuse, intimate partner abuse, or sibling abuse—can also be explained with social learning theory. People who abuse their intimate partners or children often grew up in families in which they either witnessed or were the targets of abuse (Gelles & Cornell, 1990). Growing up in a family in which some members abuse others teaches the child that not only is it acceptable to engage in physical aggression but that occupants of certain roles—such as husbands, girlfriends, or children—are also appropriate targets for aggression.

Reinforcement. Social learning theory holds that aggressive responses are acquired and maintained—like any other social behavior—through experiences of reinforcement and reward (Bandura, 1973). Individuals learn early on that aggression can be associated with desired outcomes, thereby reinforcing the behavior. Muggers may attack a person to take his or her money. One child knocks down another to obtain the toy he or she desires. Students bully other students to gain esteem or deference from their peers. Even if we do not consciously consider the rewards we might gain, we can learn that aggression leads to individual gain, thus reinforcing the behavior.

Characteristics of Targets that Influence Aggression

The preceding section introduced four potential sources of the motivation to aggress. Once aroused, such motives incline us toward aggressive behavior. Whether aggression occurs, however, also depends on the characteristics of the **target**—the person toward whom the aggressive behavior is directed. In this section, we discuss four target characteristics related to aggression: race and gender, attributions for the aggressor's attack, and retaliatory capacity.

Gender and Race

Aggression does not occur at random. If it did, we would observe aggressive behaviors by all kinds of people directed at targets of both genders, all ethnic groups, and all ages. In fact, aggression is patterned. First, aggressive behavior usually involves two people of the same race or ethnicity. This is true of aggression within the family, as most families are racially and ethnically homogeneous. But it is also true of violent crimes such as assault, sexual assault, and murder. Table 7.1 reports FBI murder statistics that demonstrate this within-race tendency.

The relationship between aggression and gender depends on the type of aggressive behavior. In cases of abuse within the family, both genders are targets. Boys and girls are equally likely to be abused by a parent. Wives abuse their husbands as often as husbands abuse their wives (Gelles & Strauss, 1988). However, the types of abuse are different. Women are more likely to slap, kick, bite, or to try to hit their partner with an object. Men are more likely to beat up their partner and to push,

Table 7.1 Race and sex of murder victim by race and sex of offender, 2009

		Race of Offender				Sex of Offender	
	Total	White	Black	Other	Unknown	Male	Female
Race of Victim							
White	3518	84.2%	12.9%	1.1%	1.7%	87.7%	8.7%
Black	2867	7.3%	90.8%	0.5%	1.4%	88.5%	10.0%
Other	181	27.6%	14.4%	57.5%	0.6%	89.5%	9.9%
Unknown	65	41.5%	33.8%	1.5%	23.1	67.7%	9.2%
Sex of Victim							
Male	4638	44.3%	52.2%	1.9%	1.6%	87.9%	10.4%
Female	1928	60.6%	34.3%	3.7%	1.4%	89.2%	9.4%

Note: This table is based on incidents in which some information about the offender is known by law enforcement. Therefore, when the offender's age, sex, and race are all reported as unknown, these data are excluded from the table. For summaries related to sex, percentages for those of an unknown sex are omitted.
Source: FBI Homicide data.

grab, or shove. In cases of violence involving current or former intimate partners, women are the victims of 74% of the murders and 85% of the assaults and sexual assaults (Greenfeld et al., 1998). These patterns are found among Blacks, Latinos, and Whites (Rennison, 2001), but the rates appear to be lower among Asian and Pacific Islanders (Johnson & Ferraro, 2000).

Although men and women are equally likely to engage in *aggressive* behavior, men engage in significantly more *violent* behavior. Of reported cases of rape or sexual assault, 95% involve a male offender and female victim. As Table 7.1 reports, men were responsible for almost 90% of murders, of both men and women, committed in 2009. Most murders and **aggravated assaults**—an attack by one person on another with the intent of causing bodily injury—involve two men.

These patterns indicate that the display of aggression is channeled by social beliefs and norms. Observing violence within one's family teaches children that violence within the family is acceptable. Similarly, beliefs and norms in U.S. society encourage men to direct physical and sexual aggression toward women and other men. For example, masculine gender norms encourage men to be dominant over women (Connell, 2005). These gender norms also associate masculinity with status and toughness, motivating men to use aggression to gain the respect of others (Thompson & Pleck, 1986). Men in our society frequently compete with each other for various rewards, such as influence over one another, status in a group, the companionship of a woman, or other symbols of success. These competitions often lead to insults that provoke anger or direct physical challenges. There are norms in some groups, cultures, or subcultures that require men to defend themselves in such situations. For example, observers have often described the American South as having a norm that requires men to defend themselves against insults—a "culture of honor" (see Box 7.1).

BOX 7.1 Research Update: The Culture of Honor

Students were milling around the cafeteria of Spring High School—just outside of Houston, Texas—before school on a September morning. Some were eating breakfast, others catching up on their homework, many simply talking with friends before the first bell rang. Just outside the cafeteria, Joshua Broussard "bumped" into Luis Alfaro as he moved through the crowded hallway. The two exchanged words. Moments later, Alfaro pulled out a knife and attacked Broussard. As students scattered, Broussard collapsed in the school hallway and died.

The attack at Spring High School is not unusual. A large number of the homicides that occur in any given year are triggered by arguments, and many of these disputes are over trivial matters, including offensive comments or name calling. However, what is most interesting about the incident is its similarity to a series of social psychological experiments conducted 20 years earlier on the "culture of honor" (Cohen, Nisbett, Bowdle, & Schwarz, 1996).

In those experiments, both "Northerner" and "Southerner"* students from the University of Michigan were invited to the laboratory for what they believed was an experiment on response times and human judgment. Upon arrival, they were asked to fill out initial paperwork and take it to a table at the end of a long, narrow hallway. Unbeknownst to the participants, the experimental treatment actually occurred during the walk to this table. As some of the participants made their way down the hallway, a confederate bumped the unsuspecting student and called him an "asshole." Observers situated in the hallway, ostensibly working on their homework, gauged the participants' reactions. Participants then participated in a series of judgment tasks to gauge their reactions to the incident.

Comparisons of the reactions of Southerners and Northerners supported the idea of a "culture of honor" in the South. Social scientists argue that individuals from places with a "culture of honor" are more likely to perceive a benign incident as an interpersonal threat. Furthermore, once offended or insulted, those who accept a "culture of honor" will feel the need to restore honor by retaliating against the insult. Sure enough, Southerners who were bumped by the confederate were more likely to see the insult as a cause for anger rather than amusement and to see violence as an appropriate reaction to an "affront." Whereas Northerners were able to brush off the insult and remain unaffected, Southerners who were insulted were primed for aggression and would act out if given the right stimulus. Later studies found that Southerners were also more prepared to aggress on a physiological level, with higher cortisol and testosterone levels than Northerners who had also been insulted.

A tremendous amount of research on the culture of honor conducted since these early studies supports these findings. Social psychologists recently considered this concept in relation to school violence and found that high school students in culture-of-honor states—including Texas—were more likely to bring a weapon to school and were at higher risk of school shootings than were students in other states (Brown, Osterman, & Barnes, 2009). Although many attributed the tragedy at Spring High to gang violence, the culture of honor may have also played an important role in the events of that September morning.

*Students were classified as "Southern" if they lived in one of the following states for at least six years: Delaware, Maryland, West Virginia, Virginia, North Carolina, South Carolina, Georgia, Florida, Kentucky, Tennessee, Alabama, Mississippi, Arkansas, Louisiana, or Texas. All other students, except those who lived in Washington, DC, were considered "Northern." On average, those classified as "Southern" had lived 87% of their lives in the South, whereas those classified as "Northern" had spent only 4% of their lives in the South.

Attribution of Intention

Direct attacks, both verbal and physical, typically produce an aggressive reaction (Geen, 1968; White & Gruber, 1982). Nevertheless, we withhold retaliation when we perceive that an attack was not intentional. We are unlikely to respond aggressively, for example, if we see that a man who has smashed his grocery cart into our car in the parking lot was trying to save a child from an on-coming car. However, we must first realize the man's intention. Aggression following harm is both more probable and stronger when we attribute the attack to the actor's intentions rather than to accidental or legitimate external pressures (Dyck & Rule, 1978). In the former case, the target of our aggressive response deserves that response more than when the harm is accidental.

The general aggression model (Anderson & Bushman, 2002), based on a dual-process model, proposes that after an initial immediate appraisal (or attribution) of an attack or hostile situation, a reappraisal of the situation only occurs if there are sufficient resources (for example, time or cognitive capacity) and the initial appraisal is somehow unsatisfactory.

These appraisals of the situation as well as related attributions for harm have important implications for our responses to aggression. In one study of 70 abused women, those living with their violent partner sometimes blamed themselves for the abuse. They attributed it to their incompetence, unattractiveness, or talking back to the partner. Other women blamed situational factors such as their partner's stress. The women most likely to leave their abusive partners were those who blamed him—rather than themselves or the situation—for the abuse (Andrews & Brewin, 1990).

An important influence on attributions is whether an attacker apologizes. An apology often states or implies that the harm another did to us was unintentional. In one study, an experimenter made mistakes that caused the participant to fail at the tasks. When the experimenter apologized, the participants refrained from acting aggressively toward her. Apologies may also lessen resulting aggression because they sometimes provide mitigating information—accounts of external causes of the offending action—that facilitate a reappraisal (Barlett & Anderson, 2011). However, it is important to note that as the severity of the harm increases, the effectiveness of apologies decreases (Ohbuchi, Kameda, & Agarie, 1989).

Retaliatory Capacity

One of the consequences that we might consider in calculating the costs (and benefits) of aggression is the likelihood of retaliation by the target.

Research suggests that the threat of retaliation reduces aggressive behavior. In one experiment, participants were told to deliver electric shocks to another person and that they could select the intensity of the shock. In one condition, participants were told that after they had delivered the shocks, the experiment would be over. In another condition, participants were told that after they had delivered shocks, they would change places with the other person. In other words, they would be in a position in which the other person would be delivering shocks (and could retaliate). Participants in the latter condition delivered significantly less intense shocks than in the former condition (Prentice-Dunn & Rogers, 1980). These findings help explain why anonymous cyber-bullying is described as more severe than nonanonymous forms of bullying. Bullies may be inclined to engage in more aggressive acts when they use fake aliases or post on anonymous websites like ask.fm because the risk of retaliation is significantly smaller.

Sometimes, there are instances of **displaced aggression**—defined as aggression toward a target that exceeds what is justified by provocation by that target. This often occurs because the aggression is instigated by a different source and then displaced onto a less powerful or more available target who had no responsibility for the initial response (Umberson, Williams & Anderson, 2002). Displaced aggression is a common explanation for aggression directed toward partners, children, or pets—"She is taking her bad day out on us."—but does it actually occur? A meta-analysis of social psychological research on the subject provides substantial evidence that displaced aggression is quite real (Marcus-Newhall, Pedersen, Carlson & Miller, 2000). Some argue that displaced aggression may partially account for higher incidences of domestic violence in poor and working-class households (Umberson, Anderson, Glick & Shapiro, 1998). Frustration with a lack of control over events outside the home, whether related to work or in other interactions, ends up directed toward family members (see the discussion of spillover from work to home in Chapter 15). Similar processes can also help explain why children who are bullied are more likely to be bullies themselves (Salmivalli & Nieminen, 2002).

Research on displaced aggression also finds that the more negative the insult, attack, or frustration and the more similar the instigator and the target, the greater the likelihood that displaced aggression will occur.

Situational Impacts on Aggression

There are a number of specific characteristics of situations that make aggression more likely. Five covered in this chapter are potential rewards, presence of models, norms, stress, and aggressive cues.

Potential Rewards

Three types of rewards that promote aggression are direct material benefits, social approval, and attention.

The material benefits that armed robbers and Mafiosi obtain by using violence support their aggression. If the material benefits are reduced—say, by vigorous law enforcement—this type of aggressive violence will decline.

Although aggression is generally condemned, social approval is a second common reward for aggressive acts. Virtually every society has norms that approve aggression against particular targets in particular circumstances. We honor soldiers for shooting the enemy in war. We praise children for defending their siblings in a fight. Most of us, on occasion, urge friends to respond aggressively to insults or exploitation.

Attention is the third type of reward for aggressive acts. The teenager who taunts or bullies a classmate basks in the spotlight of attention from peers, even as he is reproached by school authorities. Research conducted in elementary school classrooms shows that even though aggressive children are generally disliked by their peers, the aggressive behavior at school is positively reinforced with laughter and interest from classmates (Powers & Bierman, 2013). Although few today would suggest that we should ignore bullying, research does show that a strategy that coupled rewards for cooperation and ignored aggressive behavior was effective in reducing aggression among preschool children (Brown & Elliott, 1965).

Modeling

A second situational factor that increases aggression is the presence of behavioral models. Just as aggressive behavior is learned by observing and then imitating a model (Bandura, Ross, & Ross, 1961), a model's aggressive behavior in a specific situation may encourage others to behave in similar ways. This "peer contagion" (Dishion & Dodge, 2005) has been found not only among elementary students and teenagers but also among adults.

Just as the last chapter discussed the importance of models in demonstrating types of helping acts that are possible, aggressive models demonstrate the possible negative behaviors. Consider the riots that occurred in London and other parts of the United Kingdom in 2011. What began as a peaceful protest of police brutality devolved quickly into a violent clash between protestors and police that included looting, arson, and total chaos. A panel argued that social media and the 24-hour news coverage actually made the riot worse. The incident was dubbed the "BlackBerry Riots" because of the importance of mobile devices and social media in organizing riot activities, spreading inflammatory and inaccurate accounts, and circulating photos of the destruction and chaos.

Media coverage exaggerated the extent of rioting in some areas, which made rioting a self-fulfilling prophecy as it encouraged others to join in. Social media and news outlet images and film also provided aggressive models. Aggressive models provide three types of information that influence observers. First, models demonstrate specific aggressive acts that are possible in a situation. Second, models provide information about the appropriateness of aggression—about whether it is normatively appropriate in a setting. The behavior of the initial participants in the UK riots signaled that violence was appropriate. The live television coverage of the riot news stations provided unwittingly—and the social media more intentionally—transmitted this message to tens of thousands of others who could join in and add to the chaotic scenes. Finally, models provide information about the consequences of acting aggressively. Observers see whether the model succeeds in attaining goals and whether the behavior is punished or rewarded. Not surprisingly, observers are more likely to imitate aggressive behaviors that yield rewards and avoid punishment. The modeling of aggression also helps account for why prior riots in one city are associated with subsequent riots in the same city (Olzak, Shanahan, & McEneaney, 1996) and why riots seem to spread from one city to another with mass media coverage (Myers, 1997).

These models matter little when observers are not motivated to do harm. But people who feel provoked and who are suppressing any urge to aggress often lose their inhibitions after observing an aggressive model. They are the most likely to imitate aggression. In other words, the news coverage of school shootings like Columbine is unlikely to cause an observer who is not motivated to do harm to consider bringing a gun to school or to hurt a classmate. However, such coverage might provoke someone who has an underlying urge to harm their peers by showing them that lashing out violently at school is not only possible but also perhaps both common and rewarded through mass media attention (Coleman, 2004).

Norms

Just as there is a positive norm of reciprocity (see Chapter 10), there is also a *negative norm of reciprocity*. This norm—"an eye for an eye, a tooth for a tooth"—justifies retaliation for attacks. Research on the culture of honor (see Box 7.1) suggests that the belief that one should respond to an attack on one's family property or self with aggression—and even killing—varies across cultural group. There is also evidence that men are more likely to endorse this honor ideology than women are (Barnes, Brown & Osterman, 2012). Such norms influence behavior. Among ex-offenders, endorsing "an eye for an eye" and similar statements was correlated with reports of more frequent violent behavior during the past year (Markowitz & Felson, 1998).

The negative reciprocity norm requires that the retaliation be proportionate to the provocation. Numerous experiments indicate that people match the level of retaliation to the level of the attack (Taylor, 1967). In the heat of anger, however, we are likely to overestimate the strength of another's provocation and to underestimate the intensity of our own response. When angry, we are also more likely to misinterpret responses that have no aggressive intent as intentional provocation. Thus, even when people strive to match retaliation to provocation, aggression may escalate.

A study of 444 assaults against police officers revealed that escalation of retaliation due to mutual misunderstanding was the most common factor leading to violence (Toch, 1969). Typically, the police officer began with a routine request for information. The person confronted interpreted the officer's request as threatening, arbitrary, and unfair and, thus, refused to comply. The officer interpreted this non-compliance as an attack on his or her own authority and reacted by declaring the suspect under arrest. Angered further by the officer's seemingly illegitimate assertion of power, the suspect retaliated with verbal insults and obscenities. From there the incident escalated quickly. The officer angrily grabbed the suspect, who retaliated by attacking physically. This sequence illustrates how a confrontation can spiral into violent aggression even when the angry participants feel they are merely matching their opponents' level of attack.

Experiments also support this norm of negative reciprocity. Two participants engaged in a competitive reaction time task in a laboratory; after each trial, the faster person could direct a noxious blast of noise at the slower person (Bushman, Baumeister, & Strack, 1999). The experiment was rigged so the participant received the noise on one-half of the trials (randomly selected) and could deliver noise on the other half. Over time, the participant increasingly matched the noise level delivered to him or her—clear evidence of reciprocity.

Stress

Stress also increases the likelihood of aggressive behavior. Social stressors, such as chronic unemployment and the experience of discrimination, are related to aggression because of their effects on frustration and anger. A study on the impact of economic distress on violence in married and cohabiting couples found that objective indicators such as reported household income were negatively related to abuse; as household income increased, the frequency of physical violence decreased. However, regardless of actual income, when either partner wished that the other worked more hours (or earned more money), this discrepancy between desire and reality was positively related to physical violence (Fox, Benson, DeMaris, & Van Wyk, 2002).

There are several other sources of stress within couples that may lead to intimate violence. Some potential stressors include: a short relationship duration (that is, the couple doesn't know each other well), a mismatch in gender role definitions (one has traditional views, the other more modern views), substance abuse, and large numbers of children. These are related to intimate violence in part through their relationship to more frequent disagreements as well as a more heated disagreement style that causes disagreements to escalate (DeMaris, Benson, Fox, Hill & Van Wyk, 2003). This process of escalation occurs, in part, because the longer an argument or fight continues, the more likely each person is to introduce past grievances rather than focusing solely on the issue at hand.

Stress can also stem from living conditions. Research finds that intimate violence occurs more frequently in economically disadvantaged neighborhoods (Benson & Fox, 2004), even among those who are better off financially than their neighbors (Fox & Benson, 2006). These same processes suggest, though, that neighborhood characteristics can also reduce intimate violence. Research linking survey data, census data, and homicide data for the city of Chicago found that, even in disadvantaged neighborhoods, if residents share a sense of collective efficacy (for example, "people in this neighborhood can be trusted") and a sense that neighbors could be counted on, rates of intimate violence were lower (Browning & Cagney, 2003). Such sentiments could be interpreted as indicators of lower levels of stress stemming from the neighborhood environment.

Other situational stressors can also produce high levels of aggression. Several studies have shown that temperature is related to the occurrence of a number of violent crimes, including assault, sexual assault, murder, and riots (Anderson, 1987, Baron & Ransberger, 1978). This is, in part, because temperatures increase discomfort and feelings of hostility (Anderson, 2001). Recent research finds that climate controls like air conditioning have the potential to curb heat-related violence, but access to such technologies is not uniform and their reach is limited (Rotton & Cohn, 2004). Interestingly, taking into account the time of day—because more crime occurs at night, but temperatures tend to be lower then—rates of violence peak at a temperature between 80 and 90 degrees (Cohn & Rotton, 2005). Temperatures beyond that lead to reduced violence, perhaps because people want to escape the heat and break off interaction with others (Cohn & Rotton, 1997).

Heat also influences aggression indirectly by increasing the prevalence of aggressive thoughts that may subsequently lead to aggressive behavior. Researchers found that exposure to words related to hot temperatures (sunburn, boils, roasted, hot, sweats), regardless of the actual temperature in the laboratory, resulted in more aggressive thoughts and hostile perceptions than exposure to either cold (frostbite, freezes, cold, shivers) or neutral words unrelated to temperature (DeWall & Bushman, 2009).

Aggressive Cues

Situations that produce aggression often start out in ways that are ambiguous to those involved in them. Should that insult be interpreted as a good-natured joke or a challenge to a man's masculinity? Is a jovial conversation between your boyfriend and another woman perfectly innocent, friendly banter, or an unwelcome attempt at flirting? Observers and participants involved in such incidents need help from the environment to figure out what is happening and how they should respond.

Aggressive cues in the environment can increase the likelihood of an aggressive response (Berkowitz, 1989). These cues may intensify the aggressive motivation or lower inhibitions even if they are not directly involved in the immediate situation. For example, people who have been aroused or frustrated respond more aggressively when in the presence of a gun than in the presence of neutral objects, even when the object has nothing to do with the aggression (Carlson, Marcus-Newhall, &

Miller, 1990). The so-called **weapons effect** occurs when people are already aroused. The effect involves cognitive priming; the sight of a weapon makes more accessible or primes aggression-related concepts or scripts for behavior (Anderson, Benjamin, & Bartholow, 1998).

Aggressive cues also affect aggression by a process of ruminative thought (Marcus-Newhall et al., 2000). **Rumination** is a self-focused attention toward one's distress and the possible causes and consequences of the distress rather than ways to overcome it. When someone is thinking about an earlier provocation, they may respond aggressively to a mildly annoying event (a trigger). If your roommate is thinking of an incident in which her professor embarrassed her in class earlier in the day as she stirs the spaghetti sauce on the stove, she might snap at you for asking when she will be finished cooking. If she is instead thinking of the weekend ahead, she will be more likely to simply tell you that dinner will be done in a few minutes.

To test the effect of ruminating on aggression, social psychologists had a group of under-graduates participate in a three-part experiment (Bushman et al., 2005). In the first part of the experiment, the provocation phase, the participants were asked to solve difficult anagrams (for example, to unscramble NVTNIMEREON to spell ENVIRONMENT) while loud and distracting music played in the background. After a few minutes, the experimenter collected the anagram sheets, turned off the music, and left to score the sheet. The experimenter returned later and informed the participants that their score was well below average and they really should repeat the task but added—in an exasperated tone—that repeating the first part would be a waste of time and they should just proceed to part two. For part two, a random group of participants were assigned to the rumination phase and asked to respond to a number of self-focused phrases ("what kind of person you are," "why people treat you the way they do"). Others responded to externally focused or mood-enhancing phrases. In the final part of the experiment, the trigger phase, all the participants played a trivia game. When the research assistant read the trivia questions too quickly, mis-pronounced some of the names (pronouncing Leonardo da Vinci as Leon Divinsky), and occasionally mixed up the possible responses, participants who had been in the rumination condition reacted significantly more aggressively—recommending the research assistant not be hired for a permanent position and experiencing more negative emotions—than did those who had been assigned to the other groups in part two or who had not experienced an annoying trigger in the final part of the experiment (see Figure 7.2).

Reducing Aggressive Behavior

Aggressive behavior is often costly to individuals and the groups and society to which they belong. Given the problems associated with aggressive behavior, reducing aggression has been an important topic of research. Four strategies that hold some promise are reducing frustration, punishing aggressive behavior, providing nonaggressive models, and providing opportunities for catharsis.

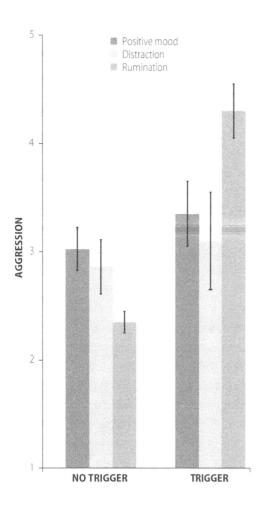

Figure 7.2   The interaction between rumination and a mild annoyance on aggression

When participants were prompted to ruminate about an aggressive provocation, a subsequent minor trigger caused a significantly more aggressive reaction than for those who were provoked but not asked to ruminate or for those who ruminated but were not exposed to the minor trigger.

Source: Figure 1, Bushman et al. (2005). "Chewing on It Can Chew You Up: Effects of Rumination on Triggered displaced Aggression." *Journal of Personality and Social Psychology*, 88, 969–983.

Reducing Frustration

Given that frustration is so central to aggression, we might be able to reduce aggressive behavior by reducing the frequency or strength of frustration. A major source of frustration in American society, for example, is inadequate resources. Studies comparing crime rates across different cities (e.g., Land, McCall, & Cohen, 1990) and nations (Gartner, 1990) find that economic deprivation is the best predictor for crime. Many cases of robbery, assault, and murder are motivated simply by a desire for money or property. Frustration and, therefore, aggression could be reduced if everyone had access to life's necessities.

Many of the frustrations we experience arise from conflicts with other people. Thus, another way to reduce aggressive behavior is to provide people with alternative means of resolving interpersonal conflicts. Recent innovations in dispute resolution involve the increasing use of professionally trained mediators and the training of selected community members in conflict-resolution techniques. These innovations have also been implemented in schools. Conflict-resolution programs using peers as mediators have been introduced partly in response to the rise in mass shootings and bullying in schools.

Punishment

Punishment is often used to control aggression because of a widely held belief that punishment is an effective deterrent. Threats can indeed be effective in eliminating aggression, but only under certain narrowly defined conditions (Baron, 1977). For threats to inhibit aggression, the anticipated punishment must be great and the probability that it will occur very high. Even so, threatened punishment is largely ineffective when potential aggressors are extremely angry.

Actual (not just anticipated or threatened) punishment can also control aggression, but again, strict conditions must be met (Baron, 1977): (1) The punishment must follow the aggressive act promptly, (2) it must be seen as the logical outcome of that act, and (3) it must not violate legitimate social norms. Unless these conditions are met, people perceive punishment as unjustified, and this increases the likelihood that they will respond with anger or aggression.

Although research demonstrates the importance of these conditions for deterrence, the criminal justice system often fails to meet these conditions. The probability than any single criminal act will be punished is low, simply because most criminals are not caught. Even when criminals are caught, punishment rarely follows the crime promptly. Moreover, few criminals see the punishment as a logical or legitimate outcome of their act. Finally, criminals often have much to gain through their aggression. A longitudinal study of adult offenders found that perception of risk of sanctions was not related to criminal activity. The most significant predictor of crime was the perception of opportunities to gain economically by breaking the law (Piliavin et al., 1986). As a result, the criminal justice system is not very effective in deterring criminal aggression.

Nonaggressive Models

Just as aggressive models may increase aggression, nonaggressive models may reduce it. Mahatma Gandhi, who led the movement to free India of British colonialism, used pacifist tactics that have since been imitated by protesters around the world. Laboratory research has also demonstrated the restraining influence of nonaggressive models. In one study (Baron & Kepner, 1970), participants observed an aggressive model deliver many more shocks to a confederate than required by the task. Other participants observed a nonaggressive model who gave the minimum number of shocks required. A control group observed no model. The results showed that the participants who observed the nonaggressive model displayed less subsequent aggression than did the participants in either the control group or the participants who saw the aggressive model. Other research shows that nonaggressive models not only reduce aggression but can also offset the influence of aggressive models (Baron, 1971).

Catharsis

Infuriated by a day of catering to the whims of her boss, Christina turned on her teenage son as he drove her home. "Why must you drive like a maniac?" she snapped in a fit of displaced aggression. Miguel was stunned. He was driving a sedate 35 miles per hour and had done nothing to provoke his mother's aggression. Did Christina feel better after venting her anger on Miguel?

Many people believe that letting off steam is better than "bottling up" hostility. A very old psychological concept captures this idea (Aristotle, *Poetics*, Book 6). **Catharsis** is the notion that one can reduce aggressive arousal by performing aggressive acts. The catharsis hypothesis states that we can purge ourselves of hostile emotions by experiencing these emotions while acting aggressively. A broader view suggests that by observing aggression as an involved spectator to drama, television, or sports, we also release aggressive emotions.

Numerous studies support the usefulness of catharsis and show that it does indeed reduce aggression (Geen & Quanty, 1977). But again, conditions are everything. For catharsis to occur, the aggressive act must be directed at the source of the frustration and not someone else. Misdirected or displaced aggression, such as kicking the dog or yelling at Miguel, often does not result in catharsis. We also must feel that the aggression we display will be viewed as acceptable by others, and we cannot feel guilty about it afterward.

In fact, with few exceptions, research has shown that performing aggressive acts will increase future aggression, not reduce it. This is true whether the initial aggression is a verbal attack, a physical attack, or even aggressive play (Bushman, Baumeister, & Stack, 1999; Geen, Stonner, & Shope, 1975). For example, research finds higher rates of both psychological and physical dating violence used by collegiate athletes in contact sports (wrestling, basketball) versus those in noncontact sports (track and field, swimming) (Burns, 2009).

Initial aggression promotes further aggression because initial aggressive acts produce disinhibition—the reduction of ordinary internal controls against socially disapproved behavior. Disinhibition is reflected in the reports of murderers and soldiers who commented that killing was difficult the first time but became easier thereafter. Second, initial aggressive acts serve to arouse our anger even further. Third, they give us experience in harming others, and thus, it becomes a more accessible part of our behavioral repertoires. Finally, if we do experience catharsis following aggression, this reinforces aggression, and behaviors we find rewarding are repeated more frequently.

Aggression in Society

Over the last two decades, there has been increasing recognition that aggressive behavior is at the heart of several major social problems. This awareness is due, in part, to the widespread publicity given to certain incidents like school shootings and other mass murders. But, fortunately, mass murders are rare. Much more common are other types of interpersonal violence, in which one person directs physical aggression toward another with the intent to injure or kill the target. This final section of the chapter on aggression discusses three specific aspects of interpersonal violence. First, it looks at the causes and consequences of sexual assault. Next, it examines the impact of pornography on sexual assault. Finally, it discusses whether television programming and video games contribute to violence.

Sexual Assault
Sexual assault is sexual touching or intercourse without consent, accomplished by coercion, manipulation, or either the threat or use of force. The greater the force used or the resulting

injury, the more severe the assault. One study of sexual coercion surveyed from 165 men and 131 women who were new members of fraternities and sororities. Men were as likely as women to report being coerced into unwanted sexual contact, but only women reported being physically forced to do so (Larimer, Lydum, Anderson, & Turner, 1999). Most cases involve offenders and victims from the same racial or ethnic group.

In some cases, the offender is motivated by sexual desire. In other cases, however, the offender's intent is to dominate, humiliate, or injure the victim. Sexual assault is one form of sexual aggression; sexual aggression is really a continuum, ranging from the use of bribes through verbal pressure, the intentional use of alcohol or drugs, physical force, and kidnapping to sexual murder (Jewkes, Sen, & Garcia-Moreno, 2002).

What Causes Sexual Aggression? There are several answers to this question. One is a specific set of cultural beliefs and practices creates conditions that encourage rape. In a rape-prone society, the sexual assault of women by men is allowed or overlooked (Sanday, 1981, 2003). Rape-prone societies share several characteristics. First, there are high levels of interpersonal violence. Second, there is an ideology of male dominance that subordinates women, suggesting that women are the property of men and should be subject to men's control. Third, men and women are regularly separated (during religious rituals, for example) in rape-prone societies. The United States is a rape-prone society. Rates of violent crime are high. Until recently, men dominated women politically, economically, and sexually. There is also a continuing separation of men and women in certain spheres (athletic programs, workplaces).

Rape-proneness has also been applied to college campuses. Researchers find that when fraternities or men's dorms are allowed to have parties, whereas sororities and women's dorms are not, men are more likely to be able to structure the party and control the movement and behavior of their guests (Armstrong, Hamilton, & Sweeney, 2006). Men also regulate and distribute the alcohol, an important factor in sexual assault on college campuses (Logan, Walker, Cole, & Keukefeld, 2002). With men as hosts, women are also expected to be nice and to defer to men in interaction, ultimately supporting male dominance in the situation and contributing to the rape-prone environment of campus parties (Armstrong, Hamilton, & Sweeney, 2006).

Perpetrators of Sexual Assault. Of course, individuals rather than societies or cultures commit rape. A second approach to determining the causes of sexual assault is to identify men's characteristics that may be related to their aggressive behavior. Research suggests that some men are sexually aggressive—that is, they rely on aggressive behaviors in their relationships with women (Malamuth, Heavey, & Linz, 1993). These men tend to score highly on measures of the desire to dominate women and of hostility toward women. They also have a variety of attitudes that facilitate aggression toward women, including rape myths, such as the belief that women secretly desire to be raped and enjoy it, that victims cause rape, and that other men are prone to rape (see Box 7.2) (Koss & Leonard, 1984; Malamuth, 1984). These men also tend to

BOX 7.2   Test Yourself: Rape Myths

Among the causes of sexual aggression are cultural beliefs that encourage rape. These beliefs are rape myths—prejudicial, stereotyped, and false beliefs about rape, rape victims, and persons who commit rape (Burt, 1980). Examples of these myths are "She asked for it," "He didn't mean to," and "It wasn't really rape." These beliefs create a climate that encourages sexual assault and is suspicious of and hostile toward victims.

An attitude scale that is widely used to assess these beliefs is the Rape Myth Acceptance Scale, developed by Burt (1980). Below are some of the items from an updated version of the scale intended for college students (McMahon & Farmer, 2011). Read each statement and circle the appropriate response: Strongly Agree (SA), Agree (A), Don't know (?), Disagree (D), or Strongly Disagree (SD).

1   If a girl goes to a room alone with a guy at a party, it is her own fault if she is raped.

   SA   A   ?   D   SD

2   If a girl doesn't physically fight back, you can't really say it was rape.

   SA   A   ?   D   SD

3   When girls go to parties wearing slutty clothes, they are asking for trouble.

   SA   A   ?   D   SD

4   If a girl initiates kissing or hooking up, she should not be surprised if a guy assumes she wants to have sex.

   SA   A   ?   D   SD

5   If a girl is raped while she is drunk, she is at least somewhat responsible for letting things get out of hand.

   SA   A   ?   D   SD

6   Rape happens when a guy's sex drive goes out of control.

   SA   A   ?   D   SD

7   A lot of times, girls who say they were raped agreed to have sex and then regret it.

   SA   A   ?   D   SD

8   Rape accusations are often used as a way of getting back at guys.

SA   **A**   **?**   **D**   **SD**

9   If a girl doesn't say "no," she can't claim rape.

SA   **A**   **?**   **D**   **SD**

10   If a guy is drunk, he might rape someone unintentionally.

SA   **A**   **?**   **D**   **SD**

Scores for each question range from 1 (strongly agree) to 5 (strongly disagree). Scores should be totaled for a cumulative score. Higher scores indicate greater rejection of rape myths. A man with a lower score likely believes that if he engages in sexual activity with a woman who comes home with him on the first date after they have both been drinking, it is not rape, even if she offers some resistance. This is one of the dangers of rape myths. They provide scripts that legitimize sexual activity to which the woman may not have overtly consented. Another type of rape myth—that claims of rape are not true—creates an environment in which such claims are not believed, and therefore, sexual assault is not punished.

There have been many studies on the correlates of endorsing rape myths. One review summarizes the findings of 72 studies (Anderson, Cooper, & Okamura, 1997). Men, older persons, and persons from lower socioeconomic backgrounds are more likely to hold such attitudes. Acceptance of rape was associated with traditional beliefs about gender roles, an adversarial view of male-female relationships, and conservative political beliefs. These results are consistent with the theory that rape myth acceptance is the result of socialization to gender types and conservative beliefs.

be sexually aroused by portrayals of rape. In laboratory studies, men who endorse rape myths are more likely to aggress against a woman who has mildly insulted or rejected them (Check & Malamuth, 1983). In addition to these specific gender attitudes, findings from research suggest that pornography use and alcohol abuse are also significant predictors of the perpetration of sexual violence (Carr & VanDeusen, 2004).

Men's tendency to be sexually aggressive is stable over time. Researchers collected data on 423 young men, including measures of hostility toward women and attitudes supportive of violence. Ten years later, they reinterviewed a number of the men and their female partners (Malamuth, Linz, Heavey, Barnes, & Acker, 1995). The characteristics measured ten years earlier predicted which men were later sexually aggressive toward their partners, as reported both by men and their partners. This research suggests that men who commit sexual assault have learned a script for heterosexual interactions that includes the use of verbal abuse or physical force to exercise influence over or obtain sexual gratification from a woman (Huesmann, 1986). Once learned, it is used to regulate behavior in various situations. Research suggests that this script is learned in childhood (Jacobson & Gottman, 1998), likely when the child observes aggression frequently, is reinforced for aggressive behavior, and is the object of aggression.

Victims of Sexual Assault. Victims of sexual assault are primarily women between the ages of 15 and 24. Some women—a minority of all victims—are assaulted by men they do not know. These assaults by strangers often occur outdoors, in parks, deserted parking lots, or in the victim's residence. The offenders in these cases are often opportunistic, attacking any woman who is available or appears to be vulnerable.

Much more often, however, women are assaulted by someone they know. This may be a man they are dating (date rape) or a neighbor or coworker (acquaintance rape). The victims in most cases of date rape are young, single women—often high school or college students. A recent study found that 78% of unwanted sexual contact on a college campus took place while "hooking up" (Flack et al., 2007). In part because of their involvement in rape-prone fraternities on campus and in the hook-up culture, White college students are at a higher risk of sexual assault than are other racial groups on campuses (Armstrong, Hamilton, & Sweeney, 2006).

Several factors contribute to the occurrence of sexual assault. One is alcohol, which is a factor in more than half of all sexual assaults (whether involving alcohol consumption by the perpetrator, victim, or both) (Abbey, 2002). Alcohol lowers internal inhibitions that might otherwise prevent aggression. It also influences judgment. Both surveys and experiments provide evidence that people are more likely to engage in risky behavior—including entering a risky situation—when they have been drinking. In fact, some men use alcohol or drugs intentionally to make a woman more likely to take risks voluntarily (Abbey et al., 2001). One study randomly assigned male participants to one of two conditions. In one, the men consumed alcohol. In the other, the participants drank a nonalcoholic beverage. The participants were then presented with an acquaintance rape scenario. Intoxicated participants found the male character's use of force to obtain sex more acceptable and were more willing to act in a similar manner than the sober participants (Abbey, 2011). The effects of alcohol were strongest for men who already held hostile attitudes toward women.

Another factor in sexual assault is misinterpreted verbal or nonverbal messages. A woman may engage in some behavior that a man incorrectly interprets as a sexual invitation (Bondurant & Donat, 1999). Misinterpretations not only increase the prevalence of sexual assault but also influence attributions about the causes of assault. When responsibility for a sexual assault is placed on the victim rather than the perpetrator, it is referred to as **victim-blame**. Those engaged in victim-blame argue that a woman's flirting or provocative dress can somehow lead a man to believe that a woman is consenting to sexual contact or intercourse. Men tend to perceive more sexual intent in women's behavior than other women do (Farris, Treat, Viken, & McFall, 2008).

Cultural beliefs are a third factor that contributes to sexual assault. According to one survey of 14- to 17-year-olds, teenagers of both genders believe that a man is justified in forcing a woman to have intercourse if she gets him sexually excited, leads him on, or has dated him for a long time (Good-childs & Zellman, 1984). Other influential cultural beliefs include that men cannot stop once they have started to become sexually aroused, that husbands cannot rape their wives, and that women enjoy rape (Edwards et al., 2011; Ryan, 2011).

Misperceptions and cultural beliefs also influence women's interpretation of forced, nonconsensual sexual activity. Many women who experience sexual assault do not perceive the experience as rape (Kahn, Mathie, & Torgler, 1994). This may be because their experience—being assaulted by someone they know during a date after some sexual foreplay—does not match their script for rape: a violent attack by a stranger (Ryan, 1988). In one study, researchers asked women to write a description "of events before, during, and after a rape" and to describe their past experiences with assault. There were some women who reported that they had been forced to have sex but who also replied "no" to the question, "Have you ever been raped?" These women were more likely to describe rape as an attack by a stranger than were women who reported that they had been raped. Similarly, women's script for a loving relationship is one of equality and romance, which encourages individuals to overlook their partner's bad behavior, with an emphasis on male rather than female sexual drive (Lloyd & Emery, 2000). An experience of aggression does not fit this script and so may be ignored. This is a good example of the power of scripts to shape experience [...].

Pornography and Violence

One possible source for scripts that encourage sexual aggression is growing up in an abusive family. Another is viewing or reading pornography (Ryan, 2011).

On August 1, 2013, Ariel Castro was sentenced to life plus 1,000 years for the kidnapping, rape, and assault of three women whom he held captive in his home in Cleveland, Ohio. At the sentencing hearing, Castro blamed his behaviors on an addiction to pornography and joined a growing number of perpetrators—including Ted Bundy, a serial murderer who confessed to killing at least 24 young women—who have used pornography addiction as a defense for their heinous actions. Such claims generate great interest in the connection between pornography and violence, a link that social psychologists have conducted considerable research to explore.

Nonaggressive Pornography. Various studies have shown that the effect of pornography on behavior depends on what the pornography portrays. Pornography that explicitly depicts adults engaging in consenting sexual activity is termed **nonaggressive pornography** or erotica. Reading or viewing nonaggressive pornography creates sexual arousal (Byrne & Kelley, 1984), usually through the mechanism of cognitive and imaginative processing.

Nonaggressive pornography by itself does not produce aggression toward women (Donnerstein & Linz, 1998). However, when the viewer's inhibitions are lowered—as they may be if he is intoxicated—or if a man is already at risk for sexual aggression, it may do so

(Vega & Malamuth, 2007). Research finds that when men are angered or frustrated and then view nonaggressive pornographic images, they show more aggressive behavior toward women (Donnerstein & Barrett, 1978). The mechanism is thought to be transfer of arousal: The sexual arousal that results from viewing pornography is added to the arousal induced by the anger, resulting in sexual aggression.

Hollywood films, while not considered pornography, increasingly include apparently consensual sexual activity that is degrading or humiliating to women. For example, a study of James Bond films found that both the sexual activity and harm to women shown in the films has been increasing steadily over time (Neuendorf et al., 2010). An experiment explored the effect of viewing scenes that objectified women. Men and women who participated in the experiment saw either selections from *9½ Weeks* and *Showgirls* or scenes from animated cartoons. Participants subsequently read and evaluated a magazine story about a date rape or a stranger rape. Men who saw the sexualized film clips were more likely to say that the victim of the data rape enjoyed it and "got what she wanted" (Milburn, Mather, & Conrad, 2000). These results have important implications given the rise of depictions of sexual violence toward women in advertising and print media (Cortese, 2004).

Aggressive Pornography. Exposure to **aggressive pornography**—explicit depictions of sexual activity in which force is threatened or used to coerce a woman to engage in sex—also influences behavior, especially aggression toward women (Malamuth, 1984; Malamuth, Addison, & Koss, 2000). Unlike erotica, aggressive pornography has lasting effects on both attitudes and behavior. In a study of its effects on attitudes (Donnerstein, 1984), men viewed one of three films featuring either aggression, nonaggressive sexual activity, or aggressive sexual activity. Following the film, the participants completed several attitude scales, including one that measured acceptance of rape myths. Men who saw the films depicting aggression or aggressive sexual activity scored higher on the rape myth acceptance scale (see Box 7.2) than did men who saw the film depicting nonaggressive sexual activity. These men also indicated greater willingness to use force to obtain sex. The fact that both films depicting aggression, even nonsexual aggression, affected attitudes more than the nonaggressive film suggests that it is aggression rather than explicit portrayals of sex that influences attitudes toward sexual aggression. Experimental research like this is important for demonstrating the effects of viewing pornography to counter the argument that the relationship between pornography and aggression only goes the other direction: that men who consume pornography already have aggressive tendencies toward women and are, therefore, attracted to aggressive pornography (Malamuth, Addison, & Koss, 2000). Although that certainly may be the case, exposure to pornography also influences sexual aggression.

In another experimental study (Donner-stein & Berkowitz, 1981), male participants were either angered or treated neutrally by a male or female confederate. The participants then viewed one of four films: a neutral film, a nonaggressive pornographic film, or one of two aggressive pornographic films. In the latter films, a young woman is shoved around, tied up, stripped, and raped. In one version, she finds the experience disgusting, whereas in the other she is smiling at the end. Following the film, the men were given an opportunity to aggress against a male or female confederate by delivering electric shocks. The films did not affect aggression toward the male confederate. However, participants who saw the aggressive films delivered more intense electric shocks to the female confederate.

The fact that aggressive pornography produces aggressive behavior reflects three influences: sexual arousal, aggressive cues, and reduced inhibitions. Some men experience high levels of arousal in response to such portrayals. Moreover, such pornography portrays women as targets of aggression. In the experiment conducted by Donnerstein and Berkowitz, the film created an association in the viewer's mind between the victim in the film and the woman who angered him, suggesting aggression toward the latter. Note that aggressive films led to increased violence toward the female confederate and not the male confederate, a finding consistent with this interpretation. These films may also reduce inhibitions to aggression by suggesting that aggression directed toward women has positive outcomes.

One important question is whether we can generalize from the results of laboratory research to natural settings. Does the viewing of aggressive pornography in nonlaboratory settings contribute to violence against women? One study found a correlation between the availability of pornography and rates of violent crime (Baron & Straus, 1984). Results suggested that the circulation index of eight "sex magazines" (including *Playboy* and *Hustler*) in a state was the strongest predictor of rape in that state. Another study examined the influence of intentional exposure to X-rated material on sexually aggressive behavior among 10- to 15-year-olds (Ybarra et al., 2011). After accounting for other potential influences related to both exposure and sexual aggression (for example, substance abuse and being a victim of sexual aggression), researchers found that boys and girls who were exposed to violent X-rated material were six times as likely to report perpetrating a sexually aggressive behavior as were those who had either not viewed X-rated material or who had only been exposed to nonviolent X-rated material.

Media Violence and Aggression

If one thing has changed about American lifestyles over the past century, it is the amount of time spent consuming entertainment and news through visual media, both online and on television. These media are replete with violence, sex, and aggressive behaviors of all kinds. Given the ubiquity of media and the widespread belief that violence—sexual, physical, and psychological—is increasing around the world, both researchers and the public are interested in the effects media exposure has on behavior.

Violent Television and Aggression. Evelyn Wagler was carrying a two-gallon can of gasoline back to her stalled car. She was cornered by six young men who forced her to douse herself with the fuel. Then, one of the men tossed a lighted match. She burned to death. Two nights earlier, a similar murder had been depicted on national television.

Violence pervades television. Both heroes and villains perform aggression on television. Not just humans, but also cartoon characters torment each other in astonishingly creative ways. During prime-time television, three to five violent incidents occur per hour of programming, and 20 to 25 violent incidents occur per hour during Saturday morning children's shows (American Psychological Association, 1993). In all, 60% of television programs and 70% of the programming intended for children contains violence (Wilson et al., 2002). By age 18, the average American child is likely to have seen about 200,000 violent acts on television, including 40,000 homicides (Plagens, Miller, Foote, & Yoffe, 1991). Only one-quarter of these violent acts results in any punishment for the perpetrators (National Television Violence Study, 1996). Although research suggests that watching violent television is correlated with aggressive behavior (Anderson et al., 2003; Coyne et al., 2011), correlation is not the same as causation.

Does exposure to television violence encourage viewers to behave aggressively? Experimental research—where one group is exposed to violent media in a controlled setting while another group is not and then both groups' behavior and attitudes are measured—suggests that there is a causal connection (Comstock, 1984; Friedrich-Cofer & Huston, 1986; Murray & Kippax, 1979). This research also points to five processes that explain why exposure to media violence might increase aggressive behavior (Huesmann & Moise, 1996).

- *Imitation.* Viewers learn specific techniques of aggression from media models. Social learning evidently played a role in the violent attack on Evelyn Wagler.
- *Cognitive priming.* Portrayals of violence activate aggressive thoughts and pro-aggression attitudes. The activation of an attitude increases the likelihood that it will be expressed in behavior.
- *Legitimization/justification.* Exposure to violence that leads to goal attainment and has positive outcomes (for example, punishes wrongdoers) legitimizes aggression and makes it more acceptable (Bushmann & Huesmann, 2001).
- *Desensitization.* After observing violence repeatedly, viewers become less sensitive to aggression. This makes them less reluctant to hurt others and less inclined to ease others' suffering.
- *Arousal.* Viewing violence on television produces excitement and physiological arousal, which may amplify aggressive responses in situations that would otherwise elicit milder anger.

Moreover, these results have been found in experiments with boys and girls of all ages, races, social classes, and levels of intelligence as well as in many countries (Huesmann & Moise, 1996). A meta-analysis of all the research available at the time reports that virtually every study—whether cross-sectional (n = 86), longitudinal (n = 46), or experimental (n = 152)—finds a significant relationship between exposure to media violence and aggression (Anderson & Bushman, 2002). This is true of television, movies, and Internet media (Ybarra, Diener-West, Markow, Leaf, Hamburger, & Boxer, 2008).

Violence on the Internet takes a number of forms, including violent videos, like some posted on the sites YouTube or Vine, or violent images and scenarios depicted in photos and ads showing physical and sexual aggression. Other violence on the Internet takes the form of psychological violence. "Hate pages" are devoted to harassing and degrading specific groups, and cyber-bullying runs rampant on Facebook, ask.fm, and other social media sites. Users—particularly adolescents who are highly susceptible to peer pressure—frequently imitate this displayed aggression, both on- and offline (Ybarra et al., 2008).

However, the relationship between violent media and aggression is not one directional. A growing body of evidence suggests that the link between aggression and media usage is actually circular (Friedrich-Cofer & Huston, 1986). Because aggressive children are relatively unpopular with their peers, they spend more time watching television as well as online and playing video games. This exposes them to more violence, teaches them aggressive scripts and behaviors, and reassures them that their behavior is appropriate. When they then try to enact these scripts in interactions with others, they become even more unpopular and are driven back to television—and the vicious cycle continues (Huesmann, 1986; Singer & Singer, 1983).

Despite all this evidence on the connection between media violence and violent behavior, scientists have been unable to convince film and television producers to decrease the amount of violence shown in television and movies. In fact, over time, film ratings have relaxed to allow more violent content in PG-13 films than was allowed in previous years (Leone & Barowski, 2011). To approach the issue from another side, researchers have turned their attention toward developing interventions to limit the negative effect of media violence (Rosenkoetter, Rosenkoetter, & Acock, 2009).

Social psychologists have used experimental methods—both in the field and the laboratory—to test strategies that parents, teachers, and others might use to counteract the deleterious effects of violent media (Rosenkoetter, Rosenkoetter, & Acock, 2009). Previous work suggests that aggression is lower among individuals who are high in empathy (Dean & Malamuth, 1997). Drawing on this, researchers tried to induce empathy among viewers. When adults ask children to empathize with the victim, children are less accepting of aggression and find the aggression in cartoons less humorous (Nathanson & Cantor, 2000). Adults can also reduce children's imitation of aggression by making negative comments about the violence. A neutral comment, however, is no less effective than no comment at all (Cantor & Wilson, 2003).

Interventions are most effective when they are long term. A year-long program for elementary students that emphasized the ways that television distorts the reality of aggression not only resulted in less positive attitudes about violence on television but also reduced identification with violent heroes and led children to watch less violent programming. Participating in the program also lowered aggressive behaviors among boys, who watch more violent program-ming than girls do (Rosenkoetter, Rosenkoetter, Ozretich, and Acock, 2004; Dodge, Coie, & Lynam, 2006).

Technological advances have greatly expanded young people's access to media, including violent media, and have limited adults' knowledge of what young people are exposed to and the opportunity to discuss the images together. © CREATISTA/shutterstock

Violent Video Games and Aggression. One late summer afternoon, an eight-year-old boy shot Marie Smothers, his elderly caregiver, in the back of the head as she sat in her living room watching television. Media reports claimed the shooting was intentional and blamed the violent video game *Grand Theft Auto*—which the boy had been playing just moments before he killed Smothers—for his violent actions. Although it is difficult to determine the causes of acts of aggression, research suggests that there is a relationship between both short- and long-term exposure to violence in video games and aggression (Anderson et al., 2010). Both men and women who report playing violent video games are more likely to report engaging in various aggressive behaviors (Bushman, Baumeister, & Stack, 1999).

Although video game playing was once restricted to arcades and television consoles, today people also play video games on computers, handheld devices, iPods, and cell phones. Technological advances have improved the sound effects and graphics, making video games more engrossing than they were in the past (Ivory & Kalyanaraman, 2007). In 2008, 97% of teenagers between 12 and 17 reported playing video games, with 31% playing every day (Lenhart et al., 2008). Many of these video games portray interpersonal violence. A content analysis of 33 popular video games found that 80% of them involved aggression or violence as part of the strategy. About half encourage violence directed at people, and 21% included violence directed at women (Dietz, 1998).

Playing video games involves a number of the psychological processes discussed earlier. Playing violent video games leads to both physiological (heart rate, body temperature) and emotional arousal (anger, hostility) (Anderson et al. 2010). Players, like the young boy discussed at the beginning of the section, might imitate what they see. More lasting, though, is acquiring the behavior patterns or scripts that include violence as a means of achieving higher scores (observational learning) and having these rewarded (reinforcement) (Funk, Flores, Buchman, & Germann, 1999). Ongoing exposure to violence also desensitizes players to violence, making it seem more normal and natural (Krahé, 2013), and primes them to later react more aggressively to minor annoyances (Anderson & Dill, 2000). This occurs, in part, through disinhibition.

Features of games either dampen or amplify the effect of violence on aggression. For example, both more visible blood in games and controllers in the shape of a realistic gun tend to heighten arousal and hostility (Barlett, Harris, & Baldassaro, 2007; Barlett, Harris & Bruey, 2008). Similarity to and identification with aggressive video game characters also increase the effects of video games on aggression (Williams, 2010). Finally, research finds that playing a video game that sexualized and objectified women—with provocative dress—increased men's rape acceptance and led them to judge rape victims more negatively than did playing an identical game with fully clothed women as characters (Stermer & Burkley, 2012).

Summary

Aggression is behavior intended to harm another person that the target person wants to avoid.

Aggression and the Motivation to Harm. There are four main theories regarding the motivation for aggression. (1) People are instinctively aggressive. (2) People become aggressive in response to events that are frustrating. (3) People aggress against others as a result of aversive emotion. (4) People are motivated by rewards and learn to use aggression as a means of obtaining what they want.

Characteristics of Targets that Affect Aggression. Once aggressive motivation has been aroused, target characteristics influence whether aggressive behavior occurs. Aggressive behavior is more likely if the target is of the same race or ethnicity. The target's gender also influences the response. When we are attacked, our response is influenced by the attributions we make about the attacker's intentions. We are less likely to engage in aggression toward a target who we believe is capable of retaliation. We may, however, engage in displaced aggression against another.

Situational Impacts on Aggression. Situational conditions are important influences on aggressive behavior. Rewards that encourage aggression include material benefits, social approval, and attention. Aggressive models provide information about available options, normative appropriateness, and consequences (or lack thereof) of aggressive acts. The negative reciprocity norm encourages aggressive behavior in certain situations. Aggressive behavior is more likely when stressors, such as high temperature, are present. Aggressive behavior is also more likely in the presence of aggressive cues, especially weapons.

Reducing Aggressive Behavior. Frustration levels could be reduced by guaranteeing everyone the basic necessities, therefore limiting aggression motivated by rewards. Punishment is effective in controlling aggression only when it promptly follows the aggressive act, is seen as the logical outcome of that act, and does not violate social norms. Nonaggressive models reduce the likelihood of aggression and can offset the effect of aggressive models. Although catharsis may follow aggressive acts, such acts may still promote later aggression.

Aggression in Society. Interpersonal violence is a serious problem in American society. Rates of sexual assault and acceptance of the behavior are influenced by societal characteristics, such as male domination of women, and by scripts that encourage male aggression toward women. Nonaggressive pornography and aggressive pornography both influence attitudes and behavior, although the latter to a much higher degree. Experimental research shows that observing violence in film, on television and the Internet, and in video games increases aggressive attitudes and behavior in everyday settings.

List of Key Terms and Concepts

affective aggression (p. 171)

aggravated assault (p. 173)

aggression (p. 166)

aggressive pornography (p. 190)

aversive affect (p. 171)

catharsis (p. 183)

displaced aggression (p. 176)

frustration (p. 168)

frustration-aggression hypothesis (p. 168)

nonaggressive pornography (p. 189)

rumination (p. 181)

sexual assault (p. 184)

target (p. 172)

victim-blame (p. 188)

weapons effect (p. 181)

Critical Thinking Skill: Applying Scientific Research to Policy Decisions

Gun violence in the United States has many people concerned. However, both politicians and citizens are divided on how best to curb this violence. Some argue that only police and the military should have guns, others argue that automatic weapons should be restricted or guns should be harder to purchase, while still others assert that access to guns is not the problem and that other measures should be taken. How should the average citizen or a policymaker decide their stance on this critical issue? The best way to make a good decision is to use the best available scientific evidence and think clearly about it. The evidence might come from correlational methods, like field studies and surveys, or from experiments.

The current discourse around gun violence centers on access. To determine whether the widespread availability of guns increases gun violence using a correlational method, a scientist might compare rates of lethal gun violence (deaths related to gunshot wounds) in countries where gun ownership is legal to the rates in countries where citizens are not allowed to buy guns through legal channels. The researchers would then see whether there is a correlation between accessibility and lethal gun violence. Suppose the correlation is positive and significant—that is, the more accessible guns are to citizens (legal to own, easy to purchase, and so forth), the larger the number of people who die from gun-related violence each year. This evidence provides support for policies that limit access to guns. However, because it is a correlational study, it cannot tell us whether access actually influences violence.

Another way to get at the question would be with an experiment. In a field experiment, scientists might choose two cities with similar rates of gun violence that are similar on other characteristics (racial diversity, economic inequality, education and income levels, and so forth). They would then have politicians institute a law that limited access to firearms in one of the cities. By tracking gun violence in the two cities, they could gauge whether restricting access lessened violence. However, there are a number of confounding factors that make such an experiment problematic and the findings difficult to interpret.

Alternatively, scientists could run a laboratory experiment in which they put subjects in a situation—something like a video game—in which they either had easy access to a gun or a gun was difficult or costly to acquire. The researchers could then expose subjects to frustrating situations in which they had the opportunity to use the gun or deal with their aggression in another way and then compare the likelihood that subjects would choose responses other than gun violence. Although laboratory experiments allow scientists significant control over conditions, the problem here is that it is a video game. Furthermore, in such a research setting, participants are acutely aware that their behavior is being tracked. Perhaps the findings would not generalize to a natural environment.

What are the benefits and limitations of the above studies? What are other studies you might conduct?

We can be most confident of a conclusion if there is converging evidence from multiple studies, both correlational and experimental. Considering these hypothetical studies together would give us more confidence in our ultimate decision because each study addresses some of the limitations of the others.

How can these studies inform a policy decision? At this point, a good policy decision would involve a cost-benefit analysis. Reducing citizens' access to guns might make those citizens more vulnerable to the violent attacks of others. Gun manufacturers and retailers would lose money if their only clients were police and military. These are costs. What are other costs? However, fewer gun deaths—whether accidental or intentional—would be a benefit. Are there other benefits?

In general, when making policy decisions when scientific evidence is available, we should evaluate the quality of that evidence and then weigh the costs and benefits of implementing policies based on the evidence.

References

Abbey, A. (2002). Alcohol-related sexual assault: A common problem among college students. *Journal of Studies on Alcohol and Drugs, 14,* 118–128.

Abbey, A., Jacques-Tiura, A. J., & LeBreton, J. M. (2011). Risk factors for sexual aggression in young men: An expansion of the confluence model. *Aggressive Behavior, 37*(5), 450–464.

Abbey, A., McAuslan, P., Zawacki, T., Clinton, A. M., & Buck, P. O. (2001). Attitudinal, experiential, and situational predictors of sexual assault perpetration. *Journal of Interpersonal Violence*, *16*(8), 784–807.

Adachi, P. J., & Willoughby, T. (2011). The effect of video game competition and violence on aggressive behavior: Which characteristic has the greatest influence? *Psychology of Violence*, *1*(4), 259.

American Psychological Association. (1993). *Summary report of the APA Commission on Violence and Youth*. Washington, DC: Author.

Anderson, C. A. (1987). Temperature and aggression: Effects on quarterly, yearly, and city rates of violent and nonviolent crime. *Journal of Personality and Social Psychology*, *52*, 1161–1173.

Anderson, C. A. (2001). Heat and violence. *Current Directions in Psychological Science*, *10*, 33–38.

Anderson, C. A., Anderson, K. B., & Deuser, W. E. (1996). Examining an affective aggression framework: Weapon and temperature effects on aggressive thoughts, affect, and attitudes. *Personality and Social Psychology Bulletin*, *22*, 366–376.

Anderson, C. A., Benjamin, A. J., & Bartholow, B. D. (1998). Does the gun pull the trigger? Automatic priming effects of weapon pictures and weapon names. *Psychological Science*, *9*, 308–314.

Anderson, C. A., Berkowitz, L., Donnerstein, E., Huesmann, L. R., Johnson, J., Linz, D., et al. (2003). The influence of media violence on youth. *Psychological Science in the Public Interest*, *4*, 81–110.

Anderson, C. A., & Bushman, B. J. (2002). Human aggression. *Annual Review of Psychology*, *53*(1), 27–51.

Anderson, C. A., & Dill, K. E. (2000). Video games and aggressive thoughts, feelings, and behavior in the laboratory and in life. *Journal of Personality and Social Psychology*, *78*(4), 772–790.

Anderson, C. A., Shibuya, A., Ihori, N., Swing, E. L., Bushman, B. J., Sakamoto, A., Rothstein, H. R., & Saleem, M. (2010). Violent video game effects on aggression, empathy, and prosocial behavior in eastern and western countries: a meta-analytic review. *Psychological Bulletin*, *136*(2), 151.

Anderson, K. B., Cooper, H., & Okamura, L. (1997). Individual differences and attitudes toward rape: A meta-analytic review. *Personality and Social Psychology Bulletin, 23*(3), 295–315.

Andrews, B., & Brewin, C. R. (1990). Attributions of blame for marital violence: A study of antecedents and consequences. *Journal of Marriage and the Family*, *52*(3), 757–767.

Armstrong, E. A., Hamilton, L., & Sweeney, B. (2006). Sexual assault on campus: A multilevel, integrative approach to party rape. *Social Problems*, *53*(4), 483–499.

Averill, J. R. (1980). A constructivist view of emotion. *Emotion: Theory, research, and experience*, *1*, 305–339.

Bandura, A. (1973). *Aggression: A social learning analysis*. Englewood Cliffs, NJ: Prentice Hall.

Bandura, A., Ross, D., & Ross, S. (1961). Transmission of aggression through imitation of aggressive models. *Journal of Abnormal and Social Psychology*, *63*, 575–582.

Barker, R. G., Dembo, T., & Lewin, K. (1941). Frustration and aggression: An experiment with young children. *University of Iowa Studies in Child Welfare*, *18*, 1–34.

Barlett, C. P., & Anderson, C. A. (2011). Reappraising the situation and its impact on aggressive behavior. *Personality and Social Psychology Bulletin*, *37*(12), 1564–1573.

Barlett, C. P., Harris, R. J., & Baldassaro, R. (2007). Longer you play, the more hostile you feel: Examination of first person shooter video games and aggression during video game play. *Aggressive Behavior*, *33*(6), 486–497.

Barlett, C. P., Harris, R. J., & Bruey, C. (2008). The effect of the amount of blood in a violent video game on aggression, hostility, and arousal. *Journal of Experimental Social Psychology*, *44*(3), 539–546.

Baron, L., & Straus, M. A. (1984). Sexual stratification, pornography, and rape in the United States. In N. M. Malamuth and E. I. Donnerstein (Eds.), *Pornography and sexual aggression* (pp. 185–209). Orlando, FL: Academic Press.

Baron, R., & Ransberger, V. (1978). Ambient temperature and the occurrence of collective violence: The "long, hot summer" revisited. *Journal of Personality and Social Psychology, 36*, 351–360.

Baron, R. A. (1971). Reducing the influence of an aggressive model: The restraining effects of discrepant modeling cues. *Journal of Personality and Social Psychology, 20*, 240–245.

Baron, R. A. (1977). *Human aggression.* New York: Plenum.

Baron, R. A., & Kepner, C. R. (1970). Model's behavior and attraction toward the model as determinants of adult aggressive behavior. *Journal of Personality and Social Psychology, 14*, 335–344.

Barnes, C. D., Brown, R. P., & Osterman, L. L. (2012). Don't tread on me: Masculine honor ideology in the US and militant responses to terrorism. *Personality and Social Psychology Bulletin, 38*(8), 1018–1029.

Benson, M. L., & Fox, G. L. (2004). When violence hits home: How economics and neighborhood play a role, Research in Brief. *NCJ, 205004.*

Berkowitz, L. (1978). Whatever happened to the frustration-aggression hypothesis? *American Behavioral Scientist, 21*, 691–708.

Berkowitz, L. (1989). Frustration-aggression hypothesis: Examination and reformulation. *Psychological Bulletin, 106*, 59–73.

Bondurant, B., & Donat, P. L. (1999). Perceptions of women's sexual interest and acquaintance rape: The role of sexual overperception and affective attitudes. *Psychology of Women Quarterly, 23*(4), 691–705.

Brown, P., & Elliott, R. (1965). Control of aggression in a nursery school class. *Journal of Experimental Child Psychology, 2*, 103–107.

Brown, R. P., Osterman, L. L., & Barnes, C. D. (2009). School violence and the culture of honor. *Psychological Science, 20*(11), 1400–1405.

Browning, C. R., & Cagney, K. A. (2003). Moving beyond poverty: Neighborhood structure, social processes, and health. *Journal of Health and Social Behavior, 44*(4), 552–571.

Burns, D. (2009). The experience and expression of anger and aggression in dating relationships for male college athletes in contact and non-contact sports. Doctoral dissertation, Oklahoma State University.

Burt, M. R. (1980). Cultural myths and supports for rape. *Journal of Personality and Social Psychology, 38*(2), 217–230.

Bushman, B., Baumeister, R., & Stack, A. (1999). Catharsis, aggression, and persuasive influence: Self-fulfilling or self-defeating prophecies. *Journal of Personality and Social Psychology, 76*, 367–376.

Bushman, B. J., Bonacci, A. M., Pedersen, W. C., Vasquez, E. A., & Miller, N. (2005). Chewing on it can chew you up: effects of rumination on triggered displaced aggression. *Journal of Personality and Social Psychology, 88*(6), 969.

Bushman, B. J., & Huesmann, L. R. (2001). Effects of televised violence on aggression. In D. G. Singer, & J. L. Singer (Eds.), *Handbook of children and the media* (pp. 223–254). Thousand Oaks, CA: Sage.

Byrne, D., & Kelley, K. (1984). Introduction: Pornography and sex research. In N. M. Malamuth & E. Donnerstein (Eds.), *Pornography and sexual aggression.* (pp. 1–15). Orlando, FL: Academic Press.

Cantor, J., & Wilson, B. J. (2003). Media and violence: Intervention strategies for reducing aggression. *Media Psychology, 5*, 363–403.

Carlson, M., Marcus-Newhall, A., & Miller, N. (1990). Effects of situational aggression cues: A quantitative review. *Journal of Personality and Social Psychology, 58*, 622–633.

Carr, J. L., & VanDeusen, K. M. (2004). Risk factors for male sexual aggression on college campuses. *Journal of Family Violence, 19*(5), 279–289.

Catalano, R., Novaco, R., & McConnell, W. (1997). A model of the net effect of job loss on violence. *Journal of Personality and Social Psychology, 72*(6), 1440–1447.

Check, J. V., & Malamuth, N. M. (1983). Sex role stereotyping and reactions to depictions of stranger versus acquaintance rape. *Journal of Personality and Social Psychology, 45*(2), 344–356.

Cohen, D., Nisbett, R. E., Bowdle, B. F., & Schwarz, N. (1996). Insult, aggression, and the southern culture of honor: An "experimental ethnography." *Journal of Personality and Social Psychology, 70*(5), 945–960.

Cohn, E. G., & Rotton, J. (1997). Assault as a function of time and temperature: A moderator-variable time-series analysis. *Journal of Personality and Social Psychology, 72*(6), 1322–1334.

Cohn, E. G., & Rotton, J. (2005). The curve is still out there: A reply to Bushman, Wang, and Anderson's (2005) Is the curve relating temperature to aggression linear or curvilinear? *Journal of Personality and Social Psychology, 89*(1), 67–70.

Coleman, L. (2004). *The copycat effect: How the media and popular culture trigger the mayhem in tomorrow's headlines.* New York: Paraview.

Comstock, G. (1984). Media influences on aggression. In A. Goldstein (Ed.), *Prevention and control of aggression: Principles, practices, and research.* (pp. 241– 272). New York: Pergamon.

Connell, R. W. (2005). *Masculinities.* Berkeley: University of California Press.

Cortese, A. J. (2004). *Provocateur: Images of women and minorities in advertising.* Lanham, MD: Rowman & Littlefield.

Coyne, S. M., Nelson, D. A., Graham-Kevan, N., Tew, E., Meng, K. N., & Olsen, J. A. (2011). Media depictions of physical and relational aggression: connections with aggression in young adults' romantic relationships. *Aggressive Behavior, 37*(1), 56–62.

Dean, K. E., & Malamuth, N. M. (1997). Characteristics of men who aggress sexually and of men who imagine aggressing: Risk and moderating variables. *Journal of Personality and Social Psychology, 72*(2), 449–455.

DeMaris, A., Benson, M. L., Fox, G. L., Hill, T., & Van Wyk, J. (2003). Distal and proximal factors in domestic violence: A test of an integrated model. *Journal of Marriage and Family, 65*(3), 652–667.

DeWall, N. C., & Bushman, B. J. (2009). Hot under the collar in a lukewarm environment: Words associated with hot temperature increase aggressive thoughts and hostile perceptions. *Journal of Experimental Social Psychology, 45*(4), 1045–1047.

Dietz, T. L. (1998). An examination of violence and gender role portrayals in video games: Implications for gender socialization and aggressive behavior. *Sex Roles, 38*(5–6), 425–442.

Dishion, T. J., & Dodge, K. A. (2005). Peer contagion in interventions for children and adolescents: Moving towards an understanding of the ecology and dynamics of change. *Journal of Abnormal Child Psychology, 33,* 395–400.

Dodge, K. A., Coie, J. D., & Lynam, D. (2006). Aggression and antisocial behavior in youth. In N. Eisenberg, W. Damon, R. L. Lerner (Eds), *Handbook of child psychology: Vol. 3. Social, emotional, and personality development* (pp. 719–788), New York: Wiley.

Dollard, J., Doob, J., Miller, N., Mowrer, O., & Sears, R. (1939). *Frustration and aggression.* New Haven, CT: Yale University Press.

Donnerstein, E. (1984). Pornography: Its effect on violence against women. In N. M. Malamuth & E. Donnerstein (Eds.), *Pornography and sexual aggression.* (pp. 53–81). Orlando, FL: Academic Press.

Donnerstein, E., & Barrett, G. (1978). The effects of erotic stimuli on male aggression toward females. *Journal of Personality and Social Psychology, 36,* 180–188.

Donnerstein, E., & Berkowitz, L. (1981). Victim reactions in aggressive erotic films as a factor in violence toward women. *Journal of Personality and Social Psychology, 41,* 710–724.

Donnerstein, E, and Linz, D. (1998). Mass media, violence and the male viewer. In M. E. Oden and J. Clay-Warner (Eds): *Confronting rape and sexual assault* (pp 181–198). Wilmington, DE: SR Books/ Scholarly Resources.

Dyck, R. J., & Rule, B. G. (1978). Effect on retaliation of causal attribution concerning attack. *Journal of Personality and Social Psychology, 36*, 521–529.

Edwards, K. M., Turchik, J. A., Dardis, C. M., Reynolds, N., & Gidycz, C. A. (2011). Rape myths: History, individual and institutional-level presence, and implications for change. *Sex Roles, 65*(11–12), 761–773.

Farris, C., Treat, T. A., Viken, R. J., & McFall, R. M. (2008). Sexual coercion and the misperception of sexual intent. *Clinical Psychology Review, 28*(1), 48–66.

Flack, W. F., Daubman, K. A., Caron, M. L., Asadorian, J. A., D'Aureli, N. R., Gigliotti, S. N., Hall, A. T. et al. (2007). Risk Factors and consequences of unwanted sex among university students hooking up, alcohol, and stress response. *Journal of Interpersonal Violence, 22*(2), 139–157.

Fox, G. L., & Benson, M. L. (2006). Household and neighborhood contexts of intimate partner violence. *Public Health Reports, 121*(4), 419–427.

Fox, G. L., Benson, M. L., DeMaris, A. A., & Wyk, J. (2002). Economic distress and intimate violence: Testing family stress and resources theories. *Journal of Marriage and Family, 64*(3), 793–807.

Freud, S. (1930). *Civilization and its discontents.* London: Hogarth Press.

Freud, S. (1950). Why war? In J. Strachey (Ed.), *Collected papers* (Vol. 5, pp. 195–216). London: Hogarth Press.

Friedrich-Cofer, L., & Huston, A. C. (1986). Television violence and aggression: The debate continues. *Psychological Bulletin, 100*, 364–371.

Gartner, R. (1990). The victims of homicide: A temporal and cross-national comparison. *American Sociological Review, 55*, 92–106.

Geen, R. G. (1968). Effects of frustration, attack, and prior training in aggressiveness upon aggressive behavior. *Journal of Personality and Social Psychology, 9*(4), 316–321.

Geen, R. G., & Quanty, M. G. (1977). The catharsis of aggression: An analysis of a hypothesis. In L. Berkowitz (Ed.), *Advances in experimental social psychology* (Vol. 10, pp. 1–37). New York: Academic Press.

Geen, R. G., Stonner, L., & Shope, G. L. (1975). The facilitation of aggression by aggression: A study in response inhibition and disinhibition. *Journal of Personality and Social Psychology, 31*, 721–726.

Gelles, R. J., & Cornell, C. P. (1997). *Intimate violence in families.* Newbury Park, CA: Sage.

Gelles, R. J., & Strauss, M. A. (1988). *Intimate violence.* New York: Simon and Schuster.

Goodchilds, J. D., & Zellman, G. L. (1984). Sexual signaling and sexual aggression in adolescent relationships. In N. M. Malamuth & E. I. Donnerstein (Eds.), *Pornography and sexual aggression* (pp. 234–243). Orlando, FL: Academic Press.

Greenfeld, L., Rand, M., Craven, D., Klaus, P., Perkins, C., Ringel, C., et al. (1998). *Violence by intimates.* Washington, DC: U.S. Department of Justice, Bureau of Justice Statistics.

Harris, M. B. (1974). Mediators between frustration and aggression in a field experiment. *Journal of Experimental Social Psychology, 10*, 561–571.

Hennessy, D. A., & Wiesenthal, D. L. (2001). Gender, driver aggression, and driver violence: An applied evaluation. *Sex Roles, 44*(11–12), 661–676.

Huesmann, L. R. (1986). Psychological processes promoting the relation between exposure to media violence and aggressive behavior by the viewer. *Journal of Social Issues, 42*(3), 125–139.

Huesmann, L. R., & Moise, J. (1996). Media violence: A demonstrated public health threat to children. *Harvard Mental Health Letter, 12*(12), 5–7.

Ivory, J. D., & Kalyanaraman, S. (2007). The effects of technological advancement and violent content in video games on players' feelings of presence, involvement, physiological arousal, and aggression. *Journal of Communication, 57*(3), 532–555.

Jacobson, N. S., & Gottman, J. M. (1998). *When men batter women: New insights into ending abusive relationships.* New York: Simon and Schuster.

Jewkes, R., Sen, P., & Garcia-Moreno, C. (2002). Sexual violence. In E. G. Krug, L. L. Dahlberg, J. A. Mercy, A. B. Zwi, & R. Lozano (Eds), *World report on violence and health* (pp. 149–181). Geneva: World Health Organization.

Johnson, M. P., & Ferraro, K. J. (2000). Research on domestic violence in the 1990s: Making distinctions. *Journal of Marriage and Family, 62*(4), 948–963.

Kahn, A. S., Mathie, V. A., & Torgler, C. (1994). Rape scripts and rape acknowledgment. *Psychology of Women Quarterly, 18*(1), 53–66.

Koss, M. P., & Leonard, K. E. (1984). Sexually aggressive men: Empirical findings and theoretical implications. In N. M. Malamuth & E. I. Donnerstein (Eds.), *Pornography and sexual aggression* (pp. 213–232). Orlando, FL: Academic Press.

Krahé, B. (2013). Violent video games and aggression. In K. E. Dill (Ed.), *The Oxford handbook of media psychology* (pp. 352–372). New York: Oxford University Press.

Krebs, D. L. (1982). Psychological approaches to altruism: An evaluation. *Ethics, 92*, 147–158.

Kulick, J. A., & Brown, R. (1979). Frustration, attribution of blame, and aggression. *Journal of Experimental Social Psychology, 15*, 183–194.

Land, K. C., McCall, P. L., & Cohen, L. E. (1990). Structural correlates of homicide rates: Are there invariances across time and social space? *American Journal of Sociology, 95*, 922–963.

Larimer, M. E., Lydum, A. R., Anderson, B. K., & Turner, A. P. (1999). Male and female recipients of unwanted sexual contact in a college student sample: Prevalence rates, alcohol use, and depression symptoms. *Sex Roles, 40*(3–4), 295–308.

Lavoie, F., Hebert, M., Tremblay, R., Vitaro, F., Vezina, L., & McDuff, P. (2002). History of family dysfunction and perpetration of dating violence by adolescent boys: A longitudinal study. *Journal of Adolescent Health, 30*, 375–383.

Lenhart, A., Kahne, J., Middaugh, E., Macgill, A. R., Evans, C., & Vitak, J. (2008). Teens, video games, and civics: teens' gaming experiences are diverse and include significant social interaction and civic engagement. *Pew Internet and American Life Project.*

Leone, R., & Barowski, L. (2011). MPAA ratings creep: a longitudinal analysis of the PG-13 rating category in US movies. *Journal of Children and Media, 5*(01), 53–68.

Lloyd, S. A., & Emery, B. C. (2000). The context and dynamics of intimate aggression against women. *Journal of Social and Personal Relationships, 17*(4–5), 503–521.

Logan, T. K., Walker, R., Cole, J., & Leukefeld, C. (2002). Victimization and substance abuse among women: contributing factors, interventions, and implications. *Review of General Psychology, 6*(4), 325.

Lorenz, K. (1966). *On aggression.* New York: Harcourt Brace Jovanovich.

Lorenz, K. (1974). *Civilized man's eight deadly sins.* New York: Harcourt Brace Jovanovich.

Malamuth, N. M. (1984). Aggression against women: Cultural and individual causes. In N. M. Malamuth & E. Donnerstein (Eds.), *Pornography and sexual aggression.* (pp. 19–52). Orlando, FL: Academic Press.

Malamuth, N. M., Addison, T., & Koss, M. (2000). Pornography and sexual aggression: Are there reliable effects and can we understand them? *Annual Review of Sex Research, 11*(1), 26–91.

Malamuth, N. M., Heavey, C. L., & Linz, D. (1993). Predicting men's antisocial behavior against women: The interaction model of sexual aggression. In G. C. N. Hall (Ed.), *Sexual aggression: Issues in etiology, assessment, and treatment* (pp. 63–97). Washington, DC: Taylor and Francis.

Malamuth, N. M., Linz, D., Heavey, C. L., Barnes, G., & Acker, M. (1995). Using the confluence model of sexual aggression to predict men's conflict with women: A 10-year follow-up study. *Journal of Personality and Social Psychology, 69*(2), 353–369.

Marcus-Newhall, A., Pedersen, W. C., Carlson, M., & Miller, N. (2000). Displaced aggression is alive and well: A meta-analytic review. *Journal of Personality and Social Psychology*, *78*(4), 670–689.

Markowitz, F., & Felson, R. (1998). Social-demographic differences in attitudes and violence. *Criminology*, *36*, 401–422.

McMahon, S., & Farmer, G. L. (2011). An updated measure for assessing subtle rape myths. *Social Work Research*, *35*(2), 71–81.

Milburn, M. A., Mather, R., & Conrad, S. D. (2000). The effects of viewing R-rated movie scenes that objectify women on perceptions of date rape. *Sex Roles*, *43*(9–10), 645–664.

Murray, J. P., & Kippax, S. (1979). From the early window to the late night show: International trends in the study of television's impact on children and adults. In L. Berkowitz (Ed.), *Advances in experimental social psychology* (Vol. 12, pp. 253–320). New York: Academic Press.

Myers, D. J. (1997). Racial rioting in the 1960s: An event history analysis of local conditions. *American Sociological Review*, *62*, 94–112.

Nathanson, A. I., & Cantor, J. (2000). Reducing the aggression-promoting effect of violent cartoons by increasing children's fictional involvement with the victim. *Journal of Broadcasting and Electronic Media*, *44*, 125–142.

National Television Violence Study. (1996). *National Television Violence Study* (Vol. 1). Thousand Oaks, CA: Sage.

Neuendorf, K. A., Gore, T. D., Dalessandro, A., Janstova, P., & Snyder-Suhy, S. (2010). Shaken and stirred: A content analysis of women's portrayals in James Bond films. *Sex Roles*, *62*(11–12), 747–761.

Ohbuchi, K. I., Kameda, M., & Agarie, N. (1989). Apology as aggression control: Its role in mediating appraisal of and response to harm. *Journal of Personality and Social Psychology*, *56*(2), 219–227.

Olzak, S., Shanahan, S., & McEneaney, E. H. (1996). Poverty, segregation, and race riots: 1960 to 1993. *American Sociological Review*, *61*(4), 590–613.

Plagens, P., Miller, M., Foote, D., & Yoffe, E. (1991, April). Violence in our culture. *Newsweek*, *51*, 46–52.

Powers, C. J., & Bierman, K. L. (2013). The multifaceted impact of peer relations on aggressive–disruptive behavior in early elementary school. *Developmental Psychology*, *49*(6), 1174–1186.

Prentice-Dunn, S., & Rogers, R. W. (1980). Effects of deindividuating situational cues and aggressive models on subjective deindividuation and aggression. *Journal of Personality and Social Psychology*, *39*(1), 104–113.

Rennison, C. M. (2001). *Violent victimization and race, 1993–98*. U.S. Department of Justice, Office of Justice Programs, Bureau of Justice Statistics.

Rosenkoetter, L. I., Rosenkoetter, S. E., & Acock, A. C. (2009). Television violence: An intervention to reduce its impact on children. *Journal of Applied Developmental Psychology, 30*(4), 381–397.

Rosenkoetter, L. I., Rosenkoetter, S. E., Ozretich, R. A., & Acock, A. C. (2004). Mitigating the harmful effects of violent television. *Journal of Applied Developmental Psychology, 25*, 25–47.

Rotton, J., & Cohn, E. G. (2004). Outdoor temperature, climate control, and criminal assault: The spatial and temporal ecology of violence. *Environment and Behavior*, *36*(2), 276–306.

Ryan, K. (1988). Rape and seduction scripts. *Psychology of Women Quarterly*, *12*, 237–245.

Ryan, K. M. (2011). The relationship between rape myths and sexual scripts: The social construction of rape. *Sex Roles*, *65*(11–12), 774–782.

Salmivalli, C., & Nieminen, E. (2002). Proactive and reactive aggression among school bullies, victims, and bully-victims. *Aggressive Behavior*, *28*(1), 30–44.

Sanday, P. R. (1981). The socio-cultural context of rape: A cross-cultural study. *Journal of Social Issues*, *37*(4), 5–27.

Sanday, P. R. (2003). Rape-free versus rape-prone: How culture makes a difference. In C. B. Travis (Ed.), *Evolution, gender, and rape*, 337–362. Cambridge, MA: MIT Press.

Singer, J. L., & Singer, D. G. (1983). Psychologists look at television: Cognitive, developmental, personality, and social policy implications. *American Psychologist, 38*, 826–834.

Stermer, S. P., & Burkley, M. (2012). Xbox or seXbox? An examination of sexualized content in video games. *Social and Personality Psychology Compass, 6*(7), 525–535.

Taylor, S. P. (1967). Aggressive behavior and physiological arousal as a function of provocation and the tendency to inhibit aggression. *Journal of Personality, 35*, 297–310.

Thompson, E. H., & Pleck, J. H. (1986). The structure of male role norms. *American Behavioral Scientist, 29*, 531–543.

Toch, H. (1969). *Violent men: An inquiry into the psychology of violence.* Chicago: Aldine.

Umberson, D., Anderson, K., Glick, J., & Shapiro, A. (1998). Domestic violence, personal control, and gender. *Journal of Marriage and the Family, 60*(2), 442–452.

Umberson, D., Williams, K., & Anderson, K. (2002). Violent behavior: A measure of emotional upset? *Journal of Health and Social Behavior, 43*(2), 189–206.

Vega, V., & Malamuth, N. (2007). The role of pornography in the context of general and specific risk factors. *Aggressive Behavior, 33*, 104–117.

White, J. W., & Gruber, K. J. (1982). Instigative aggression as a function of past experience and target characteristics. *Journal of Personality and Social Psychology, 42*(6), 1069–1075.

Williams, K. D. (2010). The effects of homophily, identification, and violent video games on players. *Mass Communication and Society, 14*(1), 3–24.

Wilson, B. J., Smith, S. L., Potter, W. J., Kunkel, D., Linz, D., Colvin, C. M., & Donnerstein, E. (2002). Violence in children's television programming: Assessing the risks. *Journal of Communication, 52*(1), 5–35.

Ybarra, M. L., Diener-West, M., Markow, D., Leaf, P. J., Hamburger, M., & Boxer, P. (2008). Linkages between Internet and other media violence with seriously violent behavior by youth. *Pediatrics, 122*(5), 929–937.

Ybarra, M. L., Mitchell, K. J., Hamburger, M., Diener-West, M., & Leaf, P. J. (2011). X-rated material and perpetration of sexually aggressive behavior among children and adolescents: Is there a link? *Aggressive Behavior, 37*(1), 1–18.

Zillman, D. (1979). *Hostility and aggression.* Hillsdale, NJ: Erlbaum.

Making Choices

Robert T. Michael

We all make choices in life. The hard thing is to live with them.

The Words (2012)

From the time you get up in the morning, you begin to make choices—about what to eat for breakfast, what to wear, and on and on. A lot of these decisions are pretty trivial. But now and then, one of them is really important, and it can impact you throughout your life.

This is a book about five big decisions that you'll face. Three of these choices have a lot to do with how and with whom you spend much of your adult life. The other two help define your capabilities, so they have a profound effect on the other three. While these are not the only big decisions you'll face, we'll focus on them because they have lifetime consequences for you and because they are interconnected. As we discuss these five, you'll see that a lot of what we consider can be useful to you in making other decisions as well.

Now, this isn't a book that tells you what to choose for any of these five life decisions. Sorry. It might, at first, seem nice if someone came along and told you what to do, how to do it, when to do it, and so forth, and relieved you of having to make choices. But when you think about it, that sounds like a terrible circumstance, since how can someone else know what's right for you? Oh, they can give you some useful advice, and this book will do that too. But since you, not them and not me, live your life, experience your activities, make your friends, feel your pleasures and your pains, no one but you can make the choices that are best for you.

That's really what it means to be an adult: to have the authority to make your own choices and the responsibility to live with them. As a child, your parents, teachers, and maybe others made a lot of choices for you. But as you become an adult, you get to define (or at least influence) your own boundaries and frame the choices as you wish, and then when you've made choices, you, not anyone else, have the opportunity and the obligation to carry them out and live with them.

Choices are so common, we often don't even realize we're making them. Because many are trivial, we don't spend a lot of effort making them. And because many are routine and repetitive, we develop rules of thumb or habits that allow us to make them almost without thinking. Some decisions, however, are pivotal, a big deal, and worth a lot of time and effort.

For now, let's begin with a piece of good news: a lot of the decisions you'll have to make probably don't really matter all that much, so don't fret over them. People may have suggested that some choices are really important that are in fact not all that critical. Take, for example, the choice of which college to attend. If you've decided to go to college and have what it takes to go, just which of quite a large number of schools you select (or that select you) really doesn't make a big difference.

Some schools will be wrong for you—too hard, too easy, too big, or whatever, so you'll want to give the choice some serious attention. But so long as you're selecting from a pool of reasonably appropriate schools, the choice of what college to go to is not so important. The experiences you'll have at one or another will be different, of course, but you can't know ahead of time which will be best or most valuable or most pleasant. Whom you pal around with when you get there, which courses you end up taking, which teacher you get for one or another class, and how diligently you apply yourself to the intellectual and social experiences at your school have a lot more to do with what you get out of college than which school it is you attend. We'll come back to this in the next chapter. However, the decision about whether or not to go to college, as we'll discuss in chapter 2, is a really important decision, one that can make a big difference in your life.

Here's another piece of pretty good news: in many of the big choices in life there's not a single "right" choice with all others being "wrong." Instead, there are better choices or poorer ones, there are some pretty foolish ones or dangerous ones to be sure, and some that are especially appealing—but very seldom is there a uniquely perfect selection. Perhaps there are absolutes in the principles that guide your life and define who you are, but when it comes to selecting this or that level of schooling, job, partner, or whatever, you'll do well to explore your options, come to understand them, and to make a sensible choice by selecting one of the better ones. But don't lose sleep over finding one perfect answer.

Why can't we just avoid making choices? There's just one simple reason: scarcity. You and I have limited resources—limited money, limited time, limited talents, and limited patience. Limits all over the place! If it weren't for scarcity, you could have it all ways, and you wouldn't need to make a choice at all. But since you do face scarcity and do have to make some big choices that can have long-lasting influence, it is a good idea to figure out how best to make wise ones. That's what this book is designed to help you do.

Since choices are so varied, you shouldn't expect to find a simple formula or a single strategy that always produces a good choice; that would trivialize the challenge you face as you consider your decisions. Instead, what you can hope to do is have a framework that gives you some guidance, enables you to consider the important elements of that choice, and helps you avoid overlooking any of these really important elements. That's what we're aiming for here. We'll learn some concepts that will be a big help and explore some facts that can shed some useful light on one or another of the alternatives.

What's in a Choice?

A good choice will reflect several things: it will reflect your *values*, your *preferences*, your *capabilities*, and your available *opportunities*. That's probably true about most of the choices you make, big and small. Like, what's for lunch? Your values can influence whether you will want a healthy lunch or not; your preferences play a big role in influencing whether it's a salad, some protein, or chips; and if you don't have much cash or credit, your limited capability may be a big factor in your "choice" of what to have for lunch and where to have it. And then, if there's not a shop nearby or a fridge to raid, your preferences and your cash won't matter all that much, so the available opportunities can also define your choice.

Your *values* influence how you behave (or they aren't really the values you live by) and what you want to achieve. There are some values that are pretty universal, like living your life with integrity and having respect and compassion for others. Different religions and various ethical principles teach values that can guide your life, but you are the boss here. You, not some philosopher or your parent, can determine your values and your personal commitment to the principles and beliefs that guide your life.

One of the fun and frightening aspects about becoming an adult is that you will want to consider what values you will live by, what truly matters to you in terms of your own self-esteem, your sense of your deeper self. This can be fun, since talking about your values with friends and people you respect can help clarify what does matter to you. It can also be frightening because, in a sense, your values really do define who you are.

Values aren't innate; you aren't born with them. You've been raised in a family that has some specific values, and because these values are familiar and because you may have seen them serve your family well over your lifetime, you'll probably be inclined to adopt them. But you must decide if those values are the ones you want to guide your behavior as an adult.

Preferences are another of those four elements involved in all your choices. Preferences are not as important as your values; they can change a lot depending on your circumstances at the time. The things you like and the things you don't like are part of your preferences. It's often hard to know where they actually came from. You'll know, however, that you like one sort of music a lot more than another or, say, that your interest in one sport or athletic activity is a lot stronger than that of your friend or your sister. One reason there's so much advertising around is that companies make an effort to inform you about a product and to persuade you that it addresses your preferences.

Preferences vary a lot in their intensity. You may have a preference for action movies over romantic ones, but it might be only a slight edge for this over that. Other preferences can be intense and can really motivate you to take one action or another.

These two elements—your values and your preferences—essentially tell you what you're aiming at, what you're after, what your objective is when you make a choice. If you didn't have any preferences or didn't consider any values important, you couldn't really make a real choice about anything, from your lunch to your life's work, since it wouldn't matter to you if you had no preferences. Values and preferences give you direction. They define your objective. That's a start.

The third element involved in your choices is your *capability*, and that's got a lot to it. One set of capabilities reflects your resources. Money matters. Your access to money is a crucial factor in making some of the choices we'll discuss (and it is a key objective when we consider others). A very different set of capabilities are your skills: the knowledge you've acquired and the personal attributes you bring to the table, like your personality, energy, and appearance. Again, some of the choices that we'll be focusing on—schooling and health habits, especially—greatly influence these capabilities.

The fourth element is your *opportunities*—the options from which you make your choices. You may have been told that you make your own opportunities, and, indeed, that can be so, but only to a degree. There's a reality out there. You were born at a particular time, grew up in some specific location (or several places), and are facing these life decisions in the context of some particular time and space, with options that are good or not so good. Recognizing and assessing the value of the opportunities you have, and understanding what opportunities you are not likely to have, are all part of making sensible decisions that we'll explore in this book.

But you have a lot to do with how well or how poorly things turn out: three of the four elements of your choice are embedded within you, and only one, the opportunities you confront, is outside yourself. That itself can be energizing. While you can't do it all on your own—and if the opportunities aren't there, it doesn't make a lot of difference how "capable" you are—a lot of what matters is within your control.

All of us have heard stories about someone who has had just incredibly bad luck but who picked themselves up, making the most of a bad situation, and turned things around despite setbacks. Everyone will have setbacks in their life. We all meet with disappointment. It's been said that what determines how successful you are in life has a lot more to do with how you handle those disappointments than how you respond to the good things that come along. So get ready to overcome the bad events and to take advantage of the good ones—you will certainly confront both.

Even if you're aware of these four elements (your values, preferences, capabilities, and opportunities), decisions can be difficult. Throughout this book we'll consider choices that are important because they can have a big influence on your life. So, yes, making choices can be somewhat scary. Also, while many of these decisions can be changed later, there's usually a cost to doing so. And when a choice really can't be undone, the stakes are high.

Another reason a lot of choices are so hard is that you often don't know exactly what will happen if you choose one option or another. Uncertainty is a pain. But since it keeps showing up when you think about the sort of decisions we'll talk about, you've got to figure out how to deal with it.

Still another reason some choices are so difficult to make is that they are often interconnected with other important decisions. That makes decision making all the more complicated. What you decide about one choice can affect what you'll want to do about another. Then you won't really know how the first one turns out before you'll face a couple more related choices, which adds to your uncertainty.

Of course, whatever you choose, a lot of stuff happens. Sometimes it may seem that you don't really have any good choices or, for that matter, any influence over how your life goes, no matter how carefully you plan. But even if you can't control everything—and you certainly cannot—it makes a lot of sense to consider your options and to make a choice, even when you can't know everything you'd like to. Punting or avoiding a choice because it's hard is almost never a smart strategy.

The good news is there is some guidance that can help you with these choices, even though it is not the case that this book, or for that matter any advice or guidance from anyone, can tell you what *you* ought to do. Again, your best choice depends on your values, your preferences, your capabilities, and your opportunities. You run your life, not your parents or your friends, not your teachers, mentors, pastor/priest/rabbi, or anyone else. You. It's your life—it's yours to make the most of, and it's you who will suffer when things go wrong or float in the clouds when things go well.

A pretty good word for this aspect of adulthood is "sovereignty": independent authority and the right to govern oneself. Since you have sovereignty over yourself, you should be skeptical when anyone seems to think they can offer you easy answers to some of these life choices—guidance, yes, suggestions, of course, but answers, no. Be careful about accepting anyone else's answers as your own.

Now, of these four elements of choice, we'll focus most of our attention on your capabilities because some of the bigger choices you'll face will help determine just what your capabilities are. We'll also emphasize some of the opportunities you have. By contrast, your values and your preferences will not be a focus here—they lie outside the boundaries of this book, despite being really important to the decisions you make.

That's where the concept of sovereignty comes in. We won't explore where your values come from, and we will only address one preference in particular, something we'll call your time preference, which has a lot to do with the choices we will be discussing. Since we're emphasizing how to make sensible decisions, all four elements will play a role, but most of the concepts we'll use relate to your capabilities and opportunities. And the facts we'll explore are facts about outcomes, not about those basic values or preferences.

Post-Reading Activities

1   Do you think your friends would be more likely to help you than strangers? Support your answer with information provided in the chapter. Test your answer by dropping your books, pencils, or wallet in front of three friends on three different occasions. Take note of how many help. Then, repeat this behavior in front of three strangers on three different occasions. Again, take note of how many help. Explain your results using the information provided in the chapter.

2   Conduct a brief Internet search of Armin Meiwes and Bernd Jürgen Armando Brandes. Does the case provide an example of aggression, based on the definition provided in the reading? Why or why not? If you determine this is a case of aggression, what explanation can you provide for the behavior?

3   Conduct a brief Internet search on Lyle and Erik Menendez. Does the case provide an example of aggression, based on the definition provided in the reading? Why or why not? If you determine this is a case of aggression, what explanation can you provide for the behavior?

4   We discussed that social behavior is goal oriented and social. Based on this understanding of social behavior, how does this influence our choice-making process?

5   What influenced you to attend the university in which you are enrolled?

UNIT IV

AREAS OF SOCIAL LIFE

Introduction

The key areas of social life introduced from a social psychology perspective are deviance, crime, attitudes, and interpersonal attraction. First, as social psychologists, we will approach the understanding of deviance and crime as "failed socialization." Social psychologists study deviance and crime with the control theory and labeling theory perspectives. Control theory illustrates the constraints placed by society on the individual through socialization. These constraints encourage individuals to abide by the positive social norms, avoiding deviant and criminal behaviors. Social bond theory, similar to control theory, highlights the bonds developed with the agents of socialization, which prevent deviant and criminal behaviors. Rather than focusing on the individual, as with control and social bond theory, labeling theory addresses society's response to the deviant or criminal behavior.

Both emotions and attitudes are evaluations. Emotions are evaluations of a social event (e.g., anger, fear, depression, and happiness). Attitudes are macro evaluations of some object or issue (i.e., like or dislike). To further distinguish between emotion and attitude, let us take an example from the media. Classic movies like *Titanic* and *Old Yeller* evoke emotions of sadness during the endings; however, many in society have positive attitudes toward these movies. Members of our society rank *Titanic* and *Old Yeller* at the top of many best-movie lists; people like (attitude) the movies despite the movies being sad (emotion).

To apply these concepts to the field of social psychology, "Crime, the Emotions and Social Psychology," by Carrabine, Cox, and Lee, assesses these various emotions in relation to crime and deviance in society. These emotions can cause crime (like hate crime) and can be a response to crime (fear of victimization). Both are presented in this reading. Further, attitude development is discussed by Mead, the classical social psychologist. Mead discusses the role of self in relation to the development of social attitudes in society.

Using our emotions and attitudes, members of society develop interpersonal attractions and close relationships. Bordens and Horowitz essentially take the spontaneity and romance out of why we like (attitudes) who we like. Social psychologists have recognized patterns in the choices individuals make in creating relationships. Many individuals make their decisions based on emotions, evaluating the way they feel with the potential friend or mate, but others have a desire to affiliate with someone or a need to belong to a relationship.

Failed Socialization

Control Theory, Social Bonds, and Labeling

Mark M. Lanier, Stuart Henry, and Desiré Anastasia

> "An abandoned child manifests evil instincts in his early childhood."
>
> —Jean-Paul Sartre, *Saint Genet: Actor and Martyr*

Robbie Hawkins's early years were filled with the trauma of witnessing physical violence between his parents, as well as being molested as a child. By the age of four he was manifesting repeated physical violence against other children at school and attacked the teachers when they disciplined him. Psychiatrists said that the four-year-old's violent behavior reflected his erratic family life, and they impressed on his parents the importance of a stable, nurturing family environment. Instead, Robbie got to witness a bitter divorce and custody battle that culminated in the arrest of his mother, Molly, for threatening behavior toward father Robert's new wife, Candice, who accused Molly of child endangerment. After this and after remarrying herself, Molly gave up visitation rights to Robbie. Now it was his stepmother, Candice, who was subjected to Robbie's anger and violence. To try to control it, Robbie's father and stepmother used various forms of restraint and violence:

> Rob's father preferred to handle his outbursts by pinning him on the floor, sometimes for longer than an hour, until he would calm down. But when it was her turn to control him, Candice, an Air Force vet, used the back of her hand. Growing up on a steady diet of psychiatric medicine and corporal punishment, Rob became more violent and withdrawn. When he was thirteen, his ongoing battle with Candice went nuclear. She searched his

backpack for cigarettes, and Rob flipped out on her. In response she slapped him across the face so hard that her ring cut his forehead. He balled up his fist and said, "I'm going to kill you." (Boal 2008, 75)

After psychiatric hospitalization for Robbie's further violence, his father gave him up to juvenile court. The Nebraska "State Department of Health and Human Services became Rob's legal guardian. ... At 16 Rob was now a veteran of institutions, having spent the last 24 months in group homes because he resisted the reconciliation with Candice that would have allowed him to rejoin the family" (Boal 2009, 75). Robbie had now been further sexually molested and suffered suicidal ideation: "Over the years he kept trying to buck the rules and talk to his biological mother, with whom he held out hopes of a reunion, but he was never allowed to call her. By now his psychological profile included the darker, more exotic ailment that would lie behind his future crimes: anti-social personality disorder, a condition that makes it difficult, if not impossible to feel empathy for strangers. It is the underlying pathology of most serial killers" (ibid., 75–76).

After two years of therapy, when Robbie was finally persuaded to apologize to Candice, she refused to accept his apology, saying that she'd never feel safe in the house and threatened to divorce Robert if he allowed his son to return home: "My stepmother is evil—she has no heart, Rob told his roommate" at the highly disciplined group home for boys where he now lived, and to whom he admitted that he missed his biological mother deeply (ibid., 76). After a period in a foster home, where he was also engaged in a variety of relatively minor crimes, including gas station stickups and selling marijuana, Robbie successfully contacted his mother: "Molly threw herself into his life as if the separation and abandonment had just been a big misunderstanding." He later had an intense relationship with a girlfriend, Kaci, who reported that he'd describe his childhood as "shitty" and his mother as "fickle." Kaci said, "He cried all the time. It was really sad because he had, like, no family. He was the saddest about his mother" (ibid., 77).

Robbie once again called his mother, Molly, and this time was allowed to visit and spent Thanksgiving 2007 with her. He was photographed smoking pot, which he shared with her, and apparently enjoying the festivities, in spite of a pending court hearing on a drunk-driving charge and the fear that Molly would take his Jeep away from him as a punishment.

One week later, on December 5, 2007, after having dinner the previous night at his mother's house, Robbie Hawkins, now an eighteen-year-old, entered the Von Maur department store in the Westroads Mall in Omaha, Nebraska, and rode the elevator to the third level, where he randomly shot eleven people, killing eight, with an AK-47 assault rifle taken from his stepfather's closet the previous night, before killing himself.

In this chapter we explore the problems of failed socialization dramatically illustrated in the case of Robbie Hawkins. First we look at the effects of inadequate parental socialization by focusing on social control theory; later we examine the negative effects of labeling by social control agents and agencies of criminal justice.

In his theory of bonding and social control and in his later theory of self-control, Travis Hirschi (1969; Gottfredson and Hirschi 1990) rejected the ideas discussed in the previous chapter: either that some people learn criminal behavior or that everyone is socialized into conformity from which some are occasionally released from the moral bind of law, to offend. Indeed, Hirschi and Gottfredson have said, "We reject the idea that 'criminal activity' requires learning in any meaningful sense of the term, nor do the 'learning processes' described by Sutherland and Akers account for 'conformity' as we define it." In contrast, Hirschi argued that some people are not socialized adequately in the first place. In control theory, being socialized is not about learning behavior, but about knowing and caring about the consequences of behavior. In fact, a main component of control theories is "the assumption that behavior is governed by its consequences" (Hirschi and Gottfredson 2006, 115). Hirschi maintained that law abiders and lawbreakers are the same in that they are all *potential* offenders. What distinguishes us is how effectively we are socialized not to break the law, not through learning behavior but through having controls instilled in us as children.

Hirschi (1969) claimed that inadequate socialization processes in children and youth allow, and can even foster, the formation of unconventional attitudes that can result in crime and delinquency. When socialization works adequately, a tie or bond is created with conventional society that prevents law violation by insulating people from temptation. Learning self-control is a crucial element in the process of resisting the impulse to law violation. What significantly affects socialization are the social bonds of attachment, commitment, involvement, and belief formed between children and conventional others, such as teachers and parents. If these bonds are weak, or do not form, children will lack self-control and will be free to violate the law. Bonding, social control, and self-control theories, then, examine the connections and controls that link people to conventional society and lead them to care about the consequences of what they do.

Control Theory: Learning Not to Commit Crime

Whereas Sutherland ([1939] 1947) and Akers (1998) focused on learning kinds of behavior, and sought to explain how some people are introduced to and adopt lawbreaking behavior, control theory (like classical theory) assumes a universal motivation to crime and deviance and instead asks why most people conform (Hirschi 1969). Control theorists' answer is that attachment and commitment to conforming people, institutions, and values produce a loyalty that protects against the temptation to deviate.

> What distinguishes social control theory as a distinct framework is (a) its focus on restraints rather than the conventional criminological focus on motivations as the key to explaining crime, and (b) its assumption that

the motives or impulses for most criminal acts are relatively normal and universal (rather than aberrant or pathological). Thus, social control theory reverses the usual explanation of crime by viewing criminal behavior as less explainable in the presence of something (deviant motivations) than in the absence of something (effective restraints). (Rankin and Wells 2006, 119)

Considering the issue of the presence or absence of restraint, it is possible to distinguish between two types of control theory, one where restraints are present but either break down or are eroded (*broken-bond theory*) and the other where they are absent (*failure-to-bond theory*).

Kinds of Social Control Theory: Broken Bonds or Failure to Bond?

Most social control theories assume that socialization into convention occurs from an early age but something breaks or weakens the bonds to convention, freeing a person to deviate. This type of control theory can be called broken-bond theory. For example, the neutralization of the moral bind of law [...] has been considered by some criminologists to be a version of this type of control theory (Akers 1994, 114). Another example of broken-bond theory is social disorganization or social ecology theory [...], which argues that the isolation and breakdown of communities can undermine a person's commitment to conform to the dominant or mainstream culture (Kornhauser 1984). Of course, when children are raised in a disorganized and fragmented community, separated from mainstream culture and values, they may not form bonds to convention in the first place, which leads us to the second type of control theory.

Failure-to-bond theory assumes that the creation of a commitment to convention is problematic. It is very difficult to persuade humans to conform to socially approved norms and values, and it requires much investment of time and energy and considerable maintenance (Box [1971] 1981). Encouraging conforming social behavior requires certain kinds of socialization and can easily go wrong: "Differences in nurturing account for variations in attachment to others and commitment to an ordered way of living" (Nettler 1984, 290). Without this attachment and commitment forming in the first place, humans are more likely to deviate and to break the law.

One of the earliest versions of failure-to-bond theory is John Bowlby's "attachment theory" (see Chapter 5). Bowlby (1951) conducted research on forty-four juvenile delinquents who were referred to his child guidance clinic (which he compared to forty-four controls). He found that children who have frequent breaks in relations with their mother in the early years of development up to the age of eight, or who have factors that mitigate against secure maternal bonding, such as child abandonment, foster care, or child abuse, develop anxiety and have difficulty forming relationships with others. The result is "affectionless characters" that lack the ability to empathize with others and do not see or feel the pain that harm may cause others. The desirable state, according to Bowlby's revised theory of attachment, is "secure attachment," which requires a responsible, lovingly responsive, and sensitive mother figure that is empathetic and able to satisfy childhood needs for emotional and physical security. Attachment theory "predicts that the most problematic individuals will be those who were abandoned at an early age, who experienced multiple placements (in foster homes and so on), who had to deal with the early absence of one or both parents, and who faced traumatic conditions in early childhood (physical, sexual or other abuse)" (Schmalleger [1999] 2002, 186).

Several other early versions of failure-to-bond theory also laid a foundation for this perspective. Drawing on Albert Reiss's ideas (1951) about offenders' failure to internalize personal self-control and the absence of direct external social controls such as law and informal social control, F. Ivan Nye (1958) distinguished between three kinds of controls: (1) direct control from the threat of punishment; (2) indirect control, which protects youths from delinquency through their wish to avoid hurting intimates, such as parents; and (3) internal control, which relies on an internalized sense of guilt.

Another early version of failure-to-bond theory was Walter Reckless's containment theory ([1950] 1973, 1961). He argued that adolescent youths are motivated toward delinquency by "pushes" from the pressures and strains of the environment and "pulls" provided by peers. Juveniles will violate the law unless protected by both internal and external controls, which he called inner and outer containments. Outer containment comes from parents and school discipline, whereas inner containment comes from a strongly developed sense of guilt and a positive self-concept. The interplay of these forces could produce more or less delinquency. In particular, a positive self-concept can be enhanced by external social approval, and this, in turn, binds the youths to the community and to conventional behavior. Conversely (and anticipating labeling theory, discussed in the next section), a negative reaction from society would result in a negative self-concept through which a reciprocity of disrespect leads to a failure to adopt conventional behavior.

Ruth Kornhauser summarized how both internal and external controls and rewards influence acts of conformity: "Social controls are actual or potential rewards and punishments that accrue from conformity to or deviation from norms. Controls may be internal, invoked by self, or external, enforced by others" (1984, 24). Kornhauser added, "Social bonds vary in depth, scope, multiplicity, and degree of articulation with each other" (ibid., 25). Travis Hirschi has been celebrated for his development of an elaborated version of the failure-to-bond version of control theory. Hirschi drew on several dimensions of these earlier theories to develop his social control theory.

Hirschi's Social Control Theory

Hirschi's book *Causes of Delinquency* (1969) embodies the essence of failure-to-bond theory and has stimulated the most research. Like the early control theorists, Hirschi drew on Jackson Toby's (1957) "stake in conformity," which referred to developing an investment in convention. Once invested, the cost of losing this stake serves as a barrier to law violation. The underlying assumption in Hirschi's argument is that all people would break the law if they did not fear the damage and consequences of getting caught. Ties or bonds to conventional parents, school, friends, employers, and so on make crime too much of a risk for most people.

For Hirschi, the "social bond" consists of four components: attachment, commitment, involvement, and belief.

Attachment refers to caring about others, including respecting their opinions and expectations, and is based on mutual trust and respect that develop from ongoing interactions and intimate relations with conventional adults.

Commitment signifies the individual's investment in conventional behavior, including a willingness to do what is promised and respecting others' expectations. Commitment involves a cost-benefit analysis of what degree of previous investment or "stake in conformity" would be lost if one were to participate in the act.

Involvement describes the time and energy spent on participation in conventional activities. Since time and energy are limited, the more time spent doing conventional activities, the less time is available for deviant acts.

Finally, the bond is solidified by *belief* in the moral validity of conventional norms and on the child's respect for the authority of those limiting their behavior. This is a fundamental and explicit assumption of control theory, which "assumes the existence of a common value system within the society or group whose norms are being violated" (ibid., 23). More broadly, belief refers to an ongoing conviction that conventional behavior and respect for its underlying principles, norms, and values are important and necessary.

The elements of bonding in Hirschi's theory are interrelated: "the chain of causation is thus from attachment to parents, through concern for persons in positions of authority, to the belief that the rules of society are binding on one's conduct" (ibid., 200).

Hirschi's bonding theory, which still stands alone as a viable explanation for crime, raises the question of whether the reason some people fail to form connections with conventional others has to do with their capacity for self-control, itself affected by parental socialization practices. These questions led Hirschi and his colleague Michael Gottfredson to *self-control theory*, considered in the next section.

Hirschi and Gottfredson's Self-Control Theory

In 1990, Hirschi and Gottfredson published *A General Theory of Crime*, which moved away from the four-component version of social-bonding theory to focus on a lack of self-control resulting in impulsive behavior. Impulsive behavior is a tendency in all humans; all are motivated to break rules and all make a rational choice decision of whether or not to do so: "All of us, it appears, are born with the ability to use force and fraud in pursuit of our private goals." Moreover, "everyone is capable of criminal or deviant acts. ... However, some are more likely than others to actually commit them" (Hirschi and Gottfredson 2001, 88). "The quality that prevents crime among some people more than it does among others ... we call 'self-control,'" which is "the tendency to consider the broader or longer-term consequences of one's acts" (2006, 114) and "the tendency to avoid acts whose long-term costs exceed their immediate or short-term benefits" (2001, 82). They identify juvenile delinquency as just one of a wide range of crimes, including embezzlement and fraud, that can be explained not so much by the absence of bonds as by a lack of self-control on the part of the offender, especially in circumstances of increased opportunity and heightened situational temptation. "Those who have a high degree of self-control avoid acts potentially damaging to their future prospects, whatever current benefits these acts seem to promise. Those with a low degree of self-control are easily swayed by current benefits and tend to forget future costs. Most people are between these extremes, sometimes doing things they know they should not do, other times being careful not to take the unnecessary risks for short-term advantage" (ibid., 82).

The difference between offenders and nonoffenders is in their awareness of and concern for the long-term costs of crime—such things as arrest, prison, disgrace, disease, and even eternal damnation. What distinguishes offenders from others is not the strength of their appetites but their freedom to enjoy the quick and easy and ordinary pleasures of crime without undue concern for the pains that may follow them. We thus infer the nature of criminality. People who engage in crime are people who neglect long-term consequences. They are, or tend to be, children of the moment. They have what we call low self-control (ibid., 90).

However, they say that "something built into people is responsible for their continued involvement or lack of involvement in such acts" (2006, 113). Criminals, according to Gottfredson and Hirschi, lack self-control because they have been poorly socialized as children, as a result of low parental investment in child rearing and poor monitoring and disciplining practices. This explains "the differential tendency of people to avoid criminal acts whatever the circumstances" (1990, 87). Matt DeLisi succinctly outlined Gottfredson and Hirschi's view of the outcome of such failed socialization:

> Abject parenting nullifies successful childhood socialization. The outcome, in persons exposed to such an environment, is low self-control. Persons with low self-control (a) prefer immediate gratification of desires, (b) pursue simple tasks rather than activities that require tenacity, (c) value physical rather than verbal or cognitive experiences, (d) enjoy quick returns instead of long-term commitments such as marriage or occupational and educational careers, (e) are employed in low-skilled versus academic endeavors, and (f) are self-centered and generally insensitive to the feelings of others. (2001, 1)

Grasmick has also developed a profile of the characteristics of poor self-control (see Table 9.1). The difference is in people's ability to suppress or restrain such urges and drives and in their needs for excitement, risk-taking, and immediate gratification. Most people do not engage in criminal acts because they have been effectively socialized by parents to exercise self-control over their behavior. Those who fail to be properly socialized have a lack of control that can also be related to "low self-esteem." Pratt and Cullen add that this "increases the likelihood that individuals will be unable to resist the easy, immediate gratification that crime and analogous behaviors seductively, and almost ubiquitously, present in everyday life" (2000, 932). Hirschi and Gottfredson describe how people develop self-control over offensive behavior: "By the age of 8 or 10, most of us learn to control such tendencies to the degree necessary to get along at home and at school. Low self-control is natural and self-control is acquired in the early years of life. Children presumably learn from many sources to consider the long-range consequences of their acts" (2001, 90).

TABLE 9.1 Grasmick's Characteristics of Low Self-Control

Impulsive

Seeks Instant Gratification

Low Levels of Diligence, Tenacity, and Persistence

Seeks Sensation and Excitement

Prefers Simple Physical Tasks over Complex, Intellectual Tasks

Self-centered

Insensitive to Others' Needs

Low Tolerance to Frustration

Addresses Conflict though Confrontation

Source: Grasmick 1993.

Developing self-control over one's behavior comes mainly from parenting practices in particular in correcting, admonishing, and punishing them when they deviate, which involves monitoring, recognizing deviance, and correcting it (ibid.).

For some children, then, the socialization process is defective, providing little protection against committing crime. Their socialization is defective not because of something biological or psychological within the individual, and not because of patterns of behavior that have been copied from others, but because the parents have failed to use adequate child-rearing practices and as a result have failed to instill self-control. Thus, early childhood is where this lack of self-control is manifested as "conduct problems" (Pratt and Cullen 2000).

As we've indicated, for Hirschi and Gottfredson, parenting involves, among other things, the control of deviant behavior or normative regulation that "requires that someone (1) monitor behavior, (2) recognize deviant behavior when it occurs, and (3) correct or punish it" (2006, 115). Rankin and Wells add, "Normative regulation is the process of 'laying down the law' and making clear what children can and cannot do. Monitoring children's behaviors for compliance or noncompliance entails supervision and surveillance. Discipline and punishment of noncompliance comprise the application of unpleasant outcomes to sanction children's misbehaviors negatively" (2006, 122–123).

"Monitoring" refers to parents or guardians watching children's behavior. Monitoring can be ineffective because of lack of care, lack of time, or the periodic physical absence of the child from its parents. "Recognizing" refers to the parents' or guardians' conception of the norms, rules, and laws of society and their readiness to identify behavior as consistent with or deviant from them. Parents may not recognize deviant behavior for several reasons, including the popular child-rearing philosophy that this practice is harmful for healthy child development. They may also not recognize deviant behavior because they are themselves unaware, are distracted (by jobs, drugs, and so on) or do not believe that such behavior is deviant.

Finally, even if they watch and recognize, parents may not provide effective punishments for deviant behavior or adequate rewards for conforming behavior. Together, inadequate monitoring, inappropriate recognition, and ineffective punishment result in dysfunctional child rearing. This will have a serious impact on children through their formative years (ages six to eight) and reduce the effectiveness of other socialization through formal schooling or informal peer groups.

Policy Implications of Control Theory

Control theory implies policy interventions based on preventive socialization designed to protect and insulate individuals from the pushes and pulls toward crime. Part of this protection comes from supervision, surveillance, and control. But rather than control being provided by the formal criminal justice system— which should remain as the punitive last resort—the major focus on preventive policy, according to control theory, should be through the informal control of children by their parents. This implies strengthening bonds to convention through developing more effective child-rearing practices and adequate childhood socialization.

Although family size and single working parents may seem to present challenges to effective parental supervision, Gottfredson and Hirschi say that "responsible adults committed to the training and welfare of the child" can carry out the child rearing, and it may be accomplished in properly run day-care facilities where children are under supervision (1990, 273). They argue that schools can be more effective than parents or families in providing the kind of supervision and control necessary to those not properly socialized by the family:

> "[Schools] can more effectively monitor behavior than the family, with one teacher overseeing many children at a time. Second, as compared to most parents, teachers generally have no difficulty recognizing deviant or disruptive behavior. Third, as compared to the family, the school has such a clear interest in maintaining order and discipline that it can be expected to do what it can to control disruptive behavior. Finally, like the family, the school in theory has the authority and means to punish lapses in self-control." (ibid., 105)

In addition, early-intervention programs include parent training and functional-family therapy that seek to reduce family conflict through dispute settlement and negotiation, reduce abuse and neglect, promote positive parent-child interaction, and teach moderate discipline (Morton and Ewald 1987). A second level of intervention for some control theorists is directed toward those "at risk" of engaging in antisocial activities. Policy here can focus on providing counseling and problem-solving and social-skills training (Goldstein, Krasner, and Garfield 1989; Hollin 1990), especially in the school context. Gottfredson and Hirschi (1990) argue that unless this kind of intervention occurs early in the child's development, it is already too late to make much difference.

These kinds of preventative interventions also have serious moral implications that go beyond the issue of economics to raise questions about the relationship between the state and the family that would need to be resolved before any such programs could be implemented on a wide scale. Admittedly, in spite of earlier statements that might appear to contradict this, Hirschi and Gottfredson have recently said, "We no longer accept the idea of obvious and necessary links to social policies. Most contemporary theories, including control theory, are efforts to understand the origins of delinquency. They are not rooted in concerns about how to fix the problem or reduce its impact. As a result they should not be judged by their alleged policy implications" (2006, 117).

Evaluation of Social Control and Self-Control Theory

Overall, social control theory has been one of the most tested of all theories. As Rankin and Kern have noted, "Among the various social control perspectives, Hirschi's (1969) version is probably most responsible for developments in family and delinquency research. It is relatively explicit, well developed, and amenable to empirical tests" (1994, 495). The bonds to convention outlined by Hirschi have been extensively studied. In one study, Costello and Vowell found the bonds to have "important direct effects" (1999, 815). Moreover, a study by Mack, Leiber, and Featherstone (2007) found that maternal attachment was the primary factor in determining levels of delinquency. One commonly identified element of the bond is religion. Baier and Wright conducted a meta-analysis (a summary and comparison of all the previous studies) of sixty studies examining religion and delinquency and concluded that "religious behavior and beliefs exert a significant, moderate effect on individuals' criminal behavior" (2001, 12). LaGrange and White (1985) pointed out that the strength of the bond to convention varies based on a number of factors, particularly age.

Although research has revealed much support for the various versions of this theory, it has also exhibited some flaws. Krohn (1991) has pointed out that Hirschi's original bonding theory fails to adequately distinguish between different elements of the bond and is unclear about the causal direction of bonding. Thus, although a lack of parental attachment can affect delinquency, delinquency can also affect parental attachment (Liska and Reed 1985). In other words, social control theory doesn't explain whether the reason that some parents fail to bond with their children is because the children themselves are the problem: "No recognition is given to evidence that children come into the world with different personalities and temperaments, and in so doing affect the behavior of parents from a very early age" (Ellis and Walsh 2000, 326). Others have criticized social control theory for failing to explain gender differences in delinquency—in other words, for failing to explain "why parents, schools, and churches throughout the world would socialize children in ways that make males form weaker bonds and have less self-control than females" (ibid.). Nor does the theory gain as much support for explaining serious adult crime. Indeed, control theory ignores the insight of Matza and Sykes concerning the subterranean values of conventional society. As a result, the theory ignores the finding that effective bonding to convention and self-control do not protect against some serious deviance. In particular, where those who have leading roles in conventional society, including parents, also indulge in unconventional behavior, from drug taking to corporate fraud, then being bonded to "convention" can also mean being bonded to crime. Finally, the question remains for control theory about how it explains a whole category of white-collar offenders, particularly financial investors, socialized effectively by parents into valuing community, convention, and capitalism and acting in the long term with full awareness of the consequences of their actions. As Rabbi David Wolpe commented after the Bernie Madoff case was revealed, "Jews have these familial ties. It's not solely a shared belief; it's a sense of close communal bonds. I'd like to believe someone raised in our community, imbued with Jewish values, would be better than this" (Pogrebin 2008).

Similarly, studies of low self-control have produced considerable support for self-control theory. Nofziger (2008) found that the level of self-control of the mother will affect her choices of punishments as well as her degree of surveillance, thus impacting the self-control of her child. When Pratt and Cullen (2000) conducted a meta-analysis of twenty-one research studies on low self-control they found that self-control, or lack thereof, is a strong predictor of crime. Likewise, DeLisi (2001), Vazsonyi et al. (2001), and Hay (2001) found self-control to be inversely related to criminal offending. Further, those who exhibited low self-control were, indeed, found to be impulsive and risk takers, and were more serious criminals (DeLisi 2001). One study found that low self-control was related to negative interactions among offenders and criminal justice personnel, which "potentially affects discretionary outcomes" (DeLisi and Berg 2006). Overall, the research on self-control theory is fairly conclusive. In another summary of existing studies, Hay found that, "with few exceptions, these studies indicate that low self-control, whether measured attitudinally or behaviorally, positively affects deviant and criminal behavior" (2001, 707). However, Akers (1994, 123) has argued that self-control theory is untestable because it is tautological or redundant: "Propensity toward crime and low self-control appear to be one and the same thing." Pratt and Cullen disagree, arguing that "the charge of tautology does not apply to studies that measure self-control with attitudinal scales that were developed to assess self-control independently of criminal behavior" (2000, 945).

BOX 9.1 The Potential for Delinquency Among Victims of Human Trafficking

Mark Lanier

One of the most heinous underreported crimes in a global context is that of human trafficking. After drug dealing, human trafficking is tied with the illegal arms industry as the second-largest criminal industry in the world today, and it is the fastest growing (J. Wilson and Dalton 2007). The US Department of State defines human trafficking as modern-day slavery, involving victims who are forced, defrauded, or coerced into labor or sexual exploitation. This modern-day form of slavery is being reported with increasing frequency throughout the world. According to the 2008 *Trafficking in Persons Report*, approximately 800,000 people are trafficked across national borders annually, with an estimated 14,500 to 17,500 victims being trafficked into the United States each year. In a special presentation at the University of Central Florida on January 12, 2009, Allen Beck, senior statistician at the Bureau of Justice Statistics, reported only 61 convictions and 140 suspects for a twenty-one-month period ending September 2008 in the United States. Why such a large disparity between arrests and the reported number of victims?

The police represent the government agency most likely to first contact victims. Unfortunately, this initial contact is often the result of a criminal offense—committed by the victim. For example, many young women are forced into prostitution; others may be forced to sell or transport drugs. When the police respond to a criminal act, they are obligated by legislative mandate to arrest the prostitute or drug runner or user. As first responders, law enforcement agencies play a key role in identifying and rescuing victims of human trafficking, but in most cases, they do not have the proper training to be able to differentiate many of these victims from criminals. This inability to identify many individuals as victims fuels a vicious cycle that allows this modern-day slavery to remain an underground phenomenon. The cycle begins with traffickers' psychological bondage on victims—constantly threatening victims that if any of them try to reach out to authorities, they will be arrested and deported back to their home country. At the same time, any bond the victim had to their prior life is destroyed. With every "faulty" arrest law enforcement makes, the traffickers' hold on their victims grows exponentially, leaving victims isolated, too afraid to come forward, and further alienated from conventional society.

Two compounding and interactive factors help perpetuate the problem and crime. One tragic consequence is that the victims, especially those taken at an early age, have inadequate positive socialization and an overabundance of improper socialization.

Bonds to conventional society, if ever formed initially, become ruptured due to the victimization. Second, victims may actually view conventional society, especially the government, as the enemy since they are repeatedly told by captors that the government will simply arrest or deport them. Sadly, too often this has been the case. The bonds that Hirschi and many others have found to reduce delinquency are thus impossible to form in victims. This vicious cycle suggests that the *victims* will actually be more likely to become delinquent—even if taken from their captors. Many have become drug addicted, many have engaged in dysfunctional sex acts, and most suffer from self-esteem issues. Finally, a life of crime may be all that they have ever bonded to!

Human trafficking is a unique problem because it transcends borders and police jurisdictions. A broad international solution is thus required. The solution must also be grounded in sound theoretical principles. If, as many empirical studies have shown, Hirschi is correct, a bond must be either established or reestablished. The first step is to make the government, especially the police, a friend and ally to the victims. The Florida Department of Law Enforcement and other international and national law enforcement agencies have recognized the problem and begun training officers to render aid rather than arrest "victims." In the United States, in October 2000, the Trafficking Victims Protection Act (TVPA) was enacted; before this, there was no federal law that existed to protect victims or to prosecute their traffickers. The three main goals (or the three Ps) of the TVPA are to prevent human trafficking overseas, protect victims, and prosecute the traffickers. Another significant change that resulted from this law was the establishment of the "T-visa," which allows victims of human trafficking to become temporary residents of the United States. After three years of having a T-visa, victims are then allowed to receive permanent residence status. Previous law would result in the deportation of many human-trafficking victims, but with the TVPA and the T-visa in place, we can now even offer victims eligibility for the witness protection program. This small first step should help the victim form positive ties (bonds) to society. In addition, the William Wilberforce Trafficking Victims Protection Re-authorization Act of 2007 makes a number of additions to the TVPA, including the allowance of prosecution for sex trafficking without proof of force or coercion (Spadanuta 2008). In 2006, the governor of Florida signed statute 787.06, which made it mandatory for law enforcement officers and prosecutors to go through basic training in human trafficking crimes (Florida Department of Law Enforcement, 2006). This statute also added racketeering to the list of offenses, which makes human trafficking a first-degree felony with a maximum prison sentence of thirty years. It is hoped these efforts and assisting victims with bonding to conventional society will show positive results.

References

Florida Department of Law Enforcement. 2006. *Violent Crime and Drug Control Council.* Tallahassee, Florida.

Spadanuta, Laura. 2008. "Cracking Down on Sex Trafficking." *Security Management* 52, no. 8: 24.

Trafficking in Persons Report. 2008. U.S. Department of State. www.state.gov/g/tip/rls/tiprpt.

Wilson, Jeremy, and Erin Dalton. 2006. "Human Trafficking in the Heartland: Variation in Law Enforcement Awareness and Response." *Journal of Contemporary Criminal Justice* 24, no. 3: 296–313.

Labeling Theory: A Special Case of Failed Socialization?

The second half of this chapter deals with the effect that society's agents of social control, such as police, schoolteachers, social workers, and probation officers, have on creating crime and criminals. Consider a second example.

Like control theorists, labeling theorists are concerned with the failure of socialization. However, instead of focusing on bonds, they examine the social reaction component of interaction with society's control agents. For labeling theorists, adequate socialization occurs when youthful indiscretions and minor rule violations are tolerated rather than labeled deviant. Labeling theorists argue that society—specifically through persons in powerful positions—creates deviance by overreacting to minor rule breaking. This results in negative socialization that, over time, can undermine a person's sense of self-worth or self-esteem and foster a commitment to deviance.

Classic labeling theorists, such as Edwin Lemert (1951, 1967) and Howard Becker ([1963] 1973), have argued that social interaction with others is important in shaping whether people eventually become offenders. Humans are not passive but are actively engaged with others in the construction of their own social identities and in creating the meaning of their world. Not all others are equally significant in this interactive process, however. Those more significant are members of powerful groups and significant individuals who seek to ban certain behavior by passing laws that are enforced via social control agents. So powerful is the impact of social control agents that otherwise minor rule breaking is magnified through criminal justice processes to have a significant impact on some perpetrators. The impact of these meaningful encounters can transform fragile social identities into criminal careers. Others have become the deviant actor that their label projected; whether this would have occurred without the labeling is the central question that labeling theorists address. Like the control theorists we have just examined, labeling theorists believe that social interaction with others is important in shaping whether people become offenders. But whereas social control and bonding theory see clear recognition of deviant behavior as an important component in the process of preventing future deviance, in contrast, labeling theory views this as an important component in creating future problems. For these theorists, the issue is not so much what this teaches us about the consequences of our behavior or how we bond to others but how our sense of self-identity is built on the views that others have of us and how this identity can be negatively impacted through other people's reactions to our behavior.

According to interactionist theory that underlies labeling theory, we discover self-identity through symbolic communication in interaction and role-play with others in social contexts. For adolescent youths, what their peers think of them and what image they project to others are of utmost importance, resulting in a concentration on style, body image, and so on. Many people define themselves, and are defined by others, according to how they appear. Yet the impact of these labels can be destructive and deadly. The spate of school violence and homicides of 1994–1999 were fueled, if not directly caused, by the negative stereotypes applied to vulnerable children who were seen as "geeks" or "nerds" before their frustration from bullying exploded into violence, as occurred at Thurston High in Springfield, Oregon, and Columbine High in Littleton, Colorado (Newman et al. 2004; Larkin 2007). Following this spate of school homicides, social control agents created a moral panic to seek out these nonconforming "odd ball killers, labeled by 'jocks' as 'The Trench Coat Mafia'" in what John Katz described as nothing short of "Geek Profiling." He relates how these marginalized "teenagers traded countless stories of being harassed, beaten, ostracized and ridiculed by teachers, students and administrators for dressing and thinking differently from the mainstream. Many said they had some understanding of why the killers in Littleton went over the edge" (1999).

The social interaction of observing differences in others, negatively stereotyping them, and then excluding, taunting, bullying, and teasing those who display these attributes, such as clothes, what they say, or how they speak, is the subject of labeling theory. This theory of how social selves, self-esteem, and social identity are formed is itself based on symbolic interactionist theory rooted in social psychology.

Symbolic Interactionist Roots of Labeling Theory

According to symbolic interactionists, we see ourselves through the mirror of others, as they react to what they see in us. Charles Horton Cooley (1864–1929) called this the "looking glass self" ([1902] 1964). Symbolic interactionism can be broken down into several easily understood propositions. The most important of these are as follows: First, we form our definition of self, or "self-identity," based on how others react to, or treat, us. Second, what people say and do are the result of how they interpret their social world. Third, humans communicate through the use of symbols—the most common symbol being language or speech. Fourth, the better a researcher can assume the role of another (the research subject) or have empathy, the better the theory can be developed. To the symbolic interactionist ideas of George Herbert Mead (1863–1931), who devised the notion of the social self, or generalized other (1934), Mead's student Herbert Blumer (1969) added that humans are actively engaged with others in the construction of their own social identities. Once formed, these identities are not fixed but continually reformed and reinterpreted as actors interact with others. Not all others are equally significant in this interactive process, however.

The most significant "others" are those in powerful groups who ban certain behavior through passing laws and those social control agents, such as police, courts, social workers, psychiatrists, school administrators, teachers, counselors, and so on, who enforce these laws. The impact on identity by agents of social control is so powerful according to labeling theorists that otherwise-minor rule breaking or differences in behavior, ideas, or appearance are magnified through criminal justice processes to have a significant effect. The impact of these officially sanctioned, meaningful encounters can transform fragile social identities into criminal careers through a process Frank Tannenbaum originally referred to as "the dramatization of evil." Either punishment or reform, argued Tannenbaum, can lead to the very "bad behavior it would suppress," such that "the person becomes the thing he is described as being" (1938, 19–20). The key to this process, according to Tannenbaum, is the "tag," or label, attached to the rule breaker.

During the 1950s, the early ideas of labeling theorists lay dormant because of the dominance of social and structural explanations (Shoemaker 1996, 191). By the 1960s, the social and political climate became very open to the view that humans are malleable. Consistent with the general criticism of tradition and established institutions of control, labeling theorists found a resonance in the idea that excessive control inhibited the potentially free human spirit that strove to be different. Along with other protest movements for women and civil rights, labeling theory, or, as some called it, the "New Deviancy Theory" (Taylor, Walton, and Young 1973), seemed, at times, to romanticize if not celebrate the lawbreaker.

Lemert's Primary and Secondary Deviance

Edwin M. Lemert (1951, 1967) argued that crime begins not with the activities of the rule breaker but with the social audience that passes laws banning certain behavior as immoral or criminal. Indeed, he maintained that rather than deviance leading to social control, "social control leads to deviance" (1967, v).

Minor rule-breaking behavior is easy for anyone to do, and many of us do it, from speeding to drinking and driving to smoking in public places, which, in several states, is now also illegal and punishable by fines. Everyone engages in forms of primary deviance, and alone it has little consequence for a person's social identity, provided that the person has a strong self-image. For example, employees who steal office equipment, use the telephone for personal calls, or overclaim expenses rarely think of themselves as "employee thieves," or embezzlers. Importantly, primary deviance "has only minor consequences for a person's status, social relationships, or subsequent behavior. Primary deviance tends to be situational, transient and idiosyncratic" (Matsueda 2001, 225).

Secondary deviance, in contrast, refers to behavior that results after a person's primary deviance is reacted to by authorities, particularly social control agents of the criminal justice system.

Secondary deviance is rule-breaking behavior that emerges from a person's social identity. This occurs partly as a result of having to deal with others' labeling and partly because of whom the person has become as a result of the social reaction to the primary deviance. This reaction produces stigmatization. "Secondary deviance is explicitly a response to societal reactions to deviance and has major consequences for a person's status, relationships and future behavior. Secondary deviance occurs when society's response to initial deviance (e.g., stigmatization, punishment, segregation) causes fundamental changes in the person's social roles, self-identity, and personality, resulting in additional deviant acts" (ibid.).

Those who are uncertain about their identity as a result of a weak self-image are vulnerable to what others think of them. Repeated forceful negative definition of these people's identity can raise serious questions for them about who they are and can eventually result in "identity transformation" through self-labeling. They come to see themselves as a deviant type and engage in subsequent deviance *because* of the stigmatized deviants they have become. They sometimes join groups of similarly labeled deviants forming a deviant or criminal subculture in which the members provide support for each other. Some gay and lesbian groups, some juvenile gangs, groups of drug abusers, and prostitute collectives may be formed through such a process. In such subcultures, members normalize each other's behavior through role adjustments (Becker [1963] 1973; Sagarin 1969). In some cases, through a process of delabeling and relabeling, group associations may result in the abandonment of the original deviant behavior—although not the problem created by the stigma, as in the case of alcoholics and narcotics users, or the obese (Trice and Roman 1970; Robinson and Henry 1977; Pfuhl and Henry 1993; Henry 2009).

Becker's Interactionist Theory: Social Reaction and Master Status

Howard S. Becker began his participant observation studies (living in the daily lives of the group being studied) in graduate school by keeping a diary on barroom musicians at the Chicago tavern where he played jazz piano (Martin, Mutchnick, and Austin 1990, 350; Debro 1970, 159). His major book on deviance, *Outsiders* ([1963] 1973), combined a theoretical analysis with the early case studies of musicians and marijuana users. He found that the effects of an activity were a consequence of how a person interprets his or her experience. Although this work has become a classic in the field, Becker, like Lemert, shifted the causality of rule breaking from the actor to the audience, arguing that "deviance is not a quality of the act a person commits but rather a consequence of the application by others of rules and sanctions to an 'offender.'" He suggested that rule breaking is the outcome of a three-stage process: social groups create deviance by (1) "making the rules whose infraction constitutes deviance," (2) "applying those rules to particular people," and (3) "labeling them outsiders." The deviant actor is the product of this process, "one to whom that label has been successfully applied; deviant behavior is behavior that people so label" ([1963] 1973, 9).

The first stage of Becker's labeling process may involve actors engaging in behavior that an audience finds offensive, such as drug use. Some people, such as minority youths, for example, may be arrested on suspicion by police for minor rule-breaking behaviors such as "loitering" or DWB (Driving While Black). What is crucial is that the audience selects a behavior that it defines as offensive. [...] [T]his definitional process can be very arbitrary and shows considerable variation culturally and historically. Importantly, Becker recognized that what becomes defined as deviant behavior and what may be criminalized depend on who has the power and whose interests they represent.

Becker coined the term *moral entrepreneur* to refer to those with more power to shape the law and therefore what is defined as crime with their own ideas of what is offensive. This is one reason the offenses of adolescents become labeled delinquency, whereas the offenses of corporations and governments more often remain violations of administrative regulations.

The second stage in the deviance process—in which control agents select people whose behavior is offensive and label their behavior—also depends on power. The process involves identifying some people's behavior as different, negatively evaluating it as offensive, finding the appropriate offense category, and supplying an interpretation of why the person's behavior is an example of that category (Henry, 2009). As Becker said in an early interview, "The whole point of the interactionist approach to deviance is to make it clear that somebody had to do the labeling. It didn't just happen. The court labeled him or his parents labeled him or the people in the community" (Debro 1970, 177).

In the third stage, the contested definition over the meaning of the signified behavior depends on who has the greater power to influence the labeling process and whether an accused has the power to resist the application of a deviance label. Young, lower-class, urban minority offenders typically do not have the resources for resistance. In contrast, middle- and upper-class offenders are typically able to redefine their activities as acceptable. Chambliss (1973), for example, found that although middle-class adolescents engage in similar delinquent activities as their lower-class counterparts, they are able to do so in greater secrecy and even when caught are protected because of their demeanor and family or community connections.

Once successfully labeled, a person is subject to the negative effects of the label itself, which provides what Becker called a "master" status. Being caught and publicly labeled as an offender "has important consequences for one's further social participation and self-image" (Becker [1963] 1973, 31). The status of "deviant" highlights certain characteristics of the person as central to his or her identity while diminishing others. This interaction with others, wrote Becker, produces a "self-fulfilling prophecy" that "sets in motion several mechanisms which conspire to shape the person in the image people have of him [or her]" (ibid., 34). Part of this process involves closing off legitimate forms of activity, which restricts the opportunities for the labeled offender to behave differently. The label also leads others to engage in retrospective interpretation.

Retrospective interpretation occurs when a review of a person's past activity highlights previous instances that can be reinterpreted as consistent with the new deviant master status. Such actions further lead to a new narrow focus by the audience, now with heightened sensitivity toward the labeled individual. This, in turn, results in more deviance being discovered. Wilkins

(1965) and J. Young (1971) described this as "deviancy amplification," since it leads to even more secrecy and interaction with similarly defined others. Deviancy amplification may eventually result in an individual accepting the label, adopting a deviant or criminal career, and joining an organized deviant group (Becker [1963] 1973, 37).

For Becker, then, the central issue was not the normal rule breaking that everyone sometimes engages in as part of human freedom and curiosity. Rather, it was others' transforming that activity into a negative, restricted force that results in new and additional offenses. In clarifying his account, Becker ([1963] 1973) argued that the secret deviant, who on the surface seems to contradict his idea that deviance does not exist until it is labeled (J. Gibbs 1966), actually refers to evolving definitions of behavior. Becker noted that at one point in time the powerful do not provide the procedures for determining a behavior's standing, yet at a subsequent time they do.

If Lemert's and Becker's work sensitized us to the power of the definition process, Erving Goffman led us to the force of stigma and spoiled identities that can result from institutionalization.

Goffman's Stigma and Total Institutions

Erving Goffman (1922–1982) used his fieldwork on a Scottish island community to write his doctorate at the University of Chicago. Although most of his work described and analyzed everyday, face-to-face interaction in a variety of noncrimino-logical settings, his work on stigma and on mental hospital institutionalization has direct relevance to criminological discussions of labeling theory. Goffman used the metaphor of drama: the world is a stage, and we are all players bringing off performances and demonstrating our strategic gamesmanship to the audience. His book *Stigma* (1963) distinguishes between the physical, moral, and racial forms of stigma, each of which is based on identified differences that others negatively evaluate and construct into "spoiled identities." The person with disabilities or suffering schizophrenia would be an example of a spoiled identity. Through interactive situations, individuals classify others into categories, some of which may be stigmatized ones. Once people are classified, we treat them as a spoiled or "virtual" identity rather than as who they actually are. For example, those with physical or mental disabilities are seen as blemished and treated as though they have numerous other deficits—and as less than human. Similarly, those racially or ethnically different from a dominant group are typically treated as deficient and inferior. Finally, those whose behavior may indicate a character flaw, such as criminal offenders, are treated as morally bankrupt, dishonest, evil, and so forth. As a consequence of this process, the stigmatized are uncomfortable with their classifiers, who they feel have unjustly exercised social and political power to deny them their full humanity.

Applied to inmates of mental hospitals or correctional settings, it is clear that the stigma process reduces the ability of those stereotyped as "spoiled" to return to a mainstream or non-criminal life (Goffman 1961). Research conducted by Bernburg, Krohn, and Rivera (2006) found that stigma increased the probability of subjects' socializing with delinquent social groups. Furthermore, a study by Funk (2004) found that stigmatization increases recidivism. The result may be an effort by the stigmatized to conceal their physical and socially constructed defects by constructing a "front" in order to pass as "normal," that is, as persons appearing to have no defects. For example, consider men who abuse their wives in the privacy of their home who in public appear to others as perfectly charming.

Goffman's notion of "total institutions," which was formulated in his study of a mental hospital, *Asylums* (1961), has had considerable impact on labeling theory generally and especially on understanding the way prisons dehumanize the inmate. A total institution is a place where similarly classified people are forced to live, work, and play together around activities consistent with the goals of the institution. This takes place under formal supervisory control governed by strict rules and procedures and within a restricted environment. The inmates in total institutions are separated formally and socially from the staff and have no input into decision making about their activities or outcomes. According to Goffman, this process is designed to force inmates to fit the institutional routine. When continued over time, the process results in inmates' dehumanization and humiliation. As a result of the adaptive behaviors inmates have to adopt in order to cope, the inmates' behavioral patterns become solidified. This changes their moral career and renders them unfit for a return to life outside the institution (ibid., 13). Goffman argued this results in a "mortification" of the self. How permanent such identity change is has been subject to controversy, but there is no question that Goffman's work added considerably to our understanding of the impact of social and institutional effects on the labeling process.

Particularly important, in light of the theories discussed in this and the previous chapter, is that labeling demonstrates the dangers inherent in attempts to intervene to change people. This is most pronounced when punitive interventions are falsely presented as reform programs that suggest a "spoiled identity."

Braithwaite's Reintegrative Shaming

John Braithwaite is an Australian criminologist whose earlier studies were on white-collar crime in the pharmaceutical industry. He is one of the most recent contributors to the labeling perspective, agreeing that the kind of stigmatization Goffman described is certainly destructive. In his book *Crime, Shame, and Reintegration* (1989), Braithwaite defined this negative stigmatization as "disintegrative shaming" and argued that it is destructive of social identities because it morally condemns people and reduces their liberty yet makes no attempt to resolve the problem by reconnecting the accused or convicted with the community. Braithwaite described a second, positive, kind of stigmatization, which he called "reintegrative shaming." This is actually constructive and can serve to reduce and prevent crime. Reintegrative shaming, while expressing social disapproval, also provides the social process mechanisms to bring those censured back into the community, reaffirming that they are morally good—only a part of their total behavior is unacceptable. Braithwaite believed this explains why numerous different communitarian societies that use a positive reintegrative form of shaming, such as Japan, have low crime rates, whereas those that use disintegrative shaming have high crime rates. In the latter cases, offenders are cut off from the mainstream society and are free from informal controls to recidivate. A number of studies have found some support for Braithwaite's theory and the detrimental effects of stigmatization (Losoncz and Tyson 2007; Murphy and Harris 2007).

Although labeling processes are a major component of Braithwaite's analysis, several commentators (Akers 1994; Gibbons 1994; Einstadter and Henry 2006) see his ideas as an integrated theory linking several of the social process theories we have discussed in this and the previous chapters (learning, control, differential association, and labeling) with those we shall discuss in the next two (cultural, subcultural, and strain).

Matsueda's Informal Negative Labeling and Differential Social Control

Ross Matsueda (1992, 2001) and colleague Karen Heimer (Heimer and Matsueda 1994) developed labeling theory to explain not only secondary deviance but also primary deviance, which for a long time was argued to be one of the weaknesses of labeling theory. This is based on their interactionist view of the social self: "The self arises through role-taking, the process of taking the role of the other, viewing one's self from the perspective of the other, and controlling one's behavior accordingly. Moreover, because role taking involves considering lines of action from the standpoint of reference groups, it follows that behavior is controlled by social groups. Self-control is actually social control" (Matsueda 2001, 224).

Matsueda (1992) argued that important parts of the labeling process occur through unofficial control agents such as parents, peers, and teachers. Matsueda's contribution suggests that the informal labeling process starts much earlier than the formal, and may continue in tandem with it. He asserted that because "the self is a reflection of appraisals made by significant others," such informal negative labeling "would influence future delinquency through the role-taking process." Heimer and Matsueda "expanded the role-taking process to include learned definitions of delinquency, anticipated reactions to delinquency, and delinquent peers" (1994, 366–368). They called this process "differential social control," arguing that it can result in a "conventional direction (e.g., when taking the role of conventional groups) or a criminal direction (e.g., when taking the role of criminal groups)" (Matsueda 2001, 235).

Policy Implications of Labeling Theory

Labeling theory has had a considerable impact on criminal justice policy, especially with regard to juveniles. Since the central tenet of labeling theory is that social reaction to minor rule breaking creates extra deviance and crime, the policy is clear. If repeated negative definition by official social control agencies transforms ambivalent social identities into criminal ones, the policy must involve reducing social reaction. This will minimize the production of secondary (or extra) rule breaking and, in particular, prevent minor rule breakers from entering criminal careers. Edwin Schur (1973) defined this overall approach as "radical nonintervention." Einstadter and Henry summarized four policy components of this perspective identified in the literature: (1) decriminalization, (2) diversion, (3) decarceration, and (4) restitution or reparation (2006, 229–232).

Decriminalization is the legalization of crimes involving consent, which [...] are also called victimless crimes (Schur 1965) and include activities such as drug use, homosexuality, gambling, and prostitution. Not only is banning these activities morally questionable (Duster 1970), but their illegality in the face of a wide public demand for them provides a basis for organized crime, gang activity, police corruption, and bribery, together with the accompanying violence necessary for "market" protection (Schur and Bedau 1974; Curran and Renzetti 1994).

Diversion is a policy that redirects those engaged in minor law violations, especially status offenses such as truancy, runaways, and curfew violation, away from the courts through informal processes leading to noncorrectional settings. The approach is credited with being responsible for the existence of the parallel system of juvenile justice, separate from and less formal than the criminal justice system for adult offenders. Juvenile justice is designed to be less stigmatizing. It involves settlement-directed talking, such as conflict resolution, mediation, and problem solving, rather than punishment.

Decarceration attempts to deal with the stigma effects of total institutions by minimizing their use and letting numerous people, such as those convicted of substance abuse offenses, out on alternatives such as probation or electronic tethers. Instead of calling for more prisons, this strategy involves stopping prison building and stopping the sentencing of offenders to prison terms for nonviolent offenses. In particular, juveniles in institutions such as reform schools and training schools were deinstitutionalized into community-based programs (Akers 1994, 131–132).

Restitution and reparation are designed to make the offender responsible for the crime by repaying or compensating either the victim (restitution) or the community or society (reparation) for the harm done. This can involve working to pay back the offender or forms of community service.

Finally, the policy implications of Braithwaite's analysis of reintegrative shaming (1989) involve providing both public exposure of harmful behavior and informal rehabilitation programs designed to bring the accused back as acceptable members of society. Like programs for the recovering alcoholic, these programs can be used as an example of how problems can be worked through. Braithwaite (1995) described this as a move toward new forms of "communitarianism" that is both a social movement and family focused. Finally, his ideas are consistent with the notion of "restorative justice," which involves bringing together offenders, victims, and the community, in mediation programs designed to reintegrate offenders back into the community and allow offenders, victims, and the community a participative role in determining the appropriate level of restitution or reparation.

In many ways, the policy implications of labeling theory are very radical and are not acceptable to most Americans, who have been fed a media diet of punishment and the quick fix ("Three strikes and you're out") from politicians. As a result, the practice of such measures as stopping prison building is confronted with the reality of massive prison-building programs; although in California the 2011 court-mandated realignment order resulted in a diversion of convicted offenders from state prisons to local jails and community corrections.

Evaluation of Labeling Theory

Labeling theory, with its commonsense truth of a "self-fulfilling prophecy," has been subject to much controversy, not least from its seemingly outrageous basic suggestion that attempts to control crime can actually make it worse. The first major criticism was that the theory does not explain why people engage in primary deviance and why some people engage in more of it than others (Gibbs 1966). Second, if deviance is only a product of public labeling, why do some, such as white-collar offenders, employee thieves, embezzlers, and so on, and some violent offenders, such as abusive husbands, engage in careers of crime without ever having been publicly labeled (Mankoff 1971)? One study found that the label applied by parents was strongly related to conceptions of delinquency, a factor that may explain more than the "official" labels that are applied. A study conducted by Johnson, Simons, and Conger (2004) found that although labeling may be one determining factor in deviance, the type of social reaction involved was also critical. Moreover, if the effects of labeling are so strong on vulnerable identities that such persons become locked into criminal careers, how do some reform? The question ultimately raised is, How resilient is the label, and is it only a coping strategy for the institutionalized?

Some critics even contest that control agents are arbitrary in their selection of offenders (Akers 1968; Wellford 1975). One researcher (Jensen 1972a, 1972b, 1980) found that the label applied differentially affects youths based on race or ethnicity. Whites accept the labeling consequences of official sanctions more than African Americans. Moreover, in a study of probationers in Texas, Schneider and McKim (2003) found that although probationers were stigmatized by others, this did not lead to self-stigmatization.

Finally, why does labeling theory tend to focus largely on the agencies of social control and on certain labeled groups—"the nuts, sluts and perverts" (Liazos 1972)—but ignore the wider structure of society and the power of the state and corporate interests in shaping the public policy of the agencies that enforce the labeling (Taylor, Walton, and Young 1973; J. Young 1981)? All these questions and more are not helped by the empirical evidence largely failing to offer support for the theory, although some question the validity of these studies (Plummer 1979; Paternoster and Iovanni 1989).

A major feature of this research is the relative lack of support for the notion that being labeled produces a negative self-image among those labeled (Shoemaker 1996). As a result, as one of its founding critics observes, it became far less dominant in the 1970s, has little to distinguish it, has lost its influence, and "no longer generates the interest, enthusiasm, research and acceptance it once did as a dominant paradigm two or three decades ago" (Akers 1994, 137). However, in recent years, the work of Ross Matsueda has created renewed interest in the theory.

Summary and Conclusion

In this chapter, we have looked at two social process theories that present a mirror image of the two we examined in the previous chapter. Social control theory rejects the neutralization idea that interactive communications may release us from the moral bind of law and instead suggests that more important is the fact that bonds form in the first place. Failure to bond to convention and ineffective socialization practices produce low self-control and allow deviance to go unchecked. For control theorists, particularly self-control theorists, if children are not socialized into thinking about the long-term consequences of their behavior, they will not develop self-control and will exhibit impulsive behavior. The key for self-control theorists is for parents to identify and call attention to the unacceptability of deviant conduct by punishing the consequences of that behavior as soon as it appears. But for labeling theorists, the very fear of the diversity of human behavior may lead to social processes of control that limit the assumed creativity of human lives, bringing about and sustaining careers focused on the very acts the controllers wish to prevent. Thus, for labeling, learning the wrong values is not the issue, nor is bonding to convention or being released from it. For labeling theorists, the issue is how difference is reacted to; how deviants are rejected and labeled is most devastating to their future sense of self, leading them to acquire deviant identities.

Although all these social-process theories sensitize us to the importance of adequate socialization and symbolic interaction, they disagree about what is helpful and what is not. Moreover, they do not offer an understanding of the wider cultural and structural forces that shape the contexts in which these social relations take place. [...]

Summary Chart: Control Theory and Labeling Theory

1. Control Theory

Basic Idea: Explains why we do not all commit crime; claims we do if the controls never form or are worn away.

Human Nature: Humans are seen as rationally calculating, self-interested, and selfish actors (as in classical theory) whose behavior is limited by connections and bonds to others who are significant reference groups for them. People learn the consequences of their behavior and develop greater or less self-control.

Society and Social Order: Consensus. Formed around major social institutions such as family, religion, community, and education.

Law, Crime, and Criminals: Law is an expression of the rules of the conventional society designed to prevent humans from exercising unbridled self-interest to satisfy short-term desires. Crime is a violation of society's laws. Criminals are those for whom bonds of caring for others never formed or are removed. We are all potential criminals, hence the need for law and punishment.

Causal Explanation: Crime is the result of a failure of people to be socialized into a bond with society and develop a stake in conformity. Social bonding consists of four elements:

(1) attachment to teachers, parents, friends, and others, and the desire not to lose them or hurt them; (2) commitment to conventional behavior, with a willingness to do what one has expressed in trust; (3) involvement in conventional activities, especially school related; and (4) belief in the need to obey conventional rules and in the institutions of society. Children who do not develop an awareness and concern about the consequences of their actions lack self-control and will act impulsively.

Criminal Justice Policy: Ensure an adequate level of bonding between youths and conventional society through intensive socialization in traditional and conventional values. Ensure adequate parental socialization of children through (1) monitoring their behavior, (2) recognizing deviance, and (3) ensuring there are consequences when the behavior departs from norms.

Criminal Justice Practice: Prevention and rehabilitation through increased bonding. Strengthened families and increased commitment to conventional occupations by work-training schemes. Reinforced participation in conventional activities at school, and through more effective parenting to instill self-control. Schools can also assist in this process, but generally if the lack of self-control persists, the criminal justice system is too late to make changes.

Evaluation: Explains crime by all social classes. Has been empirically tested and has highest level of support of all theories of crime causation, but fails to explain differences in crime rates or whether a weakened bond can be strengthened. Does not distinguish relative importance of different elements of the bond; does not explain how those highly bonded to convention commit crime or how bonding can actually be used as leverage to coerce offenders who are committed to the high rewards of other jobs and will do anything to keep them; and does not explain ethnic and class influences on beliefs or school performance. Does not consider role of delinquent peers and subcultures in breaking bond; does not consider biological and psychological differences in generating impulsive behavior.

2. Labeling Theory

Basic Idea: As a result of negative labeling and stereotyping (especially by society's control agents), people can become criminal; crime, then, is a self-fulfilling prophecy rooted in the fear that people might be criminal.

Human Nature: Humans are malleable, pliable, plastic, and susceptible to identity transformations as a result of interactions with others and based on how others see them. Human behavior is not fixed in its meaning but open to interpretation and renegotiation. Humans have a social status and are inextricably social beings who are creative and free to interact with others but when they do so become subject to their controls.

Society and Social Order: A plurality of groups dominated by the most powerful who use their power to control and stigmatize others less powerful.

Law, Crime, and Criminals: Law is the expression of the power of moral entrepreneurs and control agents to determine which behaviors are criminalized and which are not. Rules are made that impute ancillary qualities to the deviator. Conflict over legal and public definitions of crime and deviance. Crime is a status. "Criminal" is a socially constructed public stereotype or "master status" for those whom control agents identify as breaking the rules of those in power. We can all become criminals if we have the misfortune of becoming subject to processing by the criminal justice system.

Causal Explanation: Social control agents cause crime by their dramatizing of it and by their excessive reaction to people's expression of individuality and difference. Powerful groups ban behavior and then selectively enforce the ban through control agents, such as the police, psychiatrists, social workers, and so on. Some people's banned behavior is seen as significant, reacted to, and made subject to official agency processing. Lemert distinguished between primary and secondary rule breaking, or deviance. Primary deviance is the incidental and occasional rule breaking that we all do; selective application of rules to some offenders produces stigma, which Goffman described as a spoiled identity and a master status; this results in a deviant and negative self-image. Others engage in "retrospective interpretation," perceiving the actor as having always been deviant and reinterpreting past behavior for "signs" and "cues" of current status. Attempts at stereotypical designation may initially be negotiated or bargained over, as in psychiatric assessments or police discretion, but if the designation is pursued to formal processing, the result is individual role engulfment in a deviant career. Secondary deviance is the repeated rule breaking that comes from our believing that we are now the people that we have been labeled. "Deviancy amplification" comes from the expansion of deviant behavior as we now engage in other deviance in order to conceal our deviant identity and commit acts because we are not that person governed by this master status and committed to a criminal career. Parents and others exercise informal labeling that begins before formal labeling, which can have similar effects in the generation of secondary deviance.

Criminal Justice Policy: Social function of existing system is seen as moral degradation of offender's status; the alternative is to prevent the condemnation and degradation of the defendant by limiting social reaction through radical nonintervention. The perspective is critical of this process, of the shaming and social degrading of defendants as morally inferior, and of agents' control over the process. Preferred alternatives are (1) participant control over the process, (2) victim-offender interaction, (3) mediation and conciliation, and (4) action taken against defendants being influenced by their past relationships with others.

Criminal Justice Practice: Radical nonintervention, tolerance to replace moral indignation, and restitution, reparation, and rehabilitation. Minimalist approach: (1) decriminalize victimless crime; (2) diversion programs to avoid stigmatizing adolescents; (3) stop building prisons; (4) decarcerate prison population, especially nondangerous offenders; (5) develop alternative programs that allow offenders to be rehabilitated from the label; and (6) imprison only the most serious offenders.

Evaluation: Does not explain primary deviance, unless peer group and deviant group social control are incorporated; does not explain how, in spite of labeling attempts, some people never perceive self as stigmatized; does not explain perpetuity of the label (how long does it last?);

does not spend enough time on the reasons for banning behavior in first place. Some policy implications are impractical. Overemphasizes relativity of rules and laws. Does not explain common-law crimes or differences between groups or individuals in the same stigmatized category.

Discussion Questions

1 Briefly describe and explain the social bonds of attachment, commitment, involvement, and belief formed between children and conventional others; and explain how these four components of the social bond facilitate or control crime.

2 What is/are the difference(s) between broken-bond theory and failure-to-bond theory?

3 What did Hirschi and Gottfredson mean by monitoring behavior, and why do they think that is important?

4 What are the similarities and differences between social control theory and labeling theory?

5 What are the central propositions of symbolic interactionism and how do these affect or influence criminal justice policy?

6 What is the difference between primary deviation and secondary deviation and how do they relate to criminal careers?

7 What are some of the insights of labeling theory and discuss why it is so important to dealing with juvenile offenders?

References

Akers, Ronald L. 1968. "Problems in the Sociology of Deviance: Social Definitions and Behavior." *Social Forces* 46: 455–465.

———. 1994 [1999]. *Criminological Theories: Introduction and Evaluation.* Los Angeles: Roxbury Press.

———. 1998. *Social Learning and Social Structure: A General Theory of Crime and Deviance.* Boston: Northeastern University Press.

Baier, Colin J., and Bradley R. E. Wright. 2001. "If You Love Me, Keep My Commandments: A Meta-Analysis of the Effect of Religion on Crime." *Journal of Research in Crime and Delinquency* 38: 3–21.

Becker, Howard. [1963] 1973. *Outsiders: Studies in the Sociology of Deviance.* New York: Free Press.

Bernburg, Jon Gunnar, M. D. Krohn, and C. J. Rivera. 2006. "Official Labeling, Criminal Embeddedness, and Subsequent Delinquency: A Longitudinal Test of Labeling Theory." *Journal of Research in Crime and Delinquency* 43, no. 1: 67–88.

Blumer, Herbert. 1969. *Symbolic Interactionism: Perspective and Method.* Englewood Cliffs, NJ: Prentice Hall.

Boal, Mark. 2008. "Everyone Will Remember Me as Some Sort of Monster?" *Rolling Stone* 1059 (August 21): 73–80.

———. 1951. *Maternal Care and Mental Health.* Geneva: World Health Organization.

Box, Steven. [1971] 1981. *Deviance, Reality, and Society*. New York: Holt, Rinehart, and Winston.

Braithwaite, John. 1989. *Crime, Shame, and Reintegration*. Cambridge, UK: Cambridge University Press.

———. 1995. "Reintegrative Shaming, Republicanism, and Public Policy." In *Crime and Public Policy: Putting Theory to Work*, edited by Hugh D. Barlow. Boulder, CO: West-view Press.

Chambliss, William J. 1973. "The Saints and the Roughnecks." *Society* 11: 24–31.

Cooley, Charles Horton. [1902] 1964. *Social Organization: A Study of the Larger Mind*. New York: Shocken.

Costello, Barbara J., and Paul R. Vowell. 1999. "Testing Control Theory and Differential Association: A Reanalysis of the Richmond Youth Project Data." *Criminology* 37: 815–837.

Curran, Daniel J., and Claire M. Renzetti. 1994. *Theories of Crime*. Boston: Allyn & Bacon.

Debro, Julius. 1970. "Dialogue with Howard S. Becker." *Issues in Criminology* 5: 159–179.

DeLisi, Matt. 2001. "It's All in the Record: Assessing Self-Control Theory with an Offender Sample." *Criminal Justice Review* 26: 1–16.

DeLisi, Matt, and M. T. Berg. 2006. "Exploring Theoretical Linkages Between Self-Control Theory and Criminal Justice System Processing." *Journal of Criminal Justice* 34, no. 2: 153–163.

Duster, Troy. 1970. *The Legislation of Morality*. New York: Free Press.

———. 2006. *Criminological Theory: An Analysis of Its Underlying Assumptions*. 2d ed. Boulder, CO: Rowman & Littlefield.

———. 2000. *Criminology: A Global Perspective*. Boston: Allyn & Bacon.

Funk, P. 2004. "On the Effective Use of Stigma as a Crime-Deterrent." *European Economic Review* 48, no. 4: 715–728.

Gibbons, Don C. 1994. *Talking About Crime and Criminals: Problems and Issues in Theory Development in Criminology*. Englewood Cliffs, NJ: Prentice Hall.

Gibbs, Jack P. 1966. "Conceptions of Deviant Behavior: The Old and the New." *Pacific Sociological Review* 14: 20–37.

Goffman, Erving. 1961. *Asylums*. New York: Doubleday Anchor.

———. 1963. *Stigma: Notes on the Management of Spoiled Identity*. Englewood Cliffs, NJ: Prentice Hall.

Goldstein, Arnold P., Leonard Krasner, and Sol L. Garfield. 1989. *Reducing Delinquency: Intervention in the Community*. New York: Pergamon.

———. 1990. *A General Theory of Crime*. Stanford: Stanford University Press.

Grasmick, Harold G., Charles R. Tittle, Robert J. Bursik, Jr., and Bruce J. Arneklev. 1993. "Testing the Core Empirical Implications of Gottfredson and Hirschi's General Theory of Crime." *Journal of Research in Crime and Delinquency*, 30: 5–29.

Hay, Carter. 2001. "Parenting, Self-Control, and Delinquency: A Test of Self-control Theory." *Criminology* 39: 707–735.

Heimer, Karen, and Ross L. Matsueda. 1994. "Role-Taking, Role Commitment, and Delinquency: A Theory of Differential Social Control." *American Sociological Review* 59: 365–390.

———. 2009. "School Violence Beyond Columbine: A Complex Problem in Need of an Interdisciplinary Analysis." *American Behavioral Scientist* 52, no. 9: 1246–1265.

Hirschi, Travis. 1969. *Causes of Delinquency*. Berkeley, CA, and Los Angeles: University of California Press.

Hirschi, Travis, and Michael R. Gottfredson. 2001. "Self-Control Theory." In *Explaining Criminals and Crime*, edited by Raymond Paternoster and Ronet Bachman, 81–96. Los Angeles: Roxbury Press.

———. 2006. "Social Control and Self-Control Theory." In *The Essential Criminology Reader*, edited by Stuart Henry and Mark M. Lanier: 111–118. Boulder, CO: West-view Press.

Hollin, Clive R. 1990. *Cognitive Behavioral Interventions with Young Offenders*. New York: Pergamon.

Jensen, Gary F. 1972a. "Delinquency and Adolescent Self-Conceptions: A Study of the Personal Relevance of Infraction." *Social Problems* 20: 84–103.

———. 1972b. "Parents, Peers, and Delinquent Action: A Test of the Differential Association Perspective." *American Journal of Sociology* 78: 562–575.

———. 1980. "Labeling and Identity: Toward a Reconciliation of Divergent Findings." *Criminology* 18: 121–129.

Johnson, Lee Michael, Ronald Simons, and Rand D. Conger. 2004. "Criminal Justice System Involvement and Continuity of Youth Crime: A Longitudinal Analysis." *Youth and Society* 36, no. 1: 3–29.

Katz, John. 1999. "Voices from Hellmouth." slashdot.org/articles/99/04/25/1438249.shtml (accessed March 15, 2009).

———. 1984. *Social Sources of Delinquency*. 2d ed. Chicago: University of Chicago Press.

Krohn, Marvin D. 1991. "Control and Deterrence Theories." In *Criminology: A Contemporary Handbook,* edited by Joseph F. Sheley. Belmont, CA: Wadsworth.

LaGrange, Randy L., and Helene Raskin White. 1985. "Age Differences in Delinquency: A Test of Theory." *Criminology* 23: 19–45.

Larkin, Ralph W. 2007. *Comprehending Columbine*. Philadelphia: Temple University Press.

Lemert, Edwin M. 1951. *Social Pathology*. New York: McGraw-Hill.

———. 1967. *Human Deviance, Social Problems and Social Control*. Englewood Cliffs, NJ: Prentice Hall.

Liazos, Alexander. 1972. "The Poverty of the Sociology of Deviance: Nuts, Sluts and Perverts." *Social Problems* 20: 103–120.

Liska, Allen E., and Mark D. Reed. 1985. "Ties to Conventional Institutions and Delinquency: Estimating Reciprocal Effects." *American Sociological Review* 50: 547–560.

Losoncz, I., and G. Tyson. 2007. "Parental Shaming and Adolescent Delinquency: A Partial Test of Reintigrative Shaming Theory." *Australian and New Zealand Journal of Criminology* 40, no. 2: 161–178.

Mack, K. Y., M. J. Leiber, and R. A. Featherstone. 2007. "Reassessing the Family-Delinquency Association: Do Family Type, Family Processes, and Economic Factors Make a Difference?" *Journal of Criminal Justice* 35, no. 1: 51–67.

Mankoff, Milton. 1971. "Societal Reaction and Career Deviance: A Critical Analysis." *Sociological Quarterly* 12: 204–218.

Martin, Randy, Robert J. Mutchnick, and Timothy W. Austin. 1990. *Criminological Thought: Pioneers Past and Present*. New York: Macmillan.

Matsueda, Ross L. 1992. "Reflected Appraisals, Parental Labeling, and Delinquency: Specifying a Symbolic Interactionist Theory. *American Journal of Sociology* 97: 1577–1611.

———. 2001. "Labeling Theory: Historical Roots, Implications and Recent Developments." In *Explaining Criminals and Crime,* edited by Raymond Paternoster and Ronet Bachman: 223–241. Los Angeles: Roxbury Press.

Mead, George Herbert. 1934. *Mind, Self, and Society,* edited by C. W. Morris. Chicago: University of Chicago Press.

Morton, Teru L., and Linda S. Ewald. 1987. "Family-Based Interventions for Crime and Delinquency." In *Behavioral Approaches to Crime and Delinquency: A Handbook of Applications Research and Concepts*, edited by Edward K. Morris and Curtis J. Braukmann. New York: Plenum.

Murphy, K., and N. Harris. 2007. "Shaming, Shame, and Recidivism: A Test of Reintigrative Shaming Theory in the White-Collar Crime Context." *British Journal of Criminology* 47, no. 6: 900–917.

Nettler, Gwynn. 1984. *Explaining Crime*. 3d ed. New York: McGraw-Hill.

Newman, Katherine S., Cybelle Fox, David J. Harding, Jal Mehta, and Wendy Roth. 2004. *Rampage: The Social Roots of School Shootings*. New York: Basic Books.

Nofziger, S. 2008. "The 'Cause' of Low Self-Control: The Influence of Maternal Self-Control." *Journal of Research in Crime and Delinquency* 45, no. 2: 191–224.

Nye, Ivan F. 1958. *Family Relationships and Delinquent Behavior*. New York: John Wiley.

Paternoster, Raymond, and Lee Ann Iovanni. 1989. "The Labeling Perspective and Delinquency: An Elaboration of the Theory and an Assessment of the Evidence." *Justice Quarterly* 6: 359–394.

Pfuhl, Erdwin H., and Stuart Henry. 1993. *The Deviance Process*. 3d ed. Hawthorn, NY: Aldine De Gruyter.

Plummer, Ken. 1979. "Misunderstanding Labelling Perspectives." In *Deviant Interpretations,* edited by David Downes and Paul Rock. Oxford: Oxford University Press.

Pogrebin, Robin. 2008. "In Madoff Scandal, Jews Feel an Acute Betrayal." *New York Times,* December 23. www.nytimes.com/2008/12/24/us/24jews.html?hp (accessed December 28, 2008).

Pratt, Travis C., and Francis Cullen. 2000. "The Empirical Status of Gottfredson and Hirschi's General Theory of Crime: A Meta-analysis." *Criminology* 38: 931–954.

Rankin, Joseph H., and Roger Kern. 1994. "Parental Attachments and Delinquency." *Criminology* 32: 495–515.

Rankin, Joseph H., and Edward Wells. 2006. "Social Control Theory and Direct Parental Controls." In *The Essential Criminology Reader*, edited by Stuart Henry and Mark M. Lanier, 119–28. Boulder, CO: Westview Press.

Reckless, Walter C. [1950] 1973. *The Crime Problem*. Englewood Cliffs, NJ: Prentice Hall.

———. 1961. "A New Theory of Delinquency and Crime." *Federal Probation* 25: 42–46.

Reiss, Albert J., Jr. 1951. "Delinquency as the Failure of Personal and Social Controls." *American Sociological Review* 16: 196–207.

Robinson, David, and Stuart Henry. 1977. *Self-Help and Health: Mutual Aid for Modern Problems*. Oxford, UK: Martin Robertson.

Sagarin, Edward. 1969. *Odd Man In: Societies of Deviants in America*. Chicago: Quadrangle Books.

Schmalleger, Frank. [1999] 2002. *Criminology Today: An Integrative Introduction*. 3d ed. Upper Saddle River, NJ: Prentice Hall.

Schur, Edwin M. 1965. *Crimes Without Victims: Deviant Behavior and Public Policy*. Englewood Cliffs, NJ: Prentice Hall.

———. 1973. *Radical Non-intervention: Rethinking the Delinquency Problem*. Englewood Cliffs, NJ: Prentice Hall.

Schur, Edwin M., and Hugo Adam Bedau. 1974. *Victimless Crimes*. Englewood Cliffs, NJ: Prentice Hall.

Shoemaker, Donald J. 1996. *Theories of Delinquency: An Examination of Explanations of Delinquent Behavior*. 3d ed. New York: Oxford University Press.

———. [1939] 1947. *Principles of Criminology*. Philadelphia: J. B. Lippincott.

Tannenbaum, Frank. 1938. *Crime and the Community.* Boston: Ginn.

Taylor, Ian, Paul Walton, and Jock Young. 1973. *The New Criminology: For a Social Theory of Deviance.* London: Routledge and Kegan Paul.

Toby, Jackson. 1957. "Social Disorganization and Stake in Conformity: Complementary Factors in the Predatory Behavior of Hoodlums." *Journal of Criminal Law, Criminology, and Police Science* 48: 12–17.

Trice, Harrison M., and Paul M. Roman. 1970. "Delabeling, Relabeling, and Alcoholics Anonymous." *Social Problems* 17: 538–546.

Vazsonyi, Alexander T., Lloyd E. Pickering, Marianne Junger, and Dick Hessing. 2001. "An Empirical Test of a General Theory of Crime: A Four Nation Comparative Study of Self-Control and the Prediction of Deviance." *Journal of Research in Crime and Delinquency* 38: 91–131.

Wellford, Charles. 1975. "Labeling Theory and Criminology: An Assessment." *Social Problems* 22: 313–332.

Wilkins, Leslie. 1965. *Social Deviance: Social Policy, Action, and Research.* London: Tavistock.

Young, Jock. 1971. "The Role of Police as Amplifiers of Deviancy, Negotiators of Reality, and Translators of Fantasy." In *Images of Deviance,* edited by Stan Cohen. Harmonds-worth, UK: Penguin.

———. 1981. "Thinking Seriously About Crime: Some Models of Criminology." In *Crime and Society: Readings in History and Society,* edited by Mike Fitzgerald, Gregor McLennan, and Jennie Pawson. London: Routledge and Kegan Paul.

Crime, the Emotions, and Social Psychology

Eamonn Carrabine, Pam Cox, and Maggy Lee

Key Issues

- Why have the emotions been neglected in criminology?
- Is crime seductive?
- What is meant by 'fear of crime'?
- How does resentment structure 'hate' crime?
- What role does 'respect' play in violent encounters?
- Does 'shaming' restore the balance of justice between offenders, victims and the community?

Introduction

It might seem obvious that human emotions play a significant part in the commission of crime, in punishment and in social control. Indeed, the relationship between emotion and crime has fuelled the creative imagination. To take an intense emotion—passion, for instance—*la crime passionel* has inspired great works of literature, theatre, art, symphonies and the opera. It is perhaps the tragedy of crimes of passion that has inspired the artistic imagination; they are offences committed by wretched but ordinary people, not otherwise inclined to transgress. Fuelled by one or more of a myriad of emotions—the wounds of betrayal, the hurt of infidelity, broken hearts, wounded pride, spoiled virtue, jealousy, envy, and many more—they are criminalized by their acts. Passion comes to overrule reason—usually with dire consequences for the offender and the victim.

In Shakespeare's tragic tale *Othello*, the enraged Othello 'the Moor' murders his wife, Desdemona, on account of her alleged adultery, and then kills himself in deep remorse when he realizes he has been deceived into believing in her infidelity. In Bizet's *Carmen*, the smitten soldier Don José kills his love, Carmen, after she has an affair with the handsome Escamillo. In 2002, the tragic story was recast as a 'Hiphopera' by MTV and New Line Television, starring the singer Beyonce Knowles. While in the world of popular music, crimes of passion have been acted out in numerous songs. 'Delilah', the hit by Tom Jones, is a classic example of betrayal with fatal consequences and more recently Nick Cave released an entire album of 'Murder Ballads'. In this chapter we will examine how the emotions figure in criminology. We begin with describing how the emotions have been marginalized in much intellectual work, but have recently become a focal point across the humanities and social sciences.

Rediscovering the Emotions

Although crimes of passion have inspired great artistic works and enthralled audiences for centuries, the subject of emotion, it has recently been argued, has been only a peripheral interest within criminological inquiry and theory. Willem de Haan and Ian Loader, for instance, suggest that

> Many established and thriving modes of criminological reflection and research continue to proceed in ways that ignore entirely, or at best gesture towards, the impact of human emotions on their subject matter—if you doubt this, take a quick glance at almost any criminology textbook, whether of a conventional, radical or integrating bent.
>
> (2002: 243)

However, while the impact of human emotion on crime appears to be in the process of rediscovery in theoretical criminology, it has hardly been neglected in the past by research on crime and deviance. Many of these texts are among the foundational texts of social psychology, which can be defined as the systematic study of people's thoughts, feelings and conduct in social contexts. On this reckoning the emotions should not be reduced to psychological states, but as social and cultural practices that both come from within ourselves and from without—in larger structural processes that ritually shape how we feel and act.

Historically, indeed, a defining feature of Western thought is the way that emotion and reason have been regarded as opposing forces, with the emotional often seen as beneath the rational, as a sign of the lowly, primitive, natural and feminine. It has only been since the late 1970s that the sociology of emotions has become an established field within the discipline. Since then there appeared several major perspectives on the emotions and social life (Hochschild, 1983; Kemper, 1978; Scheff, 1979), as well as the repositioning of the emotions in classical and contemporary social theory (Barbalet, 1998; Williams, 2001; Shilling, 2002), while feminists have explained how the marginalization of emotion has worked to subordinate the feminine, the body and intimate desires (Spelman, 1989; Jaggar, 1989; Ahmed, 2004). Taken together these developments suggest that criminology has much to gain from engaging with this resurgence of interest in the emotions across the humanities and social sciences. Nor should this be a one-way conversation. Criminological work has a crucial place in revealing the importance of emotions in shaping our inner worlds as well as broader social and cultural practices.

Status, Stigma and Seduction

The contemporary interest in crime and the emotions can usefully be traced back to Albert Cohen's study (1955: 17) of delinquent boys, which sought to demonstrate how 'psychogenic and subcultural factors' combined to produce delinquency through the humiliating 'status frustrations' experienced by working-class boys and the alienating differences of class-based value systems. In a series of insightful pieces Erving Goffman described how all encounters are guided by certain cultural scripts that establish the ground rules for interaction. His work captures how perceptions of social worth regulate human conduct. Famously, he argued that mental patients 'suffer not from mental illness, but from contingencies' (Goffman, 1961: 135) — people who may or may not have been experiencing some degree of mental distress, but have had the misfortune to end up in an asylum and then had to adjust their self-identities in line with the 'heavy machinery of mental-hospital servicing'. In *Stigma*, Goffman (1963) examined how people managed 'spoiled identity', the pain and shame associated with being considered less than human. Crucially, he emphasized that we all move between normal and troubled worlds, and each of us falls short some of the time, such that embarrassment (and the anxious expectation of it) clouds every social interaction.

In important ways, Goffman exposed in *Stigma* the very inappropriateness of the term deviance to describe physical handicap, ethnic difference and numerous forms of social dis-affiliation. Likewise, the sharp distinction drawn between deviant and conventional values in subcultural theory was also criticized by David Matza (1964) who pointed out that juveniles intermittently drift into and out of delinquency. His focus on motivational will manages to grasp something of the immediate, intoxicating and alluring spell that delinquency casts, which he would later describe as the 'invitational edge' that deviancy offers (Matza, 1969: 111). It is this dizzying edge that Jack Katz (1988) attempts to capture in his seminal *Seductions of*

Crime through concentrating on the experiential foreground of crime across a diverse range of acts that include juvenile 'sneaky thrills', armed robbery and cold-blooded, 'senseless' murder.

Each specific crime offers distinctive ways of overcoming the mundane routines of everyday life through presenting unique emotional attractions that provide 'a dialectic process through which a person empowers the world to seduce him to criminality' (Katz, 1988: 7). While Katz's work has been influential (especially in cultural criminology) it has not escaped criticism on the grounds that it

- disregards the wider social context in which all action takes place (O'Malley and Mugford, 1994; Young, 2007a);

- fails to secure 'serious distance' (implying that offending stories are taken at face value); and

- lacks any 'systematic explanation' of the various 'motivational' accounts (I. Taylor, 1999: 224).

Yet, as Hayward (2002: 83) suggests, these objections ignore 'the failure of "background" structural theories of crime to address the fundamental question of why (under shared social conditions) one person rather than another commits crime'. It is by exploring the relationships between crime, emotion and social psychology that some of these answers are to be found.

Conceptualizing Emotions

Although there are ongoing debates over how to define exactly what are emotions, what they do and how they should best be studied (Williams, 2001; Strongman, 2003), there is now much agreement that *happiness, fear, anger* and *depression* are universal to all humans and are even said to be hardwired into human neuroanatomy (Kemper, 1987). Importantly, three of the four emotions are negatively tuned (Turner and Stets, 2005: 11) and we will be exploring how these primary emotions shape and colour other emotions like hate, shame, guilt, pride, wonder, resentment, nostalgia and dread among the many feelings encountered in our daily experiences. In his influential article Theodore Kemper (1987) argues that these secondary emotions are more socially constructed and arise from specific contexts where experiences are learnt. Guilt, for example, is derived from the primary emotion of fear and the social organization of punishment, religion or nationhood inducing some experience of shame, regret and sorrow. Table 10.1 summarizes his characterization of primary and secondary emotions, which provides a useful taxonomy of the emotions. Of course, it is important to recognize that there is considerable cultural and social variation in how these emotions are experienced, expressed and practised. We now turn from these broad conceptual issues to that emotional state which has received considerable criminological attention—fear. Indeed, it has become a well-worn observation that the problems posed by the fear of crime are potentially greater than crime itself and as we will see it was this discovery that prompted the plethora of studies on the topic.

Table 10.1 Kemper's primary and secondary emotions

Primary Emotions	Fear	Anger	Depression	Happiness
Emotions attached to primary emotions	Guilt	Shame	Ennui, sadness, resignation	Pride, loving, gratitude
Some combinations of primary emotions	Fear-anger: hate, jealousy, envy	Fear-happiness: wonder, awe, hope, shyness	Anger-happiness: vengeance, snobbery, contempt	Depression-happiness: nostalgia, yearning

Source: Adapted from Kemper, 1987; and Turner and Stets, 2005: 18.

Fear of Crime

Fear is a complex human emotion. While fear is ubiquitous and felt by every living creature, the actual sources of dread are socially distributed. Different societies have developed different ways of living with the dangers that haunt them. Yet contemporary terms like the 'politics of fear', 'fear of crime', 'age of anxiety', 'risk society' and most recently 'liquid fear' (Bauman, 2006; see also Box 10.1) each suggest that we are living in times of such heightened insecurity that danger lurks everywhere. A number of important social changes are said to herald this new era and break with the past—the mass media now provide us with round-the-clock news of crisis, disaster and trauma; rising social mobility brings a greater range of experiences, expectations and troubles; technological innovations have brought with them immense global dangers; and since 9/11 'new' forms of terrorism further contribute to the cultural climate of fear (Carrabine, 2008).

Although research on the fear of crime was established in the late 1960s—paralleling the growth in more general criminological interest and policy concerns over victims of crime—it had moved to the centre of intense empirical, political and theoretical disputes by the 1980s. Today, the 'fear of crime' is an area of criminological inquiry that constitutes a 'sub-discipline in itself' (Lee, 2001: 468) and 'is probably the main legacy of endless, and endlessly repeated, national crime surveys which have consistently identified it as a social problem of striking dimensions' (Ditton *et al.*, 1999: 83). Few issues trouble the public in Europe and the United States more than crime. Surveys have repeatedly shown that worries over victimization surpass losing a job, ill-health, road accidents and indebtedness as issues of major concern (Farall and Gadd, 2004: 127).

From the late 1960s, in the United States initially but later elsewhere around the world, interviewing citizens about their personal experiences of crime became commonplace. In addition to trying to obtain a more accurate view of victimization levels these national household crime surveys provide information on the public's beliefs and attitudes towards crime, policing, punishment and prevention. The British Crime Survey was first carried out in 1982 and has been repeated at regular intervals since. Accompanying national surveys have been an increasing number of local crime surveys, which in the UK have been carried out in various places like

BOX 10.1 Fears in Motion

The trade in safety and security is highly lucrative. To take one example, there is the quite extraordinary phenomenon of the 'Sports Utility Vehicle' (SUV) in the United States. This massive petrol-guzzling, quasi-military vehicle had at one point reached 45 per cent of all car sales in the United States and is sold as a 'defensive capsule'. It is portrayed in advertisements as offering immunity against the dangerously un-predictable urban life outside the protective armoured shell (Bauman, 2006: 143–4). According to Josh Lauer (2005) the SUV first emerged as a status symbol in the early 1980s with the introduction of the military Humvee (which stands for High Mobility Multipurpose Wheeled Vehicle) which was commissioned by the army to replace the jeep, and came to popular attention during the first Gulf War. This prompted the development of a civilian version and the continuing occupation of Iraq has only heightened their popularity.

The massive civilian Hummer was embraced as an ultra macho novelty vehicle and quickly became one of the most fashionable and popular vehicles in America, with more than a third of its sales to women drivers. Indeed, a recent television ad features a woman driving a Hummer through city streets, with the tagline, 'Slip into something more metal'. Clearly there is something more going on here than an increased fear consciousness, as the SUV is an expensive piece of 'high-end automotive jewellery' in which risk management is transformed into a symbol of conspicuous consumption (Lauer, 2005: 163–5). It is significant however that in the UK similar oversized, four-wheel-drive vehicles are frequently derided as 'Chelsea Tractors', which indicates their almost ridiculous remove from their original use among working farmers and the rural gentry (Carrabine, 2008).

Bristol, Sheffield, Merseyside, Islington and Edinburgh (Hale, 1996: 79). Typically fear of crime is often measured by responses to the question 'How safe do you feel walking alone in this area after dark?', or similar formulations, to which respondents are invited to reply by saying they feel 'very safe', 'fairly safe', 'a bit unsafe' or 'very unsafe'. The use of this question to uncover 'fear of crime' has been widely criticized, as it

- fails to explicitly mention crime (Garafalo, 1979);
- cannot do justice to the emotional complexity of fear (Box *et al.*, 1988);
- ignores the fluidity of lived experiences (Goodey, 2005: 69);
- and through questionnaires respondents are 'forced to use the same language to express very different feelings' (O'Mahony and Quinn, 1999: 232–3).

As Evi Girling and her colleagues (Girling *et al.*, 2000: 13) emphasize, these studies tend to 'discover a lack of "fit" between expert knowledge and "lay" opinion' that have come to revolve around the question of whether fear is rational or irrational in an effort to distinguish between 'warranted' estimates of risks as opposed to debilitating misperceptions of threats by particular groups of the public. Home Office research continued to find that both women and the elderly were particularly 'irrational' given the distance between their high levels of expressed fear and their low levels of actual risk. The conclusion was that women and the aged were incapable of making rational sense of the risks they faced.

Feminists quickly challenged the gendered stereotypes of women as fearful and men as fearless in much of these approaches (see, *inter alia*, Goodey, 1997; Stanko, 1997; Gilchrist *et al.*, 1998; Sutton and Farrall, 2005). Betsy Stanko (1987, 1988) was an early critic and argued that this work could not adequately grasp women's experiences and fears of sexual danger. By using alternative research methodologies (like ethnographic studies, life histories and individual interviews) significant empirical evidence was unearthed that debunked 'the myth of the safe home' (Stanko, 1988) to reveal the extent of 'ordinary violence' women regularly face and manage across public and private domains (Stanko, 1990). Such work raises 'fundamental questions of whose standards are used as markers of a reasonable or rational fear' (Walklate, 1998: 409) and suggests there are some dubious conceptual assumptions behind conventional approaches to researching fear. In any case, the debate over whether the 'fear of crime' is rational or irrational is one that can never really be resolved, as it is difficult to see what a rational fear would look like (Sparks, 1992: 10). For women fear of sexual danger is a normal condition—a 'governing of the soul' (Stanko, 1997)—such that much criminological attention has now shifted to the issue of 'ontological security' (Giddens, 1991) in an effort to grasp how inner anxieties are structured in social space.

Urbanism, Anxiety and the Human Condition

A rich seam of work has attempted to understand the ways fears and anxieties are locally constructed. Ian Taylor (1996, 1997) has argued that the fear of crime has become a condensed metaphor, which attempts to capture broader concerns over the pace of socio-economic change. As he explains, the rise of defensive middle-class suburban social movements organized around crime prevention

> are activated not just by immediately presenting sets of problems in the specific locality (stories of aggressive young people and actual violence on the hitherto peaceful local High Street) but by deeper fears about joblessness and house prices, and (in the case of parents with suburban children) schooling 'for success', child safety, moral socialization ... and a host of other increasingly agitated concerns.
>
> (Taylor, 1997: 66)

On this account, worries about crime are intimately bound up with the less easily grasped or articulated troubles generated by changes in economic, moral and social life. It is a 'fear of falling' that is the defining condition of the suburban middle class in contemporary England (Taylor and Jamieson, 1998).

A point further explored by Girling *et al.* (2000) in their study of public perceptions of crime in a prosperous English market town is that

> people's responses to crime (in its association with other matters of con-
> cern to them) are both informed by, and in turn inform, their *sense of place*;
> their sense, that is, of both *the place* they inhabit (its histories, divisions,
> trajectories and so forth), and of *their place* within a wider world of hierar-
> chies, troubles, opportunities and insecurities.
>
> (Girling *et al.*, 2000: 17; emphasis in original)

The importance of this work is that it attempts to situate people's fears in specific everyday contexts and in doing so it chimes with other recent developments that have highlighted how the individual's social location (Walklate, 1998) and inner personal senses of security (Hollway and Jefferson, 2000) shape perceptions of the wider world around them.

The introduction of psychoanalytical theory into the fear of crime debate offers much poten-tial. Wendy Hollway and Tony Jefferson (1997, 2000) draw on the key psychoanalytical insight that anxiety is the price we pay for having a sense of self. Their work emphasizes that anxiety is a universal feature of the human condition and that dynamic 'unconscious defences against anx-iety are a commonplace and constructive aspect of response to threats' (Hollway and Jefferson, 2000: 32). The specific unconscious defence mechanisms they focus on are **denial**, **splitting** and **projection** to explore how threats to the self are managed by these displacing activities. Their overall argument is that anxiety, as a pervasive yet inchoate emotion, lies behind much of the contemporary concerns over fear of crime. Drawing on their research with people living on two council estates in northern England their analysis reveals quite varied and diffuse responses to the threat of crime. The differing responses are informed by individual biography, social location and unconscious defence mechanisms. As they put it 'a rampant "fear of crime" discourse which might on the face of it be thought to exacerbate fears, could actually serve unconsciously as a relatively reassuring site for displaced anxieties which otherwise would be too threatening to cope with' (Hollway and Jefferson, 1997: 263–4).

Hollway and Jefferson (2000: 31) have introduced a notion of human subjectivity that recognizes 'the non-rational, unintentional and emotional aspects of people's actions and experience' that had largely been neglected by criminologists. Nevertheless, sympathetic critics have contended that their approach is more about 'feeling than structure' (Walklate, 1998: 411) while others argue that to 'focus only on unconscious displacement tends to ignore both the conscious strategies and various circuits of communication' (Lupton and Tulloch, 1999: 515) adopted by their respondents. But replacing the rational, unitary subject with the anxious, fragmented subject need not dispense with a socially literate understanding of subjectivity. Instead, unconscious processes combine with cognitive choices as well as social structures, like language, so that these aspects of explanation are best seen as complementary rather than alternatives (Carrabine, 2008).

Yet it would be wrong to assume that people are constantly afraid—life would be unbearable if that were so—but rather the emotional intensity varies and we find imaginative ways of ignoring or adapting to precarious environments (Tuan, 1979: 9). As Walklate (2007a: 100) has succinctly put it, fear 'is not an ever present feeling or state of mind but burns differently in different contexts'. These different contexts will include our immediate social relations, broader external forces as well as our own anxious inner worlds, such that calls for a 'psychosocial criminology' (Jefferson, 2002a; Gadd and Jefferson, 2007) will involve a greater attention to emotional life than criminologists have conventionally been prepared to pay.

Hate Crime

Perhaps one of the most explicit connections drawn between crime and a specific emotion in recent years concerns the emergence of the concept of 'hate crime' in the United States. The United States Federal Bureau of Investigation (FBI) defines hate crimes as offences that are 'motivated in part or singularly by personal prejudice against others because of a diversity—race, sexual orientation, religion, ethnicity/national origin, or disability'. While the term 'hate crime' is institutionalized in law in the United States—as in the Hate Crime Statistics Act 1990—it has gradually become a site of legal intervention in Britain:

- The Crime and Disorder Act 1998 created a number of new racially and religiously aggravated offences;

- The Criminal Justice Act 2003 introduced tougher sentences for offences motivated by hatred of the victim's sexual orientation (this must now be taken into account by the sentencing court as an aggravating factor, in addition to race or religious hate motivation);

- The Racial and Religious Hatred Act 2006 has made it a criminal offence to use threatening words or behaviour with the intention of stirring up hatred against any group of people because of their religious beliefs or their lack of religious beliefs.

The term hate crime has been adopted by the Metropolitan Police Service (MPS), and other police services and the media, and has become firmly established in popular discourse. It is contestable, however, whether 'hate crime' does in fact manifest hate.

For many people, the term hate crime arguably conjures up an image of a violent crime committed by extremists, by neo-Nazis, racist skinheads and other committed bigots—in other words, hate-fuelled individuals who subscribe to racist, anti-semitic, homophobic and other bigoted ideologies. It is not surprising that many people think this way about hate crimes, because the media focus on the most extreme incidents—as is the case with crime reporting in general. The murder of Stephen Lawrence in south London in 1993, and the subsequent media coverage of the young men suspected of the murder, and the racist views they expressed, provide a prime example. Other extreme incidents in Britain that quite understandably gained notoriety include the bombing in May 1999 of the Admiral Duncan, a 'gay pub' in Soho, London, in which three died and scores were injured. The young man convicted, David Copeland, had a history of involvement with racist organizations.

In the United States the brutality of the murder of James Byrd, an African American—who was beaten unconscious, chained to the back of a pick-up truck and dragged for miles along rural roads outside the town of Jasper, Texas, in June 1998—attracted widespread media coverage. The brutality of the murder and the fact that the two perpetrators were members of a white supremacist organization evoked painful memories of **lynching** (see Box 10.2) and historical racial violence in the United States. The callousness of the attack on the young gay man Matthew Shepard, who was pistol-whipped and left lashed to a fence in freezing conditions to die later in hospital in Wyoming in October 1998, generated considerable debate about homophobic bigotry. The incident itself and its repercussions have been portrayed in the play and film *The Laramie Project*.

Paul Iganski (2006) has demonstrated how the New Labour government's specific concerns over racially aggravated offences—influenced to some extent by US legislation and debate—has led to a gradual expansion of British law in this field, from race to religion, and also sexuality and disability. His account describes the many dilemmas surrounding such legislation: from the supporting arguments that crimes motivated by hate cause damage to the victim beyond the crime itself, that this additionally infects a wider community with fear and trauma, and constitutes an assault on the dominant values of society. Opponents criticize the legislation on the grounds that

- legislating against hate is indefensible as it suggests that hurting some kinds of people isn't quite as bad as hurting others (Jacoby, 2002);

- it is a totalitarian response to prejudice as it punishes 'thought crime' in Orwellian fashion (Phillips, 2002); and

- it treats equal crimes unequally, which goes against fundamental legal principles.

The Thrill of it All?

Given the range of victims of hate crimes, the variety of offenders involved and the different social situations in which hate crimes occur, there can obviously be no single explanation, and in any one incident there may be a range of explanations. However, one thing does appear to stand out: many incidents seem to be committed *for the fun of it*, for the kicks, for the excitement, as well as for other reasons. According to Jack Levin and Jack McDevitt:

BOX 10.2 The Politics of Lynching

Lynching is a form of extrajudicial punishment involving public torture revived in the Southern United States as a response to the perceived loss of white male domination in the nineteenth century. The passage of the Thirteenth Amendment (1865) outlawed slavery and with emancipation former slaves became 'African Americans'. It has been argued that it was 'through the process of Reconstruction, the Union attempted to restore relations with the Confederate states' (Messerscmidt, 2007: 81) and it is in this context white male mob violence quickly arose as an attempt to reassert old hierarchies. For example, in May 1866, forty-six African Americans were murdered when their schools and churches were set on fire by a white male mob in Memphis. Two months later, in July, thirty-four African Americans were killed in New Orleans at the hands of a white mob (Ayers, 1984).

The lynchings were explicitly violent and looked to ancient and medieval forms of aggravated death penalty, which included burning, castration, whipping as well as hanging. Indeed, the lynch mob insisted on punishments that were barbaric, and the fact that they would outrage liberal sensibility was all part of their appeal. They.were deliberately racialized and the lynch victim was often sought out as retribution for the alleged rape of a white woman by an African-American man. The public lynching has been understood as a carnival critique of official criminal justice and total rejection of the law's commitment to equality while reasserting local understandings of caste superiority. As Garland (2007: 147) explains, public torture lynching communicated 'impassioned sentiments that could no longer be expressed in the official idiom of the criminal law' and inflicted 'a level of suffering that had long since been officially disavowed'. In Chapter 15 we will examine how punishment arouses powerful emotions that can appeal to cruel tendencies in the human condition.

> Like young men getting together on a Saturday night to play a game of cards, certain hatemongers get together and decide to go out and destroy property or bash minorities. They want to have some fun and stir up a little excitement—at someone else's expense.

The payoff in such 'thrill-seeking hate crime', as Levin and McDevitt famously called it, is psychological as well as social:

> They enjoy the exhilaration and the thrill of making someone suffer. For those with a sadistic streak, inflicting pain and suffering is its own reward.

> In addition, the youthful perpetrators receive a stamp of approval from
> their friends who regard hatred and violence as 'hot' or 'cool'.
>
> (Levin and McDevitt, 2002: 67)

In a 'pick and mix' of bigotry, the victims of thrill-seeking hate crimes are often interchangeable.

Excitement is not the only emotion involved in so-called hate crime. Levin and McDevitt argue that resentment—to one degree or another—can be found in the personality of most hate crime offenders, and it takes many forms. There are individuals who, perhaps because of some personal misfortune, feel rejected by, estranged from and wronged by society. They look for someone to target in venting their anger.

For others, their bitterness is fuelled by a perceived or real threat to their economic security, and some strike at those they think are to blame: newcomers, immigrants, asylum seekers. Larry Ray and colleagues, drawing on research based in Greater Manchester, argue that much of the violence is related to the sense of shame and failure, resentment and hostility felt by young men who 'are disadvantaged and marginalised economically and culturally, and thus deprived of the material basis for enacting a traditional conception of working-class masculinity'. Such emotions, according to Ray *et al.*, 'readily lead to violence only in the case of young men (and occasionally for young women) for whom resorting to violence is a common approach to settling arguments and conflicts' (2003: 112).

Self-Esteem, Shame and Respect

The significance of self-esteem in violent encounters has been explored by Thomas Scheff and his colleagues. From their perspective, 'self-esteem concerns how we usually feel about ourselves. High self-esteem means that we usually feel justified pride in ourselves, low self-esteem that we often and easily feel ashamed of ourselves or try to avoid feelings of shame' (Scheff *et al.*, 1989: 178). They propose that 'shame' is a primary emotion generated by the constant, incessant but commonly unacknowledged monitoring and negative evaluation of self in the eyes of others. Shame, however, is generally unacknowledged, and as an emotion it is seen to be socially unacceptable.

Self-esteem, in short, is a 'summary concept', representing how well a person overall manages shame. People with high self-esteem have had sufficient experience of pride to outweigh their experience of shame; they can manage shame. However, when a person has had an insufficient experience of pride, then shame becomes a calamity for them. When they experience some form of humiliation, real or imagined, rather than acknowledging it, it is masked with anger. The person is then caught in a 'shame–rage feeling trap'. According to Scheff and colleagues,

> In our theory, rage is used as a defense against threat to self, that is, feeling
> shame, a feeling of vulnerability of the whole self. Anger can be a protective

measure to guard against shame, which is experienced as an attack on self. As humiliation increases, rage and hostility increase proportionally to defend against loss of self-esteem.

In short, violence is the consequence of trapped shame and anger. Crucially, Scheff and colleagues further argue that

> Pride and shame states almost always depend on the level of deference accorded a person: pride arises from deferential treatment by others ('respect'), and shame from lack of deference ('disrespect'). Gestures that imply respect or disrespect, together with the emotional response they generate, make up the deference/emotion system, which exerts a powerful influence on human behavior.
>
> (Scheff et al., 1989: 184–5)

These arguments have also proven especially influential on the role of shame in restorative justice practices, where it is argued that the community conferences that lie at the heart of reintegrative shaming (see Box 10.3) work not so much through the words said but on facial expressions, gestures and physical posture (Retzinger and Scheff, 1996). We now describe how the emotions are embodied in contemporary street cultures, where crime, hustling and violence have become a defining way of life for the ghetto poor.

BOX 10.3 Reintegrative Shaming

In his classic study *Crime, Shame and Reintegration* (1989), John Braithwaite emphasized the importance of the emotions in the restoration of justice between offenders, victims and the wider community. This work provided a powerful impetus to the 'restorative justice' movement in criminology and challenge to vindictive models of retributive punishment [...]. The book has decisively influenced studies of conflict, reconciliation and 'peace-making' as well as enabling accounts of the place of 'emotional work' in criminal justice institutions to emerge (e.g. Karstedt, 2002). His argument is that shaming the offence, and not the offender, will reintegrate the offender back into the community while giving victims a strong role in these reconciliation processes.

Crucially, though, the agents of shaming are not the victims, but the family and friends of the offender so that shame integrates rather than alienates. As he famously put it, the 'best place to see reintegrative shaming at work is in loving families' (Braithwaite, 1989: 56).

Braithwaite's arguments are closely allied to Thomas Scheff's work on shame (which suggests that one of the central features of life is our search for honour and the ways in which shaming plays a role in that search). Shame is linked to taking on the role of 'the other' (cf. Mead, 1934), and links to the pangs of conscience when confronted with the possibility of wrongdoing. We want and need the social approval of others. Shaming involves all social processes expressing disapproval that have the aim of inducing remorse in the offender. For Braithwaite, the shame that matters most is not that coming from officials such as the police, judges, courts or even victims, but that from the people we care most about. It is not stigmatizing in so far as it is aimed not at the offender per se but at the act the offender commits; the ultimate aim must be reintegration and he contends that reintegrative shaming is effective in complex societies as well as more traditional ones.

It is significant that Braithwaite developed his arguments from accounts of indigenous procedures of 'conferencing' in New Zealand and Australia, where he found that these community settings successfully combined shaming and reintegration. Critics worry whether these processes will be used against the most vulnerable groups in society or deployed only for trivial offences while conventional, custodial punishments continue to expand. It has been noted how the model of reintegrative shaming developed in Australia and currently exported around the world is one principally targeted at Aboriginal youth, intensifying police controls over this already marginalized population (Blagg, 1997). More recent Australian research has suggested that 'net-widening' may be a problem, and that more marginalized young people (including non-Aboriginal) are channelled away from youth conferencing into a youth 'justice system more punitive in its sentencing' (Cunneen and White, 2006: 107). The idealization of the family at the heart of the approach has been criticized for its reliance on defining 'others *as* others' (Ahmed, 2004: 199; emphasis in original)—those who have failed to live up to this ideal social bond—like single mothers, queer relationships, and so forth. To be fair, Braithwaite has always recognized that shaming can be used tyrannically against unpopular minorities, but it is difficult to see how the communitarian politics that informs his thinking can oppose hostile collective sentiments when that is the community's will.

Stories from the Street

The issue of 'respect' is a key theme explored by Elijah Anderson in his book *Code of the Streets* (1999). He argues that for many inner-city youths in his study, a street culture has evolved, what he calls a code of the streets—a set of informal rules governing public behaviour and the use of violence. It can be traced to the sense of hopelessness and to the alienation that the youths feel from mainstream society and its institutions, due to the joblessness and the pervasive racism they experience.

'Respect' is 'at the heart of the code', according to Anderson. Respect is about 'being treated "right", or granted the deference one deserves'. But gaining and maintaining respect has to be a constant endeavour:

> In the street culture, especially among young people, respect is viewed as almost an external entity that is hard-won but easily lost, and so must constantly be guarded. The rules of the code in fact provide a framework for negotiating respect. The person whose very appearance—including his clothing, demeanor, and way of moving—deters transgressions, feels that he possesses, and may be considered by others to possess, a measure of respect. With the right amount of respect, for instance, he can avoid 'being bothered' in public. If he is bothered, not only may he be in physical danger but he has been disgraced or 'dissed'.
>
> (Anderson, 1994: 82)

One key aspect of a person's demeanour to convey and hold respect is 'having the juice': projecting an image, a willingness to resort to violence, having the nerve to throw the first punch, to pull the trigger and, in the extreme, not being afraid to die, and not being afraid of taking another's life if needs be, if someone 'gets in their face', if disrespected.

Respect is a scarce commodity. Deprived of achieving a sense of self-esteem through participation in the jobs market, and other institutions of mainstream society, 'everyone competes', according to Anderson,

> to get what affirmation he can of the little that is available. The craving for respect that results gives people thin skins. Shows of deference by others can be highly soothing, contributing to a sense of security, comfort, self-confidence, and self-respect. Transgressions by others which go unanswered diminish these feelings and are believed to encourage further transgressions. ... Among young people, whose sense of self-esteem is particularly vulnerable, there is an especially heightened concern with being disrespected. Many inner-city young men in particular crave respect to such a degree that they will risk their lives to attain and maintain it.
>
> (1994: 89)

Similarly, Philippe Bourgois (1995) describes in his *In Search of Respect* how the street identity cultivated by men from East Harlem, which involved limited social skills, assumed gender arrogance and intimidating physical presence, made them virtually unemployable—often appearing clumsy and illiterate before prospective female supervisors in Manhattan's booming service sector economy.

In an important critique of the underclass thesis, Carl Nightingale's (1993) ethnography of the black Philadelphian ghetto maintains that the culture of the ghetto is not only a product of alienation and isolation but rather a consequence of the desperate embrace of the American Dream:

> Already at five and six, many kids in the neighborhood can recite the whole canon of adult luxury—from Gucci, Evan Piccone, and Pierre Cardin, to Mercedes and BMW ... from the age of ten, kids become thoroughly engrossed in Nike's and Reebok's cult of the sneaker.
>
> (Nightingale, 1993:153–4)

In ways that have clear echoes of Albert Cohen's earlier subcultural theory, Nightingale is arguing that structural exclusion is accompanied by an over-identification with mainstream consumer culture. As he explains:

> Inner-city kids' *inclusion* in mainstream America's mass market has been important in determining those kids' responses to the economic and racial *exclusion* they face in other parts of their lives. And, indeed, kids' experiences of exclusion and of the associated painful memories has made their participating in mass culture particularly urgent and enthusiastic, for the culture of consumption has given them a seductive means to compensate for their feelings of failure.
>
> (Nightingale, 1993: 135; emphasis in original)

The disturbing ambivalence at the heart of America's race relations is also captured in Naomi Klein's (2000: 76) discussion of companies like Tommy Hilfiger, whose marketing strategy is based on 'selling white youth on their fetishization of black style, and black youth on their fetishization of white wealth'. Jock Young (2007a: 51) has recently argued that these ghetto studies suggest that we need 'to return to the two stigmas which the poor confront, that of relative deprivation (poverty and exclusion from the labour markets) and misrecognition (lower status and lack of respect)'. Both of these are forms of humiliation, each generating powerful dynamics of resentment.

Humiliation, Rage and Edgework

At the beginning of this chapter it was observed that crimes of passion have fuelled the artistic imagination. We now turn to such crimes and draw from Jack Katz's analysis of the interrelationship of emotion and crime in his book *Seductions of Crime* (1988). In the book Katz covers a range of criminal and deviant behaviour—the ways of the 'badass', the 'hardman', the 'cold-blooded killer' and white-collar criminal—but it is instructive to focus on cases of murder that Katz analyses using a variety of documentary sources. The incidents involving what Katz calls 'Righteous Slaughter' are impassioned acts committed in moments of rage—as is the case with many murders.

In the cases that Katz analyses, the victim-to-be inflicts a humiliation upon the killer-to-be: a wife caught by her husband *in flagrante* with another man; another tortured by her husband's infidelity; a man whose virility is challenged by his partner; a neighbour offended by another neighbour parking in front of their property. In each case, humiliation arises from the violation of a respected social role, such as husband, wife, virile male, property owner. The would-be killer's reaction to the humiliation, according to Katz's analysis, is 'a last stand defence of respectability'. Their mortal act is not calculated in a premeditated sense to restore their self-worth. It is instead experienced as a compulsion, driven by rage arising from the killer's emotional comprehension of the humiliation they have suffered.

Risk, Excitement and Routine

Jack Katz (1988) is drawing attention to the exciting, pleasurable and transgressive dynamics that are very much at the 'foreground' of criminal activity in an effort to critique the 'sentimental materialism' (as Katz, 1988: 313–17, terms it) of much liberal and radical criminology. British criminologists have also explored these issues. Roger Matthews (2002) in his study of armed robbers, for instance, notes how during his interviews it was usually when his respondents were describing the actual robberies that the attractions of the crime would become all too apparent. Similarly, Mike Collison's (1996) research on masculinities and crimes connects these ideas to cultural consumption, risk-taking and drug use. For example, burgling a house is an activity laced with excitement but it is also riddled with risk. One of the respondents in his study described the dual-edged thrill and danger of getting caught, assault by the homeowner, or the police, or later on the street by failing in front of male friends. As one 20-year-old put it: 'I always used to leave the room they was sleeping in till last ... they never used to hear me for some reason ... it was scary and exciting' (Collison, 1996: 443). Few stopped to calculate the risks but rather put their faith in a mystical sense of invincibility, or hope for a run of good luck, or sometimes used drugs to ease the risk. It is useful to contrast these accounts though with Tony Kearon and Rebecca Leach's (2000) discussion of burglary where they describe the intense feelings of abjection that many victims of house theft experience.

What seems to be particularly important here, in terms of doing crime, is that this kind of 'edgework' (Lyng, 1990a, 2004) is deeply satisfying and seductive. Edgework has been described as a form of 'experiental anarchy' that is an 'experience that is much more real than the circumstances of everyday experience'. One British 19-year-old explained to Collison (1996: 435) that 'what I really want to do like to occupy my time, I'd like to jump out of planes like that, that's exciting to me, I couldn't afford things like that ... so I just pinch cars, get chases, do burglaries and enjoy myself that way'. It is important to recognize that while this edgework is an essential part of street life for underclass male youth, it also has routine features. For what comes across in all the narratives is how surprisingly ordinary this risk-taking is. But, and this is highly significant, these activities are not thought of in this way. They would be impossible to do if they were.

The important question here is why these activities are so exciting and seductive. In answering this question the crucial factor is drugs, not just in the sense of being able to 'get off your face' through Ecstasy, amphetamines and LSD, but that they form a defining part of the irregular economy in poor communities for expendable male youth in Collison's (1996) study. For young underclass men the promised land is on the TV, and it should come as no surprise to learn that their favourite film was *New Jack City*, while real life here 'stinks'. In contrast, the drug economy provides these young men with their only realistic chance of fast living and the high life in Britain. Drug crime, like other forms of street crime, creates a space for acting out predatory forms of masculinity. Street-level drug dealing, whether this is on the corner or watched on film, and the two are frequently conflated, promises action and status success. According to Collison (1996: 441) forms of predatory street crime and excessive lifestyle among some young underclass males are not a simple response to poverty, they are attempts to 'munch' their way through consumer society and fill in the spaces of structure and identity, or in other words, to get a 'reputation as mad'.

Summary

1   Criminology has an important role to play in showing how the emotions shape our inner lives and broader social practices.

2   Fear and anxiety are central characteristics of modern living.

3   Human emotions play a central role in the criminal act.

4   The study of the emotional dynamics of crime illuminates why certain crimes occur.

5   The emotions can restore justice between offenders, victims and the wider community.

Further Study

Anderson, E. (1999) *Code of the Streets: Decency, Violence and the Moral Life of the Inner City*, New York: W. W. Norton. A highly illuminating ethnographic exploration of the social and cultural dynamics of interpersonal violence in the inner city.

Bauman, Z. (2006) *Liquid Fear*, Cambridge: Polity. One of the most original sociological thinkers casts his eye over the fears and anxieties that haunt our current age.

Critical Thinking Questions

1   Why have the emotions been marginalized in Western thought?

2   Why is 'fear of crime' an ill-defined term?

3   Why might 'hate crime' legislation be a totalitarian response to prejudice?

4   How could the arguments outlined in this chapter help us understand phenomena like 'road rage', 'lynch mobs' and 'queer bashing'?

5   What are the seductions of crime?

6   How does the 'search for respect' reproduce exclusion in North American ghettoes?

Gadd, D. and Jefferson, T. (2007) *Psychosocial Criminology: An Introduction*, London: Sage. A lively demonstration of how a psychosocial approach sheds new light on the causes of many crimes, as well as challenging readers to rethink the similarities and differences between themselves and offenders.

Iganski, P. (2008) '*Hate Crime' and the City*, Bristol: Policy Press. A wide-ranging account analysing how we understand and ought to respond to crimes motivated by prejudice in the UK.

Katz, J. (1988) *Seductions of Crime: Moral and Sensual Attractions of Doing Evil*, New York: Basic Books. An indispensable analysis of the sensual and emotional dynamics of crime.

Levin, J. and McDevitt, J. (2002) *Hate Crimes Revisited:America's War on Those Who Are Different*, Boulder, CO:Westview. An invaluable evaluation of the social, cultural, motivational and policy context of hate and crime.

More Information

American Psychological Association: 'Hate Crimes Today: An Age-Old Foe in Modern Dress'
http://www.apa.org/pubinfo/hate/homepage.html
A question-and-answer site shedding some clarification on the hate crime debate.

Hate Crime.org
http://www.hatecrime.org/
Information and links to related news articles concerning current events, political choices, and victims and further information.

National Gay and Lesbian Task Force: information on hate crime laws

http://www.nglft.org/issues/issue.cfm?issueID=12

NGLTF is the national progressive organization working for the civil rights of gay, lesbian, bisexual and transgender people.

Crime reduction

http://www.crimereduction.homeoffice.gov.uk/toolkits/fc00.htm

A typical Home Office site offering advice and information on how to tackle fear and disorder in the community.

Bibliography

Ahmed, S. (2004) *The Cultural Politics of Emotion*, Edinburgh: Edinburgh University Press.

Anderson, E. (1994) 'The Code of Streets', *Atlantic Monthly*, 5: 80–94.

Anderson, E. (1999) *Code of the Streets: Decency, Violence and the Moral Life of the Inner City*, New York: W.W. Norton.

Ayers, E. (1984) *Vengeance and Justice: Crime and Punishment in the Nineteenth-century American South*, New York: Oxford University Press.

Barbalet, J. (1998) *Emotion, Social Theory and Social Structure: A Macrosociological Approach*, Cambridge: Cambridge University Press.

Bauman, Z. (2006) *Liquid Fear*, Cambridge: Polity.

Blagg, H. (1997) 'A Just Measure of Shame: Aboriginal Youth and Conferencing in Australia', *British Journal of Criminology*, 37 (4): 481–501.

Bourgois, P. (1995) *In Search of Respect*, Cambridge: Cambridge University Press.

Box, S., Hale, C. and Andrews, G. (1988) 'Explaining Fear of Crime', *British Journal of Criminology*, 28: 340–56.

Braithwaite, J. (1989) *Crime, Shame and Reintegration*, Cambridge: Cambridge University Press.

Carrabine, E. (2008) *Crime, Culture and the Media*, Cambridge: Polity.

Cohen, A. K. (1955) *Delinquent Boys: The Culture of the Gang*, Glencoe, IL: Free Press.

Collison, M. (1996) 'In Search of the High Life: Drugs, Crime, Masculinity and Consumption', *British Journal of Criminology*, 36 (3): 428–44.

Cunneen, C. and White, R. (2006) 'Australia: Control, Containment or Empowerment?', in J. Muncie and B. Goldson (eds) *Comparative Youth Justice*, London: Sage.

de Haan, W. and Loader, I. (2002) 'On the Emotions of Crime, Punishment and Social Control', *Theoretical Criminology*, 6 (3): 243–53.

Ditton, J., Bannister, J., Gilchrist, E. and Farrall, S. (1999) 'Afraid or Angry? Recalibrating the "Fear" of Crime', *International Review of Victimology*, 6: 83–99.

Farrall, S. and Gadd, D. (2004) 'Research Note: The Frequency of the Fear of Crime', *British Journal of Criminology*, 44: 127–32.

Gadd, D. and Jefferson, T. (2007) *Psychosocial Criminology: An Introduction*, London: Sage.

Garafalo, J. (1979) 'Victimisation and the Fear of Crime', *Journal of Research in Crime and Delinquency*, 16: 80–97.

Garland, D. (2007) 'Death, Denial, Discourse: On the Forms and Functions of American Capital Punishment', in D. Downes, P. Rock, C. Chinkin and C. Gearty (eds) *Crime, Social Control and Human Rights: From Moral Panics to States of Denial, Essays in Honour of Stanley Cohen*, Cullompton: Willan.

Giddens, A. (1991) *Modernity and Self-Identity*, Cambridge: Polity.

Gilchrist, E., Bannister, J., Ditton, J. and Farrall, S. (1998) 'Women and the "Fear of Crime": Challenging the Accepted Stereotype', *British Journal of Criminology*, 38 (2): 283–98.

Girling, E., Loader, I. and Sparks, R. (2000) *Crime and Social Change in Middle England: Questions of Order in an English Town*, London: Routledge.

Goffman, E. (1961) *Asylums: Essays on the Social Situation of Mental Patients and Other Inmates*, Harmondsworth: Penguin.

Goffman, E. (1963) *Stigma: Notes on the Management of Spoiled Identity*, Harmondsworth: Penguin.

Goodey, J. (1997) 'Boys Don't Cry: Masculinities, Fear of Crime and Fearlessness', *British Journal of Criminology*, 47 (3): 401–18.

Goodey, J. (2005) *Victims and Victimology: Research, Policy and Practice*, Harlow: Longman.

Hale, C. (1996) 'Fear of Crime: A Review of the Literature', *International Review of Victimology*, 4: 79–150.

Hayward, K. (2002) 'The Vilification and Pleasures of Youthful Transgression', in J. Muncie, G. Hughes and E. McLaughlin (eds) *Youth Justice: Critical Readings*, London: Sage.

Hochschild, A. (1983) *The Managed Heart: Commercialization of Human Feeling*, Berkeley: University of California Press.

Hollway, W. and Jefferson, T. (1997) 'The Risk Society in an Age of Anxiety: Situating Fear of Crime', *British Journal of Sociology*, 48 (2): 255–66.

Hollway, W. and Jefferson, T. (2000) 'The Role of Anxiety in Fear of Crime', in T. Hope and R. Sparks (eds) *Crime, Risk and Insecurity*, London: Routledge.

Iganski, P. (2006) 'Free to Speak, Free to Hate?', in L. Morris (ed.) *Rights: Sociological Perspectives*, London: Routledge.

Jacoby, J. (2002) 'Punish Crime, Not Thought Crime', in P. Iganski (ed.) *The Hate Debate*, London: Profile.

Jaggar, A. (1989) 'Love and Knowledge: Emotion in Feminist Epistemology', in S. Bordo and A. Jaggar (eds) *Gender/Body/Knowledge: Feminist Reconstructions of Being and Knowing*, New York: Rutgers University Press.

Jefferson, T. (2002a) 'For a Psychosocial Criminology', in K. Carrington and R. Hogg (eds) *Critical Criminology: Issues, Debates, Challenges*, Cullompton: Willan.

Karstedt, S. (2002) 'Emotions and Criminal Justice', *Theoretical Criminology*, 6 (3): 299–317.

Katz, J. (1988) *Seductions of Crime: Moral and Sensual Attractions of Doing Evil*, New York: Basic Books.

Kearon, A. and Leach, R. (2000) 'Invasion of the "Bodysnatchers": Burglary Reconsidered', *Theoretical Criminology*, 4 (4): 451–72.

Kemper, T. (1978) *A Social Interactional Theory of Emotions*, New York: John Wiley.

Kemper, T. (1987) 'How Many Emotions Are There? Wedding the Social and Automatic Components', *American Journal of Sociology*, 93: 263–89.

Klein, N. (2000) *No Logo*, London: Flamingo.

Lauer, J. (2005) 'Driven to Extremes: Fear of Crime and the Rise of the Sport Utility Vehicle in the United States', *Crime, Media, Culture*, 1 (2): 149–68.

Lee, M. (2001) 'The Genesis of "Fear of Crime"', *Theoretical Criminology*, 5 (4): 467–85.

Levin, J. and McDevitt, J. (2002) *Hate Crimes Revisited: America's War on Those Who Are Different*, Boulder, CO: Westview Press.

Lupton, D. and Tulloch, J. (1999) 'Theorizing Fear of Crime: Beyond the Rational/Irrational Opposition', *British Journal of Sociology*, 50 (3): 507–23.

Lyng, S. (1990) 'Edgework: A Social Psychological Analysis of Voluntary Risk Taking', *American Journal of Sociology*, 95 (4): 851–86.

Lyng, S. (2004) 'Crime, Edgework and Corporeal Transaction', *Theoretical Criminology*, 8 (3): 359–75.

Matthews, R. (2002) *Armed Robbery*, Cullompton: Willan.

Matza, D. (1964) *Delinquency and Drift*, New York: Wiley.

Matza, D. (1969) *Becoming Deviant*, Englewood Cliffs, NJ: Prentice Hall.

Mead, G. H. (1934) *Mind, Self and Society*, Chicago, IL: University of Chicago Press.

Messerschmidt, J. W. (2007) '"We Must Protect Our Southern Women": On Whiteness, Masculinities and Lynching', in M. Bosworth and J. Flavin (eds) *Race, Gender and Punishment: From Colonialism to the War on Terror*, New Brunswick, NJ: Rutgers University Press.

Nightingale, C. (1993) *On the Edge*, New York: Basic Books.

O'Mahony, D. and Quinn, K. (1999) 'Fear of Crime and Locale: The Impact of Community Related Factors upon Fear of Crime', *International Review of Victimology*, 6: 231–51.

O'Malley, P. and Mugford, S. (1994) 'Crime, Excitement and Modernity', in G. Barak (ed.) *Varieties of Criminology: Readings from a Dynamic Discipline*, Westport, CT: Praeger.

Phillips, M. (2002) 'Hate Crime: The Orwellian Response to Prejudice', in P. Iganski (ed.) *The Hate Debate: Should Hate be Punished as a Crime?*, London: Profile.

Ray, L., Smith, D. and Wastell, L. (2003) 'Understanding Racist Violence', in E. A. Stanko (ed.) *The Meanings of Violence*, London: Routledge.

Retzinger, S. and Scheff, T. (1996) 'Strategy for Community Conferences: Emotions and Social Bonds', in B. Galaway and J. Hudson (eds) *Restorative Justice: International Perspectives*, Monsey, NY: Criminal Justice Press.

Scheff, T. J. (1979) *Catharsis in Healing, Ritual, and Drama*, Berkeley: University of California Press.

Scheff, T. J., Retzinger, S. M. and Ryan, M. T. (1989) 'Crime, Violence, and Self-Esteem: Review and Proposals', in A. Mecca, N. J. Smelser and J. Vasconcellos (eds) *The Social Importance of Self-Esteem*, Berkeley: University of California Press.

Shilling, C. (2002) 'The Two Traditions in the Sociology of Emotions', in J. Barbalet (ed.) *Emotions and Sociology*, Oxford: Blackwell.

Sparks, R. (1992) *Television and the Drama of Crime: Moral Tales and the Place of Crime in Public Life*, Milton Keynes: Open University Press.

Spelman, E. (1989) 'Anger and Insubordination', in A. Garry and M. Pearsall (eds) *Women, Knowledge, and Reality: Explorations in Feminist Philosophy*, Boston, MA: Unwin Hyman.

Stanko, B. (1987) 'Typical Violence, Normal Precaution: Men, Women, and Interpersonal Violence in England, Wales and the USA', in J. Hanmer and M. Maynard (eds) *Women, Violence and Social Control*, Basingstoke: Macmillan.

Stanko, B. (1988) 'Fear of Crime and the Myth of the Safe Home: A Feminist Critique of Criminology', in K. Yllo and M. Bograd (eds) *Feminist Perspectives on Wife Abuse*, London: Sage.

Stanko, B. (1997) 'Safety Talk: Conceptualising Women's Risk Assessment as a "Technology of the Soul"', *Theoretical Criminology*, 1 (4): 479–99.

Stanko, E. (1990) *Everyday Violence*, London: Pandora.

Strongman, K. (2003) *The Psychology of Emotion: From Everyday Life to Theory*, Chichester: Wiley.

Sutton, R. and Farrall, S. (2005) 'Gender, Socially Desirable Responding and the Fear of Crime: Are Women Really More Anxious about Crime?', *British Journal of Criminology*, 45 (2): 212–24.

Taylor, I. (1996) 'Fear of Crime, Urban Fortunes and Suburban Social Movements: Some Reflections on Manchester', *Sociology*, 30 (2): 317–37.

Taylor, I. (1997) 'Crime, Anxiety, and Locality: Responding to the Condition of England at the End of the Century', *Theoretical Criminology*, 1 (1): 53–76.

Taylor, I. and Jamieson, R. (1998) 'Fear of Crime and Fear of Falling: English Anxieties Approaching the Millennium', *Arch. European Journal of Sociology*, 39 (1): 149–75.

Tuan, Y. (1979) *Landscapes of Fear*, New York: Pantheon Books.

Turner, J. and Stets, J. (2005) *The Sociology of Emotions*, Cambridge: Cambridge University Press.

Walklate, S. (1998) 'Excavating the Fear of Crime: Fear, Anxiety or Trust?', *Theoretical Criminology*, 2 (4): 403–18.

Walklate, S. (2007a) *Imagining the Victim of Crime*, Berkshire: Open University Press.

Williams, S. (2001) *Emotion and Social Theory*, London: Sage.

Young, J. (2007a) *The Vertigo of Late Modernity*, London: Sage.

Social Attitudes and the Physical World

George H. Mead

The self is not so much a substance as a process in which the conversation of gestures has been internalized within an organic form. This process does not exist for itself, but is simply a phase of the whole social organization of which the individual is a part. The organization of the social act has been imported into the organism and becomes then the mind of the individual. It still includes the attitudes of others, but now highly organized, so that they become what we call social attitudes rather than rôles of separate individuals. This process of relating one's own organism to the others in the interactions that are going on, in so far as it is imported into the conduct of the individual with the conversation of the "I" and the "me," constitutes the self.[1] The value of this importation of the conversation of gestures into the conduct of the individual lies in the superior co-ordination gained for society as a whole, and in the increased efficiency of the individual as a member of the group. It is the difference between the process which can take place in a group of rats or ants or bees, and that which can take place in a human community. The social process with its various implications is actually taken up into the experience of the individual so that that which is going on takes place more effectively, because in a certain sense it has been rehearsed in the individual. He not only plays his part better under those conditions but he also reacts back on the organization of which he is a part.

The very nature of this conversation of gestures requires that the attitude of the other is changed through the attitude of the individual to the other's stimulus. In the conversation of gestures of the lower forms the play back and forth is noticeable, since the individual not only adjusts himself to the attitude of others, but also changes the attitudes of the others. The reaction of the individual in this conversation of gestures is one that in some degree is continually modifying the social process itself. It is this modification of the process which is of greatest interest in the experience of the individual. He takes the attitude of the other toward his own stimulus, and in taking that he finds it modified in that his response becomes a different one, and leads in turn to further change.

Fundamental attitudes are presumably those that are only changed gradually, and no one individual can reorganize the whole society; but one is continually affecting society by his own attitude because he does bring up the attitude of the group toward himself, responds to it, and through that response changes the attitude of the group. This is, of course, what we are constantly doing in our imagination, in our thought; we are utilizing our own attitude to bring about a different situation in the community of which we are a part; we are exerting ourselves, bringing forward our own opinion, criticizing the attitudes of others, and approving or disapproving. But we can do that only in so far as we can call out in ourselves the response of the community; we only have ideas in so far as we are able to take the attitude of the community and then respond to it.

In the case of lower animals the response of the individual to the social situation, its gesture as over against the social situation, is what answers to the idea in the human animal. It is not, however, an idea. We use the vocal gesture to call out the response which answers to that of the community. We have, then, in our own stimulus, a reply to that response, and it is that reply which is an idea. You say that "it is my idea that such and such a thing should be done." Your idea is the reply which you make to the social demand made upon you. The social demand, we will say, is that you should pay taxes of a certain sort. You consider those taxes illegitimate. Now, your reply to the demand of the community, specifically to the tax assessor, as it takes place in your own experience, is an idea. To the extent that you have in your own conduct symbols which are the expression of your reply to the demand, you have an idea of what your assessment ought to be. It is an ideal situation in so far as you are taking the role of the tax assessor over against yourself, and replying to it. It is not like the situation in the dog-fight where the dog is actually preparing to spring and another dog takes another attitude which defeats that spring. The difference is that the conversation of gestures is a part of the actual realized fight, whereas in the other case you are taking the attitude of the tax authorities in advance and working or calling out your own response to it. When that takes place in your experience you have ideas.

A person threatens you, and you knock him down on the spot. There has been no ideal element in the situation. If you count ten and consider what the threat means, you are having an idea, are bringing the situation into an ideal setting. It is that, we have seen, which constitutes what we term mind. We are taking the attitude of the community and we are responding to it in this conversation of gestures. The gestures in this case are vocal gestures. They are significant symbols, and by symbol we do not mean something that lies outside of the field of conduct. A symbol is nothing but the stimulus whose response is given in advance. That is all we mean by a symbol. There is a word, and a blow. The blow is the historical antecedent of the word, but if the word means an insult, the response is one now involved in the word, something given in the very stimulus itself. That is all that is meant by a symbol. Now, if that response can be given in terms of an attitude utilized for the further control of action, then the relation of that stimulus and attitude is what we mean by a significant symbol.

Our thinking that goes on, as we say, inside of us, is a play of symbols in the above sense. Through gestures responses are called out in our own attitudes, and as soon as they are called out they evoke, in turn, other attitudes. What was the meaning now becomes a symbol which has another meaning. The meaning has itself become a stimulus to another response. In the dogfight the attitude of the one has the meaning of changing the attitude of the other dog, but the change of attitude now becomes a symbol (though not a language or significant symbol) to the first dog and he, too, changes his attitude. What was a meaning now becomes a stimulus. Conversation is continually going on, and what was response becomes in the field of gesture a stimulus, and the response to that is the meaning. Responses are meanings in so far as they lie inside of such a conversation of gestures. Our thinking is just such a continual change of a situation by our capacity to take it over into our own action; to change it so that it calls for a different attitude on our own part, and to carry it on to the point where the social act may be completed.

The "me" and the "I" lie in the process of thinking and they indicate the give-and-take which characterizes it. There would not be an "I" in the sense in which we use that term if there were not a "me"; there would not be a "me" without a response in the form of the "I." These two, as they appear in our experience, constitute the personality. We are individuals born into a certain nationality, located at a certain spot geographically, with such and such family relations, and such and such political relations. All of these represent a certain situation which constitutes the "me"; but this necessarily involves a continued action of the organism toward the "me" in the process within which that lies. The self is not something that exists first and then enters into relationship with others, but it is, so to speak, an eddy in the social current and so still a part of the current. It is a process in which the individual is continually adjusting himself in advance to the situation to which he belongs, and reacting back on it. So that the "I" and the "me," this thinking, this conscious adjustment, becomes then a part of the whole social process and makes a much more highly organized society possible.

The "I" and the "me" belong to the conversation of gestures. If there were simply "a word and a blow," if one answered to a social situation immediately without reflection, there would be no personality in the foregoing sense any more than there is personality in the nature of the dog or the horse. We, of course, tend to endow our domestic animals with personality, but as we get insight into their conditions we see there is no place for this sort of importation of the social process into the conduct of the individual. They do not have the mechanism for it—language. So we say that they have no personality; they are not responsible for the social situation in which they find themselves. The human individual, on the other hand, identifies himself with that social situation. He responds to it, and although his response to it may be in the nature of criticism as well as support, it involves an acceptance of the responsibility presented by the situation. Such an acceptance does not exist in the case of the lower animals. We put personalities into the animals, but they do not belong to them; and ultimately we realize that those animals have no rights. We are at liberty to cut off their lives; there is no wrong committed when an animal's life is taken away. He has not lost anything because the future does not exist for the animal; he has not the "me" in his experience which by the response of the "I" is in some sense under his control, so that the future can exist for him. He has no conscious past since there is no self of the sort we have been describing that can be extended into the past by memories. There are presumably images in the experience of lower animals, but no ideas or memories in the required sense.[2] They have not the personality that looks before or after. They have not that future and past which gives them, so to speak, any rights as such. And yet the common attitude is that of giving them just such personalities as our own. We talk to them and in our talking to them we act as if they had the sort of inner world that we have.

A similar attribution is present in the immediate attitude which we take toward inanimate physical objects about us. We take the attitude of social beings toward them. This is most elaborately true, of course, in those whom we term nature poets. The poet is in a social relation with the things about him, a fact perhaps most vividly presented in Wordsworth. The "Lines on Tintern Abbey" gives us, I believe, the social relationships of Wordsworth when he was a child and their continuation through his life. His statement of the relationship of man to nature is essentially the relationship of love, a social relation. This social attitude of the individual toward the physical thing is just the attitude which one has toward other objects; it is a social attitude. The man kicks the chair he stumbles over, and he has an affection for an object connected with him in his work or play. The immediate reaction of children to things about them is social. There is an evident basis for the particular response which we make to little things, since there is something that calls out a parental response in any small thing; such a thing calls out a parental response which is universal. This holds for physical things, as well as for animals.

The physical object is an abstraction which we make from the social response to nature. We talk to nature; we address the clouds, the sea, the tree, and objects about us. We later abstract from that type of response because of what we come to know of such objects.[3] The immediate response is, however, social; where we carry over a thinking process into nature we are making nature rational. It acts as it is expected to act. We are taking the attitude of the physical things about us, and when we change the situation nature responds in a different way.

The hand is responsible for what I term physical things, distinguishing the physical thing from what I call the consummation of the act. If we took our food as dogs do by the very organs by which we masticate it, we should not have any ground for distinguishing the food as a physical thing from the actual consummation of the act, the consumption of the food. We should reach it and seize it with the teeth, and the very act of taking hold of it would be the act of eating it. But with the human animal the hand is interposed between the consummation and the getting of the object to the mouth. In that case we are manipulating a physical thing. Such a thing comes in between the beginning of the act and its final consummation. It is in that sense a universal. When we speak of a thing we have in mind a physical thing, something we can get hold of. There are, of course, "things" you cannot get hold of, such as property rights and the imaginations of a poet; but when we ordinarily speak of things about us we refer to physical things. The characters that go to make these up are primarily determined by the hand. Contact constitutes what we call the substance of such a thing. It has color and odor, of course, but we think of these as inherent in the something which we can manipulate, the physical thing. Such a thing is of very great importance in the development of human intelligence. It is universal in the sense that it is a physical thing, whether the consummation is that of eating, or of listening to a concert. There is a whole set of physical things that come in between the beginning of an act and its consummation, but they are universal in the sense that they belong to the experience of all of us. The consummation that we get out of a concert is very different for all of us, but the physical things we are dealing with are common, universal in that sense. The actual enjoyments may take on forms which represent an experience that is accessible only to separate individuals, but what the hand handles is something that is universal. We isolate a particular locality to which any person may come. We have a set of apparatus which any person may use. We have a certain set of weights and measures by means of which we can define these physical things. In this sense the physical thing comes in to make possible a common quality within which the selves can operate.[4]

An engineer who is constructing a bridge is talking to nature in the same sense that we talk to an engineer. There are stresses and strains there which he meets, and nature comes back with other responses that have to be met in another way. In his thinking he is taking the attitude of physical things. He is talking to nature and nature is replying to him. Nature is intelligent in the sense that there are certain responses of nature toward our action which we can present and which we can reply to, and which become different when we have replied. It is a change we then can answer to, and we finally reach a point at which we can co-operate with nature.

Such is the development of modern science out of what we term magic. Magic is just this same response, but with the further assumption that physical things do think and act as we do. It is preserved in the attitude which we have toward an offending object or the trustworthy object upon which we depend. We all carry about a certain amount of this sort of magic. We avoid something because we feel it is in some way dangerous; we all respect certain omens to which we pay some attention. We keep up some social response to nature about us, even though we do not allow this to affect us in important decisions. These are attitudes which perhaps we normally cover up, but which are revealed to us in numerous situations. In so far as we are rational, as we reason and think, we are taking a social attitude toward the world about us, critically in the case of science, uncritically in the case of magic.

Notes

1 According to this view, conscious communication develops out of unconscious communication within the social process; conversation in terms of significant gestures out of conversation in terms of non-significant gestures; and the development in such fashion of conscious communication is coincident with the development of minds and selves within the social process.

2 There is no evidence of animals being able to recognize that one thing is a sign of something else and so make use of that sign. ... (1912).

3 The physical object is found to be that object to which there is no social response which calls out again a social response in the individual. The objects with which we cannot carry on social intercourse are the physical objects of the world (MS).

   We have carried our attitude in physical science over into psychology, so that we have lost sight of the social nature of our early consciousness. The child forms social objects before he forms physical objects (1912).

4 [On the social genesis and nature of the physical thing, see Section 35; also *The Philosophy of the Present*, pp. 119–39.]

From Mind, Self, and Society: The Definitive Edition, by George Herbert Mead and Charles W. Morris, pp. 178–186. Copyright © 2015 University of Chicago Press. All rights reserved. Reprinted with permission.

Interpersonal Attraction and Close Relationships

Kenneth S. Bordens and Irwin A. Horowitz

"Intimate relationships cannot substitute for a life plan. But to have any meaning or viability at all, a life plan must include intimate relationships."

— *Harriet Lerner*

Source: Max Kegfire/Shutterstock.

Key Questions

As you read this chapter, find the answers to the following questions:

1. What is a close relationship?
2. What are the roots of interpersonal attraction and close relationships?
3. What are loneliness and social anxiety?
4. What are the components and dynamics of love?
5. How does attachment relate to interpersonal relationships?
6. How does interpersonal attraction develop?
7. What does evolutionary theory have to say about mate selection?
8. How can one attract a mate?
9. How do close relationships form and evolve?
10. How are relationships evaluated?
11. What is a communal relationship?
12. How do relationships change over time?
13. What are the strategies couples use in response to conflict in a relationship?
14. What are the four horsemen of the apocalypse?
15. What is the nature of friendships?

Both Gertrude Stein and Alice B. Toklas were born in California and lived in the San Francisco Bay area. Both eventually left the United States to live in Paris. The first visit between these two people on September 8, 1907, who would be lifelong friends and lovers, did not begin well. They had become acquainted the previous night at a Paris restaurant and had arranged an appointment for the next afternoon at Gertrude's apartment. Perhaps anxious about the meeting, Gertrude was in a rage when her guest arrived a half hour later than the appointed time. But soon she recovered her good humor, and the two went walking in the streets of Paris. They found that each loved walking, and they would share their thoughts and feelings on these strolls for the rest of their lives together.

On that first afternoon, they stopped for ices and cakes in a little shop that Gertrude knew well because it reminded her of San Francisco. The day went so well that Gertrude suggested dinner at her apartment the following evening. Thus began a relationship that would last for nearly 40 years.

The one was small and dark, the other large—over two hundred pounds—with short hair and a striking Roman face. Neither was physically attractive. Each loved art and literature and opera, for which they were in the right place. The Paris in which they met in the 1920s was the home to great painters (Picasso and Matisse) and enormously talented writers (Ernest Hemingway, F. Scott Fitzgerald). Gertrude knew them all. They began to live together in Gertrude's apartment, for she was the one who had a steady supply of money. Gertrude, who had dropped out of medical school in her final year, had decided to write novels. Soon, they grew closer, their walks longer, and their talks more intimate. They traveled to Italy, and it was there, outside Florence, that Gertrude proposed marriage. Both knew the answer to the proposal, and they spent the night in a 6th-century palace. They shared each other's lives fully, enduring two wars together. In

1946, Gertrude, then 70, displayed the first signs of the tumor that would soon kill her. Gertrude handled this crisis in character, forcefully refusing any medical treatment. Not even her lifelong companion could convince her to do otherwise. When Gertrude eventually collapsed, she was rushed to a hospital in Paris. In her hospital room before the surgery, Gertrude grasped her companion's small hand and asked, "What is the answer?" Tears streamed down Alice Toklas's face, "I don't know, Lovey." The hospital attendants put Gertrude Stein on a cot and rolled her toward the operating room. Alice murmured words of affection. Gertrude commanded the attendants to stop, and she turned to Alice and said, "If you don't know the answer, then what is the question?" Gertrude settled back on the cot and chuckled softly. It was the last time they saw each other (Burnett, 1972; Simon, 1977; Toklas, 1963).

We have briefly recounted what was perhaps the most famous literary friendship of the last century, the relationship between Gertrude Stein and Alice B. Toklas. Stein and Toklas were not officially married. They did not flaunt their sexual relationship, for the times in which they lived were not particularly accommodating to what Stein called their "singular" preferences. Yet their partnership involved all the essential elements of a close relationship: intimacy, friendship, love, and sharing. Philosophers have commented that a friend multiplies one's joys and divides one's sorrows. This, too, was characteristic of their relationship.

In this chapter, we explore the nature of close relationships. The empirical study of close relationships is relatively new. Indeed, when one well-known researcher received a grant some years ago from a prestigious government funding agency to study love in a scientific manner, a gadfly senator held the researcher and the topic up to ridicule, suggesting that we know all we need to know about the topic.

Perhaps so, but in this chapter we ask a number of questions that most of us, at least, do not have the answers for. What draws two people together into a close relationship, whether a friendship or a more intimate love relationship? What influences attractiveness and attraction? How do close relationships develop and evolve, and how do they stand up to conflict and destructive impulses? What are the components of love relationships? And finally, what are friendships, and how do they differ from love? These are some of the questions addressed in this chapter.

The Roots of Interpersonal Attraction and Close Relationships

It is a basic human characteristic to be attracted to others, to desire to build close relationships with friends and lovers. In this section, we explore two needs that underlie attraction and relationships: affiliation and intimacy. Not everyone has the social skills or resources necessary to initiate and maintain close relationships. Therefore, we also look at the emotions of social anxiety and loneliness.

need for affiliation

A motivation that underlies our desire to establish and maintain rewarding interpersonal relationships.

Affiliation and Intimacy

Although each of us can endure and even value periods of solitude, for most of us extended solitude is aversive. After a time, we begin to crave the company of others. People have a **need for affiliation,** a need to establish and maintain relationships with others (Wong & Csikzentmihalyi, 1991). Contact with friends and acquaintances provides us with emotional support, attention, and the opportunity to evaluate the appropriateness of our opinions and behavior through the process of social comparison. The need for affiliation is the fundamental factor underlying our interpersonal relationships.

People who are high in the need for affiliation wish to be with friends and others more than do people who are low in the need for affiliation, and they tend to act accordingly. For example, in one study, college men who had a high need for affiliation picked living situations that increased the chances for social interaction. They were likely to have more housemates or to be more willing to share a room than were men with a lower need for affiliation (Switzer & Taylor, 1983). Men and women show some differences in the need for affiliation. Teenage girls, for example, spend more time with friends and less often wish to be alone than do teenage boys (Wong & Csikzentmihalyi, 1991). This is in keeping with other findings that women show a higher need for affiliation than do men.

The needs for affiliation and intimacy motivate us to form and sustain relationships and close, affectionate relationships.

Source: Gianluca D. Muscelli/ Shutterstock.

There is evidence that the affiliation motive operates on an implicit and an explicit level (Köllner & Schultheiss, 2014). The explicit need for affiliation is tied to more cognitive elements of affiliation, including self-concept and one's values, beliefs, and goals. The implicit system is more strongly related to the emotional aspect of affiliation (Köllner & Schultheiss, 2014). Köllner and Schultheiss conducted a meta-analysis of the literature on the explicit and implicit needs for affiliation and found a very small correlation between the two systems. This m eans that the two systems, like other implicit and explicit systems, are independent from one another and are related to different types of behavior. Additionally, they reported that the relationship between the explicit and implicit needs for affiliation is weaker for women than for men.

But merely being with others is often not enough to satisfy our social needs. We also have a **need for intimacy,** a need for close and affection- ate relationships (McAdams, 1982, 1989). Intimacy with friends or lovers involves sharing and disclosing personal information. Individuals with a high need for intimacy tend to be warm and affectionate and to show con- cern about other people. Most theorists agree that intimacy is an essential component of many different interpersonal relationships (Laurenceau, Barrett, & Pietro-monaco, 1998).

need for intimacy

A motivation for close and affection- ate relationships.

Intimacy has several dimensions, according to Baumeister and Bratslavsky (1999). One is mutual disclosure that is sympathetic and understanding. Intimate disclosure involves verbal communication but also refers to shared experiences. Another dimension of intimacy includes having a favorable attitude toward the other person that is expressed in warm feelings and positive acts such that the person is aware of how much the other cares.

The need for affiliation and intimacy gives us positive social motivation to approach other people. They are the roots of interpersonal attraction, which is defined as the desire to start and maintain relationships with oth- ers. But there are also emotions that may stand in the way of our fulfilling affiliation and intimacy needs and forming relationships. We look at these emotions next.

Loneliness and Social Anxiety

Loneliness and social anxiety are two related conditions that have im- plications for one's social relationships. Whereas the needs for affiliation and intimacy are positive motives that foster interpersonal relationships, loneliness and social anxiety can be seen as negative motivational states that interfere with the formation of meaningful relationships. In this section we shall explore loneliness and social anxiety.

Loneliness

loneliness

A psychological state that results when we perceive that there is an inadequacy or a deprivation in our social relationships.

Loneliness is a psychological state that results when we perceive an inadequacy in our relationships—a discrepancy between the way we want our relationships to be and the way they actually are (Peplau & Perlman, 1982). When we are lonely, we lack the high-quality intimate relationships that we need. Loneliness may occur within the framework of a relationship. For example, women often expect more intimacy than they experience in marriage, and that lack of intimacy can be a cause of loneliness (Tornstam, 1992).

Loneliness is common during adolescence and young adulthood, times of life when old friendships fade and new ones must be formed. For example, consider an 18-year-old going off to college. As she watches her parents drive away, she is likely to feel, along with considerable excitement, a sense of loneliness or even abandonment. New college students often believe that they will not be able to form friendships and that no one at school cares about them. The friendships they make don't seem as intimate as their high school friendships were. These students often don't realize that everybody else is pretty much in the same boat emotionally, and loneliness is often a significant factor when a student drops out of school.

Loneliness is a subjective experience and is not dependent on the number of people we have surrounding us (Peplau & Perlman, 1982). We can be alone and yet not be lonely; sometimes we want and need solitude. On the other hand, we can be surrounded by people and feel desperately lonely. Our feelings of loneliness are strongly influenced by how we evaluate our personal relationships (Peplau & Perlman, 1982). We need close relationships with a few people to buffer ourselves against feeling lonely.

Culture is also related to perception of loneliness. There is evidence that loneliness is a cross-cultural phenomenon (DiTommaso, Brannen, & Burgess, 2005). However, the way loneliness is experienced differs across cultures. For example, DiTommaso et al. found that Chinese students living in Canada reported higher levels of three types of loneliness than did Canadians. Additionally, Rokach and Neto (2005) compared Canadian and

Portuguese individuals of varying ages on several dimensions relating to loneliness. They found that Canadians were more likely to point to their own shortcomings to explain their loneliness than were Portuguese individuals. Rokach and Neto suggest that this might be due to a greater disposition of North Americans to view loneliness as a form of social failure and to different family values and structures between the two cultures. Finally, cultural expectations about relationships can also affect the experience of loneliness. For example, in Western culture, greater importance is attached to romantic relationships than in non-Western cultures (Seepersad, Mi-Kyung, & Nana, 2008). Consequently, when not in a romantic relationship, members of a Western culture (Americans) experience more romantic loneliness than those in a non-Western culture (Koreans) (Seepersad, MiKyung, & Nana, 2008).

As suggested earlier, loneliness can be associated with certain relationships or certain times of life. There are, however, individuals for whom loneliness is a lifelong experience. Such individuals have difficulty in forming relationships with others, and consequently, they go through life with few or no close relationships. What is the source of their difficulty? The problem for at least some of these people may be that they lack the basic social skills needed to form and maintain relationships. Experiences of awkward social interactions intensify these individuals' uneasiness in social settings. Lacking confidence, they become increasingly anxious about their interactions with others. Often, because of their strained social interactions, lonely people may be further excluded from social interaction, thereby increasing feelings of depression and social anxiety (Leary & Kowalski, 1995).

Beyond the psychological effects of loneliness, there are also physical and health effects. Within families, loneliness is associated with an increase in self-reported health problems and a higher rate of self-reported physical ailments (Segrin, Burke, & Dunivan, 2012). Hawkley, Burleson, Berntson, and Cacciopo (2003) report that lonely individuals are more likely to show elevated total peripheral resistance (a suspected precursor to hypertension) and lower cardiac output than nonlonely individuals. Loneliness is also associated with a higher risk for a heart condition in the elderly (Sorkin, Rook, & Lu, 2002). Loneliness and social isolation are also associated with higher levels of depression in older males (Alpass & Neville, 2003) and among male and female college students (Segrin, Powell, Givertz, & Brackin, 2003). In the Segrin et al. study, the relationship between loneliness and depression was related to relationship satisfaction. Individuals who are dissatisfied with their relationships tend to be lonely and, in turn, are more likely to experience depression. Lonely individuals get poorer-quality sleep (i.e., awaken more after falling asleep and show poor sleep efficiency) compared to nonlonely individuals (Cacioppo et al., 2002). This latter finding suggests that lonely people may be less resilient and more prone to physical problems (Cacioppo et al., 2002). Finally, loneliness among older adults has been found to be a significant predictor of an early death over a six-year period (Luo, Hawkley, Waite, & Cacioppo, 2012).

Social Anxiety

Social anxiety is one of the most widely diagnosed anxiety disorders. Social anxiety (sometimes referred to as social phobia) arises from a person's expectation of negative encounters with others (Leary, 1983a, 1983b). Socially anxious people anticipate negative interactions and think that other people will not like them very much. These negative expectations then translate into anxiety in a social situation, using "safety behaviors" (e.g., avoiding eye contact and closely monitoring one's behavior) and underestimating the quality of the impressions made on others (Hirsch, Meynen, & Clark, 2004). Socially anxious individuals tend to see ambiguous social situations more negatively than individuals without social anxiety (Huppert, Foa, Furr, Filip, & Matthews, 2003). Additionally, socially anxious individuals tend to dwell on negative aspects of social interactions more than individuals who are low in social anxiety and also recall more negative information about the social interaction (Edwards, Rapee, & Franklin, 2003). According to Edwards et al., this pattern of findings is consistent with the idea that socially anxious individuals perform a negatively biased "postmortem" of social events.

There is a cluster of characteristics that define those with social anxiety. People who suffer from social anxiety tend to display some of the following interrelated traits (Nichols, 1974):

- A sensitivity to and fearfulness of disapproval and criticism.

- A strong tendency to perceive and respond to criticism that does not exist.

- Low self-evaluation.

- Rigid ideas about what constitutes "appropriate" social behavior.

social anxiety

Anxiety tied to interpersonal relationships that occurs because of an individual's anticipation of negative encounters with others.

- A tendency to foresee negative outcomes to anticipated social interactions, which arouses anxiety.

- An increased awareness and fear of being evaluated by others.

- Fear of situations in which withdrawal would be difficult or embarrassing.

- The tendency to overestimate one's reaction to social situations (e.g., believing that you are blushing when you are not).

- An inordinate fear of the anxiety itself.

- A fear of being perceived as losing control.

Interestingly, many of these perceptions and fears are either wrong or unfounded. The research of Christensen and Kashy (1998) shows that lonely people view their own behavior more negatively than do other people. Other research shows that socially anxious individuals tend to process disturbing social events negatively immediately after they occur and a day after the event (Lundh & Sperling, 2002). Social anxiety relates directly to this *post-event rumination*. However, social anxiety also operates through negative self-evaluation of social behavior and the inordinately high amount of attention that people with social anxiety focus on their negative self-image (Chen, Rapee, & Abbott, 2013). In other words, individuals with social anxiety tend to see their own social interactions with others as very negative and spend time reinforcing their image of themselves as socially inept.

Of course, real events and real hurts may be the source of much social anxiety. Leary and his colleagues examined the effects of having our feelings hurt in a variety of ways, ranging from sexual infidelity, to unreturned phone calls, to being teased (Leary, Springer, Negel, Ansell, & Evans, 1998). The basic cause of the hurt feelings and consequent anxiety is what Leary calls *relational devaluation,* the perception that the other person does not regard the relationship as being as important as you do. Perhaps the major source of social anxiety is the feeling that you are being excluded from valued social relations (Baumeister & Tice, 1990). Having one's feelings hurt, however, leads to more than anxiety. People experience a complex sense of being distressed, upset, angry, guilty, and wounded. Leary and colleagues (1998) examined the stories written by people who had been emotionally hurt. They found that unlike the old saying about "sticks and stones," words or even gestures or looks elicit hurt feelings, last for a long time, and do not heal as readily as broken bones. Teasing is one example of what appeared to be an innocent event—at least from the teaser's point of view—that in reality imprints long-lasting hurt feelings for many victims. The males and females in the study did not differ much in their reactions to hurt feelings or to teasing.

The people who do these nasty deeds do not realize the depth of the damage that they cause, nor do they realize how much the victims come to dislike them. Perpetrators often say that they meant no harm. No harm, indeed.

Study Break

The preceding sections introduced you to the definition of interpersonal attraction and the factors that can facilitate or inhibit relationship formation. Before you go on, answer the following questions:

1   What is the need for affiliation?

2   What is the need for intimacy, and how does it differ from the need for affiliation?

3   What is loneliness, and how does it relate to the number of friends a person has?

4   How can social anxiety interfere with the formation of relationships?

5   What are the characteristics of social anxiety?

Love and Close Relationships

Psychologists and other behavioral scientists long thought that love was simply too mysterious a topic to study scientifically (Thompson & Borrello, 1992). However, psychologists have become more adventuresome, and love has become a topic of increasing interest (Hendrick & Hendrick, 1987). This is only right, because love is among the most intense of human emotions.

Love's Triangle

triangular theory of love

A theory suggesting that love is comprised of three components—passion, intimacy, and commitment—each of which is conceptualized as a leg of a triangle that can vary.

Robert Sternberg (1986, 1988) proposed a **triangular theory of love**, based on the idea that love has three components: passion, intimacy, and commitment. As shown in Figure 12.1, the theory represents love as a triangle, with each component defining a vertex.

Passion is the emotional component of love. The "aching" in the pit of your stomach when you think about your love partner is a manifestation of this component. Passion is "a state of intense longing for union with the other" (Hatfield & Walster, 1981, p. 13). Passion tends to be strongest in the early stages of a romantic relationship. It is sexual desire that initially drives the relationship. Defining passion simply as sexual desire does not

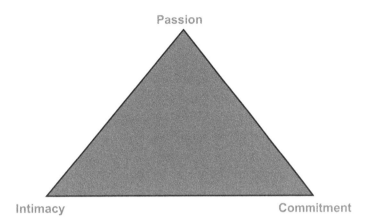

Figure 12.1 Robert Sternberg's triangular theory of love. Each leg of the triangle represents one of the three components of love: passion, intimacy, and commitment.

From Sternberg (1986).

do justice to this complicated emotion. It is not improbable that people may love passionately without sexual contact or in the absence of the ability to have sexual contact. However, as a rough measure, sexual desire serves to define passion (Baumeister & Bratslavsky, 1999).

Intimacy is the component that includes self-disclosure—the sharing of our innermost thoughts—as well as shared activities. Intimate couples look out for each other's welfare, experience happiness by being in each other's company, are able to count on each other when times are tough, and give each other emotional support and understanding (Sternberg & Gracek, 1984).

The third vertex of the triangle, *commitment*, is the long-term determination to maintain love over time. It is different from the decision people make, often in the heat of passion, that they are in love. Commitment does not necessarily go along with a couple's decision that they are in love. Sternberg defined various kinds of love, based on the presence or absence of intimacy, passion, and commitment. Table 12.1 shows each of these kinds of love and the component or components with which it is associated.

TABLE 12.1 Triangular theory and different love types

	Love Component		
Kind of Love	Intimacy	Passion	Commitment
Non-love	No	No	No
Liking	Yes	No	No
Infatuated love	No	Yes	No
Empty love	No	No	Yes
Romantic love	Yes	Yes	No
Companionate love	Yes	No	Yes
Fatuous love	No	Yes	Yes
Consummate love	Yes	Yes	Yes

According to Sternberg (1986), the components of love need not occur in a fixed order. There is a tendency for passion to dominate at the start, for intimacy to follow as a result of self-disclosure prompted by passion, and for commitment to take the longest to fully develop. However, in an arranged marriage, for example, commitment occurs before intimacy, and passion may be the laggard.

Baumeister and Bratslavsky (1999) studied the relationship between passion and intimacy and suggested that one may be a function of the other. These scholars argued that rising intimacy at any point in the relationship will create a strong sense of passion. If intimacy is stable, and that means it may be high or low, then passion will be low. But when intimacy rises, so does passion. Passion, then, is a function of change in intimacy over time (Baumeister & Bratslavsky, 1999). Research generally shows that passion declines steadily in long-term relationships, particularly among women, but intimacy does not and may increase in the late stages of the relationship (Acker & Davis, 1992). Positive changes in the amount of intimacy—self-disclosures, shared experiences—lead to increases in passion at any stage of a relationship. Finally, the relationship between relationship length and the components of love's triangle can be complex. For example, couples who are casually dating report lower levels of passion and intimacy than engaged couples. However, married couples report lower levels of passion and intimacy than engaged couples. Commitment, on the other hand, increases with relationship length (Lemiuex & Hale, 2002).

Levels of passion, intimacy, and commitment are also related to relationship satisfaction (Madey & Rodgers, 2009). Madey and Rogers found strong positive correlations between all three components and overall relationship satisfaction. They also found that intimacy and commitment showed the strongest correlations with relationship satisfaction. Additionally, they reported that individuals with a secure attachment experience higher levels of passion, intimacy, and commitment than those with a less secure attachment. Finally, intimacy and commitment mediate the relationship between attachment security and relationship satisfaction. That is, a secure attachment is related to higher levels of intimacy and commitment. In turn, these higher levels of intimacy and commitment are related to higher relationship satisfaction.

Types of Love

What, then, are Sternberg's types of love? Probably the most fascinating is **romantic love**, which involves passion and intimacy but not commitment. Romantic love is reflected in that electrifying yet conditional statement, "I am

romantic love

Love involving strong emotion and having the components of passion and intimacy but not commitment.

in love with you." Compare this with the expression reflecting consummate love, "I love you." Romantic love can be found around the world and throughout history. It is most likely to be first experienced by members of diverse ethnic groups in late adolescence or early adulthood (Regan, Durvasula, Howell, Ureno, & Rea, 2004). Additionally, concepts of romantic love are almost universally positive with characteristics such as trust and fulfilling emotional needs. One of the only negative characteristics that emerged as a "peripheral characteristic" was jealousy (Regan, Kocan, & Whitlock, 1998).

Romantic love doesn't necessarily mean marriage, however, for two main reasons. First, whereas marriage is almost universally heterosexual, romantic love need not be. Second, although some elements of romantic love may be common across cultures, some are not (de Munck, Korotayev, de Munck, & Kaltourina, 2011). Research by de Munck et al. found, for example, that intrusive thinking, happiness, passion, altruism, and improved well-being of partner were common elements to the concept of romantic love among Americans, Russians, and Lithuanians. On the other hand, there were some differences. Americans included the elements of friendship and comfort love as important to romantic love for the U.S. sample, but Russians and Lithuanians did not. Russians and Lithuanians said that romantic love was temporary, unreal, and a fairytale. Third, it is still an alien idea in most cultures that romance has anything to do with the choice of a spouse. In fact, there are still some cultures (e.g., some Indian sects) that practice arranged marriages in which commitment comes first, followed by romance. Interestingly, these arranged marriages appear to be just as satisfying as love-based marriages (Reagan, Lakhanpal, & Anguiano, 2012). Even in U.S. culture, the appeal of marrying for love seems to have increased among women in recent years, perhaps because women's roles have changed, and they no longer have so great a need to find a "good provider" (Berscheid, Snyder, & Omoto, 1989).

The importance of passion in romantic love is clear. Romantic lovers live in a pool of emotions, both positive and negative—sexual desire, fear, exultation, anger—all experienced in a state of high arousal. Intense sexual desire and physical arousal are the prime forces driving romantic love (Berscheid, 1988). One study confirms the physical arousal aspect of romantic love (Enzo et al., 2006). In this study individuals who had recently fallen in love were compared to single individuals and individuals in a long-term relationship. Enzo et al. found that the "in-love" participants showed higher levels of nerve growth factor (NGF) in their blood than single individuals or those involved in a long-term relationship. Interestingly, those "in-love" couples showed a drop in NGF if they remained together for 12 to 14 months. In fact, their blood levels of NGF were comparable to those who were in long-term relationships—perhaps providing evidence for the old adage that romance (passion) burns hot, but burns fast.

As noted, romantic love and sexual desire are likely to be seen as going together and being inseparable. This may be true in some cases. However, there is evidence that romantic love and sexual desire are two separate entities that can be experienced separately (Diamond, 2004). It is possible to experience the passion of romantic love without experiencing sexual desire. There may even be different physiological underpinnings to the two experiences (Diamond, 2004). For example, hormones associated with strong sexual desire have nothing to do with the intense bond experienced in romantic love (Diamond, 2003). Additionally, higher levels of norepinephrine and dopamine are more associated with sexual lust (i.e., the desire for sex with a willing partner without love) than with romantic love (Dundon & Rellini, 2012). Physiological mechanisms underlying the formation of strong attachments are more closely associated with activity involving naturally occurring opioids in the brain (Diamond, 2004).

Tennov (1979) distinguished a particular type of romantic love, which she called *limerence* and characterized as occurring when "you suddenly feel a sparkle (a lovely word) of interest in someone else, an interest fed by the image of returned feeling" (p. 27). Limerence is not driven solely or even primarily by sexual desire. It occurs when a person anxious for intimacy finds someone who seems able to fulfill all of his or her needs and desires. For limerent lovers, all the happiness one could ever hope for is embodied in the loved one. Indeed, one emotional consequence of limerent love is a terror that all hope will be lost if the lover leaves us (Brehm, 1988).

Consummate love combines all three vertices of love's triangle: passion, intimacy, and commitment. These couples have it all; they are able to maintain their passion and intimacy along with a commitment to a lifetime together.

Although we may fantasize about romantic love and view consummate love as a long-term ideal, other types of love can also bring happiness. Many couples are perfectly happy with *companionate love*, which has little or no passion but is infused with intimacy and commitment. Such partners are "friends for life" and generally have great trust in and tolerance for each other. Although they may regret the lack of passion, they are pragmatic and are able to live happily within the rules or limits of the relationship (Duck, 1983).

Unrequited Love

A special and very painful kind of infatuated love is love that is unfulfilled. **Unrequited love** occurs when we fall deeply and passionately in love and that love is rejected. Almost all of us have had some experience with unrequited love. In one study, 98% of the subjects had been rejected by someone they loved intensely (Baumeister, Wotman, & Stillwell, 1993). The emotional responses to unrequited love are generally negative. This is true for heterosexuals (Baumeister, et al., 1993) and gay men (Manalastas, 2011).

What makes unrequited love so painful is that both individuals feel victimized (Aron, Aron, & Allen, 1998). Very often, unrequited love ostensibly starts as a platonic friendship, but then one of the individuals admits that it was never just friendship, that he or she was always secretly in love with

consummate love

Love that includes all three components: passion, intimacy, and commitment.

unrequited love

Love expressed by one person that is rejected and not returned by the other the other (Baumeister et al., 1993). In many cases, the object of the unrequited love is often unable to express lack of interest in terms that are sufficiently discouraging. The unrequited lover takes anything as encouragement, sustains hope, and then finds the final rejection devastating. The object of unwanted love, after the initial boost to the ego, feels bewildered, guilty, and angry.

In a typical case of spurned love, a college woman took pity on a young man whom no one liked, and one night invited him to join her and some friends in a game of Parcheesi. He thought the invitation signaled something more than she intended. Much to her horror, he began to follow her around and told her how much he loved her. She wanted this to stop, but she was unable to tell him how upset she was, because she was afraid of hurting his feelings. He interpreted her silence as encouragement and persisted (Baumeister et al., 1993).

Men are more likely than women to experience unrequited love (Aron et al., 1998). This is because men are more beguiled by physical attractiveness than are women. Men tend to fall in love with someone more desirable than they are. Interestingly, people report that they have been the object of unrequited love twice as many times as they have been rejected by another. We prefer to believe that we have been loved in vain rather than having loved in vain.

Unrequited love is viewed differently depending on one's perspective: pursuer or pursued. In one study those being pursued reported being the recipients of more unwanted courtship tactics, both violent and nonviolent, than they say they used as a pursuer (Sinclair & Frieze, 2005). Some interesting gender differences emerged in this study. For example, men tended to overestimate the extent to which their romantic advances were reciprocated. Women, on the other hand, were more likely than men to report multiple attempts to clearly reject unwanted advances.

Secret Love

If unrequited love is the most painful kind of love, then *secret love* may be the most exciting. In this form of love, individuals have strong passion for one another, but cannot or will not make those feelings publicly known. Secrecy seems to increase the attraction of a relationship. Researchers have found that people continued to think more about past relationships that had been secret than about those that had been open (Wegner, Lane, & Dimitri, 1994). In fact, many individuals were still very much preoccupied with long-past secret relationships. In a study of secrecy and attraction, subjects paired as couples were induced to play "footsie" under the table while they were involved in a card game with another couple (Wegner et al., 1994). The researchers found that when the under-the-table game was played in secret, participants reported greater attraction for the other person than when it was not played in secret.

Why does secrecy create this strong attraction? Perhaps it is because individuals involved in a secret relationship think constantly and obsessively about each other. After all, they have to expend a lot of energy in maintaining the relationship. They have to figure out how to meet, how to call each other so that others won't know, and how to act neutrally in public to disguise their true relationship. Secrecy creates strong bonds between individuals; it can also be the downfall of ongoing relationships. The sudden revelation of a secret infidelity will often crush an ongoing relationship and further enhance the secret one (Wegner et al., 1994).

The Formation of Intimate Relationships

The habits of the heart may be shaped by our earliest relationships. Developmental psychologists have noted that infants form attachments with their parents or primary care-givers based on the kinds of interactions they have (Ainsworth, 1992). These patterns of attachment, or attachment styles, evolve into **working models**, mental representations of what the individual expects to happen in close relationships (Shaver, Hazan, & Bradshaw, 1988). Working models are carried forth from relationship to relationship (Brumbaugh & Fraley, 2006). So, attachment patterns we use in one relationship are likely to be transferred to subsequent relationships. Attachment theory suggests that attachment styles developed in early childhood govern the way individuals form and maintain close relationships in adulthood. Three attachment styles have been identified: secure, anxious/ ambivalent, and avoidant. Statements describing each style are shown in Table 12.2.

working models

Mental representations of what an individual expects to happen in close relationships.

TABLE 12.2 Attachment styles

	Answers and Percentages	
	Newspaper Sample	University Sample
Secure I find it relatively easy to get close to others and am comfortable depending on them and having them depend on me. I don't worry about being abandoned or about someone getting too close to me.	56%	56%
Avoidant I am somewhat uncomfortable being close to others; I find it difficult to trust them completely, difficult to allow myself to depend on them. I am nervous when anyone gets too close, and often, love partners want me to be more intimate than I feel comfortable about.	25%	23%
Anxious/Ambivalent I find that others are reluctant to get as close as I would like. I often worry that my partner doesn't really love me or won't want to stay with me. I want to merge completely with another person, and this desire sometimes scares people away.	19%	20%

From Shaver, Hazan, and Bradshaw (1988).

Attachment styles relate to how relationships are perceived and how successful they are. According to research, people who identified their attachment style as secure characterized their lovers as happy, friendly, and trusting and said that they and their partner were tolerant of each other's faults (Shaver et al., 1988). Avoidant lovers were afraid of intimacy, experienced roller-coaster emotional swings, and were constantly jealous. Anxious/ambivalent lovers experienced extreme sexual attraction coupled with extreme jealousy. Love is very intense for anxious lovers, because they strive to merge totally with their mate; anything less increases their anxiety. This experience of love for anxious lovers is a strong desire for union and a powerful intensity of sexual attraction and jealousy. It is no accident that anxious lovers, more than any other style, report love at first sight (Shaver et al., 1988). Interestingly, the relationship between attachment style and relationship quality found with white samples applies to Spanish individuals as well (Monetoliva & Garcia-Martinez, 2005). In this study, a secure attachment was associated with positive relationship experiences. Anxious and avoidant attachments were associated with more negative relationship outcomes.

Given the working model of a partner and the expectations that anxious lovers have, it will not come as a surprise to you that individuals with this style tend to have rather turbulent relationships (Simpson, Ickes, & Grich, 1999). Research shows that anxious/ambivalents have relationships that are filled with strong conflicts. One reason for this, apparently, is that anxious/ambivalent individuals have *empathic accuracy,* the ability to correctly infer their partner's thoughts and feelings. Because of this ability, they are more threatened than are other individuals and feel much more anxious (Simpson et al., 1999). This is a case of knowing too much or, at least, placing too much emphasis on their partners' present moods and feelings that may or may not tell where the relationship is going. As you might imagine, Simpson and colleagues found that of all the couples they studied, the highly anxious/ambivalent partners were much more likely to have broken up within months. Finally, males and females with an anxious attachment react to hypothetical transgressions of their partners quite negatively. Typical responses included high levels of emotional stress, attribution patterns that are damaging to the relationship, and behaviors that escalate conflict (Collins, Ford, Guichard, & Allard, 2006).

Attachment Styles and Adult Love Relationships

Fraley and Shaver (1998) showed that the ways in which we respond to our earliest care-givers may indeed last a lifetime and are used when we enter adult romantic relationships. Where better to observe how adult individuals respond to the potential loss of attachment than at an airport? The researchers had observers take careful notes on the behavior of couples when one of the members was departing. After the departure, the remaining member of the couple was asked to complete a questionnaire determining his or her attachment style.

Those with an anxious working model showed the greatest distress at the impending separation and tended to engage in actions designed to delay or stop the departure, although in reality that was not going to happen. The anxious individuals would hold on to, follow, and search for their partner, not unlike a child would for a parent under similar circumstances. So attachment styles tend to be engaged particularly when there is threat (departure in this case) to the relationship. The effects seemed stronger for women than for men (Fraley & Shaver, 1998).

It is quite likely that the behavior of those airport visitors with an anxious working model was determined in great part by the level of trust they had in their partners. Mikulincer (1998) examined the association between adult attachment style and feelings of trust in close relationships. The results of this research suggest that those with a secure working model showed and felt more trust in their partners, and even when trust was violated, secure individuals found a constructive way to deal with it. For secure individuals, the main goal of the relationship was to maintain or increase intimacy.

In contrast, anxious working model individuals, although also desiring greater intimacy, were very concerned with achieving a greater sense of security in their relationships. Avoidant individuals wanted more control. But clearly, level of trust differs significantly among the three types of attachment styles. Anxious-style individuals continually have their sense of trust undermined, because they tend to fail at relationships. Sometimes, these individuals try to start relationships that are bound to fail. As you might suspect, the likelihood of someone falling in love with another who does not love them in return is dependent on one's attachment style. Arthur and Elaine Aron found that individuals with an anxious attachment style were more likely to have experienced unreciprocated love (Aron et al., 1998). Secure individuals had been successful in the past in establishing relationships, and avoidants were unlikely to fall in love at all. Anxious individuals place great value in establishing a relationship with someone who is very desirable but are unlikely to be able to do so. They tend to fail at close relationships and, therefore, they should experience more incidents of unrequited love; indeed, that is exactly what the research findings show (Aron et al., 1998). Finally, compared to individuals with a secure or avoidant attachment, individuals with an anxious attachment are more likely to engage in negative thoughts known as rumination (Reynolds, Searight, & Ratwik, 2014). Rumination is "a maladaptive process of self-reflection, featuring a hyper-focus on internal distress and the possible causes and consequences of these cognitive-affective experiences" (Reynolds et al., 2014, para 8). Reynolds et al. also found that individuals showing a higher level of rumination also report more anxiety associated with intimate relationships.

Are attachment styles a factor in long-term relationships? A study of 322 young married couples, all under age 30, found a tendency for those with similar attachment styles to marry one another (Senchak & Leonard, 1992). Attachment style is not destiny, however, as shown by the observation that people may display different attachment styles in different relationships (Bartholomew & Horowitz, 1991). None of these findings, however, come from long-term studies on the effects of attachment styles beyond childhood. Longitudinal research that follows individuals from infancy at least until early adulthood would give us more definitive information about whether early attachment styles really influence the way we respond in adult love relationships.

Study Break

This section introduced you to love relationships and different types of love. Before you begin the next section, answer the following questions:

1   What are the three legs of the triangular theory of love, and how do they relate to one another?

2   What is romantic love, and how does culture relate to its experience?

3   What is consummate love, and what are its components?

4   What are unrequited and secret love, and how do people react when they happen?

5   What is a working model, and how does it relate to relationship formation?

6   How do different attachment styles relate to adult relationships?

Determinants of Interpersonal Attraction

What determines why we are attracted to some individuals but not others? Social psychologists have developed a number of models addressing this question. Some specific factors identified by these models that play a role in attraction are physical proximity, similarity, and physical attractiveness.

Physical Proximity: Being in the Right Place

How did you and your best friend first meet? Most likely, you met because you happened to be physically close to each other at some point in your life. For example, you might have been neighbors or sat next to each other in elementary school. The idea that you are most likely to become friends with another person you happened to be physically close to suggests that those with whom you form friendships is more happenstance (chance) than providence. Confirmation for this idea was found in a study by Back, Schmukle, and Egloff (2008). Back et al. randomly assigned freshman students to seats in a classroom at the beginning of the school year. Then the students rated each other one at a time. A year later, students were given photographs of the other students and were asked to rate the strength of their friendship with each student. Back et al. found that students who sat next to another indicated stronger friendships than those who sat in the same row or had no physical relation to each other. As this and other studies show, physical proximity, or physical immediacy, is an important determinant of attraction, especially at the beginning of a relationship.

physical proximity effect

The fact that we are more likely to form a relationship with someone who is physically close to us; proximity affects interpersonal attraction, mostly at the beginning of a relationship.

The importance of the **physical proximity effect** in the formation of friendships was also shown in a study of the friendship patterns that developed among students living in on-campus residences for married students (Festinger, Schachter, & Back, 1959). As the distance between units increased, the number of friendships decreased. Students living close to one another were more likely to become friends than were those living far apart.

Physical proximity is such a powerful determinant of attraction that it may even overshadow other, seemingly more important, factors. One study looked at friendship choices among police recruits in a police academy class (Segal, 1974). Recruits were assigned to seats alphabetically, and the single best predictor of interpersonal attraction turned out to be the letter with which a person's last name began. Simply put, those whose names were close in the alphabet and were thus seated near each other were more likely to become friends than those whose names were not close in the alphabet and were thus seated apart. The proximity effect proved more important than such variables as common interests and religion.

Why is proximity so important at the beginning stages of a friendship? The answer seems to have two parts: familiarity and the opportunity for interaction. To understand the role of familiarity, think about this common experience. You download some new music, but when you first listen to it, you are lukewarm about it. However, after repeated exposure, it "grows on you." That is, exposure to the new music seems to increase your appreciation of it. A similar effect occurs with people we encounter. These are examples of the *mere exposure effect*, in which repeated exposure to a neutral stimulus enhances one's positive feeling toward that stimulus. Since it was first identified in 1968 by Robert Zajonc, there have been over 200 studies of the mere exposure effect (Bornstein, 1989). These studies used a wide range of stimuli, and in virtually every instance, repeated exposure to a stimulus produced liking.

Physical proximity, in addition to exposing us to other people, also increases the chances that we will interact with them. That is, proximity also promotes liking, because it gives us an opportunity to find out about each other. Physical proximity and the nature of the interaction combine to determine liking (Schiffenbauer & Schavio, 1976). If we discover that the other person has similar interests and attitudes, we are encouraged to pursue the interaction.

Physical Proximity and Internet Relationships

Traditional social psychological research on the proximity effect has focused on the role of *physical closeness* in interpersonal attraction and relationship formation. However, evidence shows that more and more of us are using the Internet as a way to meet others (Rosenfeld & Thomas, 2012), which means that we must reevaluate the role of physical proximity in the attraction process. The Internet allows for the formation of relationships over great distances. One need no longer be in the same class, work at the same place, or live on the same block with another person to form a relationship. The Internet effectively reduces the *psychological distance* between people, even when the physical distance between them is great.

There is evidence that people are using the Internet to form relationships. For example, in one study 88.3% of male and 69.3% of female research participants reported using the Internet to form "casual or friendly" relationships with others. The study also found that 11.8% of men and 30.8% of women used the Internet to form intimate relationships (McCown, Fischer, Page, & Homant, 2001). In another study, 40% of college students reported using the Internet to form friendships. One of the main reasons for using the Internet in this capacity was to avoid the anxiety normally associated with meeting people and forming friendships. Finally, there was no gender difference in how the Internet was used to form relationships (Knox, Daniels, Sturdivant, & Zusman, 2001).

One concern related to the increasing use of the Internet to form friendships and other relationships is that it is somehow changing or even harming the entire concept of a friendship. However, according to Amichai-Hamburger, Kingsbury, and Schneider (2013), this does not appear to be the case. If anything, using the Internet for social relationships appears to be stimulating the quantity and quality of the interactions among people and increasing relationship intimacy (Valkenburg & Peter, 2011). The Internet provides greater opportunity to seek out others who share our interests and attitudes (Amichai-Hamburger & Hayat, 2011), which is another important factor contributing to interpersonal attraction.

How do relationships formed via the Internet stack up against relationships formed the old-fashioned way? Apparently, they stack up quite well. McKenna, Green, and Gleason (2002) found that relationships formed on the Internet were important in the lives of those who formed them. This parallels what we know about relationships formed in a face-to-face situation. Further, they found that online relationships became integrated into the participants' lives, just as face-to-face relationships do. The Internet relationships formed were stable and tended to last over a 2-year period. Once again, this parallels more traditional relationships. Finally, McKenna et al. found that women found their relationships to be more intimate than men.

There are some differences between Internet relationships and offline relationships. Chan and Cheng (2004), using a sample of participants from Hong Kong, had participants describe the quality of one Internet relationship and one traditional, offline relationship. Their results showed that offline relationship descriptions tended to show that these relationships were more interdependent, involved more commitment, and had greater breadth and depth than Internet relationships. However, both types of relationships tended to improve over time, and fewer differences between the two types of friendships were noted as the relationship matured. Another study found that romantic relationships (e.g., dating and marital) formed offline lasted longer than those formed online (Paul, 2014). Paul also found that a smaller percentage of couples who met online went on to get married (32%) than those who met offline (67%).

So, it seems clear that the Internet is serving as a medium for the formation of meaningful interpersonal relationships. Is there any downside to this method of relationship formation? The answer is yes. One other finding reported by McKenna et al. (2002) was that individuals who felt that the "real me" was represented on the Internet were most likely to form Internet relationships. These individuals also tend to be socially anxious and lonely. It is these anxious and lonely individuals who are most likely to turn to the Internet as a way to form relationships that they find threatening offline. However, the relationships that socially anxious individuals form online may not be high quality. Tian (2013) found that compared to individuals with low levels of social anxiety, socially anxious individuals formed fewer new friendships, interacted with fewer existing friends, and had lower quality relationships with existing friends on the Internet. However, they did have higher quality relationships with new friends they made on the Internet. So, is lonely people's use of the Internet to form relationships a bad thing? It depends on what one means by loneliness. Weiss (1973) suggested that there are actually two types of loneliness. *Social loneliness* consists of the negative affect associated with not having friends and meaningful relationships. *Emotional loneliness* refers to an empty feeling tied to the lack of intimate relationships (Moody, 2001). A study conducted by Moody (2001) evaluated how face-to-face and Internet relationships related to these two forms of loneliness. Moody found that face-to-face relationships were associated with low levels of both social and emotional loneliness. However, Internet relationships were associated with lower levels of social loneliness, but higher levels of emotional loneliness. In Moody's words: "the Internet can decrease social well-being, even

Although research shows that physical proximity is a strong predictor of relationship formation, more people are using the Internet for this purpose. The Internet reduces psychological distance, but not physical distance.

Source: GaudiLab/Shutterstock.

though it is often used as a communication tool" (p. 393). So, while Internet relationships can fulfill one's need for social contact, they may still leave a sense of emotional emptiness. Additionally, shyness has also been found to correlate with a condition called *Internet addiction*. The shyer the person, the more likely he or she is to become addicted to the Internet (Chak & Leung, 2004). Shyness is related to loneliness, with shy individuals being more likely to also be lonely (Jackson, Fritch, Nagasaka, & Gunderson, 2002). So, even though the Internet can help shy, lonely people establish relationships, it comes with an emotional and behavioral cost.

Similarity

Similarity between ourselves and others is another important factor in friendship formation. Similarity in attitudes, beliefs, interests, person-ality, and even physical appearance strongly influence the likelihood of interpersonal attraction. An interesting study conducted by Byrne, Ervin, and Lamberth (2004) demonstrated the effects of similarity and physical attractiveness on attraction. This study used a computer dating situation in which participants were given a 50-item questionnaire assessing person-ality characteristics and attitudes. Students were then paired. Some stu-dents were paired with a similar other and others with a dissimilar other. The pairs were then sent on a 30-minute date, after which they reported back to the experimenter to have their date assessed. Byrne et al. found that similarity and physical attractiveness, as expected, positively related to interpersonal attraction. So, there may be some validity to the claims of eHarmony.com, a company that purports to match people on a number of important dimensions, leading to successful relationships being formed!

Clearly, there are many possible points of similarity between people. Attitude similarity, for example, might mean that two people are both Democrats, are both Catholics, and in addition to their political and reli-gious beliefs, have like views on a wide range of other issues. However, it is not the absolute number of similar attitudes between individuals that influences the likelihood and strength of attraction. Far more critical are the proportion and importance of similar attitudes. It does little good if someone agrees with you on everything except for the one attitude that is central to your life (Byrne & Nelson, 1965).

What about the notion that in romantic relationships, opposites attract? This idea is essentially what Newcomb called *complementarity*. Researchers have found little evidence for complementarity (Duck, 1988). Instead, a **matching principle** seems to apply in romantic relationships. People tend

matching principle

A principle that applies in romantic relationships, suggesting that individuals become involved with a partner with whom they are closely matched socially and physically.

to become involved with a partner with whom they are usually closely matched in terms of physical attributes or social status (Schoen & Wooldredge, 1989).

Different kinds of similarity may have different implications for attraction. If you and someone else are similar in interests, then liking results. Similarity in attitudes, on the other hand, leads to respect for the other person. In a study of college freshmen, similarity in personality was found to be the critical factor determining the degree of satisfaction in friendships (Carli, Ganley, & Pierce-Otay, 1991). This study found similarity in physical attractiveness to have some positive effect on friendships but not a large one.

Why does similarity promote attraction? Attitude similarity promotes attraction in part because of our need to verify the "correctness" of our beliefs. Through the process of social comparison, we test the validity of our beliefs by comparing them to those of our friends and acquaintances (Hill, 1987). When we find that other people believe as we do, we can be more confident that our attitudes are valid. It is rewarding to know that someone we like thinks the way we do; it shows how smart we both are. Similarity may also promote attraction because we believe we can predict how a similar person will behave (Hatfield, Walster, & Traupmann, 1978).

Limits of the Similarity-Attraction Relationship

The similarity-attraction relationship is one of the most powerful and consistent effects found in social psychology. This, however, does not mean that similarity and attraction relate to one another positively in all situations and relationships. Similarity is most important for relationships that are important to us and that we are committed to (Amodio & Showers, 2005). For less committed relationships, dissimilarity was actually more strongly related to liking and maintaining a relationship over time (Amodio & Showers, 2005). Also, in supervisor-subordinate relationships within organizations, dissimilarity is associated with greater liking on the part of the subordinate for the supervisor (Glomb & Welch, 2005). In organizations, dissimilarity is most likely to translate into positive interpersonal relationships when there is a commitment to diversity (Hobman, Bordia, & Gallois, 2004).

Along the same lines, Rosenbaum (1986) argued that it is not so much that we are attracted to similar others as that we are repulsed by people who are dissimilar. Further examination of this idea that dissimilarity breeds repulsion suggests that dissimilarity serves as an initial filter in the formation of relationships. Once a relationship begins to form, however, similarity becomes the fundamental determinant of attraction (Byrne, Clore, & Smeaton, 1986; Smeaton, Byrne, & Murnen, 1989). Thus, the effect of similarity on attraction may be a two-stage process, with dissimilarity and other negative information leading us to make the initial "cuts," and similarity and other positive information then determining with whom we become close.

There also appears to be a difference between relationships formed in laboratory studies and real-life relationships with respect to the impact of similarity. Researchers have made a distinction between perceived similarity and actual similarity. *Perceived similarity* is how much similarity you believe exists between you and another person. *Actual similarity* is the actual amount of similarity that exists. A meta-analysis of the similarity-attraction literature showed that perceived similarity is a strong predictor of attraction in both the laboratory and real-life relationships. However, actual similarity predicts attraction in laboratory studies, but not in real-life relationships (Montoya, Horton, & Kirschner, 2008). In an interesting study, Ilmarinen, Lönnqvist, and Paunonen (2016) explored the relationship between personality similarity and friendship formation in a group of Finnish military cadets. The cadets completed measures of the big-five personality model (extraversion, agreeableness, conscientiousness, neuroticism, and openness to experience) and two "dark personality traits" (manipulativeness and egotism). They also rated the likeableness of their fellow cadets. Ilmarinen et al. found that similarity only predicted liking for the dark traits, especially at the low end of these dimensions. A person who scores on the low end of the manipulativeness (representing honesty) and egotism (non-egotist) scales is attracted to others with the same levels of these traits. Ilmarinen et al. suggest that this shows that people value the trait honesty when deciding whom to like.

Study Break

This section discussed some of the factors relating to interpersonal attraction. Before you go on to the next section, answer the following questions:

1   How and why does physical proximity relate to interpersonal attraction?

2   How do Internet relationships compare to more traditional relationships?

3   How does similarity relate to interpersonal attraction?

4   What is the matching principle, and why is it important in attraction?

5   What are the limits of the similarity effect?

Physical Attractiveness

Physical attractiveness is an important factor in the early stages of a relationship. Research shows, not surprisingly, that we find physically attractive people more appealing than unattractive people, at least on initial contact (Eagly, Ashmore, Makhijani, & Longo, 1991). Moreover, our society values physical attractiveness, so a relationship with an attractive person is socially rewarding to us.

In their now classic study of the effects of physical attractiveness on dating, Elaine Hatfield and her colleagues led college students to believe that they had been paired at a dance based on their responses to a personality test, but in fact, the researchers had paired the students randomly (Hatfield, Aronson, Abrahams, & Rottman, 1966). At the end of the evening, the couples evaluated each other and indicated how much they would like to date again. For both males and females, the desire to date again was best predicted by the physical attractiveness of the partner. This is not particularly surprising, perhaps, because after only one brief date, the partners probably had little other information to go on.

Physical attractiveness affects not only our attitudes toward others but also our interactions with them. A study of couples who had recently met found that, regardless of gender, when one person was physically attractive, the other tried to intensify the interaction (Garcia, Stinson, Ickes, Bissonette, & Briggs, 1991). Men were eager to initiate and maintain a conversation, no matter how little reinforcement they got. Women tried to quickly establish an intimate and exclusive relationship by finding things they had in common and by avoiding talk about other people.

There are, however, gender differences in the importance of physical attractiveness. Generally, women are less impressed by attractive males than are men by attractive females (Buss, 1988a). Women are more likely than men to report that attributes other than physical attractiveness, such as a sense of humor, are important to them.

Despite the premium placed on physical attractiveness in Western culture, there is evidence that individuals tend to match for physical attractiveness in much the same way that they match on personality and attitudinal dimensions. You can demonstrate this for yourself. Look at the engagement announcements accompanied by photographs of the engaged couples. You will find remarkable evidence for matching. Beyond such anecdotal evidence, there is research evidence for matching for physical attractiveness. Shafer and Keith (2001) found that married couples (especially younger and older couples) matched for weight.

What accounts for this matching for physical attractiveness? It turns out that physically attractive people tend to have higher standards for what they consider another person's level of attractiveness to be. For example, in one study, participants of varying levels of objective attractiveness (as rated by others) rated the attractiveness of several target individuals. The results showed that more physically attractive participants rated the target individuals lower in attractiveness than less attractive participants (Montoya, 2008). Further, more attractive participants expected less satisfaction in a relationship with targets they rated as less attractive. Additionally, attractive participants showed less fear of rejection from an attractive other than less attractive participants and saw a relationship with a target person of similar attractiveness more probable. So, people may match for attractiveness because they expect a satisfying relationship with others of similar attractiveness, have less fear of being rejected, and view a relationship with an attractive potential mate as likely to happen (Montoya, 2008).

Dimensions of Physical Attractiveness

What specific physical characteristics make someone attractive? Facial appearance has been shown to strongly affect our perceptions of attractiveness through much of our life span (McArthur, 1982; Zebrowitz, Olson, & Hoffman, 1993). Moreover, various aspects of facial appearance have specific effects. One group of researchers suspected that people find symmetrical faces more attractive than asymmetrical faces (Cardenas & Harris, 2006; Thornhill & Gangestad, 1994). Cardenas and Harris had participants examine pairs of faces, asking them to indicate which was more attractive. They found that more symmetrical faces were chosen over less symmetrical faces. Interestingly, when the researchers added asymmetrical makeup decoration to a symmetrical face, it reduced the perceived attractiveness of the symmetrical face. Similarly, Thornhill and Gangestad took photographs of males and females, fed those photos into a computer, created computer versions of the faces, and made precise measurements of the symmetry of the faces. They then asked subjects to rate the computer-generated images for attractiveness. They found that people do judge symmetrical faces to be more attractive than asymmetrical ones. Thornhill and Gangestad also asked the photographed students to fill out questionnaires about their sex and social lives. Those with symmetrical faces reported that they were sexually active earlier than others and had more friends and lovers. Finally, Mealey, Bridgestock, and Townsend (1999) report that between identical twins, the twin with the more symmetrical face is judged to be more physically attractive.

Why should symmetry and facial features in general be so important? The answer may lie more in our biology than in our psychology, an issue we explore later in the chapter.

There is a body of research that suggests that people's facial appearance plays a role in how others perceive and treat them (Berry, 1991; Noor & Evans, 2003; Zebrowitz, Collins, & Dutta, 1998; Zebrowitz & Lee, 1999). Zebrowitz and her coworkers (1998) noted that there is a **physical attractiveness bias**, a "halo," whereby individuals who are physically attractive are thought to also have other positive attributes. One cultural stereotype is that what is beautiful is good. That is, we tend to believe that physically attractive individuals possess a wide range of desirable characteristics and that they are generally happier than unattractive individuals (Dion, Berscheid, & Walster, 1972) Not only do we find attractive individuals more appealing physically, but we also confer on them a number of psychological and social advantages. We think that they are more competent and socially

physical attractiveness bias

The tendency to confer a number of psychological and social advantages to physically attractive individuals.

appealing than the average-appearing person. Moreover, unattractive individuals may experience discrimination because of their appearance. A study by Noor and Evans (2003) confirms this. They found that an asymmetrical face was perceived to be more neurotic, less open, less agreeable, and less attractive than a symmetrical face. So, individuals with symmetrical faces are associated with more positive personality characteristics than those with asymmetrical faces.

Much of this attractiveness bias is probably learned. However, there is some evidence that the attractiveness bias may have a biological component as well. In one experiment, infants 2 or 3 months old were exposed to pairs of adult faces and their preferences were recorded (Langlois, Roggman, Casey, Riesner-Danner, & Jenkins, 1987). Preference was inferred from a measure known as *fixation time,* or the amount of time spent looking at one face or the other. If the infant prefers one over the other, the infant should look at that face longer. As shown in Figure 12.2, when attractive faces were paired with unattractive faces, infants displayed a preference for the attractive faces. It is therefore quite unlikely that infants learned these preferences.

Furthermore, a number of distinctly different cultures seem to have the same biases. This doesn't necessarily mean that these biases aren't learned; various cultures may simply value the same characteristics. Studies comparing judgments of physical attractiveness in Korea and in the United States found agreement on whether a face was attractive and whether the face conveyed a sense of power. In both countries, for example, faces with broad chins, thin lips, and receding hairlines were judged to convey dominance (Triandis, 1994).

Zebrowitz and her coworkers showed that appearances of both attractive people and people with baby faces (round faces, large eyes, small nose and chin, high eyebrows) affect how others

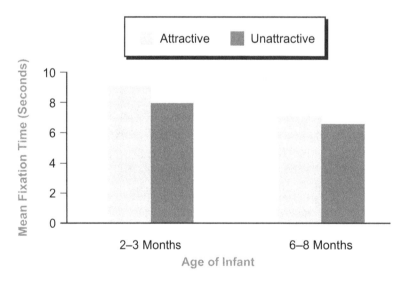

Figure 12.2 Infant fixation time as a function of the attractiveness of a stimulus face. Infants as young as 2 or 3 months old showed a preference for an attractive face over an unattractive face.

From Langlois and colleagues (1987).

treat them (Zebrowitz & Lee, 1999; Zebrowitz et al., 1998). Whereas attractive people are thought to be highly competent both physically and intellectually, baby-faced individuals are viewed as weak, submissive, warm, and naive. What happens when baby-faced individuals do not conform to the stereotype that they are harmless? In a study of delinquent adolescent boys, Zebrowitz and Lee (1999) showed that baby-faced boys, in contrast to more mature-looking delinquents, were punished much more severely. This is a contrast effect: Innocent-looking people who commit antisocial actions violate our expectations.

Although attractiveness and baby-facedness may have a downside when these individuals run afoul of expectations, the upside is, as you might expect, that the positive expectations and responses of other people shape the personalities of attractive individuals across their life (Zebrowitz et al., 1998). This is self-fulfilling prophecy, whereby attractive men who are treated positively because of their appearance become more socially secure as they get older. Similarly, Zebrowitz found that a man who had an "honest" face in his youth tended to be more honest as he got older.

For baby-faced individuals, the effect over time was somewhat different. These individuals become more assertive and aggressive over time, probably as a way of compensating for the stereotype of a baby-faced individual as submissive and weak.

However, Zebrowitz and colleagues (1998) did not observe such a self-fulfilling prophecy for women. That is, attractive young women do not become more attractive and competent socially as they age. Zebrowitz suggested further that less-attractive women may learn to compensate by becoming more socially able to counteract the negative image held of less-attractive women. This would explain the lack of significant differences in socially valued personality attributes between younger attractive and less-attractive women as they age into their fifties. Interestingly, women who had an attractive personality in their youth developed high attractiveness in their fifties, suggesting, according to Zebrowitz, that women manipulated their appearance and presentation (makeup, etc.) more than men did. It may be that this is due to women's greater motivation to present an attractive appearance because they have less power to achieve their social goals in other ways (Zebrowitz et al., 1998).

Physique and the Attractiveness Bias

Physique also profoundly affects our perceptions of attractiveness. Buss (1994) observed that the importance of physical attractiveness has increased in the United States in every decade since the 1930s. This is true for both men and women, although men rate physical attractiveness as much more important than do women. Western society has widely shared notions of which bodily attributes are attractive. We have positive perceptions of people who fit these notions and negative perceptions of those who do not. We sometimes even display discriminatory behavior against those who deviate too far from cultural standards.

People can be categorized by body type into *ectomorphs* (thin, perhaps under-weight), *mesomorphs* (athletic build), and *endomorphs* (overweight). Positive personality traits tend to be attributed to mesomorphs and negative ones to people with the other body types (Ryckman et al., 1991). There is some ambivalence about ectomorphs, especially as societal attitudes toward thinness seem to shift, influenced by such factors as an increasing health consciousness and an association of excessive thinness with acquired immunodeficiency syndrome (AIDS). Perceptions of endomorphs, in contrast, remain consistently negative. Of course, some people are more intensely attuned to physical appearance than are others. It appears that those people who are most conscious of their own appearance are the most likely to stereotype others on the basis of physique.

Certainly this is the case with regard to overweight individuals. Research confirms that obese individuals are stigmatized and are the target of negative stereotypes in our society. This bias cuts across genders. Obese men and women are likely to be stigmatized (Hebl & Turchin, 2005). These negative stereotypes exist on both the implicit and explicit level (Waller, Lampman, & Lupfer-Johnson, 2012; Wang, Brownell, & Wadden, 2004). In one study (Harris, 1990), subjects judged a stimulus person who was depicted as either normal weight or (with the help of extra clothing) obese. They evaluated "Chris," the stimulus person, along several dimensions including the likelihood that Chris was dating or married, her self-esteem, and her ideal romantic partner. The results, almost without exception, reflected negative stereotyping of an obese Chris compared to a normal-weight Chris. Subjects judged that the obese Chris was less likely to be dating or married compared to the normal-weight Chris. They also rated the obese Chris as having lower self-esteem than the normal-weight Chris and felt that her ideal love partner should also be obese.

Studies also show the practical consequences of these attitudes. For example, it has been shown that overweight college students are less likely than other students to get financial help from home (Crandall, 1991). This effect was especially strong with respect to female students and was true regardless of the resources the student's family had, the number of children in the family, or other factors that could affect parents' willingness to provide financial help. The researchers suggested that the finding might be largely explained by parents' negative attitudes toward their overweight children and consequent lack of optimism about their future. In a related domain, there is evidence that businesspeople sacrifice $1,000 in annual salary for every pound they are overweight (Kolata, 1992). Weight can also affect evaluations of employability (Grant & Mizzi, 2014). Grant and Mizzi found that an overweight potential job applicant was rated as less employable than a normal weight applicant. They also found that stereotypes about overweight people did not mediate the relationship between weight and employability ratings. They did find, however, that a "rational bias" (e.g., customers would feel uncomfortable with the overweight employee) mediated the relationship.

Interestingly, the bias against overweight people is shown by children. Children between the ages of 2 and 5 were shown two line drawings of children. One of the drawings showed a child who was 23% larger than the other. The children were asked to ascribe various characteristics to the figures in the drawing. The results showed that the children were more likely to ascribe negative qualities to the larger figure (Turnbull, Heaslip, & McLeod, 2000). This finding should not be surprising since these stereotypic images of body image are portrayed in children's literature and movies (Herbozo, Tantleff-Dunn, Gokee-Larose, & Thompson, 2004). Just think, for example, about the Disney film *The Little Mermaid*, in which the mermaid Ariel is depicted as a slim, beautiful, young woman and the sea witch (the villain) is depicted as an obese, unattractive woman.

The bias against overweight people even extends into the world of health care. For example, Waller, Lampman, and Lupfer-Johnson (2012) found a stronger implicit bias against overweight people in a medical than nonmedical context. In another study, an implicit prejudice and implicit stereotypes were shown toward overweight people by health care workers, a majority of whom were doctors (Teachman & Brownell, 2001). There was, however, little evidence for an explicit prejudice. In another study, doctors showed more negative attitudes toward hypothetical obese patients than average-weight patients and that they would spend less time with an obese patient (Hebl & Xu, 2001). Physicians indicated that they would be more likely to refer obese patients for mental health care. The good news was, however, that doctors seemed to follow an appropriate course of action with respect to weight-unrelated tests.

The bias against obese people may be culturally related. Western culture seems to place a great deal of emphasis on body image (just take a look at the models [male and female] used in advertisements). One cross-cultural study using British and Ugandan participants showed that the Ugandan participants rated a drawing of an obese figure more positively than British participants (Furnham & Baguma, 2004). Another study conducted in New Zealand found that obese job applicants were evaluated more negatively than nonobese applicants (Ding & Stillman, 2005). The bias may also have a racial component as well. One study found that black males stigmatized an obese person less than white males and that black males are less likely to be stigmatized than white males (Hebl & Turchin, 2005).

One reason obese individuals are vilified is that we believe that their weight problem stems from laziness and a lack of discipline. If we know that an individual's weight problem is the result of a biological disorder and thus beyond his or her control, we are less likely to make negative judgments of that individual (DeJong, 1980). What we fail to realize is that most obese people cannot control their weight. There is a genetic component in obesity, and this tendency can be exacerbated by social and cultural factors, such as lack of information and an unhealthy lifestyle.

Attractiveness judgments and stereotyping in everyday life may not be as strong as they are in some laboratory studies. In these studies, we make pure attraction judgments: We see only a face or a physique. When we deal with people, we evaluate an entire package even if much of what we see initially is only the wrapping. The entire package includes many attributes. A person may be overweight but may also have a mellifluous voice and a powerful personality. In a laboratory study in which subjects were exposed to a person's face and voice, the perception of the person's physical attractiveness was affected by judgments about that person's vocal attractiveness and vice versa (Zuckerman, Miyake, & Hodgins, 1991). Gertrude Stein was a woman many people found attractive even though she weighed over 200 pounds. Her striking face and her powerful personality were the main attributes that people remembered after meeting her.

Beauty and the View from Evolutionary Psychology

It is obvious that we learn to associate attractiveness with positive virtues and unattractiveness with vice, even wickedness. Children's books and movies often portray the good characters as beautiful and the villains as ugly. As noted, in the Walt Disney movie *The Little Mermaid,* the slender, beautiful mermaid, Ariel, and the evil, obese sea witch are cases in point. Such portrayals are not limited to works for children. The hunchback of Notre Dame, the phantom of the opera, and Freddy Kruger are all physically unattractive evildoers.

Evolutionary psychologists suggest that perhaps beauty is more than skin deep. Recall the research on the attractiveness of symmetrical faces. It seems that it is not only humans who value symmetry but also a variety of other species. For example, Watson and Thornhill (1994) reported that female scorpion flies can detect and prefer as mates males with symmetrical wings. Male elks with the most symmetrical racks host the largest harems.

Mate Selection: Good Genes or Good Guys?   Proponents of evolutionary psychology, a subfield of both psychology and biology, employ the principles of evolution to explain human behavior and believe that symmetry is reflective of underlying genetic quality. Lack of symmetry is thought to be caused by various stresses, such as poor maternal nutrition, late maternal age, attacks by predators, or disease, and may therefore reflect bad health or poor genetic quality. Thus, the preference for symmetry in potential mates, whether human or animal, may be instinctive (Watson & Thornhill, 1994). Indeed, even small differences matter. Twins with lower levels of symmetry are reliably rated as less attractive than their slightly more symmetrical counterpart (Mealey, Bridgstock, & Townsend, 1999).

The degree to which biology may control human mating preferences can be underscored by the finding that the type of face a woman finds attractive varies with her menstrual cycle. Perret and Penton-Voak (1999) reported a study that showed that when a woman is ovulating, she is more likely to prefer men with highly masculine features. In contrast, during other times, men with softer, feminine features are preferred. The researchers had numerous women from various countries—Japan, Scotland, England—judge male faces during different parts of their menstrual cycles. The researchers believe that these results are explained by the observation that masculine looks, in all of the animal kingdom, denote virility and the increased likelihood for healthy offspring. In a related finding, Gangestad and Thornhill (1998) reported a study that showed that females preferred the smell of a "sweaty" T-shirt worn by the most symmetrical males but only if the women were ovulating.

Of course, it is likely that more choice is involved in mate selection than would be indicated by these studies. In any event, most people do rebel against the notion that decisions about sex, marriage, and parenthood are determined by nothing more than body odor (Berreby, 1998).

Certainly we would expect those with symmetrical appearances to become aware of their advantages in sexual competition. For example, consider the following study by Simpson and his coworkers. Heterosexual men and women were told that they would be competing with another same-sex person for a date with an attractive person of the opposite sex. The experimenters videotaped and analyzed the interactions among the two competitors and the potential date. Men who had symmetrical faces used direct competition tactics. That is, when trying to get a date with the attractive woman, symmetrical men simply and baldly compared their attractive-ness (favorably) with the competitor. Less-attractive (read as less-symmetrical-faced) men used indirect competitive methods, such as emphasizing their positive personality qualities (Simpson, Gangestad, Christensen, & Leck, 1999).

Gangestad and Thornhill (1998) have argued that physical appearance marked by high symmetrical precision reveals to potential mates that the individual has good genes and is, therefore, for both men and women, a highly desirable choice. These individuals, especially men, should have fared very well in sexual competition during evolutionary history. Why? Research suggests that greater symmetry is associated with higher survival rates as well as higher re-productive rates in many species (Simpson et al., 1999). In men, it seems that certain secondary sexual attributes that are controlled by higher levels of testosterone, such as enlarged jaws, chins, and so forth, may project greater health and survival capability (Mealey, Bridgstock, & Townsend, 1999). Indeed, symmetrical men and women report more sexual partners and have sex earlier in life than less symmetrical individuals. The more symmetrical the individual—again, especially males—the more probable the person will have the opportunity for short-term sexual encounters, and the more likely, as Simpson and colleagues (1999) found, they will use direct competitive strategies to win sexual competitions.

Of course, good genes are not enough. Raising human offspring is a complicated, long-term—some might say never-ending—affair, and having a good partner willing to invest in parenthood is important. Indeed, theorists have developed what are called "good provider" models of mate selection that emphasize the potential mate's commitment to the relationship and ability to pro-vide resources necessary for the long-term health of that relationship (Gangestad & Thornhill, 1997; Trivers, 1972).

How to Attract a Mate   David Buss, a prominent evolutionary social psychologist, suggested that to find and retain a reproductively valuable mate, humans engage in love acts—behaviors with near-term goals, such as display of resources the other sex finds enticing. The ultimate purpose of these acts is to increase reproductive success (Buss, 1988a, 1988b). Human sexual be-havior thus can be viewed in much the same way as the sexual behavior of other animal species.

Subjects in one study (Buss, 1988b) listed some specific behaviors they used to keep their partner from getting involved with someone else. Buss found that males tended to use display of resources (money, cars, clothes, sometimes even brains), whereas females tried to look more attractive and threatened to be unfaithful if the males didn't shape up. Buss argued that these findings support an evolutionary interpretation of mate retention: The tactics of females focus on their value as a reproductive mate and on arousing the jealousy of the male, who needs to ensure they are not impregnated by a rival.

Jealousy is evoked when a threat or loss occurs to a valued relationship due to the partner's real or imagined attention to a rival (Dijkstra & Buunk, 1998). Men and women respond differently to infidelity, according to evolutionary psychologists, due to the fact that women bear higher reproductive costs than do men (Harris & Christenfeld, 1996). Women are concerned with having a safe environment for potential offspring, so it would follow that sexual infidelity would not be as threatening as emotional infidelity, which could signal the male's withdrawal from the relationship. Men, however, should be most concerned with ensuring the prolongation of their genes and avoiding investing energy in safeguarding some other male's offspring. Therefore, males are most threatened by acts of sexual infidelity and less so by emotional ones. Thus, males become most jealous when their mates are sexually unfaithful, whereas women are most jealous when their mates are emotionally involved with a rival (Buss, 1994; Harris & Christenfeld, 1996).

According to the evolutionary psychology view, males ought to be threatened by a rival's dominance, the ability to provide resources (money, status, power) to the female in question, whereas women ought to be most threatened by a rival who is physically attractive, because that attribute signals the potential for viable offspring. Indeed, a clever experiment by Dijkstra and Buunk (1998), in which participants judged scenarios in which the participant's real or imagined mate was flirting with a person of the opposite sex, showed that dominance in a male rival and attractiveness in a female rival elicited the greatest amount of jealousy for men and women, respectively.

Many of Buss's findings about human mating behavior are disturbing because both men and women in pursuit of their sexual goals cheat and frustrate their mates and derogate their rivals. However, some of his findings are kinder to our species. For example, he points out that the most effective tactics for men who wish to keep their mates are to provide love and kindness, to show affection, and to tell their mates of their love. That sounds rather romantic.

Indeed, evidence suggests that women are driven, at least in long-term mate selection strategies, by behavior and traits represented by the good provider models. Although men are strongly influenced by traits such as youth and attractiveness, women tend to select partners on the basis of attributes such as social status and industriousness (Ben Hamida, Mineka, & Bailey, 1998). Note the intriguing differences between traits that men find attractive in women and those that women find attractive in men. The obvious one is that men seem to be driven by the "good genes" model, whereas women's preferences seem to follow the good provider models. This preference appears across a range of cultures. One study by Shackelford, Schmitt, and Buss (2005) had males and females evaluate several characteristics that could define a potential mate. The participants were drawn from 37 cultures (including African, Asian, and European). Their results confirmed that, across cultures, women valued social status more than men, and men valued physical attractiveness more than women.

The other difference, however, is that traits that make women attractive are in essence uncontrollable: Either you are young or you are not; either you are attractive or you are not. Modern science can help, but not much. Therefore, a woman who desires to increase her value has the problem of enhancing attributes that are really not under her control (Ben Hamida et al., 1998). Male-related attributes—status, achievement—are all, to a greater or lesser extent, under some control and may be gained with effort and motivation. Ben Hamida and his colleagues argue that the uncontrollability of the factors that affect a woman's fate in the sexual marketplace may have long-term negative emotional consequences.

Before we conclude that there is an unbridgeable difference between men and women and that men follow only the good genes model and women only the good provider model, we need to take into account a recent meta-analysis showing that physical attractiveness and good earning potential mediate mate preferences for both men and women (Eastwick, Luchies, Finkel, & Hunt, 2014). We should also consider the possibility that what one wants in the sexual marketplace depends on what one's goals are and what one can reasonably expect to get. In fact, it appears that when looking for a casual sexual partner, both men and women emphasize attractiveness, and when searching for a long-term relationship, both look for a mate with good interpersonal skills, an individual who is attentive to the partner's needs, has a good sense of humor, and is easygoing (Regan, 1998). In fact, Miller (2000), an evolutionary psychologist, argued that the most outstanding features of the human mind—consciousness, morality, sense of humor, creativity—were shaped not so much by natural selection but rather by sexual selection. Miller suggested that being funny and friendly and a good conversationalist serves the same purpose for humans as an attractive tail serves peacocks: It helps attract mates.

Regan (1998) reported that women were less willing to compromise on their standards. For example, although women wanted an attractive partner for casual sex, they also wanted a male who was older and more interpersonally responsive. Men wanted attractiveness and would compromise on everything else. In fact, a woman's attractiveness seems to overcome a male potential partner's common sense as well. Agocha and Cooper (1999) reported that when men knew a potential partner's sexual history and also knew that she was physically attractive, they weighed attractiveness as much more important in the decision to engage in intercourse than the probability of contracting a sexually transmitted disease as suggested by that sexual history. However, women and men are less willing to compromise when it comes to long-term relationships. The results conform to the idea that casual sex affords men a chance to advertise their sexual prowess and gain favor with their peer group but that long-term relationships are driven by quite different needs (Regan, 1998).

Finally, students often ask about any differences between heterosexual and same-sex orientation mate preferences. The available research suggests that mate selection preferences between these groups may not differ all that much (Over & Phillips, 1997). For example, a study of personal advertisements placed by heterosexual and same-sex orientation males and females was conducted by Kenrick, Keefe, Bryan, Barr, and Brown (1995). Kenrick et al. found that mate selection patterns for heterosexual and same-sex orientation men were highly similar and showed similar patterns of change with age. Both groups of men preferred younger mates, and this preference grew stronger with age. This finding was replicated in a similar study of personal ads conducted by Burrows (2013). She found that gay men advertised for partners who were on average 13 years younger than themselves (heterosexuals advertised for someone 14 years younger). Kenrick et al. found a slight difference between same-sex orientation and heterosexual women. Younger women in both groups expressed interest in same-aged mates. However, with age, same-sex orientation women were more likely than heterosexual women to desire a younger partner. In another study, same-sex orientation women were found to be more interested in visual sexual stimulation and less in partner status than heterosexual women.

Study Break

This section explored how physical attractiveness affects interpersonal attraction. Before you begin the next section, answer the following questions:

1   Overall, how and why is physical attractiveness important in attraction?

2   What characteristics of faces contribute to the perception of facial attractiveness?

3   What is the physical attractiveness bias, and what are some of its components?

4   How and why does a person's weight relate to perceptions of attractiveness and behavior?

5   How do evolutionary psychologists explain the effects of physical attractiveness on attraction?

6   What are the factors relevant to human mate selection, and how can one attract a mate?

Dynamics of Close Relationships

We have discussed why people form close relationships and why they form them with the people they do. We turn now to the dynamics of close relationships—how they develop and are kept going, and how in some cases conflict can lead to their dissolution. But what exactly are close relationships? What psychological factors define them?

There appear to be three crucial factors, all of which we saw in the relationship between Gertrude Stein and Alice Toklas. The first factor is emotional involvement, feelings of love or warmth and fondness for the other person. The second is sharing, including sharing of feelings and experiences. The third is interdependence, which means that one's well-being is tied up with that of the other (Kelley et al., 1983). As is clear from this definition, a close relationship can be between husband and wife, lovers, or friends. Note that even when research focuses on one type of close relationship, it is usually also applicable to the others.

Relationship Development

Models of how relationships develop emphasize a predictable sequence of events. This is true of both models we examine in this section, the stage model of relationship development and social penetration theory. According to the stage model of relationship development, proposed by Levinger and Snoek (1972), relationships evolve through the following stages:

> *Stage 0, no relationship.* This is a person's status with respect to virtually all other people in the world.
>
> *Stage 1, awareness.* We become conscious of another's presence and feel the beginning of interest. When Stein and Toklas first met in the company of friends, their conversation suggested to each of them that they might have much in common.
>
> *Stage 2, surface contact.* Interaction begins but is limited to topics such as the weather, politics, and mutual likes and dislikes. Although the contact is superficial, each person is forming impressions of the other. Stein and Toklas moved into this stage the day after their first meeting and soon moved beyond it.
>
> *Stage 3, mutuality.* The relationship moves, in substages, from lesser to greater interdependence. The first substage is that of involvement, which is characterized by a growing number of shared activities (Levinger, 1988). A subsequent substage is commitment, characterized by feelings of responsibility and obligation each to the other. Although not all close relationships involve commitment (Sternberg, 1988), those that have a serious long-term influence on one's life generally do. We noted how Stein and Toklas began by sharing activities, then feelings, and then an increasing commitment to each other.

The first stages of Levinger and Snoek's model give us insight into the early stages of a relationship where people first meet. However, it does not tell us anything about *how* people meet each other, giving them a chance to form a relationship. Surprisingly, there has not been all that much research on this issue. One exception is a comprehensive study of relationship formation by Rosenfeld and Thomas (2012). In their study, Rosenfeld and Thomas studied how people meet each other and how methods of meeting others have changed over time. Figure 12.3 shows some of the ways that heterosexual and same-sex couples meet (based on data from Rosenfeld, 2010). As you can see, there are different ways that couples meet, and for some methods, there are striking differences between heterosexual and same-sex couples. Heterosexual couples are more likely to meet through family members and friends. On the other hand, same-sex couples are more likely to meet via the Internet. Rosenfeld and Thomas report that some methods of meeting have shown a decline over the past decades, and some have shown an increase. For example, there has been a decline in couples (both heterosexual and same-sex) meeting via friends from 1980 to 2010. However, there has been a sharp increase in the percentage of couples who meet via the Internet from the late 1990s through 2010, especially for same-sex couples. Further, the gap between Internet use by heterosexuals and same-sex orientation individuals is even greater when you consider only couples who have met in the past 10 years of the study (Rosenfeld & Thomas, 2012). One reason why same-sex orientation individuals use the Internet more than heterosexuals is that the more traditional ways of meeting one's partner (e.g., family, friends, and church) have never been very useful for gays and lesbians. Consequently, they are likely to turn to the Internet because it represents the best possibility of meeting other gay or lesbian partners (Rosenfeld & Thomas, 2012). Interestingly, how couples meet is not related to whether or not they stay together (Rosenfeld & Thomas, 2012).

Once couples meet, their relationship progresses in terms of the communication patterns they show. A second model of relationship development, **social penetration theory**, developed by

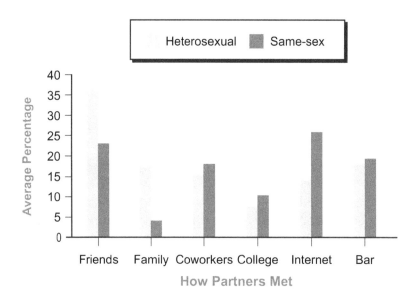

Figure 12.3 How couple's partners meet each other (average percent across relationship types).

Based on data from Rosenfeld (2010).

Altman and Taylor (1973), centers on the idea that relationships change over time in both breadth (the range of topics people discuss and activities they engage in together) and depth (the extent to which they share their inner thoughts and feelings). Relationships progress in a predictable way from slight and superficial contact to greater and deeper involvement. First the breadth of a relationship increases. Then there is an increase in its depth, and breadth may actually decrease. Casual friends may talk about topics ranging from sports to the news to the latest rumors at work. But they will not, as will more intimate friends, talk about their feelings and hopes. Close friends allow each other to enter their lives—social penetration—and share on a deeper, more intimate level, even as the range of topics they discuss may decrease.

Evidence in support of social penetration theory comes from a study in which college students filled out questionnaires about their friendships several times over the course of a semester and then again 3 months later (Hays, 1985). Over 60% of the affiliations tracked in the study developed into close relationships by the end of the semester. More important, the interaction patterns changed as the relationships developed. As predicted by social penetration theory, interactions of individuals who eventually became close friends were characterized by an initial increase in breadth followed by a decrease in breadth and an increase in intimacy, or depth.

An important contributor to increasing social penetration—or to the mutuality stage of relationship development—is *self-disclosure*, the ability and willingness to share intimate areas of one's life. College students who kept diaries of their interactions with friends reported that casual friends provided as much fun and intellectual stimulation as close friends but that close friends provided more emotional support (Hays, 1988b). Relationship development is fostered by self-disclosure simply because we often respond to intimate revelations with self-disclosures of our own (Jourard, 1971).

Dating Scripts and Relationship Formation

Once people meet one another and enter into a relationship, what ideas do they carry into their relationships? Research on how people perceive relationships has focused on dating scripts. Cognitive psychologists define a script as our knowledge and memories of how events occur. For example, you may have a script concerning a basketball game in which 10 large, athletic individuals come onto a court and try to get a round ball through a hoop. A *dating script* is your concept of how a date should progress. That is, we have an idea about what we expect to happen on a date (for example, a "first date"). These scripts

social penetration theory

A theory that relationships vary in breadth, the extent of interaction, and depth, suggesting they progress in an orderly fashion from slight and superficial contact to greater and deeper involvement.

A dating script includes ideas about what a date should be like. Men and women have somewhat different dating scripts..

Source: Jacob Lund/Shutterstock.

will guide our actions when we find ourselves in a dating situation and are derived from cultural and personal experiences (Rose & Frieze, 1989). Research shows that first-date scripts for men and women have many similarities but some important differences (Bartoli & Clark, 2006). Women, for example, have first-date scripts that are focused on the social interactions during the date. Men's first-date scripts are more action-oriented, which includes things like deciding what to do and when to initiate physical contact (Rose & Frieze, 1989). Generally, men's first-date scripts are proactive, and women's are reactive (Rose & Frieze, 1993). Additionally, men's dating scripts tend to place more emphasis on expecting sexual activity, whereas women's scripts are more likely to emphasize limiting such activity (Bartoli & Clark, 2006).

Recent research reveals some interesting things about dating scripts. First, dating scripts that conform to dominant gender-role stereotypes are seen more positively than those that do not (McCarty & Kelly, 2015). McCarty and Kelly had male and female participants rate a stereotypic (e.g., the man picks up the woman, holds the door open, etc.), counter-stereotypic (the female engaged in the behaviors depicted in the stereotypic date), or an egalitarian (none of the behaviors mentioned) date. McCarty and Kelly found that the stereotypic date was rated most positively. Additionally, the male in the stereotypic date was rated more positively (e.g., warmer, more appropriate) than in the other dating scenarios. Second, dating scripts of deaf individuals show some differences from traditional dating scripts of hearing individuals (Gilbert, Clark, & Anderson, 2012). Gilbert et al. compared the dating scripts of deaf individuals with those of hearing individuals (established in other studies) and found that a sexual outcome was not as strongly expressed among the deaf than among the hearing. In other aspects, however, the dating scripts of the deaf and hearing are very similar.

Culture provides a pretty clear set of scripts concerning heterosexual dating. There are countless movies, books, plays, and other sources of information providing a clear road map for heterosexual dating. The same does not appear to be true for dating scripts for same-sex relationships. There are differences in the dating scripts of gay men and lesbian women. The scripts of gay men tend to be more oriented toward sexual behavior and less toward emotion and intimacy. On the other hand, scripts of lesbians tend to be more oriented toward emotions (Klinkenberg & Rose, 1994). This difference parallels differences seen in heterosexual relationships, where men stress sexual and physical aspects of a date and women stress intimacy and emotion (Goldberg, 2010).

When we move from the realm of first dates and dating in general to more committed relationships, we again see that there are similarities and differences between same-sex and heterosexual couples. We must start this discussion with the fact that there are many more similarities than differences between same-sex and heterosexual couples in committed relationships (Roisman, Clausell, Holland, Fortuna, & Elieff, 2008). However, Roisman et al. report that lesbian partners work together better than partners in other relationships. Additionally, same-sex relationships tend to be more egalitarian than mixed-sex relationships (Shechory & Ziv, 2007). That is, in same-sex relationships, there is more equal distribution of household tasks and more liberal attitudes toward gender roles than in mixed-sex relationships. Generally, women in mixed-sex relationships feel less equitably treated in their relationships than women in same-sex relationships do (Shechory & Ziv, 2007). Additionally, partners in lesbian couples report a higher level of relationship quality than partners in either gay or heterosexual relationships (Kurdek, 2008). As a relationship progresses, partners in gay and lesbian couples show little change in reported relationship quality, whereas partners in heterosexual relationships show a decline in relationship quality that eventually levels off (Kurdek, 2008). Interestingly, partners in heterosexual relationships with children show two periods of declining relationship quality (Kurdek, 2008). Finally, couples in same-sex relationships are more likely to keep a romantic secret from their partners than couples in heterosexual relationships (Easterling, Knox, & Brackett, 2012).

Study Break

This section discussed how relationships form. Before you begin the next section, answer the following questions:

1 What are the stages of Levinger and Snoek's model of relationship formation, and what happens at each stage?

2 How do people tend to meet one another?

3 What dimensions underlie social penetration theory, and how do they relate to relationship formation?

4 How does self-disclosure relate to relationship formation?

5 What is a dating script, and how do scripts differ among people?

Evaluating Relationships

Periodically we evaluate the state of our relationships, especially when something is going wrong or some emotional episode occurs. Berscheid (1985) observed that emotion occurs in a close relationship when there is an interruption in a well-learned sequence of behavior. Any long-term dating or marital relationship develops sequences of behavior—Berscheid called these *interchain sequences*—that depend on the partners coordinating their actions. For example, couples develop hints and signals that show their interest in lovemaking. The couple's lovemaking becomes organized, and the response of one partner helps coordinate the response of the other. A change in the frequency or pattern of this behavior will bring about a reaction, positive or negative, from the partner. The more intertwined the couples are, the stronger are their interchain sequences; the more they depend on each other, the greater the impact of interruptions of these sequences.

Exchange Theories

social exchange theory

A theory of how relationships are evaluated, suggesting that people make assessments according to the rewards (positive things derived from a relationship) and costs (negative things derived from a relationship).

One perspective on how we evaluate relationships is provided by **social exchange theory** (Thibaut & Kelley, 1959), which suggests that people make assessments according to rewards and costs, which correspond to all of the positive and all of the negative factors derived from a relationship. Generally, rewards are high if a person gets a great deal of gratification from the relationship, whereas costs are high if the person either must exert a great deal of effort to maintain the relationship or experiences anxiety about the relationship. According to this economic model of relationships, the outcome is decided by subtracting costs from rewards. If the rewards are greater than the costs, the outcome is positive; if the costs are greater than the rewards, the outcome is negative.

This doesn't necessarily mean that if the outcome is positive, we will stay in the relationship, or that if the outcome is negative, we will leave it. We also evaluate outcomes against *comparison levels*. One type of comparison level is our expectation of what we will obtain from the relationship. That is, we compare the outcome with what we think the relationship should be giving us. A second type is a *comparison level of alternatives*, in which we compare the outcome of the relationship we are presently in with the expected outcomes of possible alternative relationships. If we judge that the alternative outcomes would not be better, or even worse, than the outcome of our present relationship, we will be less inclined to make a change. If, on the other hand, we perceive that an alternative relationship promises a better outcome, we are more likely to make a change.

A theory related to social exchange theory—*equity theory*—says that we evaluate our relationships based on their rewards and costs, but it also focuses on our perception of equity, or balance, in relationships (Hatfield, Traupmann, Sprecher, Utne, & Hay, 1985). Equity in a relationship occurs when the following equation holds:

$$\frac{\text{Person A's Benefits (rewards } - \text{ costs)}}{\text{B's Contributions}} = \frac{\text{Person B's Benefits (rewards } - \text{ costs)}}{\text{A's Contributions}}$$

Rewards may include, but are not limited to, companionship, sex, and social support. Costs may include loss of independence and increases in financial obligations. The contributions made to the relationship include earning power or high social status. The rule of equity is simply that person A's benefits should equal person B's if their contributions are equal. However, fairness requires that if A's contributions are greater than B's, A's benefits should also be greater.

Thus, under equity theory, the way people judge the fairness of the benefits depends on their understanding of what each brings to the relationship. For example, the spouse who earns more may be perceived as bringing more to the marriage and, therefore, as entitled to higher benefits. The other spouse may, as a result, increase her costs, perhaps by taking on more of the household chores.

In actual relationships, of course, people differ, often vigorously, on what counts as contributions and on how specific contributions ought to be weighed. For example, in business settings, many individuals believe that race or gender should count as a contribution when hiring. Others disagree strongly with that position.

Has the fact that most women now work outside the home altered the relationship between wives and husbands as equity theory would predict? It appears, in keeping with equity theory, that the spouse who earns more, regardless of gender, often has fewer child-care responsibilities than the spouse who earns less (Steil & Weltman, 1991, 1992).

However, it also appears that cultural expectations lead to some inequity. Husbands tend to have more control over financial matters than wives do, regardless of income (Biernat & Wortman, 1991). Moreover, a study of professional married couples in which the partners earned relatively equal amounts found that although the wives were satisfied with their husbands' participation in household chores and childrearing, in reality there was considerable inequity (Biernat & Wortman, 1991). Women were invariably the primary caregivers for the children. Men spent time with their children and did many of the household chores, but they were not the primary caregivers. This may reflect a lack of equity in these relationships, or it may mean that women simply do not fully trust their husbands to do a competent job of taking care of the children.

What happens when people perceive inequity in a relationship? As a rule, they will attempt to correct the inequity and restore equity. If you realize that your partner is dissatisfied with the state of the relationship, you might try, for example, to pay more attention to your partner and in this way increase the rewards he or she experiences. If equity is not restored, your partner might become angry or withdraw from the relationship. Inequitable relationships are relationships in trouble.

In one study, researchers measured the level of perceived equity in relationships by means of the following question and scale (Hatfield, Walster, & Berscheid, 1978, p. 121): Comparing what you get out of this relationship with what your partner gets out of it, how would you say the relationship stacks up?

+3 I am getting a much better deal than my partner.
+2 I am getting a somewhat better deal.
+1 I am getting a slightly better deal.
 0 We are both getting an equally good—or bad—deal.
−1 My partner is getting a slightly better deal.
−2 My partner is getting a somewhat better deal.
−3 My partner is getting a much better deal than I am.

Respondents were grouped into three categories: those who felt that their relationship was equitable, those who felt that they got more out of the relationship than their partners and therefore were overbenefited, and those who felt that they got less than their partners and therefore were underbenefited.

The researchers then surveyed 2,000 people and found, as expected, that those individuals who felt underbenefited were much more likely to engage in extramarital sex than those who thought that their relationship was equitable or felt overbenefited (Hatfield, Walster, & Traupmann, 1978). Generally, couples who feel that they are in an equitable relationship are more likely to maintain the relationship than those who are less equitably matched (Hill, Rubin, & Peplau, 1976).

Communal Relationships   Although the research just reviewed suggests that people make rather cold-blooded, marketplace judgments about the quality of their relationships, it is likely that they also have other ways of evaluating relationships. For example, a distinction has been made between relationships governed by exchange principles—in which, as we have seen, people benefit each other with the expectation of receiving a benefit in return—and relationships governed by communal principles—in which individuals benefit each other in response to the other's needs (Clark, 1986). In **communal relationships**, if one partner can put more into the relationship than the other, so be it. That is, people may deliberately underbenefit themselves for the sake of the relationship.

communal relationship

An interpersonal relationship in which individuals benefit each other in response to each other's needs.

Love relationships are often governed by communal principles. Clark and Grote (1998) reviewed the research concerning how couples evaluate their relationships, and although some of the results show that costs are negatively related to satisfaction as exchange theories would predict, sometimes, however, costs are positively related to satisfaction. That is, Clark and Grote found evidence that, sometimes, the more costs a partner incurs, the higher the satisfaction. How might we explain this? Well, if we consider the communal norm as one that rewards behavior that meets the needs of one's partner, then we might understand how costs could define a warm, close, and affectionate relationship. As Clark and Grote noted, it may be admirable, and one may feel good about oneself if, having helped one's partner, one has also lived up to the communal ideal. By doing so, the helping partner gains the gratitude of the other, feels good about oneself, and these positive feelings then become associated with the relationship.

One way to reconcile the different findings concerning the relationship between costs and satisfaction is to note that the costs one bears in a communal relationship are qualitatively different than those we bear in a purely exchange relationship that may be deteriorating. For example, consider the following costs borne in an exchange relationship: "She told me I was dumb." This is an intentional insult (and cost) that suggests a relationship that may be going badly. Compare this to a communal cost: "I listened carefully to what he said when a problem arose, even though I was quite busy and had other things to get done." This communal cost served to strengthen the relationship (Clark & Grote, 1998). To state the obvious, there are costs and then there are costs.

Love over Time

We have talked about how relationships get started and how the partners evaluate how that relationship is going. Now let's consider what happens to relationships over time. What factors keep them together and what drives them apart? Sprecher (1999) studied partners in romantic relationships over a period of several years. The measures of love, commitment, and satisfaction taken several times over the period of the research show that couples who maintained their relationship increased on all measures of relationship satisfaction. Couples who broke up showed a decrease in measures of relationship health just before the breakup. The collapse of the relationship did not mean that love was lost. In fact, the splintered partners continued to love each other, but everything else had gone wrong.

Sprecher's work as well as that of others suggests that intact relationships are perceived by the partners in idealistic ways and that the partners truly feel that their love and commitment grows stronger as time goes on. Intact, long-term couples are very supportive of each other and that makes it easier for them to weather difficult personal or financial problems (Gottman, Coan, Carrère, & Swanson, 1998). For example, couples who support each other during times of stress are much better able to survive periods of economic pressure that tend to cause much emotional distress in a relationship (Conger, Rueter, & Elder, Jr., 1999).

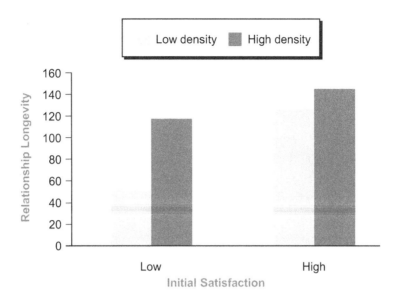

Figure 12.4   Relationship longevity as a function of belief in destiny and initial satisfaction with a relationship. Individuals who believed in romantic destiny and had initial satisfaction with the relationship tended to have longer relationships than those who did not. However, when initial satisfaction was low, individuals who believed in destiny tended not to give the relationship a chance and exited the relationship after a short time.

From Knee (1998).

Some individuals are especially idealistic and affirm a belief that they have met the person that destiny provided. Knee (1998) examined the relationships of those romantic partners who believed in romantic destiny and those who did not. He found that he could predict the longevity of the relationship by two factors: One was belief in romantic destiny and the other was whether the initial interaction was very positive. As Figure 12.4 shows, individuals who believed in romantic destiny and had that confirmed by initial satisfaction tended to have longer relationships than those who did not believe in destiny. But if things don't go quite so well at first, those who believe in destiny tend to bail out quite quickly and do not give the relationship a chance (Knee, 1998).

Sculpting a Relationship

So we see that strong relationships are idealized and are able to withstand stresses because the partners support each other rather than work at cross-purposes. How do such relationships develop? Drigotas (1999) and his coexperimenters found that successful couples have an obliging interdependence in which each, in essence, sculpts the other, much as Michelangelo carved David out of the embryonic stone. This Drigotas aptly called the *Michelangelo phenomenon* (Drigotas, Rusbult, Wieselquist, & Whitton, 1999). In a series of four studies, these researchers showed that each partner tended to become more like the ideal self that their partner envisioned for them. In other words, each partner supports the other's attempts to change. This partner affirmation of each other is strongly associated with ongoing, well-functioning couples.

Of course, one reason that successful couples have similar views of each other is that individuals tend to search for people who are similar to them. There are two types of similarity that are relevant to relationship sculpting: actual similarity and ideal similarity. Actual similarity refers to the degree to which partners possess similar traits. For example, Klohnen and Mendelsohn (1998) reported research that showed that individuals pair up with partners of approximately equal value and attributes. Note that this is in line with exchange theories discussed earlier. Therefore, people with positive self-images tend to have more positive descriptions of their ideal partner as compared to those with lesser self-images. Ideal similarity refers to "the extent to which a partner possesses attributes and traits that are part of *(a)* one's ideal self standards, or *(b)* one's ideal partner standards" (Rusbult, Kumashiro, Kubacka, & Finkel, 2009, p. 62). Klohnen and Mendelsohn (1998) reported a significant similarity between one partner's description of the ideal self and his or her description of the partner. In fact, individuals tended to bias their views of their partner in the direction of the ideal self-concepts. Rusbult et al. evaluated the contributions of actual and ideal similarity to relationship sculpting and found that both were involved. However, each contributed independently to relationship sculpting. That is, ideal similarity accounted for sculpting processing over and above that accounted for by actual similarity. Additionally, Rusbult et al. found that the level of ideal similarity in a relationship relates to the longevity of the relationship. Relationships with lower levels of ideal similarity were more likely to end than those with a higher level.

It appears then that successful relationships require that each partner work to affirm his or her beliefs about the other partner. What happens when one partner, say, gets a nasty surprise and learns that her spouse, a competent individual in social situations with people he does not know, is an awkward mutterer with close family members? Certainly, she may be upset and disillusioned. Past research by Swann (1996) has shown that when individuals confront evidence that goes against their firmly held views of themselves, they work very hard to refute or downgrade that evidence. Similarly, De La Ronde and Swann (1998) found that partners work hard to verify their views of their spouses. As Drigotas and colleagues (1999) suggested, we often enter into relationships with people who view us as we view ourselves. Therefore, we and our partners are motivated to preserve these impressions. Therefore, our surprised spouse will be motivated to see her husband as competent in social situations, as he sees himself, by suggesting perhaps that there is something about family gatherings that makes him act out of character.

There seems, then, to be a kind of unspoken conspiracy among many intact couples to protect and conserve the social world that the couple inhabits. The downside of this, of course, is when one of the partners changes in a way that violates the expectations of the other partner. For example, as De La Ronde and Swann (1998) suggested, if one partner, because of low self-esteem goes into therapy and comes out with a more positive self-image, the spouse holding the other in low regard in the first place is motivated, according to the notion of partner verification, to maintain that original negative image. Clearly, that does not bode well for the relationship.

Of course, having negative views of one's partner, as you might expect, is associated with decreased relationship well-being (Ruvolo & Rotondo, 1998). In fact, some people have a strong belief that people can change and, to go back to the example used here, that someone with a negative self-image can change for the better. Ruvulo and Rotondo (1998) measured the extent to which people involved in relationships believed that people can change. They found that when individuals had strong beliefs that individuals can change, then the views that they had of their partner were less likely to be related to the current well-being of the relationship. This means that if you saw that your partner had a negative self-image, but you were convinced that he or she could change for the better, that current image was not crucial to how you viewed the status of the relationship. However, for those individuals who did not feel that it was possible for people to change, the views of their partners were crucial to how they evaluated their relationships. So, if you believed that your partner's attributes and feelings were forever fixed, it makes sense that those views would be crucial to how you felt about the relationship. But, if things could change, probably for the better, well then these negative views won't last forever. Therefore, many successful couples behave in a manner that verifies initial images of each other.

Study Break

This section discussed a number ways that people evaluate their relationships and how relationships change over time. Before you begin the next section, answer the following questions:

1   How do exchange theories maintain that people evaluate relationships?

2   How does equity theory account for relationship evaluation, and what happens if a relationship is inequitable?

3   What is a communal relationship, and how does this approach differ from the exchange theory approach?

4   How do relationships change over time?

5   How do people go about sculpting a relationship? In your answer, describe the Michelangelo Effect.

Responses to Conflict

When relationships are deemed to be unfair, or inequitable, the result almost inevitably will be conflict. Conflict also can occur when a partner behaves badly, and everyone behaves badly at one time or another. The mere passage of time also makes conflict more likely. Couples are usually more affectionate and happier as newlyweds than they are 2 years later (Huston & Vangelisti, 1991). What happens, then, when conflicts arise? How do people in a relationship respond to conflicts? In this section we shall look at three responses to conflict: developing stories to explain conflict, accommodation, and forgiveness.

Developing Stories

Satisfied couples bias their impressions of their partner in ways that cause idealization of the partner and increase satisfaction in the relationship (McGregor & Holmes, 1999). Researchers have discovered that when satisfied couples confront a threat in the marriage due to something the partner has done (say, had a drink with another man or woman on the sly), individuals devise stories that work to diminish that threat. They construct a story to explain the event in a way that takes the blame away from their partner. The story puts the partner in the best light possible. McGregor and Holmes (1999) suggested that the process of devising a story to explain a behavior convinces the storyteller of the truth of that story. Constructing the motives of the characters in the story (the partner and others) and making the story come to a desired conclusion—all of this cognitive work is convincing to the story's author, who comes to believe in its conclusions.

Conflict in a relationship is inevitable. How couples handle conflict can determine whether the relationship continues or ends.

Source: Photographee.eu/Shutterstock.

When reality is complicated, a story that is charitable, apparently, can go far in soothing both the offending partner and the storytelling partner (McGregor & Holmes, 1999).

Sometimes, instead of escalating the conflict, couples find ways to accommodate each other, even when one or both have acted in a negative or destructive manner (Rusbult, Verette, Whitney, Slovik, & Lipkus, 1991). Typically, our initial impulse in response to a negative act such as our partner embarrassing us in front of other people is to be hurtful in return. That is, we tend toward the primitive response of returning the hurt in kind.

Then other factors come into play. That initial impulse gets moderated by second thoughts: If I react this way, I'm going to hurt the relationship and I will suffer. What should I do? Should I lash back, or should I try to be constructive? Do I satisfy the demands of my ego, or do I accommodate for the good of the relationship?

Accommodation

accommodation process

Interacting in such a way that, despite conflict, a relationship is maintained and enhanced.

These second thoughts, therefore, might lead to an **accommodation process**, which means that in interactions in which there is conflict, a partner does things that maintain and enhance the relationship (Rusbult et al., 1991). Whether a partner decides to accommodate will depend largely on the nature of the relationship. To accommodate, a person must value the relationship above his or her wounded pride. If the relationship is happy, if the partners are committed to each other, then they will be more likely to accommodate. People are also more likely to accommodate when they have no alternatives to the relationship. Interestingly, accommodation may occur spontaneously and very quickly after a negative event. In one study (Häfner & IJzerman, 2011), participants were shown a picture of either their partner's or a stranger's face showing a happy or angry expression. Participants' facial responses to the pictures were recorded. Häfner and IJzerman found that participants responded to the angry face of their partners with a smile within a second of seeing the picture. This finding was limited to participants who indicated that their relationship was strongly communal. An angry face of a stranger elicited an angry response.

Accommodation does not always mean being positive. Consistently reacting to a partner's negative behavior in positive ways may lessen the power that constructive comments can have under really serious circumstances. At times, it may be better to say nothing at all than to respond in a positive way. More important than being positive and agreeing with one's partner is to avoid being unduly negative (Montgomery, 1988). The health of a relationship depends less on taking good, constructive actions than on carefully avoiding insulting, destructive actions (Rusbult et al., 1991).

The way people in a committed relationship handle conflict, in short, is an excellent predictor of the health of the relationship. Relationship health correlates with handling conflict through accommodation, rather than ignoring conflict or focusing on negatives. Research shows a positive association between happiness in a relationship and a couple's commitment to discuss and not ignore conflicts (Crohan, 1992). Those couples who ignore conflicts report less happiness in their relationship.

Couples who tend to focus on negatives when dealing with conflict are more likely to end their relationship. An initial study showed that couples whose relationship was in difficulty tended to express negative feelings, sometimes even in anticipation of an interaction, and to display high levels of physiological arousal, whereas couples whose relationship was not in difficulty expected interactions to be constructive and were able to control their emotions (Levenson & Gottman, 1983). A follow-up study of most of the couples revealed that those couples who had recorded high physiological arousal were likely to have separated or ended the relationship (Gottman & Levenson, 1986).

As should be clear, conflict is not the cause of relationship breakup, nor is the lack of overt conflict a sign that a relationship is well. Rather, it is the way couples handle conflict that counts. Mark Twain mused that people may think of perhaps 80,000 words a day but only a few will get them into trouble. So it is with relationships. Just a few "zingers"—contemptuous negative comments—will cause great harm (Notarius & Markman, 1993). Consider the husband who thinks of himself as an elegant dresser, a person with impeccable taste in clothes. If, one day, his wife informs him during a heated exchange that she finds his clothing vulgar and is often embarrassed to be seen with him, she has struck a sensitive nerve. Her comment, perhaps aimed at damaging his self-esteem, may provoke an even more hurtful response and lead to growing ill will between the two—or to defensiveness and withdrawal. One zinger like this can undo a whole week's worth of loving and supportive interchanges.

Forgiveness

It is relatively easy to see how accommodation can solve conflict in certain situations. For example, if there is a disagreement over whether to buy a new Corvette or how to discipline the children, accommodation would be the most effective method of dealing with the conflict. However, there are events that occur in a relationship that might not be fixed by accommodation by itself. For example, an incident of infidelity may call for more than reaching an accommodation. Clinically speaking, infidelity presents one of the most serious challenges in a relationship and is one of the most difficult to handle in therapy (Gordon, Baucom, & Snyder, 2005). Infidelity is particularly damaging to an ongoing relationship when the transgressor is caught in the act or is discovered through an unsolicited third-party account (Afifi , Falato, & Weiner, 2001).

Given the potentially damaging impact of infidelity on a relationship, how can a relationship be repaired following such an event? One possibility is forgiveness, which makes conflict resolution and accommodation easier to achieve (Fincham, Beach, & Davila, 2004). In a case of infidelity the harmed partner will need to forgive the offender in order to begin the process of healing the relationship through conflict resolution and accommodation.

Most of us have some sense of what is meant by forgiveness. However, in order to study a concept like forgiveness empirically, we need a scientific definition. McCullough, Worthington, and Rachal (1997) define **interpersonal forgiveness** as changes involving a harmed individual showing decreased motivation to retaliate against one's relationship partner, a reduced tendency to maintain distance from the partner, and an increased tendency to express conciliation and goodwill toward the partner (pp. 321–322). McCullough et al. characterize forgiveness as the transition from negative motivational states (e.g., desire for revenge) to positive motivational states (e.g., conciliation) that help preserve a relationship. There are several ways in which interpersonal forgiveness can be expressed (see Table 12.3). Which method is used may depend on the nature of the relationship (e.g., married or dating) and the severity of the transgression (Sheldon, Gilchrist-Petty, & Lessley, 2014).

interpersonal forgiveness

A harmed individual's decreased motivation to retaliate against and a reduced tendency to maintain distance from one's relationship partner, and an increased willingness to express conciliation and goodwill toward the partner.

TABLE 12.3 Different methods that can be used to give forgiveness

Forgiveness Method	Description
Nonverbal	Using a nonverbal gesture to express forgiveness (e.g., a hug)
Conditional	Making forgiveness contingent on a change in behavior (e.g., I will forgive you if you don't see her any more)
Minimizing	Forgiving by minimizing the severity of the transgression (e.g., It really isn't that big of a deal that you stay out late)
Discussion-based	Changing the rules of a relationship, talking about the transgression or expressing emotions
Explicit	Overtly expressing forgiveness (e.g., stating "I forgive you")

Source: Sheldon, Gilchrist-Petty, & Lessley (2014).

As you might expect, a wronged partner's likelihood of forgiving his or her transgressing partner relates to the severity of the transgression. The more severe the transgression, the less likely forgiveness will be given (Fincham,

Jackson, & Beach, 2005). The more severe the transgression, the less likely it is that the nonverbal and minimizing methods of forgiveness will be used (Sheldon, Gilchrist-Petty, & Lessley, 2014). Forgiveness is more likely if the infidelity is a one-time occurrence rather than a pattern of behavior and if an apology is offered for the infidelity (Gunderson & Ferrari, 2008). There is also a gender difference in how men and women respond to infidelity. Men, for example, are less likely to forgive sexual infidelity (e.g., your partner engaging in a passionate sexual relationship with another person) than emotional infidelity (e.g., your partner forming an intimate bond with another person) and would be more likely to terminate a relationship after sexual infidelity than after emotional infidelity (Shackelford, Buss, & Bennett, 2002). Conversely, women would be less likely to forgive an emotional infidelity than a sexual one and would be more likely to break up with a partner who engages in emotional infidelity. Forgiveness is also more likely to occur if there is a high-quality relationship between partners before the infidelity occurs (McCullough, Exline, & Baumeister, 1998).

What are the psychological factors that mediate forgiveness for infidelity? Forgiveness is related to whether empathy for the transgressing partner is aroused (McCullough, Worthington, & Rachal, 1997). McCullough et al. report that when a transgressing partner apologizes, it activates feelings of empathy for the transgressor and leads to forgiveness. Additionally, the type of attribution made for infidelity is important. For partners in a pre-transgression relationship that is of high quality, attributions for a transgression like infidelity are likely to be "benign" and arouse empathy, which will lead to forgiveness (Fincham, Paleari, & Regalia, 2002).

Love in the Lab

John Gottman has studied marriages in a systematic and scientific manner by using a variety of instruments to observe volunteer couples who agree to live in an apartment that is wired and to have their behavior observed and recorded. Results of research from what is known as the "love lab" suggest that there are three kinds of stable marriages (Gottman, 1995). The first type is the *conflict avoiding couple,* who survive by accentuating the positive and simply ignoring the negative; the second type is the *volatile couple,* who are passionate in everything they do, even fighting. Last is the *validating couple,* who listen carefully to each other, compromise, and reconcile differences (Gottman, 1995). All these styles work because the bottom line is that each style promotes behavior that most of the time is positive. What happens if partners in a relationship are mismatched for their styles? For example, what would happen if one person has a volatile style and the other an avoiding style? When mismatches occur, it does not bode well for the relationship, especially if one partner is volatile and the other is avoiding (Busby & Hollman, 2009). With this type of mismatch, partners are less satisfied with their relationship, experience more conflict, and are more likely to experience stonewalling (see next paragraph) than are matched or other mismatched couples (Busby & Hollman, 2009). Gottman and Levenson (2002) have also found that the manner in which emotion is expressed in a marriage relates to how long a marriage lasts before divorce. Marriages with high levels of unregulated, volatile expressions of emotion (positive or negative) are shorter than those in which emotion is more neutral.

four horsemen of the apocalypse

Four factors identified as important in relationship dissolution: complaining/criticizing, contempt, defensiveness, and withdrawal from social interaction (stonewalling).

Gottman has been able to predict with uncanny accuracy the couples that are headed for divorce. He has identified four factors he refers to as the **four horsemen of the apocalypse**. These four factors are: complaining/criticizing, contempt, defensiveness, and withdrawal from social interaction (stonewalling). The last factor is the most destructive to a relationship and is a very reliable predictor of which couples divorce. There is no answer to stonewalling, but it means that communication has ceased and one partner is in the process of ostracizing the other by refusing to talk. Gottman suggested that there is a cascading relationship between the four horsemen of the apocalypse. Criticism may lead to contempt, which may lead to defensiveness and finally to stonewalling. The seeds of trouble in a marriage may be present very early in the marriage. Carrère and Gottman (1999) had newlywed couples discuss an instance of conflict that occurred in their marriages. They videotaped and analyzed how the couples interacted concerning the conflict. Carrère and Gottman found that couples who expressed negative emotion in the first three minutes of their conversation were more likely to divorce six years later than those who expressed positive emotion.

Most happy couples do not refuse to talk. Indeed, Gottman's observations in the love lab suggest that these partners make lots of attempts to repair a dispute to make sure the argument does not spiral out of control. These repair attempts, reaching out to the other, also include humor that works to defuse anger. Gottman (1995) noted that most marital problems are not easy to resolve. But happy couples realize that their relationship is more important than satisfying their own preferences and idiosyncrasies. For example, one spouse may be a "morning" person and the other is not. So when this couple goes on trips, they compromise. The "morning" person is willing to wait a bit later to start the day, and the "night" person is willing to wake up a bit earlier.

Friendships

According to Sternberg's definition mentioned earlier, liking involves intimacy without passion. Given that liking involves intimacy, does liking lead to romantic loving? The answer to this question appears to be no. Liking evidently leads only to liking. It is as if the two states—liking and loving—are on different tracks (Berscheid, 1988). People may be fond of each other and may go out together for a long time without their affection ever quite ripening into romantic love. Can we say, then, that liking and loving are basically different?

Study Break

This section introduced conflict in relationships and how conflict can be handled when it occurs. Before you begin the next section, answer the following questions:

1   How do couples use stories to handle conflict?

2   What is the accommodation process, and when is it most likely to be successful in reducing conflict?

3   How is interpersonal forgiveness used in cases of relationship infidelity, and when is it most likely to be successful?

4   What are the marriage styles described by Gottman, and how do they relate to the success or failure of a marriage?

5   What are the four horsemen of the apocalypse, and how do they relate to divorce?

Rubin (1970, 1973) thought that liking and loving were indeed essentially different. He constructed two separate measures, a liking scale and a loving scale, to explore the issue systematically. He found that although both friends and lovers were rated high on the liking scale, only lovers were rated high on the loving scale. Moreover, separate observations revealed that dating couples who gave each other high scores on the loving scale tended more than others to engage in such loving actions as gazing into each other's eyes and holding hands. A follow-up study found that these couples were more likely to have maintained the relationship than were those whose ratings on the loving scale were lower. Therefore, according to Rubin, we may like our lovers, but we do not generally love those we like, at least with the passion we feel toward our lovers.

However, even if liking and (romantic) loving are conceptually different, this does not necessarily mean that friendship does not involve love or that some of the same motives that drive romantic relationships are absent in long-term friendships. The friendships that we form during our lives can be loving and intimate and passionate. Baumeister and Bratslavsky (1999) suggested that passion can be just as strong in friendships except that the sexual component may be absent for a variety of reasons, the most obvious one being that the gender of the friend is wrong. The history of a friendship ought not to differ very much from that of a romantic relationship. When two individuals become friends, they experience attraction and affection and share disclosures and experiences. This rising intimacy leads to an increase in the passion of the friends, absent the sexual component (Baumeister & Bratslavsky, 1999).

Friendships can be either same-sex or cross-sex. Cross-sex friendships, of course, comprise a male and female friend. Although many people maintain both types of friendships, for most people same-sex friendships are more numerous than cross-sex friendships (O'Meara, 2006). O'Meara also found that men and women report having about the same number of cross-sex friends. Both same-sex and cross-sex relationships have their challenges. However, cross-sex relationships pose challenges not present in same-sex friendships. Cross-sex friendships may be fraught with sexual tension not present in same-sex friendships. Additionally, in American culture cross-sex friendships may not be seen as "normative," causing the friends to have to defend the relationship to others (O'Meara, 1989). O'Meara lists four challenges facing those in cross-sex friendships: determining the nature of the emotional bonds in the relationship, dealing with sexual tension, dealing with gender inequality within the relationship, and managing how the friendship looks to others. The good news is, however, that most people in cross-sex friendships successfully manage these problems and they become major issues in only a small percentage of cross-sex friendships (Monsour, Harris, Kurzweil, & Beard, 1994).

Gender Differences in Friendships

Female same-sex friendships and male same-sex friendships show somewhat different patterns (Brehm, 1985). Males tend to engage in activities together, whereas females tend to share their emotional lives. Richard and Don may play basketball twice a week, and while playing, they may talk about their problems and feelings, but that is not their purpose in getting together. Karen and Teri may have lunch twice a week with the express purpose of sharing their problems and feelings. Men live their friendships side by side; women live them face to face (Hendrick 1988; Wright, 1982).

The degree of this difference may be diminishing. In the last few decades, there has been a marked increase in the importance both men and women assign to personal intimacy as a source of fulfillment (McAdams, 1989). In fact, both men and women see self-disclosure as an important component in an intimate friendship. It is just that men may be less likely to express intimacy via self-disclosure (Fehr, 2004). Some research suggests that men and women self-disclose with equal frequency and perhaps intensity (Prager, Fuller, & Gonzalez, 1989). Additionally, both males and females place greater weight on the "communal" nature of friendship (i.e., friendship involving interpersonal closeness, intimacy, and trust) over the "agentic" nature (e.g., enhancing social status) of friendship (Zarbatany, Conley, & Pepper, 2004).

Men and women report having about the same number of close friends. Women tend to view their close friends as more important than men do, but men's close friendships may last longer than women's (Fiebert & Wright, 1989). Men typically distinguish between same-sex and cross-sex friendships. For men, cross-sex bonds offer the opportunity for more self-disclosure and emotional attachment. Men generally obtain more acceptance and intimacy from their female friends than from their male friends (Duck, 1988). However, for heterosexual men, cross-sex relationships are often permeated with sexual tension (Rawlins, 1992).

Women, in comparison, do not sharply distinguish among their friendships with males and females. They also see differences in their feelings for the various men in their lives. Some of their relationships with men are full of sexual tension, whereas other men may be liked, even loved, but sexual tension may be absent in those relationships.

Greater levels of interaction with females are associated with fewer episodes of loneliness for both men and women. Why? Interactions with women are infused with disclosure, intimacy, and satisfaction, and all these act as buffers against loneliness (Wheeler, Reis, & Nezlek, 1983). Women seem to make better friends than men do. It is telling that married men, when asked to name their best friend, are likely to name their wives. The expectations women have for friendship are often not satisfied by their spouse, and they tend to have at least one female friend in whom they confide (Oliker, 1989).

Friendships over the Life Cycle

Friendships are important throughout the life cycle. But they also change somewhat in relation to the stage of the life cycle and to factors in the individual's life. Sharing and intimacy begin to characterize friendships in early adolescence, as a result of an increasing ability to understand the thoughts and feelings of others. Girls have more intimate friendships in their early adolescent years than boys do, and this tends to remain true throughout life (Rawlins, 1992).

Why are boys less intimate than girls with same-sex friends? The reason might be that girls trust their friends more than boys do (Berndt, 1992). Girls tend to listen to their friends and protect their friends' feelings, whereas boys tend to tease or embarrass their friends when the opportunity arises. The more intimate the adolescent friendships, the more loyal and supportive they are. However, disloyalty and lack of support can sometimes result from pressure to conform to the peer group. Of course, these issues are not unique to adolescent friendships. Conflicts between intimacy and social pressure simply take on different forms as people get older (Berndt, 1992).

As individuals move into early and middle adulthood, the end of a marriage or other long-term intimate relationship can profoundly affect the pattern of a couple's friendships. When a woman experiences the breakup of a relationship, her friends rally around and support her (Oliker, 1989). Often, the couple's close friends will have already guessed that the relationship was in trouble. When the breakup occurs, they tend to choose one partner or the other, or to simply drift away, unable to deal with the new situation.

In later adulthood, retirement affects our friendships. We no longer have daily contact with coworkers, and thus lose a source of potential friends. With increasing age, new issues arise. The death of a spouse affects friendships perhaps as much as the breakup of a marriage. People who are recently widowed can often feel like "fifth wheels" (Rawlins, 1992). The physical problems often associated with old age can lead to a conflict between a need for independence and a need for help (Rawlins, 1992). As a result, older friends might have to renegotiate their relationships to ensure that both needs are met. Whatever the problems, friendships among the elderly are often uplifting and vital. This is well illustrated by the following statement from a 79-year-old widower: "I don't know how anyone would ever live without friends, because to me, they're next to good health, and all your life depends on friendship" (quoted in Rawlins, 1992).

Study Break

This section introduced different types of friendships and how they change over time. Before you read the Chapter Review, answer the following questions:

1   How do friendships differ from romantic relationships?

2   What are the rewards and challenges of same-sex and cross-sex friendships?

3   How does gender relate to friendships?

4   How do friendships change over the course of the life cycle?

Gertrude and Alice Revisited

Stein and Toklas are important because of their role in the vibrant literary world of Paris just after the end of World War I, a period that lasted well into the 1930s. However, aside from their historical importance, the relationship of these two individuals reflects and exemplifies the basic characteristics of close relationships. We saw how the need for intimacy overcame Alice's very strong feelings of social anxiety. Their relationship changed over time, of course, ending, finally, in a companionate one. However, they touched all the vertices of Sternberg's triangle of love: intimacy, passion, and commitment.

References

Acker, M., & Davis, M. H. (1992). Intimacy, passion and commitment in adult romantic relationships: A test of the triangular theory of love. *Journal of Social and Personal Relationships 9,* 21–50.

Afifi, W. A., Falato, W. L., & Weiner, J. L. (2001). Identity concerns after a severe relational transgression: The role of discovery method for the relational outcomes of infidelity. *Journal of Social and Personal Relationships, 18,* 291–308.

Agocha, V. B., & Cooper, M. L. (1999). Risk perceptions and safer-sex intention: Does a partner's physical attractiveness undermine the use of risk-relevant information? *Personality and Social Psychology Bulletin, 25,* 756–759.

Ainsworth, M. D. S. (1992). Epilogue. In D. Cicchetti, M. M. Greenberg, & M. Cummings (Eds.), *Attachment in the preschool years*. Chicago: University of Chicago Press.

Alpass, F. M., & Neville, S. (2003). Loneliness, health and depression in older males. *Aging and Mental Health, 7,* 212–216.

Altman, I., & Taylor, D. A. (1973). *Social penetration: The development of interpersonal relationships*. New York: Holt, Rinehart & Winston.

Amichai-Hamburger, Y., Kingsbury, M., & Schneider, B. H. (2013). Friendship: An old concept with a new meaning?. *Computers in Human Behavior, 29,* 33–39.

Amodio, D. M., & Showers, C. J. (2005). "Similarity breeds liking" revisited: The moderating role of commitment. *Journal of Social and Personal Relationships, 22,* 817–836.

Aron A., Aron, E., & Allen, J. (1998). Motivations for unrequited love. *Personality and Social Psychology Bulletin, 21,* 787–796.

Back, M. D., Schmukle, S. C., & Egloff, B. (2008). Becoming friends by chance. *Psychological Science, 19,* 439–440.

Bartholomew, K., & Horowitz, L. M. (1991). Attachment styles among young adults: A test of a four category model. *Journal of Personality and Social Psychology, 61,* 226–244.

Bartoli, A. M., & Clark, M. (2006). The dating game: similarities and differences in dating scripts among college students. *Sexuality & Culture, 10,* 54–80.

Baumeister, R. F., & Bratslavsky, E. (1999). Passion, intimacy, and time: Passionate love as a function of change of intimacy over time. *Personality and Social Psychology Review, 3,* 49–67.

Baumeister, R., & Tice, D. (1990). Anxiety and social exclusion. *Journal of Social and Clinical Psychology, 9,* 165–195.

Baumeister, R., Wotman, S., & Stillwell, A. M. (1993). Unrequited love: On heartbreak, anger, guilt, scriptlessness and humiliation. *Journal of Personality and Social Psychology, 64,* 377–394.

Ben Hamida, S., Mineka, S., & Bailey, J. M. (1998). Sex differences in perceived controllability of mate value: An evolutionary perspective. *Journal of Personality and Social Psychology, 75,* 963–966.

Berndt, T. J. (1992). Friendship and friends' influence in adolescence. *Current Directions in Psychological Sciences, 1,* 156–159.

Berreby, D. (1998, June 9). Studies explore love and the sweaty t-shirt. *The New York Times,* B14.

Berry, D. (1991). Attractive faces are not all created equal: Joint effects of facial babyishness and attractiveness on social perception. *Personality and Social Psychology Bulletin, 17,* 523–528.

Berscheid, E. (1985). Compatibility, interdependence, and emotion. In W. Ickes (Ed.), *Compatible and incompatible relationships*. New York: Springer-Verlag.

Berscheid, E. (1988). Some comments on the anatomy of love: Or what ever happened to old fashioned lust? In R. J. Steinberg & M. L. Barnes (Eds.), *The psychology of love* (pp. 359– 374). New Haven, CT: Yale University Press.

Berscheid, E., Snyder, M., & Omoto, A. M. (1989). The relationship closeness inventory: Assessing the closeness of interpersonal relationships. *Journal of Personality and Social Psychology 57,* 792–807.

Biernat, M., & Wortman, C. (1991). Sharing of home responsibilities between professionally employed women and their husbands. *Journal of Personality and Social Psychology, 60,* 844–860.

Bornstein, R. F. (1989). Exposure and affect: Overview and meta-analysis of research, 1968–1987. *Psychological Bulletin, 106,* 265–289.

Brehm, S. (1985). *Intimate relations*. New York: Random House.

Brehm, S. (1988). Passionate love. In R. J. Steinberg & M. L. Barnes (Eds.), *The psychology of love* (pp. 232–263). New Haven, CT: Yale University Press.

Brumbaugh, C. C., & Fraley, R. C. (2006). Transference and attachment: How do attachment patterns get carried forward from one relationship to the next? *Personality and Social Psychology Bulletin, 32,* 552–560.

Burnett, A. (1972). *Gertrude Stein.* New York: Atheneum.

Burrows, K. (2013). Age preferences in dating advertisements by homosexuals and heterosexuals: From sociobiological to sociological explanations. *Archives of Sexual Behavior, 42,* 203–211.

Busby, D. M., & Holman, T. B. (2009). Perceived match or mismatch on the Gottman conflict styles: Associations with relationship outcome variables. *Family Process, 48,* 531–545.

Buss, D. M. (1988a). Love acts: The evolutionary biology of love. In R. J. Steinberg & M. L. Barnes (Eds.), *The psychology of love* (pp. 100–118). New Haven, CT: Yale University Press.

Buss, D. M. (1988b). From vigilance to violence: Tactics of mate retention in American undergraduates. *Ethology and Sociobiology, 9,* 291–317.

Buss, D. M. (1994). *The evolution of desire: Strategies of human mating.* New York: Basic Books.

Byrne, D., Clore, G. L., & Smeaton, G. (1986). The attraction hypothesis: Do similar attitudes affect anything? *Journal of Personality and Social Psychology, 51,* 1167–1170.

Byrne, D., Ervin, C. R., & Lamberth, J. (2004). Continuity between the experimental study of attraction and real-life computer dating. In H. T. Reis & C. E. Rusbult (Eds.), *Close relationships: Key readings* (pp. 81–88). Philadelphia, PA: Taylor & Francis.

Byrne, D., & Nelson, D. (1965). Attraction as a linear function of proportion of positive reinforcements. *Journal of Personality and Social Psychology, 1,* 659–663.

Cacioppo, J. T., Hawkley, L. C., Berntson, G. G., Ernst, J. M., Gibbs, A. C., Stickgold, R., & Hobson, J. A. (2002). Do lonely days invade the night? Potential social modulation of sleep efficiency. *Psychological Science, 13,* 384–387.

Cardenas, R. A., & Harris, L. J. (2006). Symmetrical decorations enhance the attractiveness of faces and abstract designs. *Evolution and Human Behavior, 27,* 1–18.

Carli, L. L., Ganley, R., & Pierce-Otay, A. (1991). Similarity and satisfaction in roommate relationships. *Personality and Social Psychology Bulletin, 17,* 419–427.

Carrère, S., & Gottman, J. M. (1999). Predicting divorce among newlyweds from the first three minutes of a marital conflict discussion. *Family Process, 38,* 293–301.

Chak, K., & Leung, L. (2004). Shyness and locus of control as predictors of Internet addiction and Internet use. *CyberPsychology and Behavior, 7,* 559–570.

Chan, D., K-S., & Cheng, G. H-L. (2004). A comparison of offline and online friendship qualities at different stages of relationship development. *Journal of Social and Personal Relationships, 21,* 305–320.

Chen, J., Rapee, R. M., & Abbott, M. (2013). Mediators of the relationship between social anxiety and post-event rumination, *Journal of Anxiety Disorders, 27,* 1–8.

Christensen, P. N., & Kashy, D. (1998). Perceptions of and by lonely people in initial social interaction. *Personality and Social Psychology Bulletin, 24,* 322–329.

Clark, M. S. (1986). Evidence for the effectiveness of manipulations of desire for communal versus exchange relationships. *Personality and Social Psychology Bulletin, 12,* 414–425.

Clark, M. S., & Grote, N. K. (1998). Why aren't indices of relationship costs always negatively related to indices of relationship quality? *Personality and Social Psychology Review, 2,* 2–17.

Collins, N. L., Ford, M. B., Guichard, A., & Allard, L. M. (2006). Working models of attachment and attribution processes in intimate relationships. *Personality and Social Psychology Bulletin, 32,* 201–219.

Conger, R. D., Rueter, M. A., & Elder, G. H., Jr. (1999). Couple resilience to economic pressure. *Journal of Personality and Social Psychology, 76,* 54–71.

Crandall, C. S. (1991). Do heavyweight students have more difficulty paying for college? *Personality and Social Psychology Bulletin, 17,* 606–611.

Crohan, S. E. (1992). Marital happiness and spousal consensus on beliefs about marital conflict: A longitudinal investigation. *Journal of Social and Personal Relationships, 9,* 89–102.

De La Ronde, C., & Swann, W. B., Jr. (1998). Partner verification: Restoring the shattered images of our intimates. *Journal of Personality and Social Psychology, 75,* 374–382.

de Munck, V. C., Korotayev, A., de Munck, J., & Kaltourina, D. (2011). Cross-cultural analysis of models of romantic love among U.S. residents, Russians, and Lithuanians. *Cross-Cultural Research, 45,* 128–154.

DeJong, M. (1980). The stigma of obesity: The consequence of naive assumptions concerning the causes of physical deviance. *Journal of Health and Social Behavior, 21,* 75–87.

Diamond, L. M. (2004). Emerging perspectives on distinctions between romantic love and sexual desire. *Current Directions in Psychological Science, 13,* 116–119.

Diamond, L. M. (2003). What does sexual orientation orient? A biobehavioral model distinguishing romantic love and sexual desire. *Psychological Review, 110,* 173–192.

Dijkstra, P., & Buunk, B. (1998). Jealousy as a function of rival characteristics: An evolutionary perspective. *Personality and Social Psychology Bulletin, 42,* 1158–1166.

Ding, V. J., & Stillman, J. A. (2005). An empirical investigation of discrimination against overweight female job applicants in New Zealand. *New Zealand Journal of Psychology, 39,* 139–148.

Dion, K., Berscheid, E., & Walster, E. (1972). What is beautiful is good. *Journal of Personality and Social Psychology, 24,* 285–290.

DiTommaso, E., Brannen, C., & Burgess, M. (2005). The universality of relationship characteristics: A cross-cultural comparison of different types of attachment and loneliness in Canadian and visiting Chinese students. *Social Behavior and Personality, 33,* 57–68.

Drigotas, S. M., Rusbult, C. E., Wieselquist, J., & Whitton, S. (1999). Close partner as sculptor of the ideal self: Behavioral affirmation and the Michelangelo phenomenon. *Journal of Personality and Social Psychology, 77,* 293–324.

Duck, S. W. (1983). *Friends for life.* New York: St. Martin's Press.

Duck, S. W. (1988). *Handbook of personal relationships.* New York: Wiley.

Dundon, C. M., & Rellini, A. H. (2012). Emotional states of love moderate the association between catecholamines and female sexual responses in the laboratory. *Journal of Sexual Medicine, 9,* 2617–2630.

Eagly, A. H., Ashmore, R. D., Makhijani, M. G., & Longo, L. C. (1991). What is beautiful is good, but … : A metaanalytic review of research on the physical attractiveness stereotype. *Psychological Bulletin, 110,* 109–128.

Easterling, B., Knox, D., & Brackett, A. (2012). Secrets in romantic relationships: Does sexual orientation matter? *Journal of GLBT Family Studies, 8,* 196–208.

Eastwick, P. W., Luchies, L. B., Finkel, E. J., & Hunt, L. L. (2014). The predictive validity of ideal partner preferences: A review and meta-analysis. *Psychological Bulletin, 140,* 623–665.

Edwards, S. L., Rapee, R. M., & Franklin, J. (2003). Postevent rumination and recall bias for a social performance event in high and low socially anxious individuals. *Cognitive Therapy and Research, 27,* 603–617.

Enzo, E., Politi, P., Bianchi, M., Minoretti, P., Bertona, M., & Geroldi, D. (2006). Raised plasma nerve growth factors associated with early stage romantic love. *Psychoneuroendocrinology, 31,* 288–294.

Fehr, B. (2004). Intimacy expectations in same-sex friendships: A prototype interaction-pattern model. *Journal of Personality and Social Psychology, 86,* 265–284.

Festinger, L., Schachter, S., & Back, K. W. (1959). *Social pressures in informal groups: A study of human factors in housing.* New York: Harper & Row.

Fiebert, M. S., & Wright, K. S. (1989). Midlife friendships in an American faculty sample. *Psychological Reports, 64,* 1127–1130.

Fincham, F. D., Beach, S. R. H., & Davila, J. (2004). Forgiveness and conflict resolution in marriage. *Journal of Family Psychology, 18,* 72–81.

Fincham, F. D., Jackson, H., & Beach, S. R. H. (2005). Transgression severity and forgiveness: Different moderators for objective and subjective severity. *Journal of Social and Clinical Psychology, 24,* 860–875.

Fincham, F. D., Paleari, F. G., & Regalia, C. (2002). Forgiveness in marriage: The role of relationship quality, attributions, and empathy. *Personal Relationships, 9,* 27–37.

Fraley, R. C., & Shaver, P. R. (1998). Airport separations: A naturalistic study of adult attachment dynamics in separating couples. *Journal of Personality and Social Psychology, 75,* 1198–1212.

Furnham, A., & Baguma, P. (2004). Cultural differences in the evaluation of male and female body shapes. *International Journal of Eating Disorders, 15,* 81–89.

Gangestad, S. W., & Thornhill, R. (1997). Human sexual selection and developmental instability. In J. A. Simpson & D. T. Kenrick (Eds.), *Evolutionary social psychology* (pp. 169– 195). Mahwah, NJ: Erlbaum.

Gangestad, S. W., & Thornhill R. (1998, May 22). Menstrual cycle variation in women's preferences for the scent of symmetrical men. *Proceedings of the Royal Society of London, 265,* 927.

Garcia, S., Stinson, L., Ickes, W., Bissonette, W. & Briggs, S. R. (1991). Shyness and physical attractiveness in mixed-sex dyads. *Journal of Personality and Social Psychology, 61,* 35–49.

Gilbert, G., Clark, M., & Anderson, M. (2012). Do deaf individuals' dating scripts follow the traditional sexual script? *Sexuality & Culture, 16,* 90–99.

Glomb, T. M., & Welch, E. T. (2005). Can opposites attract? Personality heterogeneity in supervisor-subordinate dyads as a predictor of subordinate outcomes. *Journal of Applied Psychology, 90,* 749–757.

Goldberg, A. E. (2010). *Lesbian and gay parents and their children: Research on the family life cycle.* Washington, D.C.: American Psychological Association.

Gordon, K. C., Baucom, D. H., & Snyder, D. K. (2005). Treating couples recovering from infidelity: An integrative approach. *Journal of Clinical Psychology, 61,* 1393–1405.

Gottman, J. M. (1995). *Why marriages fail or succeed.* New York: Fireside.

Gottman, J. M., Coan, J., Carrère, S., & Swanson, C. (1998). Predicting marital happiness and stability from newlywed interactions. *Journal of Marriage and the Family, 60,* 5–22.

Gottman, J. M., & Levenson, R. W. (1986). Assessing the role of emotion in marriage. *Behavioral Assessment, 8,* 31–48.

Gottman, J. M., & Levenson, R. W. (2002). A two-factor model for predicting when a couple will divorce: Exploratory analyses using 14-year longitudinal data. *Family Process, 41,* 83.

Grant, S., & Mizzi, T. (2014). Body weight bias in hiring decisions: Identifying explanatory mechanisms. *Social Behavior and Personality, 42,* 353–370.

Gunderson, P. R., & Ferrari, J. R. (2008). Forgiveness of sexual cheating in romantic relationships: Effects of discovery method, frequency of offense, and presence of apology. *North American Journal of Psychology, 10,* 1–14.

Häfner, M., & IJzerman, H. (2011). The face of love: Spontaneous accommodation as social emotion regulation. *Personality and Social Psychology Bulletin, 37,* 1551–1563.

Harris, C. R., & Christenfeld, N. (1996). Gender, jealousy, and reason. *Psychological Science, 7,* 364–366.

Harris, M. B. (1990). Is love seen as different for the obese? *Journal of Applied Social Psychology, 20,* 1209–1224.

Hatfield, E., Traupmann, J., Sprecher, S., Utne, M., & Hay, J. (1985). Equity and intimate relationships: Recent research. In W. Ickes (Ed.), *Compatible and incompatible relationships* (pp. 91–117). New York: Springer-Verlag.

Hatfield, E. (Walster), Aronson, V., Abrahams, D., & Rottman, L. (1966). Importance of physical attractiveness in dating behavior. *Journal of Personality and Social Psychology, 4,* 508–516.

Hatfield, E. H, Walster, G. W., & Berscheid, E. (1978). *Equity theory and research.* Boston: Allyn & Bacon.

Hatfield, E. H., Walster, G. W., & Traupmann, J. (1978). Equity and premarital sex. *Journal of Personality and Social Psychology, 36,* 82–92.

Hatfield, E., & Walster, G. W. (1981). *A new look at love.* Reading, MA: Addison-Wesley.

Hawkley, L. C., Burleson, M. H., Berntson, G. G., & Cacioppo, J. T. (2003). Loneliness in everyday life: Cardiovascular activity, psychosocial context, and health behaviors. *Journal of Personality and Social Psychology, 85,* 105–120.

Hays, R. B. (1985). A longitudinal study of friendship development. *Journal of Personality and Social Psychology 48,* 261–273.

Hays, R. B. (1988b). The day-to-day functioning of casual versus close friendships. *Journal of Social and Personal Relationships, 5,* 261–273.

Hebl, M. R., & Turchin, J. M. (2005). The stigma of obesity: What about men? *Basic and Applied Social Psychology, 27,* 267–275.

Hebl, M. R., & Xu, J. (2001). Weighing the care: Physicians' reaction to the size of a patient. *International Journal of Obesity, 25,* 1246–1252.

Hendrick, C. (1988). Roles and gender in relationships. In S. Duck (Ed.), *Handbook of personal relationships* (pp. 429–448). New York: Wiley.

Hendrick, S. S., & Hendrick, C. (1987). Love and sex attitudes: A close relationship. In W. H. Jones & D. Perlman (Eds.), *Advances in personal relationships* (Vol. 1). Greenwich, CT: JAI Press.

Herbozo, S., Tantleff-Dunn, S., Gokee-Larose, J., & Thompson, J. K. (2004). Beauty and thinness messages in children's media: A content analysis. *Eating Disorders, 12,* 21–34.

Hill, C. A. (1987). Affiliation motivation: People who need people … but in different ways. *Journal of Personality and Social Psychology, 52,* 1008– 1018.Hill, C. T., Rubin, Z., & Peplau, L. A. (1976). Breakups before marriage: The end of 103 affairs. *Journal of Social Issues, 32,* 147–168.

Hirsch, C., Meynen, T., & Clark, D. M. (2004). Negative self-imagery in social anxiety contaminates social interactions. *Memory, 12,* 496–506.

Hobman, E. V., Bordia, P., & Gallois, C. (2004). Perceived dissimilarity and work group involvement: The moderating effects of group openness to diversity. *Group & Organization Management, 29,* 560–587.

Huppert, J. D., Foa, E. B., Furr, J. M., Filip, J. C., & Matthews, A. (2003). Interpretation bias in social anxiety: A dimensional perspective. *Cognitive Therapy and Research, 27,* 569–577.

Huston, T. L., & Vangelisti, A. L. (1991). Socioemotional behavior and satisfaction in marital relationships: A longitudinal study. *Journal of Personality and Social Psychology, 61,* 721–733.

Ilmarinen, V., Lönnqvist, J., & Paunonen, S. (2016). Similarity-attraction effects in friendship formation: Honest platoon-mates prefer each other but dishonest do not. *Personality & Individual Differences, 92,* 153–158.

Jackson, T., Fritch, A., Nagasaka, T., & Gunderson, J. (2002). Toward explaining the relationship between shyness and loneliness: A path analysis with American college students. *Social Behavior and Personality, 30,* 263–270.

Jourard, S. M. (1971). *Self-disclosure: An experimental analysis of the transparent self.* New York: Wiley.

Kelley, H. H., Berscheid, E., Christensen, A., Harvey, J. H., Huston, T. L., Levinger, G., McClintock, E., Peplau, L. A., & Peterson, D. R. (1983). *Close relationships.* New York: Freeman.

Kenrick, D. T., Keefe, R. C., Bryan, A., Barr, A., & Brown, S. (1995). Age preferences and mate choice among homosexuals and heterosexuals: A case for modular psychological mechanisms. *Journal of Personality and Social Psychology, 69,* 1169–1172.

Klinkenberg, D., & Rose, S. (1994). Dating scripts of gay men and lesbians. *Journal of Homosexuality, 26,* 23–35.

Klohnen, E. C., & Mendelsohn, G. A. (1998). Partner selection for personality characteristics: A couple-centered approach. *Personality and Social Psychology Bulletin, 24,* 268–278.

Knee, C. R. (1998). Implicit theories of relationship: Assessment and prediction of romantic initiation, coping, and longevity. *Journal of Personality and Social Psychology, 74,* 360–370.

Knox, D., Daniels, V., Sturdivant, L., & Zusman, M. E. (2001). College student use of the Internet for mate selection. *College Student Journal, 35,* 158–161.

Kolata, G. (1992, November 24). After kinship and marriage, anthropology discovers love. *New York Times,* p. B9.

Köllner, M. G., & Schultheiss, O. C. (2014). Meta-analytic evidence of low convergence between implicit and explicit measures of the needs for achievement, affiliation, and power. *Frontiers in Psychology, 5* (Article 826), 1–20.

Kurdek, L. A. (2008). Change in relationship quality for partners from lesbian, gay male, and heterosexual couples. *Journal of Family Psychology, 22,* 701–711.

Langlois, J. H., Roggman, L. A., Casey, R. I., Riesner Danner, L. A., & Jenkins, V. Y. (1987). Infant preferences for attractive faces: Rudiments of a stereotype? *Developmental Psychology, 23,* 363–369.

Laurenceau, J. P., Barrett, L. F., & Pietromanaco, P. R. (1998). Intimacy as an interpersonal process: The importance of self-disclosure, partner disclosure, and perceived partner responsiveness in interpersonal exchanges. *Journal of Personality and Social Psychology, 74,* 1238–1251.

Leary, M. R. (1983a). Understanding social anxiety: *Social, personality, and clinical perspectives* (Vol. 153, Sage Library of Social Research). Beverly Hills, CA: Sage.

Leary, M. R. (1983b). Social anxiousness: The construct and its measurement. *Journal of Personality Assessment, 47,* 66–75.

Leary, M. R., & Kowalski, R. M. (1995). *Social anxiety.* New York: Guilford.

Leary, M. R., Springer, C., Negel, L., Ansell, E., and Evans, K. (1998). The causes, phenomenology, and consequences of hurt feelings. *Journal of Personality and Social Psychology, 74,* 1225–1237.

Lemiuex, R., & Hale, J. L. (2002). Cross-sectional analysis of intimacy, passion, and commitment: Testing the assumptions of the triangular theory of love. *Psychological Reports, 90,* 1009–1014.

Levenson, R. W., & Gottman, J. M. (1983). Marital interaction: Physiological linkage and affective exchange. *Journal of Personality and Social Psychology, 45,* 587–597.

Levinger, C., & Snoek, J. D. (1972). *Attraction in relationships: A new look at interpersonal attraction.* Morristown, NJ: General Learning Press.

Levinger, G. (1988). Can we picture "love"? In R. J. Sternberg & M. L. Barnes (Eds.), *The psychology of love* (pp. 139–158). New Haven, CT: Yale University Press.

Lundh, L.-G., & Sperling, M. (2002). Social anxiety and the post-event processing of distressing social events. *Cognitive Behaviour Therapy, 31,* 129–134.

Luo, Y., Hawkley, L. C., Waite, L., & Cacioppo, J. T. (2012). Loneliness, health, and mortality in old age: A national longitudinal study. *Social Science & Medicine, 74,* 907–914.

Madey, S. F., & Rodgers, L. (2009). The effect of attachment and Sternberg's triangular theory of love on relationship satisfaction. *Individual Differences Research, 7,* 76–84.

Manalastas, E. J. (2011). Unrequired love among young Filipino gay men: Subjective experiences of unreciprocated lovers. *Social Science Diliman, 7,* 63–81.

McAdams, D. P. (1982). Intimacy motivation. In A. J. Stewart (Ed.), *Motivation and society.* San Francisco: Jossey-Bass.

McAdams, D. P. (1989). *Intimacy.* New York: Doubleday.

McArthur, L. Z. (1982). Judging a book by its cover: A cognitive analysis of the relationship between physical appearance and stereotyping. In A. Hastorf & A. Isen (Eds.), *Cognitive social psychology* (pp. 149–211). New York: Elsevier/ North Holland.

McCarty, M. K., & Kelly, J. R. (2015). Perceptions of dating behavior: The role of ambivalent sexism. *Sex Roles, 72,* 237–251.

McCown, J. A., Fischer, D., Page, R., & Homant, M. (2001). Internet relationships: People who meet people. *CyberPsychology and Behavior, 4,* 593–596.

McCullough, M. E., Exline, J. J., & Baumeister, R. F. (1998). An annotated bibliography of research on forgiveness and related concepts. In E. L. Worthington (Ed.), Dimensions of forgiveness: *Psychological research and theological perspectives* (pp. 193–317). Philadelphia: Templeton Press.

McCullough, M. E., Worthington, E. L., Jr., and Rachal, K. C. (1997). Interpersonal forgiving in close relationships. *Journal of Personality and Social Psychology, 73,* 321–336.

McGregor, I., & Holmes, I. G. (1999). How storytelling shapes memory and impressions of relationships over time. *Journal of Personality and Social Psychology, 76,* 406–419.

McKenna, K., Green, A., & Gleason, M. (2002). Relationship formation on the Internet: What's the big attraction? *Journal of Social Issues, 58,* 9–31.

Mealey, L., Bridstock, R., & Townsend, G. C. (1999). Symmetry and perceived facial attractiveness: A monozygotic twin comparison. *Journal of Personality and Social Psychology, 76,* 151–158.

Milkulincer, M. (1998). Attachment working models and the sense of trust: An exploration of interaction goals and affect regulation. *Journal of Personality and Social Psychology, 74,* 1209–1224.

Miller, G. (2000). Evolution of human music through sexual selection. In N. L. Wallin, B. Merker, & S. Brown (Eds.), *The origins of music* (pp. 329–360). Cambridge, MA: MIT Press.

Monetoliva, A., & Garcia-Martinez, J. M. A. (2005). Adult attachment style and its effect on the quality of romantic relationships in Spanish students. *Journal of Social Psychology, 145,* 745–747.

Monsour, M., Harris, B., Kurzweil, N., & Beard, C. (1994). Challenges confronting cross-sex friendships: 'Much ado about nothing?'. *Sex Roles, 31,* 55–77.

Montgomery, B. M. (1988). Quality communication in personal relationships. In S. Duck, D. F. Hay, S. E. Hobfoll, W. Ickes, B. M. Montgomery (Eds.), *Handbook of personal relationships: Theory, research and interventions* (pp. 343– 359). New York: Wiley.

Montoya, R. (2008). I'm hot, so I'd say you're not: The influence of objective physical attractiveness on mate selection. *Personality and Social Psychology Bulletin, 34,* 1315–1331.

Montoya, R. M., Horton, R. S., & Kirchner, J. (2008). Is actual similarity necessary for attraction? A meta-analysis of actual and perceived similarity. *Journal of Social and Personal Relationships, 25,* 889–922.

Moody, E. J. (2001). Internet use and its relationship to loneliness. *CyberPsychology and Behavior, 4,* 393–401.

Nichols, K. A. (1974). Severe social anxiety. *British Journal of Medical Psychology, 74,* 301–306.

Noor, F., & Evans, D. C. (2003). The effect of facial symmetry on perceptions of personality and attractiveness. Journal of Research in Personality, *37,* 339–347.

Notarius, C., & Markman, H. (1993). *We can work it out: Making sense out of marital conflict.* New York: Putnam.

O'Meara, D. J. (1989). Cross-sex friendship: Four basic challenges of an ignored relationship. *Sex Roles, 21,* 525–543.

O'Meara, D. J. (2006). Cross-sex friendships: Who has more? *Sex Roles, 54,* 809–820.

Oliker, S. J. (1989). *Best friends and marriage: Exchange among women.* Berkeley: University of California Press.

Over, R., & Phillips, G. (1997). Differences between men and women in age preferences for a same-sex partner. *Behavioral and Brain Sciences, 20,* 138–140.

Paul, A. (2014). Is online better than offline for meeting partners? Depends: Are you looking to marry or to date? *Cyberpsychology, Behavior & Social Networking, 17,* 664–667.

Peplau, L. A., & Perlman, D. (1982). Perspectives on loneliness. In L. A. Peplau & D. Perlman (Eds.), *Loneliness: A source-book of current theory research, and therapy* (pp. 1–18). New York: Wiley.

Perrett, D. L., & Penton-Voak, I. (1999, February 25). Reply. *Nature, 397,* 661.

Prager, K., Fuller, D. O., & Gonzalez, A. S. (1989). The function of self-disclosure in social interaction. *Journal of Social and Personal Relationships, 4,* 563–588.

Rawlins, W. K. (1992). *Friendship matters: Communication, dialectics, and life course.* New York: Aldine De Gruyter.

Regan, P. C., Durvasula, R., Howell, L., Ureno, O., & Rea, M. (2004). Gender, ethnicity, and the timing of first sexual and romantic experiences. *Social Behavior and Personality, 32,* 667–676.

Regan, P. C., Kocan, E. R., & Whitlock, T. (1998). Ain't love grand: A prototype analysis of the concept of romantic love. *Journal of Social and Personal Relationships, 15,* 411–420.

Reagan, P. C., Lakhanpal, S., & Anguiano, C. (2012). Relationship outcomes in Indian-American love-based and arranged marriages. *Psychological Reports, 110,* 915–924.

Reynolds, S., Searight, H. R., & Ratwik, S. (2014). Adult attachment style and rumination in the context of intimate relationships. *North American Journal of Psychology, 16,* 495–506.

Roisman, G. I., Clausell, E., Holland, A., Fortuna, K., & Elieff, C. (2007). Adult romantic relationships as contexts of human development: A multimethod comparison of same-sex couples with opposite-sex dating, engaged, and married dyads. *Developmental Psychology, 44,* 91–101.

Rokach, A., & Neto, F. (2005). Age, culture and the antecedents of loneliness. *Social Behavior and Personality, 33,* 477–494.

Rose, S., & Frieze, I. H. (1989). Young singles' scripts for a first date. *Gender & Society, 3,* 258–268.

Rose, S., & Frieze, I. H. (1993). Young singles' contemporary dating scripts. *Sex Roles, 28,* 499–509.

Rosenbaum, M. E. (1986). The repulsion hypothesis: On the nondevelopment of relationships. *Journal of Personality and Social Psychology, 51,* 1156–1166.

Rosenfeld, M. J. (2010). Meeting online: The rise of the Internet as a social intermediary. Retrieved from *http://paa2010.princeton.edu/papers/100828*

Rosenfeld, M. J., & Thomas, R. J. (2012). Searching for a mate: The rise of the Internet as a social intermediary. *American Sociological Review, 77,* 523–547.

Rubin, Z. (1970). Measurement and romantic love. *Journal of Personality and Social Psychology, 16,* 265–273.

Rubin, Z. (1973). *Liking and loving: An invitation to social psychology.* New York: Holt, Rinehart & Winston.

Rusbult, C. E., Kumashiro, M., Kubacka, K. E., & Finkel, E. J. (2009). "The part of me that you bring out": Ideal similarity and the Michelangelo phenomenon. *Journal of Personality and Social Psychology, 96,* 61–82.

Rusbult, C. E., Verette, J., Whitney, G. A., Slovik, L. F., & Lipkus, I. (1991). Accommodation processes in close relationships: Theory and preliminary empirical evidence. *Journal of Personality and Social Psychology 61,* 641–647.

Ruvolo, A. P., & Rotondo, J. L. (1998). Diamonds in the rough: Implicit personality theories and views of partner and self. *Personality and Social Psychology Bulletin, 24,* 750–758.

Ryckman, R. M., Robbins, M. A., Thornton, B., Kaaczor, L. M., Gayton, S. L., & Anderson, C. V. (1991). Public self-consciousness and physique stereotyping. *Personality and Social Psychology Bulletin, 18,* 400–405.

Schiffenbauer, A., & Schavio, S. R. (1976). Physical distance and attraction: An intensification effect. *Journal of Experimental Social Psychology 12,* 274–282.

Schoen, R., & Wooldredge, J. (1989). Marriage choices in North Carolina and Virginia, 1969–71 and 1979–81. *Journal of Marriage and the Family 51,* 465–481.

Seepersad, S., Mi-Kyung, C., & Nana, S. (2008). How does culture influence the degree of romantic loneliness and closeness. *Journal of Psychology, 142,* 209–220.

Segal, M. W. (1974). Alphabet and attraction: An unobtrusive measure of the effect of propinquity in a field setting. *Journal of Personality and Social Psychology, 30,* 654–657.

Segrin, C., Burke, T., & Dunivan, M. (2012). Loneliness and poor health within families. *Journal of Social and Personal Relationships, 29,* 597–611.

Segrin, C., Powell, H., Givertz, M., & Brackin, A. (2003). Symptoms of depression, relational quality, and loneliness in dating relationships. *Personal Relationships, 10,* 25–36.

Senchak, M., & Leonard, K. (1992). Attachment styles and marital adjustment among newlywed couples. *Journal of Social and Personal Relationships, 9,* 221–238.

Shackelford, T. P., Buss, D. M., & Bennett, K. (2002). Forgiveness or breakup: Sex differences in responses to a partner's infidelity. *Cognition and Emotion, 16,* 299–307.

Shackelford, T. P., Schmitt, D. P., & Buss, D. M. (2005). Universal dimensions of human mate preferences. *Personality and Individual Differences, 39,* 447–458.

Shafer, R. B., & Keith, P. M. (2001). Matching by weight in married couples: A life cycle perspective. *Journal of Social Psychology, 130,* 657–664.

Shaver, P., Hazan, C., & Bradshaw, D. (1988). Love as attachment: The integration of three behavioral systems. In R. Sternberg & M. Barnes (Eds.), *The psychology of love* (pp. 68–99). New Haven, CT: Yale University Press.

Shechory, M., & Ziv, R. (2007). Relationships between gender role attitudes, role division, and perception of equity among heterosexual, gay and lesbian couples. *Sex Roles, 56,* 629–638.

Sheldon, P., Gilchrist-Petty, E., & Lessley, J. A. (2014). You did what? The relationship between forgiveness tendency, communication of forgiveness, and relationship satisfaction in married and dating couples. *Communication Reports, 27,* 78–90.

Simon, L. (1977). *The biography of Alice B. Toklas.* Garden City, NY: Doubleday.

Simpson, J. A., Gangestad, S. W., Christensen, P. N., & Leck, K. (1999). Fluctuating symmetry, sociosexuality, and intrasexual competition. *Journal of Personality and Social Psychology, 76,* 159–172.

Simpson, J. A., Ickes, W., & Grich, J. (1999). When accuracy hurts: Reactions of anxious-ambivalent dating partners to a relationship-determining situation. *Journal of Personality and Social Psychology, 76,* 754–769.

Sinclair, H. C., & Frieze, I. H. (2005). When courtship persistence becomes intrusive pursuit: Comparing rejecter and pursuer perspectives of unrequited attraction. *Sex Roles, 52,* 839–852.

Smeaton, G., Byrne, D., & Murnen, S. K. (1989). The repulsion hypothesis revisited: Similarity irrelevance or dissimilarity bias. *Journal of Personality and Social Psychology, 56,* 4–59.

Sorkin, D., Rook, K. S., & Lu, J. L. (2002). Loneliness, lack of emotional support, lack of companionship, and likelihood of having a heart condition in an elderly sample. *Annals of Behavior Medicine, 24,* 290–298.

Sprecher, S. (1999). "I love you more today than yesterday": Romantic partners' perceptions of changes in love and related affect over time. *Journal of Personality and Social Psychology, 76,* 46–53.

Steil, J. M., & Weltman, K. (1991). Marital inequality: The importance of resources, personal attributes, and social norms on career valuing and the allocation of domestic responsibilities. *Sex Roles, 24,* 161–179.

Steil, J. M., & Weltman, K. (1992). Influence strategies at home and at work: A study of sixty dual-career couples. *Journal of Social and Personal Relationships, 9,* 65–88.

Sternberg, R. J. (1986). A triangular theory of love. *Psychological Review, 93,* 119–135.

Sternberg, R. J. (1988). Triangulating love. In R. J. Sternberg & M. L. Barnes (Eds.), *The psychology of love* (pp. 119–138). New Haven, CT: Yale University Press.

Sternberg, R. J., & Gracek, S. (1984). The nature of love. *Journal of Personality and Social Psychology, 47,* 312–329.

Swann, W. B., Jr. (1996). *Self-traps: The elusive quest for higher self-esteem.* New York: Freeman.

Switzer, R., & Taylor, R. B. (1983). Sociability versus privacy of residential choice: Impacts of personality and local social ties. *Basic and Applied Social Psychology, 4,* 123–136.

Teachman, B. A., & Brownell, K. D. (2001). Implicit anti-fat bias among health professionals: Is anyone immune? *International Journal of Obesity, 25,* 1525–1531.

Tennov, D. (1979). *Love and limerence: The experience of being in love.* New York: Stein & Day.

Thibaut, J. W., & Kelley, H. H. (1959). *The social psychology of groups.* New York: Wiley.

Thompson, B., & Borrello, C. M. (1992). Different views of love: Deductive and inductive lines of inquiry. *Psychological Science, 1,* 154–155.

Thornhill, R., & Gangestad, S. W. (1994). Human fluctuating asymmetry and sexual behavior. *Psychological Science, 5,* 297–302.

Tian, Q. (2013). Social anxiety, motivation, self-disclosure, and computer-mediated friendship: A path analysis of the social interaction in the blogosphere. *Communication Research, 40,* 237–260.

Toklas, A. B. (1963). *What is remembered.* New York: Holt, Rinehart & Winston.

Tornstam, L. (1992). Loneliness in marriage. *Journal of Social and Personal Relationships, 9,* 197–217.

Triandis, H. C. (1994). *Culture and social behavior.* New York: McGraw-Hill.

Trivers, R. (1972). *Social evolution.* Meno Park, CA: Benjamin/Cummings.

Turnbull, J., Heaslip, S., & McLeod, H. A. (2000). Preschool children's attitudes to fat and normal male and female stimulus figures. *International Journal of Obesity, 24,* 705–706.

Valkenburg, P. M., & Peter, J. (2007). Preadolescents' and adolescents' online communication and their closeness to friends. *Developmental Psychology, 43,* 267–277.

Waller, T., Lampman, C., & Lupfer-Johnson, G. (2012). Assessing bias against overweight individuals among nursing and psychology students: An implicit association test. *Journal of Clinical Nursing, 21,* 3504–3512.

Wang, S. S., Brownell, K. D., & Wadden, T. A. (2004). The influence of the stigma of obesity on overweight individuals. *International Journal of Obesity, 28,* 1333–1337.

Watson, P. W., & Thornhill, P. (1994). Fluctuating asymmetry and sexual selection. *Trends in Ecology and Evolution, 9,* 21–25.

Wegner, D. M., Lane, J. D., & Dimitri, S. (1994). The allure of secret relationships. *Journal of Personality and Social Psychology, 66,* 287–300.

Weiss, R. (1973). *Loneliness: The experience of emotional and social isolation.* Cambridge, MA: The MIT Press.

Wheeler, L., Reis, H., & Nezlek, J. (1983). Loneliness, social interaction, and sex roles. *Journal of Personality and Social Psychology, 45,* 943–953.

Wong, M. Mei-ha, & Csikzentmihalyi, M. (1991). Affiliation motivation and daily experience. *Journal of Personality and Social Psychology, 60,* 154–164.

Wright, P. H. (1982). Men's friendships, women's friendships and the alleged inferiority of the latter. *Sex Roles, 8,* 1–21.

Zarbatany, L., Conley, R., & Pepper, S. (2004). Personality and gender differences in friendship needs and experiences in preadolescence and young adulthood. *International Journal of Behavioral Development, 28,* 299–310.

Zebrowitz, L.A., Collins, M. A., & Dutta, R. (1998). The relationship between appearance and personality across life-span. *Personality and Social Psychology Bulletin, 24,* 736–749.

Zebrowitz, L. A., & Lee, S. Y. (1999). Appearance, stereotype-incongruent behavior, and social relationships. *Personality and Social Psychology, 25,* 569–584.

Zebrowitz, L. A., Olson, K., & Hoffman, K. (1993). Stability of babyfaceness and attractiveness across the lifespan. *Journal of Personality and Social Psychology, 64,* 453–466.

Zuckerman, M., Miyake, K., & Hodgins, H. S. (1991). Cross-channel effects of vocal and physical attractiveness and their implications for interpersonal perception. *Journal of Personality and Social Psychology, 60,* 545–554.

Post-Reading Activities

1   Assuming you agree with control theory as the cause of deviant behaviors, how would you prevent deviant behavior in society? In other words, what are the social implications of control theory?

2   Now, assume you agree with labeling theory. How would you prevent deviant behavior in society with labeling theory as your policy guide?

3   Select either control theory or labeling theory. How would you help a person cope with an overwhelming emotion of fear of victimization?

4   How would labeling theory assist policy makers in preventing hate crimes?

5   Think about a close relationship that you have. Using social psychology, why are you attracted to this person? Why do you love this person?

UNIT V

GROUP DYNAMICS

Introduction

As we move to the end of this anthology, we move our conversation to that of group behaviors. Crowd behaviors can be peaceful and aggressive. Crowd behaviors can influence individual behaviors. Individuals in crowds may do things out of their normal behavior (deindividuation) because of a crowd. Crowd behavior can incite contagion, where the individuals within the crowd begin to imitate the behaviors of other crowd members. Crowds can also lead to social movements and positive changes in a society. Larrick, Mannes, and Soll provide the first reading in the unit, which discusses the wisdom of crowds. When considering group behavior, one must also explain conformity. "The Psychological Explanation of Conformity" discerns information on conformity and why individuals conform to the crowds or groups or individual leaders.

The Social Psychology
of the Wisdom of Crowds

Richard P. Larrick, Albert E. Mannes, and Jack B. Soll

Picture yourself taking part in a classroom psychology experiment on perception. You and nine other subjects are being asked to judge the lengths of lines in a vision test. The experimenter holds up a large card that contains three lines of different lengths, marked A, B, and C, and a target line. The subjects are asked: Which of A, B, or C is the same length as the target? For each card, all subjects take turns reporting which line matches the target. The first few sets of cards are unremarkable. Everyone states what is clear to the eye. On the fifth trial, the obvious answer to you is B, but the first person says C (you find this mildly amusing). However, the second person also says C. The third says C, and then the fourth. Everyone says C. When it is your turn to answer, what do you say? Before hearing the response of others, you thought the answer was obviously B. But the unanimous opinion of others is C.

All students of social psychology recognize the famous Asch (1955) experiment, and most remember that three of four subjects at some point conform to a group answer that defies their own perceptions. Deutsch and Gerard (1955) introduced the term *normative social influence* to characterize the tendency for people to give public responses that allow them to fit in with others even when they privately disagree. However, Asch's classic study has come to symbolize more. In its own time—an era of totalitarian governments that repressed individualism and McCarthyite pressures in the United States that did likewise—Asch's study reinforced a suspicion of groups and a celebration of the lone, independent individual.

Early conformity research was criticized for leaving the widely held but misleading impression that people yield too much to the judgments of others, thereby harming themselves. Some authors (Allen, 1965; Campbell, 1961) suggested that this pessimistic conclusion is misleading because it was foreordained by the experimental design. In the Asch study, the other nine group members were only pretending to be subjects and had been planted to give consistently false answers before the true subject responded. Allen observed, "[M]ost psychological experiments in this area have been designed in such a manner that conformity was by necessity maladaptive: factually incorrect, detrimental to the group and the individual, or simply dishonest" (1965, p. 136).

In response, some authors stressed the adaptive value of conformity. Under uncertainty, people look to others for information (Deutsch & Gerard, 1955; Festinger, 1954), and groups are usually a valid source of information (Campbell, 1961). Allen observed that "a person may go along with beliefs expressed by most of the other people around him because he realizes that opinions shared by many are often more likely to be correct than the opinions held by a single individual. ... In some situations conformity is constructive and appropriate; in other situations it is not" (1965, pp. 136–137). (See Kameda & Tindale, 2006, and Krueger & Massey, 2009, for recent analyses of the adaptiveness of conformity.)

This chapter builds on the questions raised by classic social psychology experiments on conformity to examine the wisdom of relying on crowds. We review two general sets of questions. The normative questions ask what is rational or optimal: How accurate are the judgments of collectives? When individuals disagree with the judgments of others, should they change their judgment or hold firm to their initial opinion (Bell, Raiffa, & Tversky, 1988)? The descriptive questions ask what people actually do when they have access to the judgments of others: Do individuals understand why they should listen to others? Do they effectively decide when to listen to others (Bell, Raiffa, & Tversky, 1988)?

To address these questions, we build on a research tradition that differs markedly from the Asch tradition. The Asch situation was by nature misleading. In more mathematical terms, the answers from the false group members were unrepresentative of true answers. Brunswik (1955) famously argued that decision makers need to be presented with representative stimuli to assess how well they use information (Dami, Hertwig, & Hoffrage, 2004). To understand whether groups yield accurate answers and whether subjects are able to benefit from group accuracy, one needs to study processes in which representative judgments are elicited and shared with decision makers.

The remainder of the chapter is divided into two main sections. First, we describe recent research on the wisdom of crowds. This innovative literature combines decades of research in different fields showing the benefits of combining information across people. We analyze the conditions that make crowds effective to answer the normative questions of how and when crowds are wise. We then examine the descriptive question of how people use the judgments of others. We review a growing body of research showing that people are egocentric in their use of judgments: They rely too much on their own judgments and miss the opportunity to learn from others.

The Wisdom of Crowds

Some of the earliest studies in social psychology examined whether groups were fundamentally different from individuals. In the 1920s, researchers examined whether groups were smarter than individuals (see Larrick & Soll, 2006, for a historical review). In one early study students estimated the temperature in a classroom. When the estimates were averaged, the result was more accurate than the estimate of a typical group member. It should be noted that individual members of this "group" never interacted with one another. Where did the benefits come from? Early authors were surprised by this result and attributed it to some mysterious group property. As one writer put it, "In every coming together of minds ... [t]here is the Creative Plus, which no one mind by itself could achieve" (Overstreet, 1925, as cited in Watson, 1928). In time, researchers recognized that the power of groups came from something much simpler but still elegant: Combining judgments takes individual imperfection and smoothes the rough edges to isolate the collective's view of the truth. Or, to put it more mathematically and mundanely, averaging cancels error.

Subsequent research in the forecasting literature demonstrated that simple combination methods that weight people equally, such as averaging judgments, often perform as well as more sophisticated statistical methods of combination (Armstrong, 2001; Clemen, 1989). The power and simplicity of averaging was summed up in the title of James Surowiecki's 2004 best-selling book, *The Wisdom of Crowds*.

Consider a brief example that illustrates the power of averaging. Imagine two professors estimating the number of students who are likely to apply to a program in neuroscience. Their goal is to get as close to the truth as possible. Being too high or too low is equally bad (e.g., being 5 high or 5 low will be treated as a miss of 5). Professor L estimates 40. Professor H estimates 60. Their average guess is 50. If the truth turns out to be 47, the judges have missed by 7 and 13, respectively, and their average miss is 10. But the average of the judges' guesses, 50, missed the true value of 47 by only 3—a substantially smaller error than the average miss of 10. Why does this happen? The judgments of 40 and 60 "bracket" the truth: The high error and low error offset each other. It is bracketing that gives averaging its power (Larrick & Soll, 2006; Soll & Larrick, 2009).

Now suppose that the truth is 37. Both professors have overestimated (by 3 and 23, respectively), and the average performance of the professors has missed by (3 + 23)/2 = 13. The average guess of 50 also misses by 13. In cases like this—where both judges fall on the same side of the truth—averaging "locks in" the average individual error. This is the worst case scenario for averaging. With bracketing, averaging will be more accurate than the average individual error.

Of course, Professor L is more accurate than Professor H in both examples. Picking Professor L's lone judgment would have done well in the second scenario although fallen short of the average in the first scenario. It is tempting to declare Professor L smarter than the average. Research on groups frequently compares group performance to the performance of the "best member."

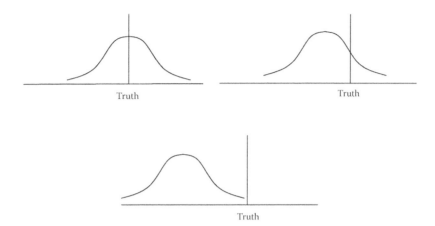

Figure 13.1   Three distributions of individual judgments in which judgments are evenly distributed around the truth (top left panel), bracket the truth (top right panel), or are biased below the
truth (bottom panel).

It is important to point out, however, that in judgments under uncertainty the best member
standard can be misleading when defined post hoc. Even when there is skill in judgment, there
is luck as well, and it takes a large sample to know whether one judge is truly more accurate than
another. The critical questions are whether (a) one judge is *reliably* better than another judge
by *a substantial margin* over time and (b) whether the difference in ability is *detectable* from
available cues in advance. In this example, could one know anything in advance about Professors
L and H (or their answers) that would lead one to heavily favor the judgment of one over the
other before knowing the outcome? Averaging is powerful, because, thanks to bracketing, it must
perform better than the average judge and can often perform much better. This performance
makes it superior to choosing individual judges when judges are roughly similar in ability or
when it is hard to distinguish their ability in advance.

The idea of bracketing generalizes to larger crowds.[1] To illustrate, the *Wall Street Journal*
surveys a panel of about 50 economists every six months to make macroeconomic forecasts
about inflation, unemployment, and so forth. The resulting diagram of forecasts often looks
like a reasonable approximation of a normal distribution (see three hypothetical examples in
Figure 13.1). When the truth is added to the plot six months later, it is often the case that the
crowd of economists is roughly centered on the truth (top left panel). Even when the distribution
is not centered on the truth, it often brackets the truth (top right panel). Given some degree
of bracketing, the average of the crowd is by mathematical necessity more accurate than the
average individual.[2] When there is no bracketing—that is, the whole crowd is biased strictly
above or below the truth as in the bottom panel—the average of the crowd is still as accurate as
the average individual. Averaging the answers of a crowd, therefore, ensures a level of accuracy
no worse than the average member of the crowd and, in some cases, a level better than nearly
all members.

Conditions for Crowds to be Wise

Crowds, of course, are not always wiser than individuals. The degree to which crowds are more accurate than individuals is a function of two factors: expertise and diversity. First, the crowd needs to consist of individuals with some knowledge or expertise about the issue in question. This could be based on past education or past experience. In quantitative judgments, expertise allows individuals to use imperfect evidence to make predictions that will fall close to the truth over many judgments.

Second, the crowd needs to hold diverse perspectives on the judgment in question. As a result of holding diverse perspectives, different individuals will bring different areas of expertise to bear on a judgment and therefore make different mistakes. For example, imagine two professors predicting the academic ability of graduate school applicants. One professor tends to focus on past research experience; the other focuses on grades. Both cues are valid—both cues are predictive of future performance. Moreover, the cues are not perfectly correlated, so over many cases, they often lead to conflicting conclusions. Thus, when one professor is optimistic about a student who has a good deal of research experience and the second professor is pessimistic because the student has low grades, their average assessment is more complete and likely to be more accurate than their individual assessments. Relying on a subset of cues introduces errors that can be offset by including the additional valid cues used by other judges.

To appreciate the effect of diversity on judgment, consider its absence. Imagine a marketing team evaluating the revenue potential of new possible products. If all of the marketers have worked in the same company on the same past products at the same period of time, they have developed a shared set of experiences that guide their judgment about which new products are best. As a result, they are likely to hold shared opinions such as "customizability is more attractive to people under 40 than to people over 40." The consequence is that they share the same expertise—and the same blind spots. Forecasting researchers term this pattern "positively correlated forecast errors" and show mathematically that it reduces the value of aggregating judgments across people because similar errors cannot cancel each other. Sociologists who study social networks refer to shared patterns of knowledge as *redundant* (Burt, 1992, 2004). The word redundant evokes the right image: In the extreme, the knowledge of one person is a pretty good substitute for another person's. From a wisdom-of-crowds perspective, it is as if you do not have a crowd; your crowd is effectively one.

There are two ways to foster diversity. Differences in perspective are created through who is in the group (composition) and how they share information (process).

Composition

Research in the forecasting literature (Clemen & Winkler, 1986) has demonstrated the value of combining forecasts from different econometric models based on different economic schools of thought. The organizational literature has emphasized cross-functional teams as the best source for new ideas (Cronin & Weingart, 2007). A company does not want a new product designed by marketers alone—marketers will give it a fantastic look with many features but may pay less attention to the cost of production. The company needs expertise in other areas (finance, engineering, etc.) to ensure that the product meets a more optimal set of objectives.

Network sociologists propose enhancing diversity by finding gaps in the social network (Burt, 1992). The premise is that in tightly knit groups, people talk a great deal, and come to know and value the same things. They become redundant. From a group's vantage point, new ideas and new perspectives lie outside their own boundaries—even in other closely knit groups. The beauty of separation is that separated groups are likely to have evolved different views that are redundant *within* a group but nonredundant *between* them (Burt, 2004).

Creating diversity through composition can be challenging. One obstacle is that in-groups that share a similar perspective often look down on out-groups (DiDonato, Ullrich, & Krueger, 2011). Members of the marketing group suspect that members of the finance group are just bean counters who will stifle creativity. A second obstacle is that real differences in language and thinking impede collaboration between groups (Cronin & Weingart, 2007). These obstacles tend to lead people to associate with similar others. Sociologists term this tendency *homophily*; informally, it is the tendency for birds of a feather flocking together. Thus, when people assemble teams, they often select members based on common experience, common training, and common attitudes. This facilitates harmony but limits diversity.

Process The second source of diversity is the process a group or collective uses to elicit judgments. A good group process ensures that individuals think independently before sharing their judgments. Why is independence important? Imagine being in an experiment in which you are asked to estimate the years in which important events happened. Imagine also that before you see a question, you see the real answer from another subject. For example, you see 1300 followed by the question "In what year was the Magna Carta written?" To what extent is your answer influenced by first seeing the answer of another subject? Koehler and Beauregard (2006) found that when answers were given without seeing other answers—that is, when answers were independent—they were typically 50 years apart (median value). When answers were given after seeing someone else's answer, however, they differed by only 10 years from the answer that was seen. Cognitive psychologists have called this general phenomenon *anchoring* (Tversky & Kahneman, 1974). Anchoring occurs because people start with a number, such as the year 1300, and unconsciously recruit evidence consistent with it (Chapman & Johnson, 1999; Mussweiler & Strack, 1999) and then fail to adjust sufficiently from it (Epley & Gilovich, 2001).

Whether a deliberate strategy or an unconscious anchoring process, people rely on others to form their judgments. Deutsch and Gerard (1955) called this tendency *informational influence* and contrasted it with the *normative influence* illustrated in the Asch study. Recall that participants in the Asch experiment would often publicly report an answer with which they disagreed privately. Informational influence, on the other hand, occurs when people use the judgments of others to reduce their own uncertainty. It results in a new opinion—public and private—that incorporates the beliefs of others.

Because of anchoring and informational influence, single judgments in a group can propagate through the judgments of others if the others have not first formed an opinion. For example, having one person start a discussion with an opinion ("we should increase inventory by 20%") tends to lead others to think in small variations of that opinion. The result is that both the initial accuracy and the initial error in the first judgment are spread to those who hear it (economists have studied this phenomenon under the name *information cascades*; see Krueger & Massey, 2009, for a review). Anchoring and informational influence produce *positively correlated error* and *redundancy*, which amount to reducing the effective sample size.

Better group processes ensure that members think independently to form their judgments before sharing them. Research on brainstorming has found that working independently leads to a bigger and better pool of ideas than working face to face (Girota, Terwiesch, & Ulrich, 2010; Paulus & Yang, 2000). This effect occurs, in part, because independent ideas are generated in parallel, whereas face-to-face conversations require taking turns. But some of the effect is due to groups developing a common way of thinking about a question due to anchoring and informational influence. The danger of anchoring during group discussion has led one forecasting expert (Armstrong, 2006) to propose that many decisions would be better made if groups shared information without ever meeting.

Crowds Versus Individual Experts

To say that a crowd is wise invites the question, "Compared to what?" The implicit comparison in these examples has been to the average individual in the crowd. Indeed, for quantitative judgments, the average of the crowd can never be worse than the average individual in the crowd. With a high rate of bracketing, averaging will be far superior to the average individual. However, the average individual is not the only standard by which to judge a crowd. One can also ask how well averaging performs compared with the best member of the crowd (Luan, Katsikopoulos, & Reimer, in press). For this comparison to be informative, it is important to predict beforehand who the best judge will be. As noted earlier, it is always possible to determine the best performer after the fact.

There can be significant barriers to accurate identification of expertise. If there is no reliable track record of performance, one needs to rely on other cues. In a group discussion, members often rely on confidence and verbosity as cues to expertise (Littlepage, Robison, & Reddington, 1997). Unfortunately, cues like confidence often correlate weakly with actual accuracy (Burson, Larrick, & Klayman, 2007). Consequently, group members often inaccurately rank order the expertise of the members of their group (for example, Miner, 1984).

Even if one has access to past performance, the sample may not be large enough to allow a valid inference of stable ability. If you track the best performers in *The Wall Street Journal* data from one period to the next, they are no more accurate than the average judge in later periods

(Mannes, Soll, & Larrick, 2011). Why? Performance is a function of both skill and luck. More formally, apparent experts in one period of time regress to the mean of performance in the next period (for a discussion of regression to the mean, see Chapter 10 by Fiedler and Krueger in this volume).[3] As a result, one is better off using the average of the whole sample of economists in the current period than to bet on the winner from the last survey.

Whether one should pick a single expert or rely on a crowd depends not just on access to valid evidence about the ability of judges, but also the presence of a large difference between the best judge and other judges. The benefits of diversity are so strong that one can combine the judgments from individuals who differ a great deal in their individual accuracy and still gain from averaging. In a two judge case, one judge can be 50% more accurate than another judge and averaging will still outperform the better judge with realistic rates of bracketing (Soll & Larrick, 2009). For example, if over many prediction periods one economist tends to miss true GNP (gross national product) increases by $50 billion on average and a second economist tends to miss by $75 billion, there is still a benefit to combining their judgments. It takes a large difference in ability to justify choosing one judge instead of averaging.

In sum, there are many advantages to averaging a crowd over choosing single experts. First, when judges are similar in ability, it allows their errors to cancel. Second, when judges differ in ability but differences are hard to detect, an averaging strategy is sure to give at least some weight to the best performers; by contrast, trying to pick a single expert based on available cues could put all the weight on a less accurate judge. Finally, an averaging strategy can be implemented even in the absence of evidence about relative expertise.

Types of Crowd Judgments

Most of the examples offered so far have focused on quantitative judgments under uncertainty. But the benefits of crowds can apply to many tasks. When choosing among options, majority rule performs well compared to more complex approaches (Hastie & Kameda, 2005; Sorkin, Luan, & Itzkowitz, 2004). In the popular game show *Who Wants to be a Millionaire?* the studio audience answered the trivia questions correctly 91% of the time (Surowiecki, 2004). More qualitative tasks also benefit from crowds. Research on creativity has shown that once a person has pursued one approach to solving a problem, it is hard for the person to generate other approaches. Brainstorming overcomes this problem by tapping the diverse perspectives of a group to gener- ate a larger and more complete pool of ideas (Girotra et al., 2010; Paulus & Yang, 2000). Bond, Carlson, and Keeney (2008) asked business students to generate objectives for their summer job (e.g., pay level, location, growth opportunities, relevance to future career plans, and so forth). They found that students listed about seven objectives on average. However, when students were then presented with both their own objectives along with a list of objectives generated by others, they tended to find another seven objectives that were as important as the ones they had generated on their own. Groups are smarter than individuals in creating a wider range of creative ideas, objectives, and alternatives.

Technology has made it easier to draw on the wisdom of crowds. Some tools are as simple as aggregating average ratings on consumer Web sites. Others are more complex, such as prediction markets, in which people wager real or pretend money to bet on future events, such as sports. (A famous but short-lived Department of Defense market had people betting for and against the timing of future terrorist attacks; betting "for" an attack was perceived as distasteful.) Similarly, corporations have used internal "idea jams" to tap employee perspectives on innovation opportunities and have used external "crowd sourcing" to reach a broad pool of diverse entrepreneurs to address unsolved technological problems they currently face.

The Individual as a Crowd

Research on the wisdom of crowds supports the old saying that two heads are better than one. It is interesting that the insights from this literature have also been used to show that one head can be nearly as good as two (Herzog & Hertwig, 2009; Vul & Pashler, 2008), as long as a judge follows the principles of relevant knowledge and diverse perspectives. The key insight is that people typically rely on only a sample of the evidence available to them at any given time. But what if people had a reset button, so that they could retrieve facts from memory anew or handle the same facts in a new way?

One way to free people from their original answers is to delay a second answer (Vul & Pashler, 2008) so that people forget their initial perspectives and think about the problem differently the second time around. Another way to free people is to have them try to construct a fresh perspective. To demonstrate this possibility, Herzog and Hertwig (2009) had participants make estimates about quantitative values they did not know with certainty (specifically, dates in history). All participants gave two answers to the same question, and the authors constructed an average of the first and second judgments for each individual. In one condition, participants simply gave a second estimate following their first estimate. This condition did little to increase diversity—people simply anchored on their initial opinions—and there was no benefit from averaging. In a second condition, participants were told to assume that their first answer was incorrect, think of some reasons it might be wrong, and then "based on this new perspective, make a second, alternative estimate" (p. 234). This process of *second guessing* increased bracketing; as expected, the average of the first and second judgments was significantly more accurate than the first estimate. A lesson of Herzog and Hertwig's study is that we each carry around our own crowd, but we gain the wisdom only if we ask different members of the crowd.

How well do People use Crowds?

Strategies for Combining Judgments

Given that crowds are often wise, an important question for social psychology is whether people understand the value of combining knowledge across people. How well do people use judgments of others? This has become a growing area of research in recent years. Most research has focused on a very simple version of a crowd: two-person collectives involving the self (Sniezek & Buckley, 1995; Yaniv & Kleinberger, 2000). In these studies, people make estimates and then learn actual, representative estimates of others. The source of estimates is often called an *advisor* and the literature as a whole has come to be known as "advice taking." The advice-taking literature has used a wide range of quantitative stimuli, including estimating ages or weights of people from photographs, years in which historical events occurred, temperatures of cities, and so on. Studies that have focused on accuracy then compare initial and revised estimates to the truth and typically pay subjects for the closeness of their judgment. A smaller amount of research has looked at how people use the estimates of larger collectives of which they might or might not be members. We consider these two areas of research separately.

Using Advice from one Other Person One of the most robust findings in the advice-taking literature is that people underweight advice from another and overweight their own opinions (see Bonaccio & Dalal, 2006, for a review). A common result is that, on average, people tend to adjust their estimates 20% to 30% of the way toward advice (Harvey & Fischer, 1997; Soll & Larrick, 2009; Yaniv, 2004), a phenomenon that Yaniv and Kleinberger (2000) labeled *egocentric discounting*. For example, imagine estimating the age of someone from a photograph. You might make an initial estimate of 42 years old, see an advisor's estimate of 50, and adjust your answer to 44. The initial estimate and advice in this example are 8 years apart. The revised answer of 44 reflects a movement of 2/8, which translates to putting 25% weight on advice (WOA) and keeping 75% weight on your initial answer.

Subsequent research has found that 20% to 30% weight on advice is not descriptive of how people actually revise their judgments. The common pattern of 20% to 30% weight on advice is an average result of more extreme underlying behavior. Soll and Larrick (2009) showed that people often either choose one of the two answers (typically their own) or use an equal-weighted average. In their studies, the 30% mean weight on advice reflected a pattern of frequently ignoring advice entirely (0% WOA), sometimes averaging their initial estimates with advice (50% WOA), and occasionally ignoring their own initial estimates and fully accepting advice (100% WOA). The most common response in these studies was 0% weight on advice. Such an extreme strategy takes no advantage of the error-canceling benefits of a two-person crowd and significantly hurts final accuracy. Subjects would have formed more accurate final estimates if they had given *equal* weight to their own estimates and advice (Soll & Larrick, 2009).[4]

Why do people put so much weight on their own estimates? Several explanations have been offered. First, many people have an incorrect theory of combining judgments (Larrick & Soll, 2006), believing that averaging leads to mediocrity. Specifically, they incorrectly believe that the average judgment in a crowd is no more accurate than the average judge. Holding this incorrect belief is significantly related to ignoring advice (Larrick & Soll, 2006).

Other explanations for ignoring advice have focused on more psychological assumptions. Harvey and Harries (2004) proposed that people believe that the advisor is substantially less accurate than oneself. Yaniv and his colleagues (Yaniv, 2004; Yaniv & Kleinberger, 2000) proposed that people weight their own answers more highly because they know the reasons for their own judgments but not those behind the judgments of others. Soll and Mannes (2011) tested both explanations by directly measuring subjects' perceptions of their accuracy relative to their advisor and by systematically providing or withholding cues at the time of revision (where seeing cues can remind subjects of their reasons for their initial answer). They found some evidence for inflated perceptions of the self, but not enough to explain the frequent use of 0% WOA. Moreover, they found no effect of having access to reasons on WOA. They proposed that the tendency to hold on to one's judgment may be less cognitive and more motivational: One's judgments are part of oneself and, like possessions, letting go of them is painful. Moreover, there may be an asymmetry in the regret of changing one's mind. Actively giving up an initially accurate answer for a worse one may lead to more regret than passively holding on to an inaccurate answer and foregoing improvement [...].

The advice-taking literature has found that a number of factors affect the weight placed on advice. Some factors are rational: Subjects weight advice more heavily when advisors are more experienced or knowledgeable (Harvey & Fischer, 1997; Soll & Larrick, 2009), when advisors express greater confidence in the quality of their advice (Sniezek & Buckley, 1995; Sniezek & Van Swol, 2001; Soll & Larrick, 2009), and when the subject finds the task difficult (Gino & Moore, 2007). As long as people use these advisor characteristics according to their validity, shifting weight to more expert advisors is an effective response to these cues. Other factors are more psychological: Decision makers weight advice less heavily when they feel powerful (See, Morrison, Rothman, & Soll, 2011) and when they experience emotions that increase feelings of certainty, such as anger (Gino & Schweitzer, 2008). This research identifies a practical set of factors that reduces the use of advice and can help practitioners in different fields, such as business and medicine, recognize when egocentric discounting will be at its greatest.

Combining Judgments from a Collective A smaller stream of research has focused on how people combine the opinions of multiple others. Most studies in this area have looked at how people combine judgments across a panel of experts. In these studies, subjects have not made their own initial judgment but are neutral arbiters deciding how to balance the judgments of others (Budescu, 2006; Harvey, Harries, & Fischer, 2000; Yaniv, 1997). Budescu and colleagues (Budescu, 2006; Budescu, Rantilla, Yu, & Karelitz, 2003) have found that people tend to weight expert judgments in proportion to the expertise of different judges.

Two studies in this area have looked at advice taking from a group. As in the two-person advice research, these studies involve having people make an initial judgment and then revise it after seeing the estimates of a group (Mannes, 2009; Yaniv & Milyavsky, 2007). Yaniv and Milyavsky (2007) found that people cherry-pick the advice from a larger crowd, focusing on the judgments most consistent with their own. Subjects effectively use their first guess as a standard of accuracy and dismiss discrepant advice. From a wisdom-of-crowds perspective, this is dangerous: It ignores the benefits of incorporating diverse perspectives to cancel error. Mannes (2009) explored the extent to which people listen to the average judgment from crowds of different sizes. Normatively, subjects would be wise to put less weight on themselves and more weight on the crowd as the crowd grows in size (reflecting a basic principle in statistics known as the *law of large numbers*). In addition, if all judges are expected to be equally accurate in advance, subjects would be wise to put the same weight on themselves as they do on each member of the crowd (i.e., a $1/n$ weight on their own judgment and a $(n - 1)/n$ weight on the crowd's advice). Mannes found that people put more weight on larger crowds, as they should from a normative perspective, but not enough weight. They put only 60% weight on advice from a nine-person crowd where equal weighting would require more than 90% weight. The consequence of egocentric weighting is that subjects paid a significant price in the accuracy of their final judgments.

Future Directions for the Psychology of the Wisdom of Crowds

The main conclusion from existing research is that people use crowds too little: They put too much weight on their own judgment and thereby miss out on the benefit of diverse perspectives for reducing error. This is a young and growing area of research. What are some of the unanswered questions? Perhaps a key issue that arises in the existing work is that advice is quantitative, impersonal, and unsolicited—it consists of seeing numerical estimates made by others (including group averages) and making conscious decisions about how best to combine them with one's own independent estimates. The use of crowd judgments should be explored in other ways.

First, advice *seeking* could be an important variable to study. How often do people seek advice? Perhaps the easiest way to reduce error in judgment is to seek other's opinions, and the failure to do so has the same negative consequences as ignoring advice. We suspect people seek advice less often than they should. How does seeking advice affect its use? The act of seeking advice is likely to increase the extent to which advice is used (Gino, 2008) and thereby improve judgment. It is also possible that seeking advice will lead people to pick a single expert and put too much faith in that single piece of advice.

Second, other advice-taking contexts may change openness to advice, such as face-to-face interactions or interactions with richer information sharing. Richer information sharing may lead to deeper information processing. Face-to-face interactions may evoke processes such as empathy and mimicry that produce greater yielding to others.

Third, the benefits of independence should be carefully examined. Earlier we argued that independence increases diversity of perspective and thereby makes a crowd more accurate. Asch captured this idea when writing that "consensus, to be productive, requires that each individual contribute independently out of his experience and insight" (1955, p. 34). In this view, individual judgments are "inputs" to a combination process and they are more valuable if they are independent. However, individual judgments can also be "outputs" from exposure to the judgments of collectives. Egocentric discounting of advice is an example of an inferior output. In output situations there may be a benefit if the individual does *not* have an independent opinion: Anchoring on a crowd may actually yield more accurate judgments because it ensures that individual judges are using a larger sample—even if unwittingly.

Consider a study that predates Asch. Jenness (1932) asked students to estimate the number of beans in a jar. They made their estimates in a prescribed sequence: first individually, then by consensus in a three-person group, and then individually again. The initial individual guesses missed the true value (811) by 305 on average. The group consensus answers missed the value by just 91, producing a substantial improvement over their initial individual guesses. Strikingly, however, their final individual guesses missed by 122 on average—worse than the group answers. What went wrong? By reasserting their independence and deviating from the group answer, the subjects in Jenness's study were less accurate than if they had simply placed their faith in the crowd.

Thus, we can think of crowd processes as having two stages. Independence is important at Stage 1, the input stage, because the effective sample size is increased when different judges make different errors. However, independence may be unimportant or even detrimental at Stage 2, the output stage, when a decision maker uses others' judgments to form a final opinion that he or she is going to act on. Campbell adopted the Stage 2 perspective when he argued that, "[I]n Asch's famous situation, the single true subject might rationally decide that, since everybody's eyes are imperfect, and since it would be so extremely infrequent that so many Swarthmore students would deliberately lie in a situation like this, it is more probable that his own eyes are wrong than that all of the others are wrong. He might, therefore, rationally decide that, if asked to bet, he would bet with the majority" (1961, p. 123). In contrast to the view inherited from the Asch tradition, social influence may actually be beneficial. Normative and informational influence may serve as a *cognitive repair* (Heath, Larrick, & Klayman, 1998) that mitigates depending too much on one's own judgments. Influence ensures that people incorporate the wisdom of the crowd in their own judgments.

Notes

1 One can conceive of bracketing in a group as the rate at which randomly selected pairs bracket the truth or as a ratio of the proportion of the crowd falling on each side of the truth. For example, if 60% of the crowd is high and 40% low, the pairwise bracketing rate is $1 - [(.6 \times .6) + (.4 \times .4)] = .48$, and there is a 1.5 (.6/.4) ratio.

2 This mathematical necessity can be proven by applying Jensen's inequality. Let Judge *i*'s estimate on quantity *j* be represented as $X_{ij} = T_j + D_{ij}$, where T_j is the correct answer and D_{ij} is the deviation, $i = 1, 2, ..., n$, and $j = 1, 2, ..., m$. Let $w_1, w_2, ..., w_n$ be the weights assigned to *n* judgments, where $W_i = 1$. Accuracy on a given estimate is a function of the deviation, $f(D)$. Typically, $f(D)$ is increasing in

|D|, so higher scores reflect lower accuracy. For a quantity *j*, the deviation for a weighted average is the weighted average of the deviations of the individual estimates:

$$f(w_1 x_{1j} + w_2 x_{2j} + \ldots + w_n x_{nj} - T_j) = f\left(\sum_{i=1}^{n} w_i D_{ij}\right).$$

The right-hand side of the preceding equation gives the accuracy of a weighted average. If *f* is a convex function, then Jensen's inequality states that

$$\sum_{i=1}^{n} w_i f(D_{ij}) \geq f\left(\sum_{i=1}^{n} w_i D_{ij}\right).$$

In this chapter, we focus on absolute error as our accuracy standard because it is neutral in punishing larger versus small errors. Past forecast research has focused on squared error as the loss function, which implies that larger errors are worse than smaller ones. When squared error is used as the loss function, averaging is more accurate than the average judge even when there is no bracketing.

Aggregation also improves judgment using other criteria for accuracy, such as correlations with the truth.

3 Denrell and Fang (2010) showed that when a *Wall Street Journal* economist "wins" one period with more extreme judgments—that is, judgments that are outliers compared to the rest of the group—they are actually less accurate than the average judge in subsequent periods.

4 In these studies, subjects made judgments independently (yielding bracketing rates of 30% to 40%), were randomly assigned advisors from their own subject population (yielding small average differences in expertise between judges), and given cues to expertise such as self-expressed confidence or a small sample of past performance (which are weak cues). All of these features, which favor averaging, were known by subjects.

References

Allen, V. L. (1965). Situational factors in conformity. *Advances in Experimental Social Psychology, 2,* 133–175.

Armstrong, J. S. (2001). *Principles of forecasting: A handbook for researchers and practitioners.* Boston: Kluwer Academic.

Armstrong, J. S. (2006). Should the forecasting process eliminate face-to-face meetings? *Foresight: The International Journal of Applied Forecasting, 5,* 3–8.

Asch, S. E. (1955). Opinions and social pressure. *Scientific American, 193,* 31–35.

Bell, D., Raiffa, H., & Tversky, A. (1988). *Decision making: Descriptive, normative, and prescriptive interactions.* Cambridge, UK: Cambridge University Press.

Bonaccio, S., & Dalal, R. S. (2006). Advice taking and decision-making: An integrative literature review, and implications for the organizational sciences. *Organizational Behavior and Human Decision Processes, 101,* 127–151.

Bond, S. D., Carlson, K. A., & Keeney, R. L. (2008). Generating objectives: Can decision makers articulate what they want? *Management Science, 54*, 56–70.

Brunswik, E. (1955): Representative design and probabilistic theory in a functional psychology. *Psychological Review, 62*, 193–217.

Budescu, D. V. (2006). Confidence in aggregation of opinions from multiple sources. In K. Fiedler & P. Juslin (Eds.), *Information sampling and adaptive cognition* (pp. 327–352). Cambridge, UK: Cambridge University Press.

Budescu, D. V., Rantilla, A. K., Yu, H.-T., & Karelitz, T. M. (2003). The effects of asymmetry among advisors on the aggregation of their opinions. *Organizational Behavior and Human Decision Processes, 90*, 178–194.

Burson, K. A., Larrick, R. P., & Klayman, J. (2006). Skilled or unskilled, but still unaware of it: how perceptions of difficulty drive miscalibration in relative comparisons. *Journal of Personality and Social Psychology, 90*, 60–77.

Burt, R. S. (1992). *Structural holes*. Cambridge, MA: Harvard University Press.

Burt, R. S. (2004). Structural holes and good ideas. *American Journal of Sociology, 110*, 349–399.

Campbell, D. T. (1961). Conformity in psychology's theories of acquired behavioral dispositions. In I. A. Berg & B. M. Bass (Eds.), *Conformity and deviation* (pp. 101–142). New York: Harper & Brothers.

Chapman, G. B., & Johnson, E. J. (1999). Anchoring, activation and the construction of values. *Organizational Behavior and Human Decision Processes, 79,* 115–153.

Clemen, R. T. (1989). Combining forecasts: A review and annotated bibliography. *International Journal of Forecasting, 5,* 559–609.

Clemen, R. T., & Winkler, R. L. (1986). Combining economic forecasts. *Journal of Business and Economic Statistics, 4,* 39–46.

Cronin, M. A., & Weingart, L. R. (2007). Representational gaps, information processing, and conflict in functionally diverse teams. *Academy of Management Review, 32*, 761–773.

Dami, M. K., Hertwig, R., & Hoffrage, U. (2004). The role of representative design in an ecological approach to cognition. *Psychological Bulletin, 130*, 959–988.

Denrell, J., & Fang, C. (2010). Predicting the next big thing: Success as a signal of poor judgment. *Management Science, 56*, 1653–1667.

Deutsch, M., & Gerard, H. B. (1955). A study of normative and informational social influences upon individual judgment. *Journal of Abnormal and Social Psychology, 51*, 629–636.

DiDonato, T. E., Ullrich, J., & Krueger, J. I. (2011). Social perception as induction and inference: An integrative model of intergroup differentiation, ingroup favoritism, and differential accuracy. *Journal of Personality and Social Psychology, 100*, 66–83.

Epley, N., & Gilovich, T. (2001). Putting adjustment back in the anchoring and adjustment heuristic: Differential processing of self-generated and experimenter-provided anchors. *Psychological Science, 12,* 391–396.

Festinger, L. (1954). A theory of social comparison processes. *Human Relations, 7*, 117–140.

Gino, F. (2008). Do we listen to advice just because we paid for it? The impact of cost of advice on its use. *Organizational Behavior and Human Decision Processes*, *107*, 234–245.

Gino, F., & Moore, D. A. (2007). Effects of task difficulty on use of advice. *Journal of Behavioral Decision Making, 20*, 21–35.

Gino, F., & Schweitzer, M. (2008). Blinded by anger or feeling the love: How emotions influence advice taking. *Journal of Applied Psychology, 93*, 1165–1173.

Girotra, K., Terwiesch, C., & Ulrich, K. T. (2010). Idea generation and the quality of the best idea. *Management Science, 56,* 591–605.

Harvey, N., & Fischer, I. (1997). Taking advice: Accepting help, improving judgment, and sharing responsibility. *Organizational Behavior and Human Decision Processes, 70,* 117–133.

Harvey, N., & Harries, C. (2004). Effects of judges' forecasting on their later combination of forecasts for the same outcomes. *International Journal of Forecasting, 20,* 391–409.

Harvey, N., Harries, C., & Fischer, I. (2000). Using advice and assessing its quality. *Organizational Behavior and Human Decision Processes, 81,* 252–273.

Hastie, R., & Kameda, T. (2005). The robust beauty of majority rules in group decisions. *Psychological Review, 112,* 494–508.

Heath, C., Larrick, R. P., & Klayman, J. (1998). Cognitive repairs: How organizations compensate for the shortcomings of individual learners. *Research in Organizational Behavior, 20,* 1–37.

Herzog, S. M., & Hertwig, R. (2009). The wisdom of many in one mind: Improving individual judgments with dialectical bootstrapping. *Psychological Science, 20,* 231–237.

Jenness, A. (1932). The role of discussion in changing opinion regarding a matter of fact. *Journal of Abnormal and Social Psychology, 27,* 279–296.

Kameda, T., & Tindale, R. S. (2006). Groups as adaptive devices: Human docility and group aggregation mechanisms in evolutionary context. In M. Schaller, J. Simpson, & D. Kenrick (Eds.), *Evolution and social psychology* (pp. 317–341). New York: Psychology Press.

Koehler, D. J., & Beauregard, T. A. (2006). Illusion of confirmation from exposure to another's hypothesis. *Journal of Behavioral Decision Making, 19,* 61–78.

Krueger, J. I., & Massey, A. L. (2009). A rational reconstruction of misbehavior. *Social Cognition, 27,* 785–810.

Larrick, R. P., & Soll, J. B. (2006). Intuitions about combining opinions: Misappreciation of the averaging principle. *Management Science, 52,* 111–127.

Littlepage, G. E., Robison, W., & Reddington, K. (1997). Effects of task experience and group experience on group performance, member ability, and recognition of expertise. *Organizational Behavior and Human Decision Processes, 69,* 133–147.

Luan, S., Katsikopolous, K. V., & Reimer, T. (in press). The "less-is-more" effect in group decision making. In R. Hertwig, U. Hoffrage, & the ABC Research Group. *Simple heuristics in a social world.* New York: Oxford University Press.

Mannes, A. E. (2009). Are we wise about the wisdom of crowds? The use of group judgments in belief revision. *Management Science, 55,* 1267–1279.

Mannes, A. E., Soll, J. B., & Larrick, R. P. (2011). *The wisdom of small crowds.* Unpublished manuscript.

Miner, F. C. (1984). Group versus individual decision making: An investigation of performance measures, decision strategies, and process losses/gains. *Organizational Behavior and Human Performance, 33,* 112–124.

Mussweiler, T., & Strack, F. (1999). Hypothesis-consistent testing and semantic priming in the anchoring paradigm: A selective accessibility model. *Journal of Experimental Social Psychology, 35,* 136–164.

Paulus, P. B., & Yang, H. C. (2000). Idea generation in groups: A basis for creativity in organizations. *Organizational Behavior and Human Decision Processes, 82,* 76–87.

See, K. E., Morrison, E. W., Rothman, N. B., & Soll, J. B. (2011). *Powerful and unpersuaded: The implications of power for confidence, advice-taking, and accuracy.* In press.

Sniezek, J. A., & Buckley, T. (1995). Cueing and cognitive conflict in Judge-Adviser decision making. *Organizational Behavior and Human Decision Processes, 62,* 159–174.

Sniezek, J. A., & Van Swol, L. M. (2001). Trust, confidence, and expertise in a judge-advisor system. *Organizational Behavior and Human Decision Processes, 84,* 288–307.

Soll, J. B., & Larrick, R. P. (2009). Strategies for revising judgment: How (and how well) people use others' opinions. *Journal of Experimental Psychology: Learning, Memory and Cognition, 35,* 780–805.

Soll, J. B., & Mannes, A. E. (2011). Judgmental aggregation strategies depend on whether the self is involved. *International Journal of Forecasting, 27,* 81–102.

Sorkin, R. D., Luan, S., & Itzkowitz, J. (2004). Group decision and deliberation: A distributed detection process. In D. Koehler & N. Harvey (Eds.), *Handbook of judgment and decision making* (pp. 464–484). New York: Oxford University Press.

Surowiecki, J. (2004). *The wisdom of crowds: Why the many are smarter than the few and how collective wisdom shapes business, economies, societies, and nations.* London: Little, Brown.

Tversky, A., & Kahneman, D. (1974). Judgment under uncertainty: Heuristics and biases. *Science, 185,* 1124–1131.

Vul, E., & Pashler, H. (2008). Measuring the crowd within: Probabilistic representations within individuals. *Psychological Science, 19,* 645–647.

Watson, G. B. (1928). Do groups think more efficiently than individuals? *Journal of Abnormal and Social Psychology, 23,* 328–336.

Yaniv, I. (1997). Weighting and trimming: heuristics for aggregating judgments under uncertainty. *Organizational Behavior and Human Decision Processes, 69,* 237–249.

Yaniv, I. (2004). Receiving other people's advice: Influence and benefit. *Organizational Behavior and Human Decision Processes, 93,* 1–13.

Yaniv, I., & Kleinberger, E. (2000). Advice taking in decision making: Egocentric discounting and reputation formation. *Organizational Behavior and Human Decision Processes, 83,* 260–281.

Yaniv, I., & Milyavsky, M. (2007). Using advice from multiple sources to revise and improve judgments. *Organizational Behavior and Human Decision Processes, 103,* 104–120.

The Psychological Explanation of Conformity

Guandong Song, Qinhai Ma, Fangfei Wu, and Lin Li

Conformity occurs when the subject demonstrates the same behavior or attitude as the object. The subject is the individual who conforms. The object(s) may be individuals, groups, organizations, policies, rules and regulations, or the experience or natural instinct of the subject. Conformity is divided into 2 categories: irrational conformity (herd behavior) and rational conformity (abidance, compliance, and obedience). In this study we explain the meaning of abidance, compliance, obedience, and herd behavior. The conclusions have implications in the fields of commerce, education, service, politics, management, religion, and more.

Keywords: conformity, abidance, compliance, obedience, herd behavior.

What is conformity?

The pioneering research on conformity was conducted by Sherif in 1935 (cited in Friedman, Sears, & Smith, 1984). Psychologists such as Asch (1951) and Milgram (1963) subsequently conducted similar experimental studies (see also, Milgram, Bickman, & Berkowitz, 1969). *Conformity* is *the change of actions or attitudes caused by the pressure from some real or notional groups* (Myers, 2010).

Guandong Song, Qinhai Ma, Fangfei Wu, and Lin Li, "The Psychological Explanation of Conformity," *Social Behavior and Personality*, vol. 40, no. 8, pp. 1365-1372. Copyright © 2012 by Scientific Journal Publishers Limited. Reprinted with permission. Provided by ProQuest LLC.

However, when we analyze the process of conformity and its causes we find that there are at least two limitations of the experiment. First, the group is not a prerequisite for the conformity of individuals. In Sherif's (1935) experiment (cited in Friedman et al., 1984), the majority conformed to the minority when it was conducted by one assistant. In Asch's (1951) study the conforming percentage was 2.8% with one assistant and in Milgram's (1963) research, one assistant stopped 4% of all pedestrians, while 42% of the pedestrians looked on without stopping. Second, conformity is not absolutely irrational herd behavior. In most cases, conformity is a result of rational reflection, although mistakes can be made.

The conforming action can, therefore, be divided into rational conformity and irrational conformity. Rational conformity is behavior guided by thinking, judgment, or reasoning. It occurs as a result of the influences exerted by the object's behavior or attitude and includes abidance, compliance, and obedience. Irrational conformity or herd behavior is the behavior the subject presents when they are guided by intuitionistic and instinctive activities and influenced by the behavior or attitude of the object (Figure 14.1). Generally speaking, there are a variety of factors that cause conforming behavior, such as individuals, organizations, and policies. Conformity can thus be divided into narrow conformity and generalized conformity (Figure 14.2).

Narrow conformity means that the individual's actions or attitudes are consistent with those of the majority. It is a special form of generalized conformity, which we will discuss in this paper.

Conformity

Conformity is defined as *a subject's behavior or attitudes following those of the object*. The subject is the individual who conforms. The object can be external or internal factors that cause conforming actions, in the form of individuals, groups, organizations, policies, rules and regulations, or the experience and natural instinct of the subject.

The Conforming Subject as an Individual. First, considering an individual as the conforming subject can make the study easy to understand. It can also help researchers grasp micropsychological reactions and the real causes of conformity. Second, it is convenient to design, operate, get statistics from, and analyze the experiment. Furthermore, the psychological condition of conformity of groups can be reflected by analyzing one or more individuals in the group.

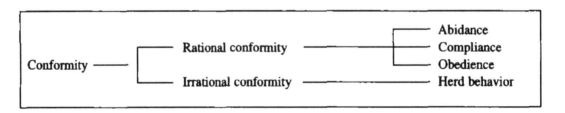

Figure 14.1 Classification chart of conformity.

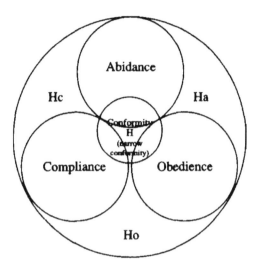

Figure 14.2   Generalized conformity.

Note: The three medium-sized tangent circles are, respectively, abidance, compliance, and obedience. The small circle passing through the three tangent points is narrow conformity. The four blank areas (H, Ha, He, Ho) are herd behaviors. The excircle represents generalized conformity.

The Conformity Object can be External or Internal. The object can be external, such as individuals, groups, organizations, policies, rules, and regulations; or internal, including the experience and genetic instinct of the subject.

The Definition of Conformity Synthesizes all the Factors that Might Cause such Behaviors. Firstly, conformity does not literally mean *conforming*. The quest for the essence of conformity lies in which kind of conformity is caused by groups. Furthermore, majority is only one of the influential factors of conforming, thus varied patterns (Asch, 1951) of conformity are generated.

The Internal Reasons for Conformity. Conformity is defined according to the presentation of external behaviors. But we must also discuss the internal reasons for conformity. Only in this way can we grasp the essence of the problem and the psychological reason. It is extremely significant to our work and life. For instance, if parents use threats of violence to force their children to study, the children will obey their parents in order to evade punishment. This leads to psychological pressure which is not good for children's study or growth. However, if parents cultivate children's learning interests and adopt a step-by-step approach, they will be aware of the significance of learning and their learning interests will be enhanced. Eventually, they will conform to the parents' wishes and work hard. This is beneficial not only in maintaining children's learning motivation but also in facilitating their physical and mental health.

Abidance

Abidance occurs when the subject is about to learn or do something. The subject acts consistently with the object, whose behavior or attitude is considered to be the guidance of his judgment and reasoning process in an uncertain psychological condition.

The Cause. The ambiguous condition and certain behaviors and attitudes of the object are the direct external cause. The emergence of abidance depends on the ambiguous condition or problems faced by the follower. Such ambiguity may be objective (Sherif's experiment; cited in Friedman et al., 1984) or man made (Asch's 1951 experiment). The uncertain condition enhances the subject's trust of the information provided by the object, and thus abidance occurs (Guandong, 1997, 2002).

The Purpose. Under conditions of uncertainty or psychological ambiguity, the individual must follow the cues of others. For example, in Sherif's experiment, the participants were told to judge the distance a light spot moved. Although the individual had received some visual information, the situation was still quite uncertain until the individual found a person who seemed to be completely confident about the answer. The individual thought that the person was likely to have more useful information, and were likely to go along with him (Friedman et al., 1984).

Theoretical Assumption. The notable characteristic of abidance is that the subject abides to the object. The subject abides by regarding the actions and attitudes of the object as guides for his/her judgment and reasoning and subjectively agrees with the object. Thus, there is internal consistency among the purpose, reason, mental process, and emotional experience of the subject's activity (Guandong, 2004). The internal and external consistency of abidance is called self-identity theory.

Function. The concept and theory of abidance are reliable. They help us to know how individuals, groups, or organizations influence the public, how to make effective policies, rules, and regulations, and how to recognize the existent foundation of religions.

Compliance

Hogg and Vaughan (2010) state that compliance is an agreeable behavioral response to a request made by another individual. But from the sociocognitive perspective, compliance means that the subject assumes the same actions or attitudes as the object's expectations after summarizing, judging, and deducing his/her action and attitude, even though he/she may not think it is right (Guandong & Lei, 2007). The subject is the compliant individual, while the object refers to individuals, groups, and organizations that the subject conforms to.

The Purpose and Theoretical Assumption. The purpose of meeting the expectations of the object is to exhilarate others. Exhilaration is remarkable in compliance and it is the only standard for judging whether a conforming behavior is the compliance. In daily life, people tend to believe that compliance is a duty children have to their parents as a way of showing respect. Exhilarating others is called exhilaration theory in compliance.

Emotional Feeling and Thinking Processes. When disagreement exists the subject usually shows negative tendencies in emotional feeling. The thinking process of compliance is either active or passive in performance because of the various ways of thinking (Guandong, 2004).

Function. The theory of compliance has theoretical and practical significance for establishing and maintaining good relationships among people.

Obedience

Traditionally, obedience is the behavior produced by the commands of authority (Kassin, Fein, & Markus, 2011). But in our opinion, obedience means that the subject keeps the action and attitude the same as that of the object to seek rewards or avoid punishments after summarizing, judging, and deducing the object (Guandong, Zhitian, & Miao, 2008). The subject is the individual who obeys. The object can be individuals, groups, organizations, policies, rules and regulations, and the internal experience of the subject. The explanation is as follows:

The Purpose and Theoretical Assumption. The subject is subordinate to the object for the purpose of seeking rewards or avoiding punishment. The reason for obedience is the valence (the subjective value) generated directly or indirectly by the object. When the subject believes the valence is positive and the expectancy (the subjective judgment of the possibility that the subject can realize his goals through the object) is strong, obedience will emerge. This is called expectation theory.

The precondition of obedience is the obvious or potential valence of the object for the subject. For example, in Milgram's obedience experiment, he paid $4.50 as the valence in each trial (Milgram, 1963).[1] The occurrence of obedience depends on the subject's expectancy for the realization of the goals. Only if the valence and expectancy are positive, can obedience be inspired.

Emotional Feeling and Function. Because the obedient situation is often related to payment or subjective and negative emotional feelings, the purpose, reason, thinking process, and emotional feelings of the subject's negative obedient behavior has internal consistency (Guandong, 2004). The obedience research is significant for theories of management.

The Relationship between Abidance, Compliance, and Obedience

Abidance, compliance, and obedience are three different presentations of rational conformity. The common characteristic in the presentations is that the subject's rational behavior is consistent with that of the object under normal conditions. Differences in perceptions of rational conformity result in the various theoretical assumptions, behavioral attributions, psychological characteristics, and definitions of the nature of conformity (see Table 14.1).

The three presentations are not isolated from each other. Instead, they can be transformed into each other. For instance, a person might show obedience to the traffic rules at the beginning.

Table 14.1 The Distinctions and relationships among abidance, compliance, and obedience

	Abidance	Compliance	Obedience
Subject	individual of abidance	individual of compliance	individual of obedience
Object	individuals, groups, organizations, policies, rules, regulations, as well as the natural instinct or experience of the subject	individuals, groups, and organizations	individuals, groups, organizations, policies, rules, regulations, as well as the natural instinct or experience of the subject
Theoretical assumptions	self-identify theory of abidance	exhilaration theory of compliance	expectation theory of obedience
Reason	the understanding of the subject	the feeling of the object	the need of the subject
Purpose	to understand things or take actions	to meet the expectations of the object	to seek rewards and avoid punishment
External causes	the ambiguous situation and the certain behavior and attitude of the object	the expectation of the object	the requirement of the object
Features of thinking	active	uncertain	passive
Emotional feelings	positive	negative tendency	negative
Behavior and attitude	consistent	inconsistent	inconsistent
Presentation of the behavior	consistent	consistent	consistent
Character of the behavior	candid behavior or attitude	exhilarating behavior or attitude	self-regarding behavior or attitude
Application fields	commerce, advertisement, education, management, propaganda, and other public service fields	interpersonal relationships, family relationships, and other social fields	politics, administration, business management, and other managing fields

However, after a traffic accident, he abides by traffic regulations more consciously. The passive obedience to traffic regulations is transformed into conscious abidance.

Herd Behavior

Even though the herd behavior experiment was designed on the basis of the genetic instinct of worms, it is applicable to human beings. Distorted perceptions in Asch's (1951) "lines comparison" experiment were examples of herd behavior.

Herd behavior occurs when the subject accepts the behaviors or attitudes of the object according to his or her intuition and genetic instinct. The subject is influenced by the herd behavior of objects such as individuals, groups, organizations, policies, rules, regulations, and the internal experience or natural instinct of the subject.

The Cause and Purpose. Herd behavior has a close relationship with experience and genetic instinct. The psychological reason for herd behavior is the stable psychology which originates from the experience and genetic instinct of human beings.

But herd behavior does not mean behavior without purpose. Usually, the purpose is clear. For example, a clerk may follow the orders of his/her superior because he/she can benefit by doing so. In this case, his/her purpose is very clear. Of course, herd behavior can also be purposeless, for example, the instinctive reflex of organisms.

Transformation. Herd behavior can sometimes be transformed from rational conformity. When rational conformity develops and becomes the changeless experience of the subject, it will easily be replaced by herd behavior. Herd behavior can also evolve into rational conformity.

Herd behavior often results in negative effects. In order to overcome it, it is essential to abandon the habit of relying on intuition and relying instead on rational thinking.

Conclusion

Scientific ideology is an important standard for scientific research. Sherif's (1935; cited in Friedman et al., 1984) research on conformity is behaviorism-oriented. Asch's (1951) research was based on the view of group dynamics (Shultz, 1981). Behaviorists abandon the study of consciousness, while Gestalt psychologists focus on perceptive consciousness. As a result, when scientific operating rules are adopted for studying conformity, there will be a lack of comprehensive understanding of the issue. In this paper we integrate behavior theory, humanistic-oriented theory, cognitive theory, and other psychological theories. It is a comprehensive and scientific summary in the nature of its phenomenon, the changes of its presentation, and the reasons for conformity.

Notes

1 In Milgram's experiment, abidance may occur since the participants agree with the information provided and want to finish the experiment; compliance may occur since the participants cater to the psychologist; and obedience may occur due to the instinct.

References

Asch, S. E. (1951). Effects of group pressure upon the modification and distortion of judgment. In H. Guetzkow (Ed.), *Groups, leadership, and men* (pp. 177–190). Pittsburgh, PA: Carnegie.

Friedman, J. L., Sears, D. O., & Smith, J. M. (1984). *Social psychology* [Trans. D. Gao & J, Gao] (pp. 437–457). Heilongjiang: Heilongjiang People's Publishing House.

Guandong, S. (1997). A new view on conformity. *Psychological Science, 20,* 88–90.

Guandong, S. (2002). More on the realization of conformity. *Psychological Science, 25,* 202–204.

Guandong, S. (2004). An investigative study of conformity. *Psychological Science, 27,* 657–661.

Guandong, S., & Lei, Z. (2007). A discussion of the concept of compliance [In Chinese]. *Social Science Journal, 6,* 37–41.

Guandong, S., Zhitian, Y., & Miao, C. (2008). A psychological study of obedience in psychology. *Psychological Science, 31,* 249–252.

Hogg, M. A,, & Vaughan, G. M. (2010). *Essentials of social psychology.* Harlow, UK: Pearson Education.

Kassin, S., Fein, S., & Markus, H. R. (2011). *Social psychology* (8th ed.). Belmont, CA: Wadsworth/ Cengage Learning.

Milgram, S. (1963). A behavioral study of obedience. *Journal of Abnormal and Social Psychology, 67,* 371–378. **http://doi.org/ccdgzs**

Milgram, S., Bickman, L., & Berkowitz, L. (1969). Note on the drawing power of crowds of different size. *Journal of Personality and Social Psychology, 13,* 79–82. **http://doi.org/cqxbtk**

Myers, D. G. (2010). *Social psychology* (10th ed.). New York: McGraw-Hill.

Shultz, D. P. (1981). *The history of modern psychology* [Trans. L. Yang]. Beijing: People's Education Press.

Post-Reading Activities

1   Why do you think individuals are reluctant to use information from crowds?

2   What might be the pros and cons of using crowd-based information?

3   Based on the readings, how can you resist conforming to antisocial behaviors?

CONCLUSION

The purpose of this textbook is to provide an overview of social psychology from a sociological perspective. Again, social psychology forms a bridge between psychology and sociology. Throughout this text, we have emphasized the social psychology theorists of Mead, Cooley, Blumer, and Goffman. These theories were highlighted in the Buechler reading, "How We Become Who We Are." They explain the development of identity. Not only does an individual have a personal development, but also a social development. As we have discussed throughout this text, the social development influences our day-to-day lives in great detail as in studying altruism, aggression, and persuasion. With their perspectives, we have come to the understanding of our social world influencing our individual behaviors like altruism, aggression, decision making, deviance, and conformity. It is imperative that both disciplines—psychology and sociology—be employed. Otherwise, we miss macro influences of the social world. The macro influences allow for researchers to acknowledge the role "others" play in the behavior of individuals. For example, the total fertility rate (number of babies born) to a woman does incorporate a personal decision of the woman, but it also incorporates the level of education, the rights and freedoms of a woman in society, the predominant religions of the society, the availability of family planning information, and the level of medical assistance available.

So, how do you think you would explain social psychology to a sociologist? How would a sociology social psychologist, as opposed to a psychologist, understand and research altruism or aggression?

CPSIA information can be obtained
at www.ICGtesting.com
Printed in the USA
LVHW042132031218
599113LV00001B/2/P

9 781516 539703